# MULTIPLE-CHOICE & FREE-RESPONSE QUESTIONS IN PREPARATION FOR THE AP PSYCHOLOGY EXAMINATION

## (Third Edition)

**Michael Sullivan**
Hopkinton High School
Hopkinton, Massachusetts

**Michael Hamilton**
Hopkinton High School
Hopkinton, Massachusetts

**D&S MARKETING SYSTEMS, INC.**
1205 38th Street • Brooklyn, New York 11218

w w w . d s m a r k e t i n g . c o m

ISBN # 1-934780-14-6

Printed in the U.S.A.

# About the Authors

**Michael Sullivan** received his BA from the University of Massachusetts at Amherst and his MA from the University of Massachusetts at Boston. He served four years on the Test Development Committee for the Advanced Placement Psychology Examination, and has been a Reader for the AP Psychology Exam.

Michael spent parts of three summers as a staff member at the Teaching the Science of Psychology summer institute for high school psychology teachers supported by the National Science Foundation and the Northern Kentucky University Foundation. He had previously played the same role at the Texas A&M University Summer Institute for the Teaching of Psychology, also funded by the National Science Foundation.

Michael has won a District Teacher of the Year award and been a nominee for the Massachusetts Teacher of the Year. In 2000, he received the Mary Margaret Moffett Memorial Teaching Excellence Award, given by the American Psychological Association.

In 2004, Michael was one of six public school teachers in Massachusetts invited to take part in the GoodWork Project out of Harvard University's Project Zero, run by Howard Gardner.

**Mike Hamilton** received both his BA and MA from the University of Northern Iowa. After teaching for several years in Iowa, Mike moved to Massachusetts and began working at Hopkinton High School in 2006. He has taught psychology in a high school setting for the past 10 years.

Mike is currently a Member-at-Large on the board of Teachers of Psychology in Secondary Schools (TOPSS), a division of the American Psychological Association. Mike is also a Reader for the AP Psychology Exam.

He has conducted various regional and national workshops on the teaching of high school psychology. He recently co-led the 2010 APA/Clark University Workshop for High School Teachers funded by the American Psychological Foundation, Clark University, and APA.

# Acknowledgements

We owe a great debt of gratitude to our editors, who have certainly made this book and its accompanying teacher's manual better. Bill James of Milford (MI) High School did a very perceptive and conscientious job editing this student preparation book. It is reassuring to know that such a skilled teacher spent so much time analyzing our work. Cheryl Perreault, formerly of Northeastern University in Boston, offered many helpful insights (and some much needed kind words!) during her diligent review of both the student text and the teacher's manual. Aaron Portenga of Grand Haven (MI) High School applied his substantial teaching and content expertise in reading both products, and we are grateful for his discerning eye.

Thank you to Kevin Galipeau for his generosity and expertise in reading much of this work.

The following students from the Hopkinton High School Class of 2010 also volunteered their services as editors, and did a marvelously helpful job in that capacity.

| | |
|---|---|
| Alice Beecher | Alice Lagoy |
| Samantha Bertschmann | Anna Lipkin |
| Amanda Carbonneau | Lauren O'Loughlin |
| Shaye Ellis | Michelle Surka |
| Olivia Eori | Hannah Weinsaft |

Special mention goes to Gretchen Sileo (Class of 2010) and Elise LeCrone (Class of 2011), who each did an incredibly professional job reading many chapters of this book. Their efforts were especially kind, and their work especially impressive.

Our hearty thanks also go out to the following artists, who contributed their significant skills in bringing most of the cartoon ideas in this book to fruition:

Alejandro Yegros, cartoonist (alejandroyegros.com)

Leah Raczynski (HHS Class of 2013)

Dan Quigley (HHS Class of 2011)

Caroline Olney (HHS Class of 2011)

Samantha Levitre (HHS Class of 2010)

Stephanie Planchard (HHS Class of 2010)

Jaclyn Perreault (HHS Class of 2009)

John Hinkel (HHS Class of 2009)

Sandy Valpey Cordtts (valpeystudios@mac.com)

Special thanks to Renée Cammarata Hamilton for her enthusiastic support and limitless patience throughout this process. It was comforting to know that you were always available for advice and guidance.

Thank you to Mazalit Lehrfeld, of MazDesign, for her consistent and conscientious efforts in typesetting.

# Table of Contents

# AP Psychology
## *Introduction*

Psychology is an ever-evolving discipline. Much of what we summarize in this book may turn out to be wrong, or at least incomplete, as more research is conducted and more insight gained. We've done our best, knowing that the study of psychology is dynamic and invites constant update and renewal.

We hope this book will clarify and illuminate areas of confusion that arise from the plethora of television shows, movies and books purporting to be about 'psychology'. While many people have the misconception that psychology is merely a matter of applying labels to common sense intuitions, psychologists are trained to rely on evidence, systematically gathered, rather than gut feelings. Much of what we intuitively believe to be true turns out to be more complicated when it is carefully and empirically investigated.

Psychologists examine

- why people do what they do, and how biological, social and cognitive factors influence those behaviors.
- how people make decisions and arrive at judgments.
- how people perceive the world and events in it.
- human dysfunction, but also human flourishing. One of the growing sub-fields within psychology is that of *positive psychology*, which emphasizes human potential, strengths and happiness. Psychologists also examine the coping strategies humans use in adapting to life's challenges.

Psychologists do not

- engage in voodoo or magic, some student perceptions to the contrary!
- constantly "psychoanalyze" people.

  If you are known to be a student of psychology, people will often wonder aloud if you are "psychoanalyzing" them, which reveals another common misconception about psychology. 'Psychoanalysis' is actually a particular perspective within the field, not a generic term for theorizing about people and their possible motivations.
- rely merely on intuition, but rather gather data to test hypotheses

A strong case could be made that every high school student should take psychology before they graduate. In the first place, it's no accident that psychology is perennially one of the most popular majors on college campuses - it is a terrifically interesting field, so almost all high school students will find it accessible and intriguing. But the major selling point for such a proposal is the relevance of psychology. Whether or not a student plans to go to school after grade twelve, a fundamental understanding of human behavior, emotion and mental processes will serve them well in life. As many of our students say, "Psychology is everywhere!" The more one knows about principles of human perception, the more aware and insightful about even the most mundane events one becomes. The more one knows about learning and motivation, the easier it is to understand and even influence the behavior of others in the workplace and in the world at large. The more one knows about human judgment, decision making and attitudes the better able one is to think for themselves and to wisely evaluate the thinking of others. The more one knows about psychological disorders or the roots of personality, the more sensitive and tolerant one becomes. In fact, it's hard to imagine teaching and learning about psychology without making connections to one's own life. After all, psychology is *about* one's own life - our perception, our thinking, our feeling, our motivations, our quirks and our quest for happiness, fulfillment and meaning.

The Advanced Placement Psychology curriculum is designed to give you a university level survey of this very broad field while you are still in high school. This book can serve most of the functions of a full-length, hardcover college psychology textbook in your preparation for the advanced placement examination. It provides all the content and practice you need in order to excel on the AP exam. You may, however, wish to secure another text to serve as a resource; this is especially true if you are preparing entirely on your own. If you do, make certain it is a college level introductory text. Some teachers of Advanced Placement Psychology believe that the textbook choice is the single most important decision one makes in preparing for the exam. If, however, you are taking a legitimate psychology course taught by a capable and diligent instructor, you are obviously at an advantage no matter what text you use.

The practice items you will see in this book will prepare you for the kinds of questions you will see on the test itself. Those items are useful both for practice and for "diagnosis" of strengths and weaknesses. **Each chapter includes a set of multiple-choice items** that mirrors the range of difficulty and breadth of content you will encounter on the AP Examination. If you follow the directions for **time management** and self discipline that this book provides, each section will give you a true sense of where you stand in that particular unit. Later, when you try one of the **three full-length practice examinations,** you will discover that it's pretty easy to identify your weaker and stronger content areas. This will make your studying more effective and less time consuming.

**In each chapter there is an "Essay Themes" section**, which highlights the big picture of each unit. Of course, there's no guarantee that those particular themes will show up on a particular essay, but reflecting on them will certainly help you to bring the unit into focus and help you tie what otherwise might appear to be a bunch of disparate "facts" into a coherent whole. The essay portion of the exam (the authors of the test prefer to call it the "free response" section) will almost always ask you to think thematically, so we'll practice that kind of thinking all along the way in this book.

Psychology is such a multi-faceted field that it is difficult to study it *without* thinking thematically. And there is a great deal of overlap between the many sub-fields within the discipline, even though there are many who actually contend that 'psychology' isn't really one discipline at all anymore. Such thinkers might argue that study of say, "Personality Theory" is very different in content and approach from the study of "The Biological Bases of Behavior", but the AP curriculum still emphasizes study of each of those and much more under the one umbrella of 'psychology'.

The Advanced Placement Psychology Examination is made up of **100 multiple-choice items** (worth 2/3 of your entire exam score) and **two free response or essay questions** (collectively worth 1/3 of your overall score). There is no choice on the free response section as there is, for example, on the AP US History test. Every student is asked to "present a cogent argument" in response to the same two items. The multiple-choice section lasts **70 minutes**; the free response section, distributed only after the multiple-choice portion has been collected by the test proctors, is **50 minutes** long. There's no hard and fast rule on this, but in very general terms students tend to feel more "rushed" on the essays than on the multiple-choice. Again, disciplined time management is especially important on that part of the examination. You should try to adhere to the pacing guidelines suggested at various points in this book; **the importance of time management on the AP Psychology Examination cannot be overstated.**

Advanced Placement Exams are scored on a **one to five scale.** Most colleges and universities award advanced placement credit for scores of three or above; some accept only four's and five's, and a very few highly selective schools will only grant credit for a five. The College Board and the Educational Testing Service have conducted at least two "comparability studies" to validate the test. They found that high school advanced placement psychology students perform at least as well as college students on advanced placement exams, which indicates that those students are indeed receiving a genuine college psychology experience.

Generally speaking, 67 - 70% of the over 175,000 test takers each year earn a score of three or above in AP Psychology. Despite what you may hear from teachers and other students, there is no strict threshold for any particular score. Your score is more of **a ranking** of how you performed in comparison to all the other test takers than it is anything else. There is no cut-off established beforehand for "four-ness" or "five-ness". For instance, if there was a year in which students did poorly nationwide on one essay, the overall raw scores would be lower, but students who were the best of the best, however good or not-so-good "best" was that year, would still receive "fives".

The AP Psychology curriculum consists of fourteen content areas. In this book we break one of those, "Cognition", into its two major parts, "Memory" and "Thought and Language". We also incorporate the "History of Psychology" into the rest of the program rather than treating it separately. **The majority of units will make up seven to ten percent of the multiple-choice items** on the big exam. You'll see some exceptions to this, although that won't impact your preparation very much. The percentages do *not* apply to the free response section of the text. Anything is fair game in those. The authors of those questions try hard to reference concepts from several different content units in each free response item. But their basic goal in developing free response prompts is to come up with fair but challenging questions that will differentiate between student levels of mastery, not to cover any particular content area. So it's a losing battle to try to use previous tests to predict what might be on this year's exam. On past exams there was once a very loose tendency to place one "harder science" item (on "statistics and methodology" or "biopsychology" for example) with a "softer science" question (from "personality theory" or "social psychology" for instance), but items are not written or chosen based on thinking like "We need a 'memory' question - we haven't had one of those in years" or "We have to come up with more difficult questions because the students are doing too well!". It isn't done that way.

If you read the book and follow the tips offered in this chapter and throughout the text you will succeed on the AP exam. We have included over 450 multiple-choice questions and six free response questions in this edition. These will serve as great practice and will also allow you to determine where your areas of weakness lie. We hope you find the text engaging and easy to navigate. It is our sincerest wish that you find this course to be among the best you have ever taken.

## Course Outline

### I. Research Methodology and Approaches (8-10%)

The meat of this unit focuses on experimentation in the social sciences. You will learn how to design and critically evaluate experiments. You'll also study other kinds of research: naturalistic observations, longitudinal and cross-sectional studies, correlational research, the case study approach and survey methodology. There's a bit about statistics in this unit - don't worry, you don't need to be a "math person" to understand these basic concepts!

### II. The Biological Bases of Behavior (8-10%)

This unit does frighten people, but mastery of it is essential for understanding of later topics. You can't really claim to understand 'psychology' if you don't know about the biological underpinnings of what we do, think and feel. By the time you're finished here, you'll have a nice grasp of how specific brain regions seem to operate, how the body sends its messages through neurons in the brain and through the glands of the endocrine system and how a "genetic predisposition" can give us a push in one behavioral direction or another.

### III. Sensation and Perception (6-8%)

Many college psych textbooks break this into two separate chapters, but the AP curriculum quite reasonably joins them together. That makes for a large unit, but fortunately many of the concepts can be demonstrated to you, which makes them easy to assimilate and retain. Basically, the 'sensation' part of this unit covers the physiological information gathering systems in humans, while the 'perception' segment involves study of the psychological interpretation of that sensory input.

### IV. States of Consciousness (2-4%)

Like many students, you'll probably find this a very high interest topic, although it has relatively small weight on the AP Exam. The main focus here is on sleep and dreams: Why do we sleep? What are the characteristics of a "typical" night's sleep? Do dreams have significance, or do we simply attempt to attach significance to what is essentially random brain activity? What is the nature of hypnosis - is it an "altered state of consciousness" or is a hypnotized subject simply very relaxed and thus more suggestible than he would be otherwise? You'll also learn a bit about the action of psychoactive drugs in this mini-unit.

### V. Learning Theory (7-9%)

Here you will learn about classical conditioning, operant conditioning, social or observational learning and some different types of cognitive learning. Some of the best-known studies in the history of psychology are in learning theory; you'll find it pretty easy to remember Ivan Pavlov's classical conditioning of salivation in dogs, John B. Watson's classical conditioning of fear in a little boy, and Albert Bandura's famed "Bobo" study in which young children imitate the aggressive behavior of adult models. This unit is very important because it foreshadows your later study of the "Behavioral" school of psychological thought in units on Motivation, Personality Theory, Abnormal Psychology and Treatment.

### VI. Cognition (including Memory and Thought and Language) (8-10%)

Here is another topic that is often split into two chapters in textbooks. Concepts in memory are often easy to actively demonstrate, and it's easy to think of real life examples of such phenomena, so they should be relatively easy to remember! The second half of the unit focuses on human judgment, planning and decision-making and on language acquisition. The latter topic serves as a nice lead-in to the unit on developmental psychology, so this book is organized with that in mind.

### VII. Developmental Psychology (7-9%)

This book is laid out a bit differently than the AP unit chronology, in that this unit is placed immediately after the unit on Cognition, and is then followed by study of Motivation and Emotion. You'll understand more on the reasoning behind that placement later. Developmental Psych is the study of how humans progress through life in terms of physical and social growth, thinking and moral reasoning.

### VIII. Motivation and Emotion (6-8%)

Again, in this book, this unit is placed *after* Developmental Psychology, although the AP Psychology curriculum places it after Cognition. Either sequence is easily defensible. Stop someone on the street and ask them "What is psychology?", and they may well say "it's the study of why people do what they do" - and that is the thrust of the first part of this chapter, which is yet another example of a topic that is sometimes split in two in college psych textbooks. In the second half of the unit, we will examine how human emotions unfold, whether or not they are universally experienced and perceived, and the nature of specific emotions like love and aggression.

### IX. Personality Theory (5-7%)

This will supply you with a nice overview of the big "schools of thought" in psychology, which is essential for success on the AP Psych Exam.  Much of the history of psychology is tied into these different perspectives and you will need to understand how each group views the origins and development of personality. Several free response questions on past AP Psychology Exams have revolved around those major perspectives, and you'll see a whole lot of overlap between this unit and several others in the course, so give it careful attention.

### X. Testing and Individual Differences (5-7%)

This used to be referred to as "Intelligence and Assessment", and that pretty much tells you what it is about. You'll learn about several theories, which attempt to define 'smart', and various ways to try to assess that elusive quality. You'll also explore the concepts of reliability (the consistency of the scoring of a test) and validity ("does this test really test what it says it tests?") in assessment. You will find powerful connections here to your own educational experiences.

### XI. Abnormal Psychology (7-9%)

Many people think this is 'psychology'; the study of the characteristics and origins of mental disorders. It *is* a very important and quite fascinating topic, but it is only one of many under the big tent of 'psychology'. It's also almost always placed rather late in psychology textbooks and curriculum progressions. In Abnormal Psych you'll learn about several different categories of psychological disorder ranging from mood disorders to anxiety disorders to various kinds of schizophrenia. You'll also explore the difficulties professionals face in delineating the lines between 'normal' behavior and clinically 'abnormal' behavior. You'll undoubtedly leave this unit more sensitive about the complexities of human behavior and dysfunction.

### XII. Treatment of Psychological Disorders (5-7%)

Your study of this unit will go well if you got a good grip on the major theoretical perspectives in psychology during the chapter on Personality Theory. There is significant overlap between the two topics, but in this chapter you'll focus more on specific therapeutic techniques used by clinicians from different psychological orientations - psychoanalytic strategies to uncover unconscious conflict, cognitive techniques to restructure self-destructive thinking, behavioral approaches designed to model or condition healthier behaviors, drug interventions from the biomedical perspective, and more.

### XIII. Social Psychology (8-10%)

Because this is almost always placed at the end of textbooks and course outlines, it sometimes gets less attention than it deserves. Don't overlook it! For one thing, it carries substantial weight on the AP Exam, but more importantly, it contains engaging material which is readily linked to your own lives. Social Psych is the study of individual behavior in group and societal contexts. The specific topics in this unit include obedience to authority, conformity to group pressure, helping behavior, group dynamics, attitudes, prejudice and attraction. That's a pretty broad menu, and it makes for stimulating discussions!

### XIV. History of Psychology (2-4%)

We have not included a separate chapter that focuses only on the history of psychology because you'll pick up what you need to know in the course of studying the units mentioned above. Most of the history that you would see on the exam involves the different perspectives (schools of thought) in psychology and the people who were instrumental in developing those perspectives.

### Top Ten Things to Remember in Taking the Multiple-Choice Section of the AP Psychology Exam

In getting ready to try the multiple-choice practice items use the "test preparation" **graphic organizers** provided for you at the end of each chapter, or, better yet, make your own. Simply engaging in the process of creating a visual representation of the material you know or wish to know is an invaluable learning tool - it's very hard to create a graphic organizer unless you have a pretty good grasp of the stuff you're representing. There are many suggested formats for graphic organizers available, but individually tailoring the look of it so it makes sense to *you* is the best approach.

10. If you are well prepared, you probably won't feel rushed on the multiple-choice, so **you can afford to slow down.**

9. **Practice time management,** using the review items at the end of each chapter and the three full-length practice examinations in this book. Knowing about pacing strategies is not the same thing as being able to actually execute those strategies - the only way to gauge your ability to do that is to try them. You might also ask your teacher to design his or her unit tests to mirror the pacing of the actual AP Exam, to give you year-long practice in time management.

8. As you proceed through the exam, **make a mark next to items you want to revisit** later. You may not have time to review all 100 items, so it'll be useful to have highlighted those that most require a second look.

7. If you do have "review time" after running through all 100 questions, look only at those you marked earlier. While research conducted by Justin Kruger and others suggests that one shouldn't be afraid to review and actually change answers on multiple-choice questions, on a strictly timed exam like this one **it's simply not feasible to re-evaluate every decision you've made** during the course of the test.

6. The items in the multiple-choice section are arranged in **order of difficulty,** based on pretesting data and the judgment of the committee that constructs the test, so it is a useful strategy not to "out think yourself" on items placed early in the test. Sometimes well-prepared students feel an answer is "too easy" and talk themselves out of it, but it's important to remember that items early in the test *are* likely pretty easy for a well-prepared student!

5. **Consider covering the answer choices as you read the stem** of each question, and try to answer before looking. This can make some of the distractor items less distracting. It takes practice to get yourself to actually do this consistently, so try it out early in the year when answering review items at the end of each chapter.

4. There is a small section in this book, immediately preceding the three practice exams, entitled "Preparation to Take the Examination". Try some of the exercises in that section. Learning "test taking strategies" isn't enough for you to succeed on a challenging standardized test - there's no substitute for knowing the content. But **practice with process of elimination and other techniques can certainly help on specific items**. Again: *knowing about* such approaches is not enough - you have to try them out.

3. The multiple-choice section of the AP Psychology Exam **is worth 2/3 of your total test score.** That's a lot of weight. Lots of students (and their teachers!) worry more about the free response section of the test, but do not underestimate the importance of these 100 questions.

2. This book will help you **space your practice** over the course of the school year, but you should also **do the same for your studying.** Generally speaking, "distributed rehearsal" is more effective than "massed rehearsal", although last minute cramming can be valuable if you're essentially relearning material you had mastered earlier. If, however, you're trying to assimilate new material in large amounts at the last minute, you are going to struggle.

1. **Think.** Don't simply react in "I know it or I don't" mode. You can reason out a lot more than you might at first believe by applying your general knowledge of psychology, even if at first you feel you don't "know" the answer to a question. This approach requires attention and practice. You have to train yourself to slow down and not simply *react* to an item.

### Top Ten Things to Remember in Answering the Free Response Questions on the AP Psychology Exam

10. From the start of the school year, **practice pacing**. Time yourself on essays your teacher gives you on unit tests. That will help you gradually develop an internal "clock" which will serve you well on the AP Exam in May.

9. **Budget your time.** Actually write down your projected "start" and "finish" time when you begin writing. This step can help discipline you to give fair treatment to both of the essays. You might consider giving yourself 22 or 23 minutes on your first essay, and the same amount on your second, which will still leave you a few minutes at the

end to go back and add a flourish or clean up a loose end. Also remember that the **two free response questions have equal weight;** even though one might look bigger than another, don't let that fool you!

8. **Do the item you know best first.** This is to insure that you get full credit for what you really know. It's pretty frustrating to spend a lot of time on an item you're struggling with only to get to a question you know very well with too little time to do it justice.

7. **Highlight key elements of each question** and respond directly to them. If the question asks you to "compare *and* contrast", it'll hurt you if you don't actually do both, and the best way to avoid such an oversight is to highlight everything you need to do.

6. Take a breath and **reflect for a moment**. You may only have moments to do this, but that little snippet of time can help you focus on what you know, how to organize it and how to express it to a reader.

5. **This is a specific kind of writing and time is very much a factor,** so you don't need an introductory paragraph, especially if it is only going to restate the question, nor do you necessarily need to follow a strict "five paragraph essay" format. The free response prompts are often laid out in a kind of outline format. You can use that layout as an organizing principle in your essay, perhaps by simply beginning a new paragraph for every new concept you're asked to consider. Look at the free response questions in the practice exams at the end of this book and you'll get a sense of how this would work.

4. **A fellow human *will* be reading this,** and he or she deserves your consideration. Those readers are very capable people, and they're usually pretty nice too, so they want to give you the credit you deserve, but it's your job to make that easy for them. So you do want the occasional paragraph break, you do want to remember **this is an essay,** not a series of short answers, and you do want to write as legibly as you can.

3. Think of your audience as an intelligent but uninformed child. He or she can understand things quite well, but doesn't know anything about the field, and it's your job to **"teach" them what *you* know about it.**

2. **Say it clearly, and move on.** You don't have the time to do much else, and the readers appreciate it when students are direct and concise. Continually reminding yourself of what your audience needs and wants can help guide you in the writing process.

1. **Use terminology from the field of psychology.** Your goal is to impress upon the reader that you thrived in a rigorous college level psychology course, and that you're not merely relying on episodes of "Law and Order" or "CSI" or "Oprah" for your knowledge.

The College Board makes each year's Free Response Questions available to both AP Psychology teachers and students. You may find it useful to use these past questions to help you study. More importantly, you can use them to practice the above tips. You can access these questions by going to:

http://www.collegeboard.com/student/testing/ap/psych/samp.html?phych   (Although the last part of this link may look like a typographical error, it is correct)

# Chapter 1
# *Statistics and Research Methodology*

### Introduction

Psychology is the systematic, scientific study of human behavior and mental processes. This opening unit on research methods is an introduction to how psychologists do their work. Psychologists and the teachers who construct the advanced placement exam are committed to presenting psychology as a social science.

Social scientists use systematic methods to gather, interpret and evaluate information that will allow them to assess the credibility of claims and to arrive at a belief or a course of action. The study of the social sciences requires acceptance of the reality that at times we may be unable to arrive at a solution, and recognition of the fact that there is often more than one "right answer." In many of the units presented in this course you may actually leave with more questions than answers. Social scientists also actively look for possible flaws in their theories and research, and view contradictions as opportunities to further explore the truth. Above all, study of the social sciences requires the disposition to develop and utilize such skills in critical thinking.

For as long as the Advanced Placement Psychology program has existed, this unit has been a significant area of focus on the AP examination. Simply stated, you are in trouble on the test if you do not give this unit your full attention. In it you'll be considering questions like:

- How do we meaningfully evaluate the validity of any claim?
- As we assess research, what evidence is meaningful and why?
- To what extent should one insist on asking "What's the evidence?" Can such persistence "paralyze" us intellectually?
- To what degree can one truly control experimental conditions so as to reasonably ascertain cause and effect?
- Has the research finding been replicated?

### Experimentation in Psychology

The bulk of this chapter revolves around **experimentation** in psychology. Most people refer to research in general as 'experimentation', but an experiment is a specific type of research, as are correlational research, case study approaches, survey approaches, naturalistic observations, cross-sectional studies and longitudinal studies. You must have a basic understanding of how each of those is conducted, with a sense of their strengths and limitations as well.

The basic goal in an experiment is to determine if some variable you manipulate (the **independent variable** or **IV**) has a cause and effect relationship on some outcome that you measure (**the dependent variable** or **DV**). Essentially, you are testing the effect of the independent variable on the dependent variable. When you are asked to identify these components of an experiment, it may be useful to re-frame the experimental set-up each time by saying "They're testing the effect of _____ on _____". The first blank is the IV, the second is the DV. Discriminating between these two types of variables can be difficult, so be sure to know them. You could also think of the independent variable as being an intravenous treatment in a hospital; the doctor "puts something into you" with the IV and then measures what effect it has on you.

A researcher states a **hypothesis,** which is a prediction of the effect of the independent variable on the dependent variable, and then attempts to control for possible **confounding variables** (variables other than the IV that might account for a difference between groups in the experiment). These variables can confuse and often invalidate research results so experimenters go to great lengths to make sure that these extraneous variables do not influence the study.  Here's an example: if you were testing the effect of two different teaching styles (the IV) on AP Psychology examination performance (the DV), you would want to make certain that any difference between the two groups on the AP Exam was in fact the result of being taught differently. You would not want one group to do better than the other because one took the exam when bright and fresh at 9 a.m. while the second group took the test at 4:30 p.m. after a full day of classes. You would not want one group to take the exam in an air-conditioned room while the second group slogged through the thing in unpleasantly hot conditions. The differences in time of day and testing environment might account for the differences in performance between the two groups, so you need to control for those possible confounding variables.

| INDEPENDENT VARIABLE (I.V.) | DEPENDENT VARIABLE (D.V.) | CONFOUNDING VARIABLE |
|---|---|---|
| What the experimenter manipulates; What they "do to" the members of the experimental group(s) | What the experimenter measures in the end; Theoretically, it is "dependent upon" whether or not the participants received the IV | Variables the experimenter did not control for that may have affected the results |

A scientific hypothesis must be falsifiable – that is, it can be shown to be untrue by the research findings. An assertion that is not falsifiable is really a matter of opinion. That's fine, but it's not 'science'. The best studies in psychology have stood up to repeated attempts to falsify them. More than trying to "prove" their hypothesis, social scientists actually try in their research to disprove **the null hypothesis**, which is the statement that the independent variable will have no effect on the dependent variable. We assume the null hypothesis is correct until we can encounter scientific evidence to reject it. No matter what data were gathered in the experiment described in the preceding paragraph, it would be difficult to say that one had proven that one teaching style was superior to all others. But if the data show a statistically significant difference between the groups it does suggest that using a particular teaching approach had some effect on student test performance.

Experimenters must always attempt to gather a **representative sample** of all members of the group they wish to study, called the **population,** and they assign those volunteers to **control** and **experimental groups** so that each is representative of the whole target group. That way, one can **generalize** from the outcomes of the experiment to the entire population. Random selection of subjects and random assignment of them to experimental or control groups is generally all that is needed to insure that you have a representative sample overall and in each of your groups. To choose **"at random"** simply means that all members of the population have an equal chance of being chosen. A researcher might simply pick names out of a hat or use a computer algorithm to establish a representative set of groups. Another way to insure representativeness in each group is to use **group matching.** In this procedure, one systematically assigns individuals to each group to guarantee balance. If you used group matching to choose fair teams for an informal basketball game, you might place the two best players on opposite teams, the two worst players on opposite teams, and so on.

Often, it is necessary for experimenters to establish **operational definitions** (a definition of a concept or phenomenon which provides for specific ways to measure whether that thing exists or occurs) of the concepts under study. This helps especially in the measurement of the dependent variable. It is difficult to measure something that is poorly defined. Having clear and precise operational definitions allows for **replication,** in which other researchers repeat an experiment to confirm its conclusions. Replication is an essential component of the scientific method.

| EXPERIMENTAL GROUPS | CONTROL GROUPS | PLACEBO GROUPS |
|---|---|---|
| Participants receive the independent variable | Participants do not receive the independent variable; A comparison group | Participants are led to believe they are receiving the independent variable, but they do not; Tests the possible effect of expectancy on the results |

You must also know about **double blind** designs as a means of eliminating possible experimenter bias. In a double blind design, neither the participants in the study nor the experimenters (or the experimental assistants who gather the data) know which participants belong to the control group and which belong to experimental groups. This helps prevent **confirmation bias,** in which an experimenter might consciously or unconsciously look to confirm what they already believe about their hypothesis.  In addition to utilizing **double blinds,** many experiments (especially those involving medications) utilize a **placebo** group. Members of this group unknowingly receive a medication that contains no active ingredient. They actually get no treatment (or independent variable) at all. This is done to account for the **self-fulfilling prophecy** known as the "placebo effect" in which a participant's belief that they are receiving a treatment may produce an outcome rather than the treatment (or IV) itself. You might find it interesting to discuss with your classmates whether it is ethical to require placebo groups in a study designed to evaluate the effectiveness of a new drug. Volunteers randomly assigned to that group might thus miss out on the benefits of the new medication if it *does* turn out to be effective.

The greatest strength of experimental methodology is that it is the only research method from which we can infer direct cause and effect relationships. Experiments allow us to control conditions and variables in order to see the exact extent to which our IV affects our DV.

One limitation of experimental methodology is that lab results may not always translate to real-life situations. Experiments can also be costly to conduct and intrusive on the lives of those being tested. Of course, there are also phenomena that we cannot practically test with an experiment. We'll investigate alternative ways to study such phenomena later in this chapter.

We'll wrap up our look at experimental methodology by laying out a hypothetical experiment testing the effect of a drug designed to treat depression.

- **Population:** Adults in the US suffering from depression

- **Operational Definition:** 'Adult' defined as age 21 to 65; all meet clinical criteria for a diagnosis of major depression

- **Hypothesis:** "Drug X will alleviate the symptoms of depression"

- **Null hypothesis:** "Drug X will have no effect on the symptoms of depression"

- **The IV:** Drug X

- **The DV:** Symptoms of depression

- **Randomly select a sample** of the target population and then randomly assign those participants to three groups

- **Experimental Group:** Receives the independent variable- Drug X

- **Placebo Group:** Receives a treatment with no active ingredient

- **Control Group:** Receives no treatment

- **Double Blind Design:** The participants do not know whether they are receiving Drug X or the placebo, and the researcher evaluating the levels of depression is not aware of the hypothesis nor the groups to which the participants were assigned.

### Ethics in Experimental Methodology

The American Psychological Association (APA) has established a strict set of **ethical guidelines** that researchers must adhere to when conducting research with human subjects. To ensure that all experiments follow these guidelines, researchers must first have their experiment approved by an **Institutional Review Board (IRB).** The IRB reviews the proposal and rejects experiments that do not abide by these ethical requirements. The table below contains the major ethical guidelines that you will need to know for this course.

| | |
|---|---|
| **Informed consent** | Before the experiment starts the subjects must be informed of the nature and purpose of the experiment and any potential risks that are involved. Participants must be willing volunteers. Once informed of the details of the experiment, subjects sign a formal consent form. |
| **Confidentiality** | The researchers may not release or publish the names of anyone participating in the experiment. |
| **Protection of participants** | All participants are protected from physical, mental and emotional harm. |
| **Right to discontinue** | Participants have the right to end their participation during any phase of an experiment. |
| **Minimum of deception** | Researchers have an obligation to avoid deceiving participants whenever possible. There are cases where some degree of deception is necessary, but in these cases researchers must demonstrate a strong scientific or medical justification. |
| **Obligation to debrief** | After the experiment is complete all participants have a right to full disclosure of the nature of the research including the findings that the study produced. |
| **For more information:** | http://www.apa.org/ethics/ |

Later, in the unit on Learning Theory, you'll learn about a study from the 1920's in the classical conditioning of fear. In it, behaviorist John B. Watson conditioned a very young orphan (known as Little Albert) to fear a white rat that the boy originally liked. Even without the details you will examine in that later chapter, you can see some obvious ethical issues in Watson's work, such as an intense amount of distress imposed on a child who is being taught to fear something and lack of informed consent, just to mention two. In the last unit of this course, on Social Psychology, you'll learn about Stanley Milgram's work in the early 1960's on obedience to authority; this too sparked much ethical debate and contributed to the standards that now exist in the field of psychological research. Milgram asked male volunteers to "teach" word pairs to other volunteers, using painful electric shocks as punishment for incorrect responses. In fact, the "learner" was part of the experiment, and did not actually receive shocks, although the teacher did not know that as he heard the learner pretend to yell in protest and pain in a nearby room. Milgram's real intent was not to study the effect of punishment on learning, but to examine whether an individual would obey an authority figure (the researcher conducting the study) even when doing so would cause harm to another. Did Milgram place his volunteers under too much stress? Was there too much deception inherent in his research design? Did he inform volunteers that they had the right to discontinue participation at any time? (In fact, he did not - that present day guideline evolved partly as a direct response to Milgram's study) Was his post-study debriefing sufficient to relieve any distress his work may have caused? You may be able to consider these questions more deeply later as your studies progress, especially after you examine Milgram's research further at the end of the course.

## Use of Animals in Research

Today less than 10% of psychological research involves animals – still, much of what we know in psychology has been derived from experiments done with animals. Although most research today inflicts no harm on the animals being tested, there have been studies in the past that would seem highly unethical using today's standards. This invites the question: When is the harm worth the benefit, if ever? Responsible people can disagree on the answer to that question, but it may reassure you to know that the APA has developed very specific rules and procedures for using animals in research. Much like the IRB, animal research requires that the Institutional Animal Care and Use Committee (IACUC) evaluate and approve potential experiments to avoid the mistreatment or abuse of animals. If you are interested in animal research go to www.apa.org/science/anguide.html for a detailed description of this set of ethical guidelines.

## Other Research Methods

There are several other ways to conduct research in psychology. One of those is through **correlational research.** The aim here is to examine the link (the co- relationship) between variables; do two variables tend to occur together, and, if so, in what direction? For example: does the weight in pounds of professional baseball players correlate with the number of home runs players hit? If so, is it that heavier players tend to hit more home runs (a **positive correlation**), that home run totals go down as weight increases (a **negative correlation**), or is there no apparent statistical connection between the two variables? The strength of such correlations is measured in **correlation coefficients.** A "perfect" positive correlation is represented as r = +1.0, a "perfect" negative correlation as r = -1.0. If the 'r' value is near 0.00 then you can infer that the variables under study do not tend to occur together. In real-world research, you would never get a perfect correlation, in which the two variables you are studying always move in exact proportion to each other. But, as one example, you might find a rather strong positive correlation, perhaps r = +.70, for height and weight in American males. Taller individuals do tend to be heavier than shorter individuals. A key point to remember is that, no matter how strongly correlated two variables are, one cannot assume that one variable causes the other to occur. For example, in an urban setting we might find a very strong positive correlation between the number of physical assaults and the sales of ice cream. Does this mean that buying ice cream causes assaults, or that being assaulted encourages victims to buy more ice cream? Both explanations are unlikely. What seems to be at work here is a *third variable* – perhaps air temperature. Both physical assaults and ice cream purchases increases in the summer months, when the temperature is higher.

To repeat: be cautious in interpreting correlational data. A strong statistical correlation indicates the *possibility* of a causative link but it does not *prove* that a cause and effect relationship exists. The only way to demonstrate cause and effect would be to conduct a controlled experiment.

**Scatterplots** are often used to chart data gathered from correlational research. For your reference, here are some fictional scatterplots:

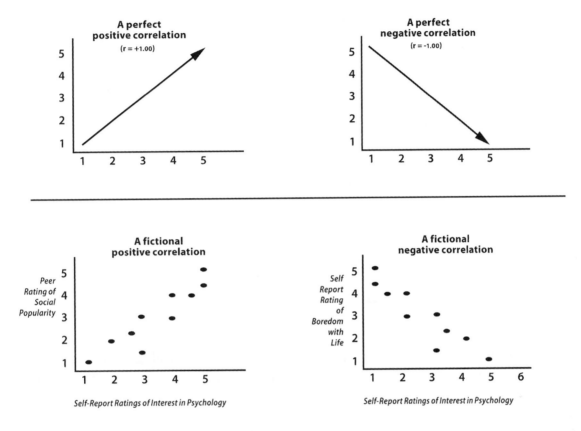

Some psychological research is done through the use of surveys. As with experiments, in survey methodology you need to choose a truly representative sample of the population you are studying to ensure that you are getting accurate and useful results.  Some things you must consider in administering a survey (which can come in the form of an interview or a written questionnaire) are demand characteristic, social desirability bias and framing. At times those who are taking a survey sense what the researcher seems to want of them; they then supply the responses they feel they're expected to give. This is an example of a **demand characteristic,** and it is one argument for keeping the person who is administering the survey "blind" as to the hypothesis or the agenda of the lead researcher. That way, the administrator cannot unwittingly cue the respondents. In **social desirability bias,** the survey respondent offers responses they deem to be socially acceptable. For example: if asked to report the number of times they drink alcohol per week, college students may well give responses that are in line with accepted standards of the culture, especially if they feel their actual behaviors are excessive in either direction.

"Demand Characteristic"

(Sullivan - Levitre-Valpey)

The way that questions are **framed** or worded can dramatically impact the results of your survey. Even the order of words in a question can have subtle effects. What if we asked high school students the following?

*Does the school administration deal with students fairly or unfairly?*

Might we get different results if we asked it this way?

*Does the school administration deal with students unfairly or fairly?*

Simply flipping the order of the word 'fairly' and 'unfairly' might well affect the survey respondents. Researchers need to be cognizant of how these *wording effects* can influence responses and thus threaten the validity of a survey.

Surveys can be relatively inexpensive to conduct while allowing researchers to gather a lot of data in a short amount of time. However, they rely on self-reported attitudes that are vulnerable to dishonesty and self-deception. The difference between what people say they do and what they actually do is easy to see in the following example. A recent survey reported by CNN asked men if they washed their hands after using a public restroom. Ninety-five percent of respondents confirmed that they did wash their hands, but a *naturalistic observation* revealed that only 65% actually washed their hands. We can surmise that such responses to the survey may well have been affected by *social desirability bias.*

In **naturalistic observations,** a researcher observes subjects while the subjects do whatever they do in a natural setting. This is an attempt to see what people and other animals really do in typical environments and scenarios, as compared to what they *report* they do on surveys or other self-report inventories. Therefore, it is essential that the researcher remain unobtrusive – that is, he or she makes sure the subjects do not know they are being watched. Before conducting the observation, researchers need to *operationally define* the behaviors that they will observe and measure. This helps reduce subjectivity and increases **inter-rater reliability** (consistency between the scores of multiple observers).

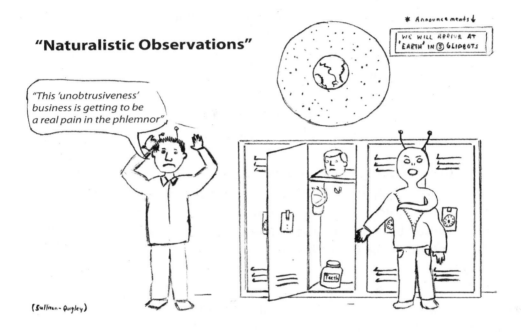

Case study approaches serve a similar purpose in that they take a single case and study its elements and implications. Often, such real life cases offer the opportunity for insights that one could never or would never attempt to gain through artificially designing an experiment. One of the more famous case studies in psychology comes from 1964. A 28 year-old woman named Kitty Genovese was assaulted near her apartment in Queens, New York. Over the course of thirty minutes, she was stabbed repeatedly and sexually assaulted; she eventually died of her wounds. When the police investigated, they found over three-dozen individuals who'd heard the commotion and the victim's cries for help, but had done nothing. Once police were finally notified, they arrived on the scene only after Genovese had passed away. Over the years, the facts of this case have been questioned. Did these people actually do nothing at all? Is the police report of the aftermath completely accurate? Controlled studies into what has come to be called **the bystander effect** have since been conducted, and they largely confirmed what psychologists had concluded from the Genovese case - generally speaking, the larger the group witnessing an event in which someone is in need of help, the less likely it is that any one individual will intervene. In these situations people *diffuse the responsibility* and convince themselves that someone else will help. People in such circumstances sometimes rely on *social referencing* (looking at the actions of others as a guide to inform one's own behaviors) and if no one else is taking action, they sometimes convince themselves that no action needs to be taken. This is sometimes called *pluralistic ignorance.*

"Jonestown" is another famous case study in Social Psychology. Jim Jones created a church called the People's Temple that thrived for some time in San Francisco. As questions of abuse and coercion arose around the group and its leader, Jones convinced hundreds of his followers to leave their families behind to construct a communal village, to be called "Jonestown", in the jungles of Guyana in South America. Tragically, in 1978, California congressman Leo Ryan, who was visiting the group on a fact-finding mission, was shot and killed at Jonestown. Jones, fearing the dissolution of the group, convinced members to drink juice laced with cyanide. In what is considered the largest mass suicide in modern history, over 900 members of the People's Temple died.

A case like this brings up many questions about human nature and behavior. Under what circumstances do people **conform to group pressure**? What conditions lead people to **obey an authority figure**? From this case we have learned much about the psychology and mentality of group behavior and the influence of a powerful leader. You will read more about such concepts in Social Psychology.

Case studies give us in-depth information on one particular incident. However, a major weakness of the case study method is that its implications may be specific to only that situation. One goal of research is to predict what would happen in similar circumstances, but a single case study may not allow us to make useful generalizations.

In a **longitudinal study,** researchers follow the same subjects over an extended period of time. Filmmaker Michael Apted made a movie in the mid-1960's he called "7 Up". In it, he interviewed a number of seven year olds in England. Since then, he's tracked those individuals down every seven years to make other documentaries (entitled "14 Up", "21 Up" and so on). The result is a compelling series examining the lives of the same people over the course of a lifespan. Another famous longitudinal study in psychology was conducted by Lewis Terman. Starting in the 1920s Terman began a decades long study of 1500 "gifted" California schoolchildren who had IQ scores over 135 (35 points above the average IQ). He found that this group tended to be happier, healthier, and more successful academically and professionally than people with average IQ scores.

Such an approach obviously takes many years and intensive commitment, and there is a potential problem with losing subjects along the way (sometimes called *subject mortality*), so **cross-sectional studies** are often conducted instead. In these, one examines a representative sample of different ages here and now. For example, if we were interested in the development of linguistic intelligence, we might select representative samples of 20 year-olds, 40 year-olds, 60 year-olds and 80 year-olds and compare their performances on various verbal tasks.

## Statistics in Psychology

There are some statistical concepts an AP Psychology student must know. For our purposes, statistics can be broken into two general categories: **descriptive statistics and inferential statistics. Descriptive statistics** do what they say they do- they summarize and describe data. **Inferential statistics** allow us to infer and draw conclusions from research. They involve analyzing sets of data to determine whether they are the result of mere chance or are actually the result of a manipulation made by the researchers.

The most important **inferential statistic** for this course is **statistical significance.** A finding is generally deemed to be statistically significant if there is a 95% or greater chance that the differences between groups in an experiment are not merely due to chance occurrence. This is represented as $p < .05$, which suggests the probability that the outcome is a chance occurrence is 5% or less. That in turn supports the notion that the results of our experiment were indeed the result of manipulating the independent variable. Thus, establishing statistical significance helps to reject the null hypothesis. An AP Psychology student does not have to know how to calculate a value for statistical significance, but should certainly understand it conceptually.

**Descriptive statistics** include **measures of central tendency (mean, median and mode)** and measures of **variability**. We've already discussed *correlational data*, which measures the relationship between variables – this too is a kind of descriptive statistic.

**The mean** is the arithmetic average of a set of values, **the median** is the middle value in a set (think of the median strip running down the middle of a highway), such that half the values fall above it and half below it (Remember to put the values in order first! the median value of the set of scores 3,8,5 is five, not eight...it is just such a seemingly simple item on the multiple choice section of the AP Exam that confuses test-takers, if they are moving too quickly), and **the mode** is the value that occurs most frequently in a set of scores (think "mo" for mode and "mo" for most). Knowing the mean is often very useful when looking at data, but there are times when the median or mode would be more useful. For example, if you were sitting in a restaurant with several of your friends and a billionaire took a seat at the table next to you, the mean salary of those in the restaurant would suddenly change dramatically. Extreme outliers, like the billionaire's salary, can affect the mean - in this case the median and mode would more accurately represent the salaries of the group.

"The importance of the mode"

In addition to knowing the measures of central tendency it may be useful to look at the variability or spread of scores in your data. The **range** and **standard deviation** are basic measures of variability. You calculate the range by simply subtracting the lowest number in your data set from the highest number in your data set. This number gives you a general idea of variation in your data but it only takes into account the two most extreme scores. A more informative measure is the standard deviation, which tells you the typical difference between any one score and the mean of all of the scores. The formula for standard deviation is the square root of the **variance,** which is a calculation of the differences between each score and the mean. A low standard deviation tells you that the data points were clustered around the mean and there were relatively few outliers. Here's a quick example of the calculation of variance and standard deviation in reference to the fictional data for two home run hitters in baseball supplied below. Without doing any calculations, ask yourself – which player's performance over the years will have the higher standard deviation?

| Season | Homeruns-Player A | Homeruns-Player B |
|--------|-------------------|-------------------|
| 1 | 10 | 19 |
| 2 | 34 | 20 |
| 3 | 17 | 25 |
| 4 | 36 | 17 |
| 5 | 11 | 15 |
| 6 | 13 | 20 |
| 7 | 40 | 24 |

### Measures of Central Tendency

|        | Player A | Player B |
|--------|----------|----------|
| N      | 7        | 7        |
| Mean   | 23.0     | 20.0     |
| Median | 17.0     | 20.0     |
| Mode   | None     | 20.0     |

### Calculating the Variance and Standard Deviation

| Player A | | | Player B | | |
|----------|------------------------|------------------------------|----------|------------------------|------------------------------|
| Value | Difference from mean | Square of the difference | Value | Difference from mean | Square of the difference |
| 10 | -13 | 169 | 19 | -1 | 1 |
| 34 | +11 | 121 | 20 | - | - |
| 17 | -6 | 36 | 25 | +5 | 25 |
| 36 | +13 | 169 | 17 | -3 | 9 |
| 11 | -12 | 144 | 15 | -5 | 25 |
| 13 | -10 | 100 | 20 | - | - |
| 40 | +17 | 289 | 24 | +4 | 16 |

| Player A | Player B |
|----------|----------|
| Total of squares of difference = 1028<br>Divide total by n-1 = 1028/6 = 171.33<br>Variance = 171.33<br>S.D. is the square root of the variance = 13.09 | Total of squares of difference = 76<br>Divide total by n-1 = 76/6 = 12.67<br>Variance = 12.67<br>S.D. is the square root of the variance = 3.56 |

On the average, Player A hits more homeruns year-to-year, but his performance is more variable, as we can see from the statistics above. If you were looking for a homerun hitter, which player would you prefer to have?

A well-prepared student should also have a basic grasp of **normal and skewed distributions**, and **percentiles**. If data about a variable are graphed and fall on a symmetrical, "bell shaped" curve, the distribution is referred to as a "normal distribution" or a "normal curve". In a skewed distribution, scores tend to cluster in one direction or another. The "skewedness" of such a curve is determined by the rare scores, the outliers. Thus, if a distribution is pushed to the right, with the hump of the curve at the high end of scores, this is called **a negative skew,** as the less typical scores are on the low end of the distribution. In **a positively skewed distribution,** high scores are the outliers (when you graph this, it looks a little like a 'p' lying on its back, which could cue you that the data are positively skewed). This is counterintuitive for many AP students, so be careful with it.

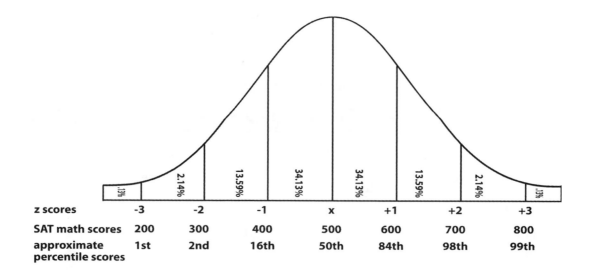

| z scores | -3 | -2 | -1 | x | +1 | +2 | +3 |
|---|---|---|---|---|---|---|---|
| SAT math scores | 200 | 300 | 400 | 500 | 600 | 700 | 800 |
| approximate percentile scores | 1st | 2nd | 16th | 50th | 84th | 98th | 99th |

Sometimes data are reported as **z scores** (also called standard scores). A *z score* simply tells you how many standard deviations a score is away from the mean. In the above example if your score was $z = +2$ (meaning you scored two standard deviations above the mean), your SAT score would be 700. When you take a standardized test such as the SAT, you will typically receive your raw score and a **percentile** score. A **percentile** score tells you where you rank in comparison to others. If, for example, you scored at the 84th percentile on an exam, it means you performed as well as or better than 84% of those who took the same test.

In our later study of intelligence and assessment, you will encounter an example of a normal distribution for intelligence quotient (IQ) scores. There is a visual representation of that in chapter eleven of this book.

There are a few more statistical concepts that you are less likely to encounter on the AP exam but which we will quickly summarize below:

- **The gambler's fallacy:** In figuring probabilities, many people commit this error. Essentially, they wrongly assume some occurrence is due to happen even when that occurrence is purely a matter of chance; if you are playing a card game and "need" an ace, you cannot assume that you are due for an ace because you haven't had one for a long time. If the cards are shuffled appropriately, when the first card is dealt you have a 1 in 13 chance (since there are four aces among the 52 cards in the deck) of receiving an ace.

- **Polygons:** A flashy name for a line graph; you might see reference to the term, but it shouldn't trouble you on the exam.

- **Histograms:** A flashy name for a bar graph; again, just recognizing that you might see the term is all you need to worry about.

This is not a particularly large unit, but it is necessary that you have a good grip on it in order to understand much of the data you encounter throughout your year of study and also to succeed on an exam, which places a premium on mastery of this material.

### Name Hall of Fame

At the end of each unit we include a "Name Hall of Fame." In this section we will revisit the most important individuals from that particular unit, and we will also help you to determine which names are essential to know in order to be successful on the AP Psychology Exam.

In this unit, there really are no clear-cut, indisputable inductees into the Name Hall of Fame. However, in your study of experimental methodology, you've heard about **John B. Watson** and his work in classical conditioning with a young orphan named **"Little Albert"**. You also explored **Stanley Milgram's** study on obedience to authority, often referred to in high school classes as "the electric shock study". Both of these offer much material for a debate on ethics in research methodology, and the Milgram study in particular provides a marvelous opportunity to discuss multiple variations one can build onto the basic design of a study (The Milgram study is not really an 'experiment' per se, as it did not have two or more experimental groups or an experimental group and a control group, but many would see that as nit-picking). Many teachers and textbooks refer to the example of **"Clever Hans"** to introduce the idea of using the experimental method and implementation of a double blind procedure. Hans was a horse who won acclaim in Europe for his alleged ability to count and do other tricks not typically within the skill set of a horse. It turns out that his owner was not a charlatan, but was unconsciously guilty of signaling Hans when he approached a correct answer to the owner's queries. This was revealed when a set of questions was given to Hans by a questioner who did not himself know the answers; thus, he was unable to cue the animal. Hans, who was certainly a bright horse but not a magically gifted one, now had no unconscious signal to read, and his performance dipped to chance percentages.

Finally, there are names that are usually associated with the history of psychology that might come up on the AP Exam. Two that are notable are **Wilhelm Wundt,** who established the first formal psychology laboratory in Leipzig, Germany in 1879, and **William James,** the great American psychologist whose text book, *Principles of Psychology* was published in 1890 but is still respected for its insights. Other names from the history of the field, like **Hermann Ebbinghaus, Edward Thorndike, Alfred Binet, Sigmund Freud, John B. Watson** and **Ivan Pavlov,** to name but a few, will be covered in other content areas:

- Edward Thorndike, John B. Watson and Ivan Pavlov in *Learning Theory*
- Hermann Ebbinghaus in *Memory*
- Sigmund Freud in *Developmental Psychology, Personality Theory and Treatment*
- Alfred Binet in *Testing and Individual Differences.*

Please see the next page for more information on the history of psychology.

## NOTABLE NAMES IN THE HISTORY OF PSYCHOLOGY (In order of birth date)

| | |
|---|---|
| **Wilhelm Wundt** (1832-1920) | Established the first experimental psychology lab in Leipzig, Germany in 1879. Many consider this the beginning of the study of psychology as a science. |
| **William James** (1841-1910) | Often viewed as the first "great" American psychologist. He wrote an influential text entitled Principles of Psychology and was a leader of the school of thought known as functionalism, which focuses on the purposes consciousness and cognitions play in helping one to adapt to environmental demands |
| **G. Stanley Hall** (1844-1924) | Established the first experimental psychology laboratory at Johns Hopkins. Became the first President of Clark University in 1889, and the first President of the American Psychological Association in 1892. Led the Clark Conference in 1909, attended by Sigmund Freud and Carl Jung. |
| **Edward Titchener** (1862-1920) | Studied with Wilhelm Wundt prior to becoming a psychology professor at Cornell University. Titchener's ideas created the basis for a school of thought called structuralism, which studies the components of our conscious experience. |
| **Mary Whiton Calkins** (1863-1930) | Denied a PhD by Harvard though she met the doctoral requirements, but later became first female president of the American Psychological Association (APA) |
| **Margaret Floy Washburn** (1871-1939) | First woman to receive a PhD in psychology, from Cornell, she later became the 2nd female president of the APA |
| **Francis Sumner** (1895-1954) | First African-American man to receive a PhD in psychology, from Clark University in 1920 |
| **Inez Prosser** (1897-1934) | First African-American woman to receive a PhD in psychology, from the University of Cincinnati in 1933 |

**Essay Themes**

One of the most common themes in past advanced placement psychology exam essays has been the **designing and critiquing of experiments.** In the first decade of the program, almost one third of the free response items revolved around this theme. This does not mean that the authors of the test are "due" for another such question anytime soon, but it does say something about the importance of knowing all you can about how to conduct research in psychology.

Other exam questions have asked students to compare the different methods of research and to state pros and cons for using each particular approach. You should be able to evaluate the effectiveness of various research methods in studying the same phenomenon.

It's a good general rule in every unit in the AP Psychology course to reflect upon areas of controversy and debate, which require genuine critical thinking, as these offer rich topics for intelligent essay test construction. For example:

- Are the conclusions any particular researchers reach valid? That is, did the research they conducted truly test what it claimed to test, can the results be reliably replicated, and is the procedure sound?

- Is there a trade-off between adherence to ethical research standards and the "need to know"? Is what we learned from Stanley Milgram's research into obedience to authority "worth" the ethical compromises? Is it ethical to require placebo groups in a study designed to evaluate the effectiveness of a new drug when volunteers randomly assigned to that group might thus miss out on the benefits of the new medication if it does turn out to be effective?

# Statistics and Research Methodology

## Experimentation in Psychology

- Exploring cause and effect
- Control groups, experimental groups and placebo groups
  - IV
  - DV
  - Confounding variables
- Operational definitions
- Hypothesis and null hypothesis
- Choosing a representative sample of your target population
  - Randomization
  - Group matching
- Experimenter bias and double blind procedures
- Replication

## Other Research Methods

- Naturalistic Observation
  - Ethical guidelines
  - Case Studies
- Correlational Research
  - Longitudinal Studies
  - Cross-Sectional Studies
- Survey Methodology
  - Demand characteristic
  - Social desirability bias
  - "Saying vs. doing"
  - Framing

## Statistics in Psychology

- Descriptive vs. Inferential statistics
- Statistical Significance
- Probabilities, and The Gambler's Fallacy
- Correlation vs. Causation
- Correlation coefficients and scatterplots
- Positive correlation
- Negative correlation
- Zero correlation

## More Statistics in Psychology

- "The normal curve"
- Percentiles
- The Standard Deviation
- Positive Skews
- Negative Skews
- Measures of Central Tendency:
  - Mean
  - Median
  - Mode

21

**Practice Items**

- **Time yourself** on this section, and record how long it takes you; this information will be useful to you later on

- If you work at the pace you will need on the actual AP Exam, this section should take you no more than 10 minutes and 30 seconds

- If it takes you only three minutes and you get them all correct, more power to you! If you are done in less than seven minutes and you make 3 or more errors, then you ought to consider slowing down a bit

- THESE SECTION ITEMS ARE **NOT** IN ORDER OF DIFFICULTY!


1.  A survey indicates that children who have been exposed to training in playing a musical instrument academically outperform children with no such background. School administrators in the area conclude that playing musical instruments early in childhood makes children more intelligent. This conclusion is flawed because

    (A) the administrators did not accurately identify the independent variable
    (B) survey methodology is notoriously inaccurate
    (C) there was no control for confounding variables
    (D) the administrators wrongly inferred causation from correlation
    (E) no such conclusion can be reached with only nominal data


2.  The term 'gambler's fallacy' refers to

    (A) the need of some individuals to bet on sporting events in order to make the event worth watching
    (B) the tendency to assume that purely random events are "due" to occur, simply because they haven't occurred in some time
    (C) believing another person is intentionally misleading you when he or she is not
    (D) an attempt to place a bet on a meaningless event with someone who does not believe in gambling
    (E) a miscalculation in placing a bet in a poker game

3.  A teacher assigns a team of five students to observe their classmates for evidence of helping behaviors in the school cafeteria. She asks each of them to come up with a score sheet and to simply record the number of pro-social behaviors each observes over the course of one week. Which of the following is a significant limitation of this study?

    (A) There is no independent variable in the study
    (B) There is no operational definition of pro-social behaviors
    (C) No null hypothesis is stated
    (D) There is no counterbalancing
    (E) There is no double blind procedure


4.  If a researcher wanted to demonstrate that a cause and effect relationship exists between frustration and aggressive behaviors in children, he or she should use which of the following research methods?

    (A) A correlational study
    (B) A controlled experimental design
    (C) A survey
    (D) Case studies
    (E) A cross-sectional study


5.  One advantage of a case study approach over a survey approach in psychological research is that

    (A) there is often a significant difference between what individuals report they would do in a certain circumstance and what they actually do in such a circumstance
    (B) over 90% of subjects have been proven to knowingly lie in responding to surveys
    (C) it is impossible to ever get a truly representative sample of respondents when administering surveys
    (D) the case study method allows for relatively easy control of confounding variables
    (E) the case study method allows for the gathering of more specific empirical data

    **The next <u>three</u> questions (#6, #7, #8) refer to the following scenario:**
    In an experiment entitled Expectation and Its Impact on Performance, a group of new 4th grade students who have done poorly in school through grade three are randomly split into three groups. One group is assigned to a teacher who is given complete and accurate information on each student; the second group is assigned to a teacher who is told that all her kids have shown unusual ability and motivation in previous years, and the third group is assigned to a teacher who is told nothing about the students. At the end of the year, the students' performances are compared using a standardized test measure.

6.  The null hypothesis in this example

    (A) states that the 4th graders will continue to do poorly in the future
    (B) states that the teachers' expectations will have no effect on the students' performance
    (C) states that students' expectations of their teacher will impact their performance
    (D) suggests that the standardized test at the end of the year will be greatly influenced by the teachers' expectations
    (E) suggests that the experimental group will outperform the control group

7.  What, respectively, are the independent and the dependent variables in this example?

    (A) The students' behavior and the teachers' performance
    (B) The teachers' performance and the students' behavior
    (C) The teachers' expectations are both the IV and the DV in this experiment
    (D) The teachers' expectations and the students' performance, respectively
    (E) The students' performance and the teachers' expectations, respectively

8.  Which group is the control group in this experiment?

    (A) The group about which the teacher is given complete and accurate information
    (B) The group the teacher was told had unusual ability
    (C) The group the teacher was given no information about
    (D) Each of the groups in this experiment can be considered control groups
    (E) This experimental design does not have a control group

9.  A writer for a local newspaper enters the high school and stops the first 20 students she encounters, asking them to take a brief survey. She takes half of them and asks "On a scale of 1 to 10, how happy are you with the idea of lengthening the school day by one hour?" Meanwhile, her assistant takes the remainder of the volunteers and asks them if they are "very unhappy", "unhappy", "neutral", "happy" or "very happy" with the idea of lengthening the school day. When the writer tallies the responses she finds 89% of the students responded with a '2' or below or said they were "very unhappy" about lengthening the school day. The title of her article the next day is "Smith High School Students Strongly Oppose Lengthening the School Day." Which of the following best summarizes two errors in this methodology?

    (A) Her sample is not representative of "Smith High School", and her use of two different versions of the question confounds the results
    (B) Her sample is too small and the question is framed in an unethical manner
    (C) She has no independent variable in her study and there is no control group
    (D) She did not get the consent of the students and there is too much deception in the methodology
    (E) Survey methodology is never reliable and using a "one to ten" scale is outdated

10. Which of the following is the most likely value for "r" in a study examining the correlation in adult males between age in years and amount of hair on the head?

    (A) r= +1.25
    (B) r= -.97
    (C) r= -.44
    (D) r= +.79
    (E) r= -1.17

11. In random sampling, it is essential that

    (A) the standard deviation be small
    (B) there is a 5% margin for error
    (C) there is an equal number of males and females in the sample
    (D) you include at least 50% of the target population in your sample
    (E) all members of the target population have an equal chance of being chosen

12. Which of the following accurately describes the three measures of central tendency for the following scores on a quiz? 3, 7, 6, 10, 4

    (A) The S.D. is < 2, there is no mode, and the median is 6
    (B) The S.D. is > 2, the mean is 6, and the variance is 4
    (C) The mean is 6, the mode is 3, and the median is 6
    (D) The mean is 6, there is no mode, and the median is 6
    (E) The range is 6, the mean is 5, and the median is 4

13. Two psychologists are debating the merits of different approaches for studying the consistency of extroversion over a lifespan. Psychologist #1 argues for a longitudinal study, psychologist #2 for a cross sectional study. The best argument psychologist #2 might offer in opposition to his colleague's position is

    (A) a longitudinal study would not allow for generalizability
    (B) a longitudinal study would not allow for selection of a representative sample
    (C) a longitudinal study is potentially limited by subject mortality
    (D) a cross-sectional study offers more consistency within the subject pool
    (E) a cross-sectional study is the only valid method for examining development over the lifespan

14. In a normal distribution of IQ scores with a mean of 100 and a standard deviation of fifteen, approximately what percent of scores would fall between z = -1 and z = +2?

    (A) 34%
    (B) 57%
    (C) 68%
    (D) 82%
    (E) 97%

15. When scores in a distribution are negatively skewed

    (A) the mean, median, and mode are the same
    (B) the median value will be higher than the mean value
    (C) the median value will be the same as the mode
    (D) the mode and the mean will be the same
    (E) the range will be the same as the median

# Chapter 2
# *The Biological Bases Of Behavior*

### Introduction

- In the words of neuroscientist Matt Ridley: To what extent are our newborn brains a "recipe" and to what extent a "finished meal"?

- Where's the balance between "free will" and "biological determinism"?

You will consider questions like these in this chapter on **BioPsychology,** which examines the biological roots of what we do and how we think, specifically in terms of two message-sending mechanisms (the electro-chemical "neural chain" and the endocrine system), the function of various brain structures, and the role of *genetic predispositions* in human behavior and mental processes. Although we will look at some specific functions of these various systems and structures, it is essential to keep in mind that each is a part of an integrated whole. **None of these systems work independently of the others.** Human biology is a complex, interactive system, which is remarkably flexible and "plastic."

This unit lays a physiological foundation that will facilitate your understanding in pretty much all of the units to follow. Although our understanding of the human brain is limited, it is constantly evolving, especially with the advancement of new technologies that allow for more detailed examination of the brain at work. These technologies have allowed for tremendous discoveries in **neuroscience,** the scientific study of neurons and the nervous system. New discoveries are made everyday in this growing field, so don't be surprised if some of what you read in this chapter is updated or modified in the near future.

This unit is not as difficult as it might at first appear, and you will have ample opportunity to revisit major concepts in it as the course progresses, since there is so much overlap between "BioPsych" and the other sub-disciplines within psychology. The multiple-choice section of the AP Exam will feature at least eight items from here, and it's entirely possible that at least one free response item will require some mastery of this material as well, so give the chapter careful attention.

### The Neural Chain

How does the brain work? A complicated question, no doubt, but when asked to explain how the brain works in five words or less, famed scientist Stephen Pinker quipped "brain cells fire in patterns." In essence everything that you experience in your mental and physical world begins by cells firing in a certain pattern. The cells Pinker refers to are called neurons and we open our exploration of the nervous system with a look at these special cells.

**Neurons** are the basic building blocks of the nervous system and although estimates vary significantly, the consensus is there are about 100 billion of these cells. There are many different types of neuron, but all contain the following basic parts:

• **Dendrites:** The branch-like projections that receive messages from other neurons; sometimes referred to as dendritic branches; Robert Sapolsky of Stanford University aptly refers to them as "the ears of the neuron."

• **The soma:** The cell body, made up of a nucleus which is surrounded by cytoplasm, all of which is held together by a membrane.

• **The axon:** The "tail" of the neuron along which electrical signals are conducted; this signal results from a brief change in the electrical charge of the cell, at the axon hillock, (the juncture between the cell body and the axon itself) called **the action potential,** which radiates down the axon. Many axons are wrapped in a white fatty substance called myelin. This sheath of **myelin** protects the axon and increases the speed of the action potential allowing for much faster communication. Myelin develops over time and the myelination of cells continues well into your twenties. Dysfunction in myelin can cause dramatic health problems as in the case of multiple sclerosis (MS). In MS, the body's immune system attacks the myelin causing significant disruption in communication between neurons. This results in loss of strength, muscle control and coordination, among an array of other possible symptoms.

• **Axon terminals or terminal buttons:** Knobs at the end of each axon from which chemical messengers called neurotransmitters are released into the synapse, the gap between the terminal buttons of the presynaptic sending neuron and the dendrites of the postsynaptic receiving neuron. Each neuron can have thousands of these terminals, which means that a single neuron could potentially communicate with the dendrites of thousands of other neurons.

**The anatomy of a neuron**

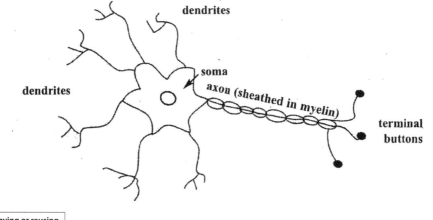

This web of interconnections between cells is often referred to as **the neural chain.** The neurotransmitters carry information, which is the foundation of behaviors and mental processes. Neurotransmitters may be **excitatory,** stimulating the firing of messages, or **inhibitory,** slowing the transmission of neural messages. For example, the caffeine in the coffee you drink increases the activity of **glutamate,** the major excitatory neurotransmitter that therefore serves as a stimulant to the central nervous system. Simultaneously, caffeine blocks some inhibitory activity; in essence, it is stepping on the accelerator of the car, while draining some brake fluid. If there is more excitatory than inhibitory input, then messages are sent along their way. If there is a majority of inhibitory input, messages are slowed or stopped. To complicate things a bit, some neurotransmitters can be excitatory or inhibitory, depending on **the receptors** to which their molecules bind. **Acetylcholine** is one example of such a chemical.

Some students find it useful to think of these inhibitory mechanisms as the safety catch on a gun, and the **"gun analogy"** also holds up in terms of other operations in the firing of a neuron. Cell excitation begins the process of **depolarization.** When this happens positively charged sodium ions rush into the cell and potassium ions flow out temporarily, leaving the cell more positively charged on the inside. If there is enough input the neuron reaches its **firing threshold.** Once it does so, it fires in an **"all or none"** fashion. In pulling the trigger of a gun, there is a point at which the gun will fire, no matter how slowly or gently you have pulled the trigger. Pulling the trigger slowly will not make the bullet fly more slowly. After the neuron fires its electrical signal, there is a very brief **refractory period** in which the cell cannot fire again. This is analogous to the time after firing a pistol that one has to re-cock the gun in order to shoot again. It's easy to confuse the concepts of refractory period and resting state. When a neuron is in its **resting state** or **resting potential,** it is more negatively charged (at -70 millivolts) inside the cell - it *could* fire, it just isn't firing at the moment. During the absolute refractory period, the cell temporarily cannot fire at all, and during the relative refractory period that follows, it is much more difficult for the cell to fire than when in its resting state. It's not likely that you'll run into this distinction on the AP Exam, but if it comes up you'll be ahead of the competition.

When the electrical signal reaches the end of the axon it causes the release of the neurotransmitter housed in **the vesicles** of the terminal buttons. The chemical enters the synapse, where it locks into the receptor sites of the receiving, or **postsynaptic neuron** (the neuron that sends the message is considered **presynaptic**). Any excess neurotransmitter left in the synapse is re-collected by the transmitting neuron. This is called **reuptake**. Some neurotransmitters are "cleaned up" from the synapse not by the process of reuptake but by enzymes that break the chemical down.

Neuroscientists often use the **"lock and key"** analogy to help students understand how cells communicate, and also how drugs can act to block or stimulate neurotransmitter activity. For example, some drugs designed to control schizophrenia work like a piece of tape covering a keyhole. The presence of schizophrenia is correlated with higher than normal levels of **dopamine** activity, and several medications used to treat the disease basically do not allow that neurotransmitter (the key) to bind to the receptor site (the keyhole or lock) of the postsynaptic neuron. Such a drug, one that inhibits or impedes the action of a neurotransmitter, is called an **antagonist;** drugs that enhance or amplify the action of a certain neurotransmitter are called **agonists.** In a sense cocaine is a kind of agonist, although it does not so much mimic the action of dopamine as it stimulates a higher than normal level of dopamine activity by *blocking the reuptake* of that chemical. Dopamine molecules are thus left out in the synapse and continue to bind to receptors, elevating the level of dopamine activity.

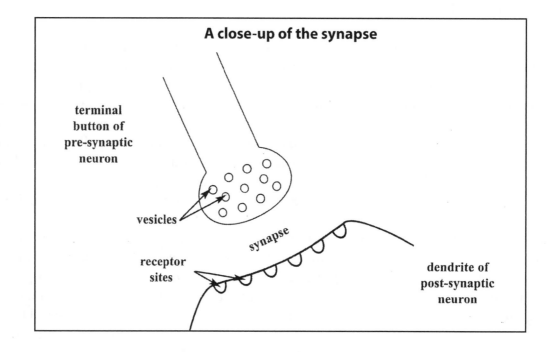

**A close-up of the synapse**

terminal button of pre-synaptic neuron

vesicles

synapse

receptor sites

dendrite of post-synaptic neuron

In later units on Memory, Motivation and Emotion, Abnormal Psychology and others you will learn more about the action of specific neurotransmitters. For example, low levels of **acetylcholine (ACh)** are correlated with the presence of Alzheimer's Disease. But it also clearly sends messages regarding muscular contraction as well. Curare is a poison that acts as an ACh antagonist. It causes paralysis because it blocks transmission of ACh. On the other hand, black widow spider venom stimulates ACh activity. Exposure to it results in powerful muscle contractions and convulsions.

Arousal of the **fight or flight mechanism** when an organism is under stress stimulates the release of neurotransmitters like **norepinephrine** (adrenaline) and the body's natural pain-killers, **endorphins**. The aptly named **Substance P** is the neurotransmitter responsible for the sending of pain messages. **Serotonin** seems connected to mood regulation and eating drives, among other things. The aforementioned **dopamine** is often linked to pleasure; several recreational drugs seem to operate on dopamine neurons. Some estimate that as many as one third of all neurons are **G.A.B.A. (gamma-aminobutyric acid)** neurons. G.A.B.A. is the most abundant inhibitory neurotransmitter in the brain. Many seizure disorders are correlated with lower than normal levels of G.A.B.A. activity, resulting in lower than normal levels of inhibition - simplistically stated, it's as if the brakes are failing in the car. Alcohol is a G.A.B.A. agonist in that its molecules bind to G.A.B.A. receptors sites causing a slowdown of the central nervous system.

### Some Important Neurotransmitters

Please keep in mind that it is difficult to summarize the various functions of these chemical messengers, and our understanding of their operation will undoubtedly deepen in the near future. But you may need to know about some specific neurotransmitters and their activity on the AP Exam, so we do the best we can to help you with this table.

| Neurotransmitter | Major Functions | Related Disorders |
|---|---|---|
| Acetylcholine (ACh) | Voluntary muscle movements; memory | Alzheimer's Disease is linked to a loss of ACh producing neurons |
| Dopamine | Pleasure; muscular control; learning; attention | Excess activity is associated with schizophrenia; low levels of activity are associated with Parkinson's disease |
| Endorphins | Alleviating pain | Some chronic pain and fibromyalgia sufferers have dramatically reduced endorphin activity |
| Norepinephrine; Epinephrine | Involved in alertness and arousal | Low levels are often correlated with depression |
| G.A.B.A. (gamma-aminobutyric acid) | The primary inhibitory neurotransmitter in the brain | Low levels may be involved in anxiety, and seizure disorders |
| Glutamate | The primary excitatory neurotransmitter in the brain | Too much glutamate activity can be associated with seizure disorders; glutamate may also play a role in many degenerative disorders of the central nervous system, and with bipolar disorder |
| Serotonin | Appetite, sleep, mood | Low levels are associated with depression; serotonin levels may also be a factor in anxiety disorders and many other problems |
| Substance P | Sends pain messages | May be linked to fibromyalgia, a disease marked by enduring pain and tenderness in joints, muscles and tendons; may also be linked to other pain disorders |

You might see reference on the AP Exam to the basic process by which **afferent, or sensory neurons,** carry messages to **interneurons** in the brain and spinal cord which then transmit the message out to the muscles and glands (the **effectors**) via **efferent, or motor neurons.** In a *reflex arc*, the sensory input of an uninvited projectile flying toward your eye is carried by afferent neurons directly to the spinal cord and then back out to your eye and head muscles even before your brain is engaged. As a result, you reflexively flinch. A common strategy to keep these two types of cell straight is to link "A" for 'afferent', "A" for 'approach', and "E" for 'efferent', "E" for 'exit'.

There are far more **glial cells** (a 10 to 1 ratio by most estimates) in your brain than there are neurons. The term 'glial cell' is fairly easy to remember because its name sounds something like 'glue', and glials function as support cells that essentially hold together the message-sending neurons and support their functioning. There are at least three different types of glial cell. Some provide nutrients to the message-sending neurons, some specifically supply the myelin that surrounds axons, while others function as immune cells in the brain. Until recently it was thought that glial cells were merely support cells, but now it seems clear that some of them have their own message-sending capacities as well.

**Mirror neurons** are another type of cell that has recently attracted interest from scientists. Basically, when we see someone else do something, neural pathways in our brains fire as if we ourselves were performing the task. Mirror neurons are especially common in an area of the brain called the motor cortex. Although there is still much to discover about mirror neurons, they may well form the basis for social learning (learning from observing others) and empathy.

### The Nervous System

You must have a general understanding of the difference between the **central nervous system (the CNS)** and the **peripheral nervous system (the PNS)**. The CNS is made up of the brain and spinal cord, both of which are encased in bone. The PNS is comprised of all the nerves throughout your body that are not part of the CNS. Many students struggle with the distinction between the **somatic system** and the **autonomic system**, the two subdivisions of the PNS. In Greek 'soma' means 'body', which might help you to remember that the somatic system (also known as the skeletal system) is involved with the voluntary actions of the body, while the autonomic system is largely involuntary. Many teachers teach the autonomic system by referring to it as *automatic*, but students are usually familiar with the term 'autonomous' from history classes, and it is more accurate to refer to this as a system that pretty much acts on its own, as an autonomous country would. The autonomic system is further broken into **sympathetic** and **parasympathetic** systems. The former is analogous to an emergency response system (ratcheting up heart rate, dilating the pupils, inhibiting digestion and salivation to ready the body for immediate action), the latter to its opposing process, working to return you to balance. Thus, the sympathetic and parasympathetic systems are often referred to as antagonistic systems.

### The Brain

Think of the brain as being broken into three general areas: **the hindbrain, the midbrain, and the forebrain.** The hindbrain includes **the medulla, pons, and cerebellum. The medulla** helps to control breathing, swallowing, blood circulation, vomiting, and digestion. **The pons** plays a role in some of these same vital functions and also serves as a bridge between brain regions. It is also believed to play a role in sleep, dreaming, and overall attentiveness. The medulla and pons are in the brainstem where the spine enters the skull. As you may know, the left side of the brain controls the right side of the body (and vice versa) and that crossover takes place in this brainstem area. Lastly, the **cerebellum** is a center for balance, coordination of limbs and smooth muscle movements.

**The reticular formation** is a system of neurons that extends from the hindbrain into the midbrain. One part of this network, **the reticular activating system (R.A.S.),** controls alertness and attention to incoming stimuli. You may encounter different usages of these two labels *('reticular formation'* vs. *'reticular activating system'),* but for our purposes they are synonymous. The key word is reticular. This area is analogous to the bell that rings over the entrance to a store, signaling the proprietor that there is a customer who requires attention. In essence, it is a sensory filter that selects which environmental stimuli we most need to attend to.

The **midbrain** receives and integrates many types of sensory information. It is also a bridge between the older hindbrain and the more recently evolved parts of the forebrain. Sitting atop the midbrain, **the thalamus,** is often referred to as the switchboard of the brain. It sorts and relays sensory information (for all senses but smell, which is routed through the emotional limbic system) to appropriate "higher brain" destinations. Interestingly, the thalamus is considered part of the forebrain, which we summarize next.

### The Limbic System

Please remember that all of the following parts of the forebrain play a role in many different integrated activities. We will try to summarize the most important aspects of their functions here.

The hippocampus, the amygdala and the hypothalamus are all part of the **limbic system,** often thought of as the seat of emotion and basic motivation. **The hippocampus** is only peripherally involved in such processes however. It seems mostly responsible for the formation of new memories. **The amygdala** is associated with anger, fear and to some extent sex drive - it may also be viewed as the spot in the brain most responsible for evaluating the "emotional relevance" of <u>any</u> incoming information. **The septum** also plays a role in fear response. Finally, **the hypothalamus,** located at the base of the brain, helps regulate appetite, thirst, sex drive, the sleep/wake cycle, body temperature, and the 'fight or flight' response. This region is only about the size of a pea, but neuron-for-neuron it may serve more functions than any other brain structure.  It also works in concert with the pituitary gland to govern the endocrine system making it the "center of the endocrine world" according to Robert Sapolsky. You'll read a bit more about the endocrine system later.

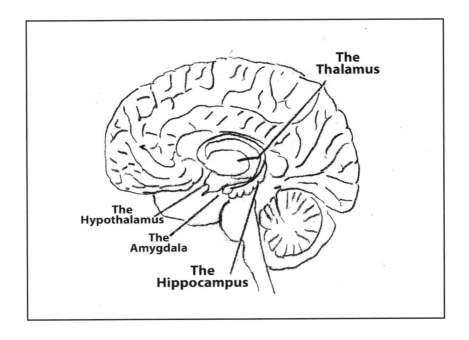

### The Cerebral Cortex

The wrinkled, convoluted shell of the brain is called **the cortex.** It is divided into four lobes: frontal, parietal, occipital, temporal. Generally speaking (all of these summaries of the functions in each of the four lobes are open to debate and to change)**, the frontal lobes** play a role in speaking and muscular activity and the **prefrontal** area of the frontal lobes acts as the executive of the brain, carrying out planning, decision making, judgment and self-control. T**he motor cortex,** responsible for voluntary muscle movement, is located in the rear of the frontal lobe, near the border of **the parietal lobe,** which houses **the somatosensory area** of the cortex. This section governs the sense of touch, temperature and pain. **The visual cortex** is located in **the occipital lobe,** in the rear of the cortex. Many students find this odd and thus easy to remember - they are surprised to learn that the area of the brain given over to the processing of visual information is actually at the back of the head. Meanwhile, **the**

**auditory cortex,** which processes information from both ears, is located in the **temporal lobes,** to the side of the head, just above the ears. The temporal lobes also contain an area essential to your sense of smell, the *olfactory cortex.* Neuroscientists have identified areas in the temporal lobes that serve as a visual recognition center. Damage to this area could result in the inability to recognize even the most familiar faces and objects in your life. Last but hardly least is the **association cortex**, which makes up a huge portion (perhaps as much as 3/4) of the entire cortex. It is difficult to specifically localize its functions, but it seems to be responsible for linking relevance and meaning to sensory input and, in the frontal lobe, for much of the highest level thinking that humans do.

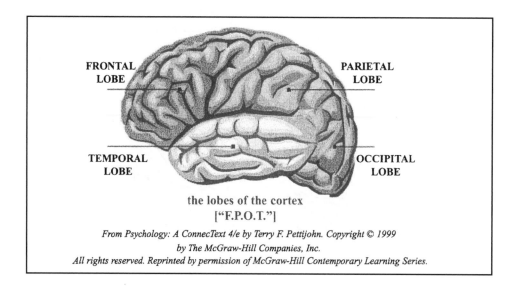

FRONTAL
LOBE

PARIETAL
LOBE

TEMPORAL
LOBE

OCCIPITAL
LOBE

the lobes of the cortex
["F.P.O.T."]

*From Psychology: A ConnecText 4/e by Terry F. Pettijohn. Copyright © 1999*
*by The McGraw-Hill Companies, Inc.*
*All rights reserved. Reprinted by permission of McGraw-Hill Contemporary Learning Series.*

## Split-Brain Research and Hemispheric Specialization

Any chapter on the brain would be incomplete without a description of Roger Sperry's Nobel Prize winning work with **"split-brain" patients**, from which we have learned so much about the function of the left and right sides of the human brain. Sperry conducted experiments on the perceptions of patients who had had their corpus callosum severed in a surgical procedure designed to control severe seizures. The **corpus callosum** is a thick connecting bundle containing millions of neurons that links the two halves, or hemispheres, of the brain. The surgery thus isolates each hemisphere from the other, which has no overt impact on functioning; however, Sperry (and his collaborator, Michael Gazzaniga) discovered that it *did* have some effect. When, for instance, he asked such a patient to look at a dot in the middle of a divided screen and instantaneously flashed separate images to the two sides of the screen, he found that the participants could not verbally report what they had "seen" on the left half of the screen. He knew they had indeed seen the image, because they could identify it by touch and through illustration using the left hand, but they couldn't *verbally report* it. Sperry knew that the left side of the body is governed by the right side of the brain, and vice versa. From this, he surmised that the right side of the brain, the side that would have first received the image (which, remember, had been seen only in the left visual field), must have limited language capability. The left side of the brain must house the major centers for language. Images flashed to the right visual field, and thus the left hemisphere of the brain, were readily identified verbally by the split-brain patients. When intact, the corpus callosum instantaneously allows the two halves of the brain to communicate with each other, but the surgical procedure these patients had undergone cut that connection. Split-brain patients adapt to the change over time, but Sperry's work told us much about language function in the brain.

Research such as this (along with improvements in brain imaging technologies) demonstrates that the two hemispheres of the brain have some specialized functions. This hemispheric specialization is called **lateralization**. The right hemisphere of the brain tends to be better at visual, spatial, artistic and musical tasks while the left hemisphere tends to be the center for mathematical, logical, analytical and linguistic abilities.

You should also be familiar with two of the brain's primary language centers, **Broca's Area and Wernicke's Area**. Broca's Area is involved in the ability to produce and express speech while Wernicke's Area is involved in the comprehension of speech. Both language sites are typically found in the left hemisphere. Damage to these can result in disruptions of speech production or speech comprehension called **aphasias.**

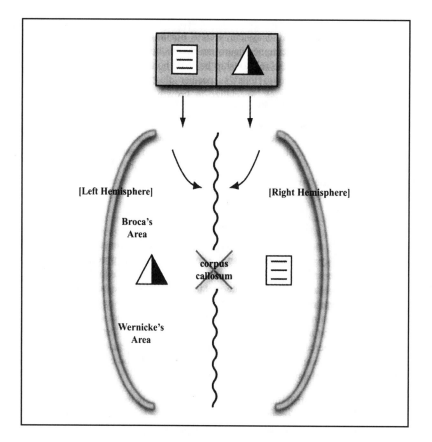

*The split-brain volunteer*
*would verbally report seeing only "a two-tone triangle"*

### Methods for Examining Brain Structure and Function

Early researchers in brain function largely relied on case studies of people who had suffered damage to the brain to infer which regions of the brain served which purposes. Later, researchers intentionally destroyed, or lesioned parts of the brain in animals to examine the changes in behavior that resulted from the damage.  Today, science has moved to a new frontier of brain exploration that allows us to see in great detail which parts of the brain are active in response to different stimuli.

Some commonly used tools to view brain structure and measure brain activity include: magnetic resonance imaging **(MRI)**, computerized axial tomography **(CAT)**, electroencephalograph **(EEG)** and positron emission tomography **(PET)**. MRI's and CAT scans show remarkably detailed pictures of *the structure* of the brain.  An EEG measures changes in the brain's electrical *activity*.  A PET scan requires patients to receive a non-harmful injection of a radioactive substance that helps highlight the metabolism of glucose, the fuel of the brain.  As a subject performs different tasks, glucose flows to the parts of the brain that are activated. A computer tracks the glucose and provides colorful images that tell us which parts of the brain are activated. A newer brain scan called a functional MRI (**fMRI**) shows both the structure *and* activity of different brain regions.  It produces high-resolution images.

It is fair to say that you would not be asked a question on the AP Exam about any of these brain-imaging technologies without reference to both its name *and* its acronym.

## Brain Plasticity

The technologies discussed above have allowed us a much greater understanding of how the brain works.  It has also challenged some long-held beliefs about the nature of neurons and brain organization.  It was once believed that humans are born with all of the neurons that they will ever have and that all brain pathways are laid down early in life.  Both of these notions are no longer accepted.  We now know that the brain creates new neurons (especially in the hippocampus) throughout life, a process called **neurogenesis**. There is some evidence that neurogenesis is promoted by sleep and exercise.

Our learning is facilitated by a brain that is remarkably plastic. It seems able, even as we age, to wire and re-wire its synaptic connections in response to new situations, information and environmental stimuli. This concept of **brain plasticity** is supported by many striking examples of humans whose brains have somehow rewired themselves to compensate for the loss of function resulting from injury or illness. Among others, Matt Ridley argues that the world in which we live and function helps to "build a brain", and that our "nature" manifests itself only via interaction with the environment.

New neural networks are formed through a process called **Long-Term Potentiation (LTP).** Triggering the same sequence of neurons over time creates faster and more efficient pathways to allow quick access to the new information. It may be useful to draw an analogy here. When it first snows and you walk from the parking lot to the school (assuming it hasn't been plowed) you have to trudge through the drifts. However, the more times you take that route, the smoother the pathway becomes, allowing for faster, easier access. This is essentially what neurons do – wearing away pathways that are frequently traveled. As Donald Hebb has said, "Neurons that fire together, wire together." It seems that LTP is the neural foundation of learning and memory.

## The Endocrine System

As mentioned earlier the hypothalamus joins the **pituitary gland** in directing the other glands of **the endocrine system.** Thus, the pituitary is sometimes called *the master gland*, although many argue this label is too simplistic. In addition to directing other glands, the pituitary releases *oxytocin* (a chemical involved in bonding, especially in terms of parent to child connection) and *H.G.H.* (human growth hormone).

The glands of the endocrine system secrete **hormones**, another type of chemical messenger. Unlike the aforementioned neurotransmitters however, hormones are carried in the bloodstream. Some liken the relationship between hormones and neurotransmitters to post office mail (the hormonal system) as compared to today's speedier electronic mail (the neural chain). The **thyroid and parathyroid glands,** in the neck, specialize in growth and metabolism. The **adrenal glands**, at the midsection of the body, near the kidneys, govern "fight or flight" responses, through secretion of adrenaline and noradrenaline (also called epinephrine and norepinephrine) and cortisol. The **pineal gland,** located deep in the brain, secretes the sleep-inducing hormone **melatonin**. The **pancreas**, just below the adrenals, secretes insulin that works in the metabolism of blood sugar. **The ovaries** produce estrogen and progesterone **and testes** produce androgens, most notably testosterone. The hormones produced by the testes and ovaries are responsible for the development at puberty of **primary sex characteristics**, which are involved directly in reproduction, and **secondary sex characteristics** such as breast development in females and growth of facial and body hair in males.

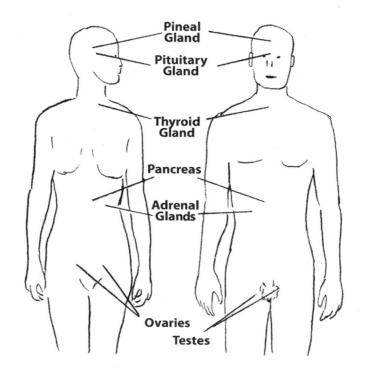

### Genetics

Much of what you need to know about genetics for AP Psychology you may already have learned in a biology course. You probably already know something about **dominant and recessive genes** and that you inherit a total of 46 chromosomes (23 from mom and

23 from dad). Your sex is determined by the last chromosomal pair - **males have XY chromosomes and females have XX**. You always get an X from mom, but dad can give you an X or Y. You may have also learned that **genotype** refers to one's genetic make-up while **phenotype** refers to the outward manifestations that results from the interaction between those genetics and the environment. Phenotype is essentially what you see when you look at an organism. **Behavioral genetics** is the study of the interaction between genetics and environment. Certain environmental factors are more likely to encourage the expression of certain genetic predispositions.

You understand most of what you need to know about genetics in an advanced placement psychology course if you grasp the difference between **genetic predispositions** and genetic determinism. The term 'genetic predisposition' refers to the idea that humans are born with a tendency toward certain behaviors or characteristics, but only a tendency. Many students misinterpret this to mean that we "are born with" certain traits, but the concept of genetic or biological predisposition only suggests a push in one direction or another, a nudge that relies on environmental influences as well. For example, there does seem to be a genetic predisposition (but not genetic *determinism*) for body weight and body fat percentage, for schizophrenia, for major depression, and so on. You will encounter more such examples in later units, especially when you examine *twin studies* in the units on Developmental Psychology and Personality Theory.

There are some things that are truly "genetic" such as eye color and sex. For success on the AP Exam, you should also be familiar with the following genetically determined conditions.

- **Down Syndrome** is a genetic abnormality that is particularly relevant in psychology. It is caused by an extra chromosome on the 21st chromosome pair, and results in various levels of mental retardation, some limitations in physical development, and characteristic features of appearance.

- **Turner Syndrome** results from an incomplete set of sex chromosomes. These females have a normal X, but their second sex chromosome is missing or incomplete (XO). They typically do not have functioning ovaries and do not develop secondary sex characteristics at puberty.

- **Williams Syndrome** is a rare genetic disorder in which a substantial number of genes are missing from a chromosome. This results in mild to moderate retardation and significant spatial weaknesses. Although they have measurable cognitive deficits they tend to be highly sociable and gravitate toward people. They have a remarkable capacity for kindness toward others and recent research indicates that they do not carry the same prejudices and biases toward others that most people have.

- **Phenylketonuria (PKU)** results when both parents pass on a mutated gene that leaves a child without an enzyme that breaks down the amino acid phenylalanine. If this accumulates it can be toxic and cause mental retardation. Babies are routinely screened for this because if it is caught at birth, a strict diet can prevent such problems. PKU stands out from other so-called genetic abnormalities because although it is genetically determined an environmental intervention can head off complications.

A concept that is often misunderstood is **heritability.** This refers to the amount of *difference between individuals* that seems to be accounted for by heredity. If we were to say that body fat percentage was 40% heritability it would *not* mean that 40% of your body weight comes from genetics, but that 40% of the difference between you and some other individual seems due to genetics.

## Name Hall of Fame

There are no shoo-ins for the Hall of Fame in this unit. You may encounter **Roger Sperry's** name in reference to his split-brain research, and you might see **Wilder Penfield's** name in regard to his work in the middle of the 20th century in mapping the motor and sensory areas of the cortex. Almost every teacher and textbook refers to the 1848 case of **Phineas Gage**, who was injured in a horrifying accident while doing railroad work. Gage was 25 years old, 150 pounds, and a very reliable worker, but his personality was significantly altered after a 3 1/2 foot, 13-pound metal rod was driven through his skull in an explosion. Although he somehow recovered physically from this trauma, the damage to his frontal lobes and an apparent severing of the connection between that section of the brain and his limbic system left him an impulsive, highly emotional man, unable to perform much in the way of goal directed activity. From this frightening case study, scientists learned much about the functions of all healthy human brains.

## Essay Themes

While it is unlikely that you would see a free response item that was completely based on understanding of the biological bases of behavior, you still ought to have a general grip on the concept of **how neurotransmitters and hormones work to effect behavior**. You will also benefit from knowing the **basic functions of the structures of the brain** summarized in this unit. When in doubt in searching for a biological justification for some behavior or characteristic, you always have the concept of **genetic predispositions** to fall back on, especially as more and more such genetic tendencies are uncovered. That is also a possible topic for a critical thinking essay, which might require you to organize and evaluate evidence on the predominance of biological vs. environmental influences on human behavior and mental processes.

You might encounter a question that asks you to explain psychological abnormalities with a focus on BioPsych mechanisms. In addition the **plasticity of the human brain** is a hot topic in neuroscience so an understanding of this will be helpful on the AP Exam.

# The Biological Bases of Behavior

## The Neural Chain

- D.S.A.T. (neuron mnemonic); myelin sheath
  - Resting state/resting potential
    - firing threshold
    - all-or-none law
    - refractory period
    - re-uptake
  - excitation vs. inhibition
  - agonists and antagonists
    - glutamate
    - G.A.B.A.
- mirror neurons
- afferent/sensory neurons
- inter-neurons
- efferent/motor neurons

- effectors
- the reflex arc
- glial cells
  - substance p
  - endorphins
  - epinephrine/ norepinephrine
  - acetylcholine
  - serotonin
  - dopamine
- the gun analogy
- the toilet analogy
- the lock and key analogy
  - brain plasticity; LTP; neurogenesis

## The Nervous System

- Case study: Phineas Gage
- The C.N.S.:
  - the cerebral cortex
  - the 4 lobes of the cortex
  - the reticular activating system
  - the cerebellum
  - the medulla
  - the thalamus
  - the hypothalamus
  - the amygdala
  - the hippocampus
- The P.N.S.:
  - the somatic system
  - the autonomic system:
    - sympathetic
    - parasympathetic
- Split Brain research
- Brain Lateralization
- Broca's and Wernicke's Areas
  - EEG; CAT; MRI; fMRI; PET

## The Endocrine System

- What is it?
- How does it function?
- the pituitary gland (note: oxytocin)
- the pineal gland (note melatonin)
- the thyroid and parathyroid glands (note: thyroxin)
- the pancreas (note: insulin)
- the adrenals (note: adrenaline/epinephrine)
- the ovaries and testes (note: androgen and estrogen)

## Genetics

- phenotype
- genotype
- Genetic Predispositions
  - Twin Studies
- Genetic Abnormalities:
  - Down Syndrome
  - Turner Syndrome
  - Williams Syndrome
  - Phenylketonuria (PKU)
- For Discussion:
  - genetics and body weight?
  - genetics and alcoholism?
  - genetics and schizophrenia?

44

## Practice Items

- **Time yourself** on this section, and record how long it takes you. This information will be useful to you later on

- If you work at the pace you will need on the actual AP Exam, this section should take you no more than 10 minutes and 30 seconds

- If it takes you only three minutes and you get them all correct, more power to you! If you are done in less than seven minutes and you make 3 or more errors, then you ought to consider slowing down a bit

- THESE SECTION ITEMS ARE **NOT** IN ORDER OF DIFFICULTY!

1. For a brief time after firing a single-shot handgun, you cannot fire the gun again. This is analagous to what in cell firing?

   (A) Reaching the firing threshold
   (B) The resting state
   (C) The refractory period
   (D) The action potential
   (E) Inhibitory neurotransmitter activity

2. A heavily myelinated neuron and a non-myelinated neuron differ in

   (A) the speed at which neural messages can be transmitted
   (B) their dendritic sensitivity
   (C) the capacity of their terminal buttons
   (D) their location, the former in the brain, the latter in the muscles
   (E) their firing thresholds

3. Afferent neurons differ from efferent neurons in that

   (A) afferent neurons carry messages to the central nervous system and efferent neurons carry messages from the central nervous system to the muscles and glands
   (B) afferent neurons release epinephrine and efferent neurons release dopamine
   (C) afferent neurons are found only in the central nervous system and efferent neurons are found only in the autonomic nervous system
   (D) afferent neurons are found in the endocrine system and efferent neurons are found in the peripheral nervous system
   (E) afferent neurons have an extremely high firing threshold while efferent neurons have a very low firing threshold

4.  Reduced control of bladder contraction and inhibition of salivation and digestion are characteristic of

    (A) cerebral entropy
    (B) endocrine activation
    (C) the firing of neural messages
    (D) parasympathetic nervous system activation
    (E) sympathetic nervous system activation

5.  The pleasure humans derive from food, water and sexual activity is most correlated with activity of which of the following neurotransmitters?

    (A) G.A.B.A.
    (B) Acetylcholine
    (C) Substance P
    (D) Norepinephrine
    (E) Dopamine

6.  Which of the following house the auditory cortex and the visual cortex respectively?

    (A) The limbic system and the endocrine system
    (B) The sympathetic system and the parasympathetic system
    (C) The occipital lobe and the parietal lobe
    (D) The temporal lobe and the occipital lobe
    (E) The temporal lobe and the parietal lobe

7.  Damage to the frontal lobes would most likely result in

    (A)  an inability to visually perceive environmental stimuli
    (B) an inability to feel bodily sensations from various limbs
    (C) difficulty in decision making and social judgment
    (D) difficulty in the ability to recognize faces of people you know
    (E) a loss of motivation to carry out basic life functions such as eating and drinking

8.  If a neuron were missing its dendrites, the effect would be

    (A) a subtle slowing of the speed of electrical signals
    (B) a potentially dangerous increase in the speed of neural transmission
    (C) a decrease in reuptake capability
    (D) an inability of the neuron to receive chemical input from other neurons
    (E) re-allocation of chemical molecules to alternative storage sites

9.  Agonists differ from antagonists in that

    (A) agonists suppress activity in the endocrine system and antagonists boost activity in the endocrine system
    (B) agonists enhance the function of a neurotransmitter and antagonists inhibit the function of a neurotransmitter
    (C) agonists work primarily on hormones and antagonists influence neurotransmitters
    (D) agonists decrease neural firing and antagonists increase neural firing
    (E) agonists influence only serotonin and antagonists influence only dopamine

10. A split brain patient is instantaneously flashed an image of a truck to the left visual field and a cow to the right visual field. When asked to verbally report what he saw,

    (A) he will be unable to meaningfully respond
    (B) he will report seeing a truck
    (C) he will report seeing a cow
    (D) he will report seeing a truck on the left and a cow on the right
    (E) he will report seeing both images, but will reverse their proper placement on the screen

11. If a patient reported that she was experiencing some immobility in one or more body parts, her doctor may do well to investigate which of the following?

    (A) Levels of ACh, the motor cortex and the cerebellum
    (B) Levels of oxytocin, the somoatosensory cortex and the medulla
    (C) Levels of endorphins, levels of substance p, and the temporal lobe,
    (D) The pituitary gland, the amygdala and the motor cortex
    (E) The limbic system, the thalamus and the pineal gland

12. The brain produces natural pain killing opiates called

    (A) hormones
    (B) endorphins
    (C) adrenals
    (D) parathyroids
    (E) oxytocin

13. An individual suffering from Broca's Aphasia would likely experience

    (A) difficulty understanding the speech of others
    (B) difficulty producing and expressing speech
    (C) a mood disorder such as depression
    (D) increased activity in the facial recognition center of the brain
    (E) a decline in alertness and overall attention

14. In the peripheral nervous system, the somatic (or skeletal) branch

    (A) operates as an opposing process vs. the autonomic system

    (B) serves as part of the central nervous system

    (C) is made up of sensory and motor neurons which largely govern voluntary muscular responses

    (D) essentially governs involuntary processes such as breathing, blinking, swallowing and heart rate

    (E) essentially governs speech areas that allow humans to comprehend and express language

15. The thalamus and the hypothalamus in the human brain are most accurately described as performing what basic functions, respectively?

    (A) The center for emotional arousal; the center for higher level decision making

    (B) The relay station or switchboard of the brain; regulation of appetite and thirst

    (C) The center for formation of new memories; regulation of sex drive

    (D) A sensory processing center; the center for storage of newly formed memories

    (E) Regulation of appetite and thirst; a sensory processing center

# Chapter 3
# *Sensation And Perception*

## Introduction

Sensation and Perception is another area of psychology with a heavy focus on biology. It is a rather large unit in the AP Psychology curriculum, but happily, a high percentage of the concepts in it can be demonstrated to you, which makes them relatively easy to retain. We will also include a few visuals in this chapter that we hope will clarify some difficult concepts. So, while there is a lot to digest here, if you actively engage in the study of this unit you will certainly leave it with a new perspective on how we take in and interpret information from the world.   Here are some of the questions you will want to consider in Sensation and Perception:

- How much of our experience of the world is "real" and how much is it merely our interpretation of what's real, based on our expectations?

- To what extent is human sensory and perceptual experience learned, and to what extent is it "hard wired"?

- To what extent do the human senses interact with each other as in the case of the influence of smell on our sense of flavor?

- To what extent are the human brain and sensory systems "plastic" and adaptable, even in the case of extreme damage or deprivation?

## Sensation

**'Sensation'** refers to the process of attending to and taking in stimuli from the environment. It involves what-is-out-there and the physical processes engaged when we see, hear, taste, touch or smell it. On top of those five familiar senses we also have a sense of whole body balance or equilibrium, the **vestibular sense**, housed in the inner ear, and a sense of body part position and movement, **the kinesthetic sense**. We'll say more about those later in the chapter. **'Perception'** refers to the interpretation and organization of sensory information. As you will discover in this unit, it is remarkable how much of our experience is influenced by our individual attention, memories, past experiences, previous learning and motivations. For that reason, perception is sometimes called **"top-down" processing** while 'sensation' is thought of as **"bottom-up" processing**. There is a kind of bottom-to-

top flow transferring sensory input into individual perception of that input. For example: visual information is received by layers of cells in your retina and is transmitted to the visual cortex, from which it is sent to a higher brain area for color recognitions. From there it goes to a still higher brain area to encode it and to associate it with other information in your brain. You and your best friend might each attend to the same red chair and "see" it largely in the same manner, but your perceptions of it could be notably different. It may, for instance, remind you of a chair you sat in when asking your favorite person to the prom although it has no such significance for your friend. On an even less emotionally laden level, each of you might "see" the chair using the same basic sensory processes but, due to top-down processing, one might describe it as "big," another as "small," one might add features to their recall of the chair that are not present in the actual chair, one might miss or forget fairly obvious features of the chair that the other considered prominent, and so on.

The earliest work in the field we now call 'psychology' was led by researchers like Ernst Weber, Gustav Fechner and Wilhelm Wundt in the area of **'psychophysics'.** This involved the study of the links between physical stimuli in the world and the psychological experience of those stimuli. You can see that this is the essence of what we label today as 'sensation and perception.' The earliest researchers in psychophysics relied on introspection, asking subjects to reflect upon and describe their sense experiences. This is a useful but imperfect way to quantify the experience of sensory stimuli. As the focus on psychophysics grew, it was Fechner that led the field in establishing more reliable methods to measure sensory thresholds.

Imagine that you are ushered into an examination room with several classmates and given a set of earphones. Each of you will close your eyes and be exposed to tones of varying volume. You are instructed to raise your hand if / when you hear a tone. One goal of such a test is to determine your **absolute threshold** for hearing. This is defined as the minimum amount of stimulus you can detect at least fifty percent of the time it is presented. If the examiner were to identify a tone that all of the students could hear, and then presented another tone and asked the students to report whether it was louder or softer than the previous tone, he or she would be measuring the **difference threshold**, or the just noticeable difference (**the JND**). This is the smallest difference between two stimuli which a subject can detect at least fifty percent of the time. Some experts might argue that the difference threshold and the JND are not exactly synonymous, but this is a distinction that would not be made on the Advanced Placement Examination.

People tend to notice the age difference when an eighteen-year-old is dating a fourteen-year-old. Few, however, would think twice about a 38-year-old dating a 34-year-old. This is the essence of **Weber's Law**. If a very loud tone were presented to the students and then an only *marginally* louder tone was presented, Weber's Law would predict that the listeners would be unlikely to notice the difference in the tones. Weber's Law is actually a formula that supports the principle that two stimuli must differ by a constant *proportion*, not a constant *amount*, for a difference between them to be detected. For example, the JND for weight is about 2%. Simply stated, the louder a sound is, the brighter a light is, the more pungent an aroma is, the more you would have to change it, proportionally, to notice a difference.

The law does not apply as well to very high and very low levels of stimulus. Anyone who has lifted weights can see this is so: according to Weber's Law, if an individual can bench press 300 pounds, a significant weight, adding only 5 pounds to the bar, a relatively small amount, should not be noticeable. Of course, it is quite noticeable if the lifter is already at the ceiling of his or her performance.

Study of detection thresholds leads inevitably into study of attention. It would be much more difficult for the students taking the hearing test to perform well if they did not attend to the stimuli in the first place, or even to the *idea* that stimuli may be presented. And background interference (known as *'noise,'* which can be interference in any sensory modality, not merely hearing) can also influence one's ability to detect a stimulus. In **signal detection theory**, if a tone is presented and an individual detects it, it is called a "**hit**". If a tone is presented and the individual does not detect it, it is a "**miss**". If no tone is presented and the individual reports there *was* a tone, this is a "**false alarm**" (or a *false positive*) and, if no tone is presented and the listener reports that there was no tone, we use the term "**correct rejection**". There are all kinds of real-life examples to illustrate signal detection theory, from parents listening for the possible cries of their newborn baby to radar and sonar operators and their reliability in the detection of signals to doctors identifying tumors or fractures in bones.

### Signal Detection Theory

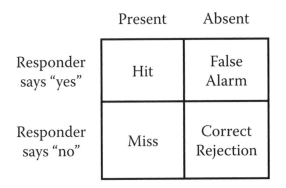

As you might surmise from your own experience, repeated exposure to any stimulus can make you so desensitized that you no longer attend to it. This **adaptation** happens on a psychological level, but can also occur on a *physiological* level. In **sensory adaptation,** the receptors for any particular sense actually no longer respond in the same way to repeated stimulation. You've likely experienced this when you have gone swimming. At first, the water seems unbearably cold, but quickly your sense receptors adapt to the temperature of the pool. However, if a stimulus threatens your survival your senses are slower to adapt to it. To protect you, your body needs to be responsive to potentially dangerous stimuli. Developmental psychologists ingeniously determine how much infants, who can't verbally tell us about their preferences, favor someone or something by how long they attend to it. Once they essentially adapt to the input they may no longer give it attention _until it changes_. This is referred to as **habituation**.

You will also have to know about **selective and divided attention** and **dichotic listening and viewing** studies. The two types of 'attention' essentially explain themselves, especially if you have ever attended a party in which much auditory, visual and olfactory stimulation is reaching your sensory system and you _choose to attend_ to some of it but not to all of it. Of course, the very fact that you can attend to _some_ of it implies that you can _divide your attention_ between multiple sensory inputs. This is examined in the laboratory through the use of dichotic listening tasks, in which you might be asked to wear a set of headphones, which simultaneously play two competing messages, one in the left ear and one in the right. You may be asked to selectively attend to only one or attempt to divide your attention between both, and, in either case, might then be tested for what you retained from either or both sets of input. What outcomes would you predict from such studies? The **cocktail party effect** is a vivid example of selective attention. It refers to your ability to easily attend to one voice or conversation even in a busy and noisy social setting. However, if someone across the room said your name, it would instantly grab your attention even though you hadn't been specifically paying attention to that person.

When we selectively attend to something in our environment we often miss or are blind to other incoming stimuli. This is often referred to as **inattentional blindness.** A striking demonstration of inattentional blindness stems from a famous dichotic viewing test that superimposes two teams of men playing catch with a ball onto a television screen and asks you to attend to one group while tuning out the other. While participants count the passes completed by the members of one team, a lady with an umbrella strolls through the middle of the screen. A majority of the participants were so focused on the assigned task that they simply missed the woman walk across the screen. **Change blindness** is a specific form of inattentional blindness in which we fail to notice changes in our environment. For example, when participants are asked to view a series of photographs of the same room they often fail to notice that the experimenters have rearranged the contents of the room in each of the different pictures.

The concepts of selective and divided attention have garnered increased attention as technology has developed. To what extent does cell phone use or texting distract one from performing day-to-day tasks? Are those who grew up with near constant exposure to such technologies better able to juggle multiple tasks simultaneously? Recent research by Eyal Ophir, Clifford Nass and Anthony Wagner suggests that individuals who identify themselves as frequent and able "media multi-taskers" actually do less well in filtering out irrelevant stimuli. Perhaps modern life is making it more challenging to identify what to pay attention *to*. Can the brain actually multi-task? Or is that term a misnomer? More fMRI and PET brain imaging research might help sort this out in the future.

"Not surprisingly, the dog failed to notice the lady with the umbrella"

(Sullivan-Valpey)

The remainder of the 'sensation' portion of the unit involves specific study of each sensory system. The Advanced Placement Examination often places more weight on the visual and auditory systems, although this is not by design; it may merely result from the fact that there is more content to test on in those areas. In any case, it is important to be familiar with the basics of all seven senses.

### Vision and Hearing

What follows is a detailed description of each of your sensory systems. It may however, be useful to start by looking at some things that your senses have in common. Each system contains receptor cells that are capable of **transduction**. Transduction occurs when the receptor cells take incoming physical or chemical energy and change that energy into neural impulses. Neural impulses from each sense (except smell) then travel to the thalamus where they are rerouted to their appropriate destination in the brain. Smell has a more direct route to the brain and is wired to an area near your hippocampus.

Each of the following systems is also capable of *sensory adaptation.* As noted earlier, when receptor cells are exposed to an unchanging stimulus they adapt by reducing their firing rate until the stimulus changes.

As you read you may also think of examples of **sensory interaction**. How many of your experiences result from two or more senses working together? For example, your sensation of flavor is aided greatly by the aroma, appearance, texture and temperature of the food.

### The Visual System

**Receptors**: Rods and cones are located in the back of **the retina**. **Rods** are far more numerous and are specialized for black/white, light/dark vision, while **cones** are specialized for color vision and for visual clarity or acuity. All told, there are approximately 120 million rods and six million cones in each eye. Cones are largely clustered in **the fovea**. Thus, in order for us to see an object clearly, the image must fall on the fovea, which is in the center of the retina. Further, in order for us to really discern color, an image must fall on the fovea - rods predominate in our peripheral vision. The energy of the light waves is transduced by the rods and cones into electrical signals, which are then transmitted to a layer of a few million bipolar cells, which in turn communicate with about 1.5 million ganglion cells. This organization, extending from so many rods and cones down to far fewer ganglion cells is called *summation.* The axons of those ganglion cells form the optic nerve, upon which the neural message is carried to the thalamus and then to the visual cortex.

**The visual cortex**: The portion of the brain responsible for the processing of visual information; it's located in the occipital lobe, at the back of the head. The primary visual cortex is sometimes called *Area V1.*

**The blind spot**: The point on the retina where the optic nerve exits the back of the eye, headed for the visual cortex. At that spot, there are no rods and cones, and thus no receptors for vision. An image that falls directly on the blind spot would not be seen, although head and eye movements and the teamwork between the two eyes, each compensating for the other, allows us to avoid "blind spots" in our vision. The following may help you in visualizing all of this.

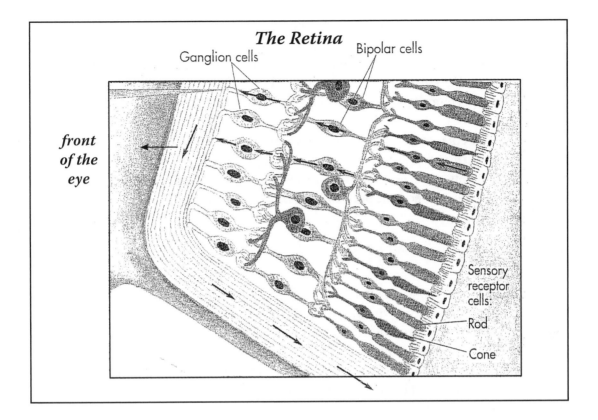

*The Retina*

Ganglion cells        Bipolar cells

front of the eye

Sensory receptor cells:

Rod

Cone

**Dark adaptation**: The process of the rods and cones adjusting to changes in levels of light. Rods and cones both adapt when you enter a darkened movie theater, although the rods do so for a longer period of time.

**Color vision theories**: According to the **trichromatic theory** (also known as Young-Helmholtz Theory) there are three different types of color receptors, that are specialized to respond to red, green and blue. These fire at different rates to allow us to see other colors. Developed in the 1800s, this theory has stood the test of time. Research done in the 1960s confirmed that we do indeed have cones that are particularly sensitive to three different wavelengths of light. This theory helps to explain **color blindness**. Actually complete color blindness is quite rare- *color deficiency* is a more accurate description. Most individuals who are considered "color blind" actually do see some color, but have trouble discriminating the differences between certain hues. Genetically, males are much more likely to be color deficient. The most common deficiency is due to a malfunction in red or green sensitive cones.

**Opponent process theory** states there are two kinds of cones, one of which responds to red and green, the other to blue and yellow, while the rods, of course, respond to black and white input. Each element of the pair works in opposition to the other - when one color in a pair is excited, the other is inhibited. Thus, if you stare for about 30 seconds at a green dot, and then avert your gaze to a neutral background, you will likely experience a *red* **color afterimage**. This is because the intense exposure excites the "green" element of the cone while inhibiting the "red" system. When that environmental exposure stops and you avert your gaze to a white background, the opposing red system is briefly excited. Your brain thus creates a visual experience that does not actually exist in the "bottom-up" world.

Trichromatic theory and opponent process theory are both widely accepted by scientists. Each theory holds true for a different level of visual processing. Trichromatic theory seems to explain color vision at the level of the cones while opponent process theory may account for color vision in the subsequent path to the visual cortex.

### The Auditory System

**Receptors**: **Hair cells**, located on the basilar membrane in **the cochlea**. The energy from sound waves is transduced into electrochemical energy, and sensory neurons then carry that information to the auditory cortex. The sound waves travel into the auditory canal, which vibrates the tympanic membrane (eardrum), which in turn vibrates three small bones called ossicles. Those bones are named the hammer (or malleus), the anvil (or incus) and the stirrup (or stapes). The ossicles pass the vibrations on to the oval window and into the cochlea (see diagram below).

**Auditory cortex**: The portion of the brain responsible for processing hearing. It is located in the temporal lobes.

**Conduction deafness**: Deafness resulting from blockage of the transmission of sound waves. Ear wax, for example, blocks the conduction of sound waves through the auditory canal, just as damage to the bones (the ossicles) in the middle ear might impede the transfer of sound waves from the eardrum to the oval window, so the information never reaches the hair cells in the cochlea.

**Sensorineural (nerve) deafness**: Deafness caused by damage to the hair cells or the auditory nerve. The following visual may help you picture the basic auditory mechanisms.

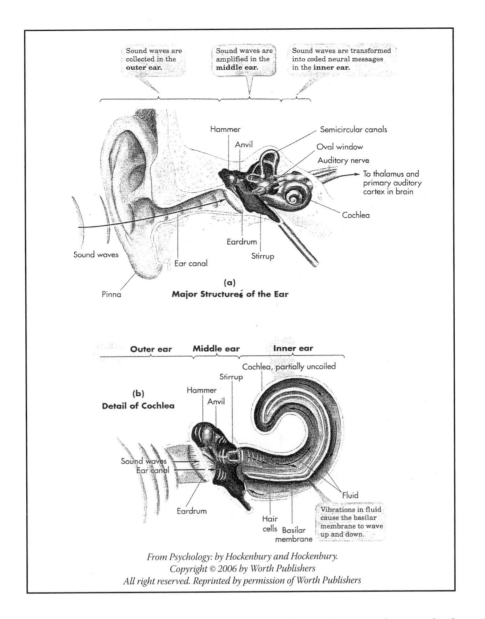

Sound waves are collected in the **outer ear.**

Sound waves are amplified in the **middle ear.**

Sound waves are transformed into coded neural messages in the **inner ear.**

Hammer

Anvil

Semicircular canals

Oval window

Auditory nerve

To thalamus and primary auditory cortex in brain

Cochlea

Eardrum

Stirrup

Sound waves

Ear canal

Pinna

**(a)**
**Major Structures of the Ear**

Outer ear    Middle ear    Inner ear

Cochlea, partially uncoiled

Stirrup

**(b)**
**Detail of Cochlea**

Hammer

Anvil

Sound waves
Ear canal

Eardrum

Hair cells    Basilar membrane

Fluid

Vibrations in fluid cause the basilar membrane to wave up and down.

*From Psychology: by Hockenbury and Hockenbury.*
*Copyright © 2006 by Worth Publishers*
*All right reserved. Reprinted by permission of Worth Publishers*

**Place theory**: This suggests we identify the pitch of sounds according to the location of vibrations on the basilar membrane. This works something like plucking a string on a violin or guitar while pressing down on the string at different spots on the neck. Place theory works well in locating high-pitched sounds, but lower frequency regions are less easy to locate on the basilar membrane.

**Frequency theory**: This suggests our brain identifies the pitch of sounds according to how rapidly the nerve impulses fire. At very high frequencies, nerves fire one after another (**the volley principle**), since no one cell could fire quickly enough to accommodate such frequencies. In the auditory cortex the number of impulses fired per second is "translated" into hertz, the unit of measure for the frequency of a sound. For example, a 90-hertz frequency produces 90 action potentials per second.

## The Chemical Senses

Gustation (taste) and olfaction (smell) are both labeled chemical senses because their receptor cells respond to chemicals rather than physical energy. Our olfactory sense detects chemical molecules from the air we breathe and our gustatory sense detects chemicals that come into contact with the taste receptors in our mouths.

### The Olfactory System

**Receptors**: **Olfactory cells** are located along the olfactory bulb in the nasal cavity. There are at least 100 different kinds of olfactory receptor sites, and about 10 million total olfactory cells. When different sequences of odor receptors fire, we are able to identify an estimated 10,000 distinct scents.

**Olfactory cortex**: Located in the temporal lobes, this is "wired" closely with the amygdala and the hippocampus, both of which are in the emotional limbic system, which may account for the power of emotionally charged memories triggered by smells. As mentioned earlier, the other senses are "wired" through the thalamus, the relay station of the brain. By the way, the phenomenon of a sense cueing a memory is called *redintegration.*

**Anosmia**: The term for the loss of the sense of smell.

**Pheromones**: Chemically produced odors that send signals (of sexual readiness, territory etc.) to other members of that species. The question is, "Do humans emit and respond to pheromones?" Many animal species clearly communicate through pheromones, but whether or not people do remains open to debate.

### The Gustatory System

**Receptors: Taste cells**, clustered in groups called taste buds, are located within the small bumps of the tongue, called papillae. Their sensitivity tends to decline with age, especially in the case of those specialized most for **bitter** and **sour** tastes. Two other types of taste cells respond largely to **sweet** and **salty** tastes, which tend to be the preferred tastes of children. Recently, researchers have discovered a fifth taste category called **umami**. Umami receptors respond to savory or hearty flavors present in meats, cheeses, and foods that contain monosodium glutamate (MSG).

The five basic receptors for taste are located across the surface of the tongue. Many older textbooks have "tongue diagrams" that suggest specific localization of each of these taste areas on the tongue although we now know that these taste locales are *not* so strictly localized. Your gustatory sense is unique in that the receptor cells regenerate every week or two. As you age, however, these cells die off, which helps to explain our ever-evolving taste preferences.

Much of the sense of taste comes from *interaction* with the sense of smell, which you can demonstrate to yourself by holding your nose while beginning to eat some chocolate or a jellybean. If you then release your nose, you should get a burst of that flavor, indicating it is largely an olfactory phenomenon. In addition to taste and smell, factors such as texture, temperature, appearance, and expectations all greatly influence your food preferences. There is also evidence to suggest a genetic component to taste preferences. **Supertasters**, the 25% of people born with an especially high number of taste buds, are very sensitive to potent tastes. **Nontasters**, on the other hand, have far fewer taste buds. The rest of the population falls in between these extremes.

### The Body Senses

### The Sense of Touch

**Receptors**: There are several different types of receptors located in **the skin**. However, the Advanced Placement Examination would not include questions about specific receptors like Meissner corpuscles, Ruffini endings or Merkel disks. These touch receptor cells respond to pain, pressure and temperature. Although the interaction among these cells is not completely understood, they appear to fire in various combinations, resulting in our experience of different touch sensations.

**Sensory cortex**: Located in the **parietal lobe** at the crown of the head. The left parietal lobe receives information from the right side of the body, while the right parietal lobe gets the information from the left side of the body. The more sensitive the area of the body is, the more surface area in the cortex is given over to that body part. For example, your fingertips and lips take up a large cortical area, whereas your forearm does not. You will see below a *sensory homunculus*, representing how we would look if our body parts were proportional to the layout of our sensory cortex.

**"The Homunculus"**

**Pain:** Pain is a great example of the interaction between *bottom-up* and *top-down processing*. Two people could suffer the exact same injury to the exact same part of the body, yet they may report drastically different experiences of pain. Why is this? There must be more to it than simple *sensation*. Your perception of pain is likely influenced by past experiences, the culture you grew up in, and individual biological factors.

No theory completely explains the mystery of pain, but it is widely accepted that there are two different pain systems. Two distinct sets of nerve fibers carry pain signals from the skin to the spine. *A-delta fibers,* which are heavily myelinated, work as an alarm system carrying the sharp immediate pain you feel to your brain. The dull and aching pain you later feel is carried to the spine and brain by *C fibers* that are processed partly in the limbic system, which may explain some of the emotional reactions that accompany pain.

**The gate-control theory of pain** suggests there is a kind of neurological "gate" in the spinal cord which opens and closes to both allow pain messages through to the brain and to stop those messages. Small fibers are thought to open the "gate" by sending pain signals. This gate can be closed by stimulating larger fibers in the injured area, which may explain why rubbing an injured area can temporarily relieve pain. The gate may also be affected by psychological factors. Anxiety and fear may open the gate while laughing or other mental distractions close the gate.

You may also find it interesting to look into **phantom limb pain**, a curious phenomenon found in people who have had a limb amputated or, in some cases, an organ removed. Long after the body part is gone, some people still report strong sensations of pain in the missing limb. What accounts for this? Perhaps the brain retains a kind of map of the missing body part and continues to send messages about it, despite its physical absence. Indeed, it may be the fact that the body part no longer exists that is at the root of the problem. A person with a painfully clenched hand can simply release the tension of the hand, providing relief from the pain. But if the brain is sending "Painfully clenched hand!" signals and there is no hand to unclench, the pain signals might well continue because of that lack of physical feedback.

### The Kinesthetic System

**Receptors**: Proprioceptors (specialized sensory neurons) are found in joints, tendons, and muscles. They give us information as to the position of individual body parts and movement. When we perform any movement we rely greatly on this system.

### The Vestibular System

This sense originates in the fluid-filled **semicircular canals** in the inner ear and governs whole body orientation and balance. It responds to changes in motion and body position, allowing us to maintain equilibrium. As you may have guessed, this system is closely tied to the cerebellum, which also plays a critical role in balance.

You might find it interesting to explore **synesthesia**, a fascinating and rare ability in some people who vividly experience one sense in terms of another; that is, to "see" musical notes or to "hear" certain colors. It's a highly engaging and mystifying topic to study.

## Perception

*"What the caterpillar calls the end, the rest of the world calls a butterfly"*
*(Lao-Tzu)*

As we've already seen, 'perception' involves how we interpret sensory input from the top down - that is, from our brain/mind down to the world "as it is." It may help you to know that some refer to this top-down processing as *organismic variables*, which include all the things an individual organism brings to each sensory experience and which thus can make that sensory experience into a very different 'perception'. For example, each of us has a different **frame of reference**. A 7 foot tall man might describe an alleged bank robber as rather short while a young preschooler would be more likely to describe the same bank robber as being quite tall. Each of us is also often influenced by **perceptual set** (also called **perceptual expectancy**), in which what we expect to see, hear, taste, touch or smell *actually influences* what we experience. A closely related concept is that of a **schema**, which is a kind of framework we have in our heads based on previous experience. If asked to look at a photo of an office, we already expect certain things to be part of that office and might well be surprised to see things that do not fit our "office schema". A professional football player given a quick look at a panoramic image of a play in motion would be better able to "remember" details of that image because his experience has supplied him with a schema for where particular players would most typically be. **Context**, the impact of the surrounding environment on our judgments, can also play a significant role in our perception of images and events. Think of how easily you can decipher someone's handwriting by piecing together what a letter or word must be in the context of the surrounding words. There are also **contrast effects** in perception. A gray bar on a white background can appear to be a different shade of gray than the same gray bar on a black background.

According to **Gestalt psychologists**, humans have a tendency to want to organize their perceptions into meaningful units or wholes. They argue that the whole is different (and sometimes greater) than the sum of its parts. One basic principle of Gestalt psychology is the Law of Pragnanz, which states that our brain organizes patterns in the simplest way possible. There are several other Gestalt Grouping Principles as well. We often finish off incomplete images based on our prior knowledge. This is called **closure**. We group **similar** perceptions together, as we do items in close **proximity** to one another, and objects that seem to "flow" together (called **good continuation**). We also sometimes infer the presence of something we cannot directly perceive, again based upon previous exposure to similar situations. For example, when driving we do not need to directly see the rest of the road over the horizon to infer that there is indeed a "rest of the road".

One of the most basic rules for organizing our perceptions is called **figure-ground perception**. Each time we look at something we perceive a figure as set apart from the background. For example, when looking at a map of Hawaii, the islands would be the figure and the ocean would be the ground. The *cocktail party effect* is an auditory figure-ground example. In a loud environment the voice you are listening to would be the figure and the background noise would be the ground.

We also infer things about the shape and size of objects even when the image we "see" of it changes. If we see a plane in the sky, we know it is a large plane even though the image of it that falls on our retina (called the **proximal stimulus**) is tiny. We know it remains **a constant size** (the **distal stimulus**, referring to how the thing really is in the world) despite its appearance. To visualize the concept of **shape constancy**, think of a door viewed from multiple angles. If you see the door closed, or ajar, or wide open, you still perceive it as a door, despite the differing shapes projected onto your retina.

There are at least two theories as to how we recognize objects in the world. How, for instance, do we know that the letter 'K' is the letter 'K'? According to **feature analysis theory**, we first break it into its pieces and decide what those features could comprise. Support for this comes from the Nobel Prize winning work of David Hubel and Thorsten Weisel, who discovered that there are cells in the visual cortex (conveniently labeled **feature detector cells**) which are specialized to fire only in response to particular angles or lines in the visual field. You might want to think of this as *parts-based object recognition*. Conversely, according to **prototype matching theory**, we have stored a small number of models or paradigms of each letter and compare each new whole to those prototypes. This is therefore a form of *image-based object recognition*.

You will need to familiarize yourself with several cues for perceiving depth and distance. Here is a quick list of those most likely to show up on an Advanced Placement Exam:

Each of the following is a **monocular depth cue**, meaning that they require only one eye. Look around the room you're sitting in and you can find an illustration of many of these:

- **Accommodation**: Changes in the curvature of the lens of the eye to adjust and focus on objects at various distances

- **Brightness**: Objects nearer to you appear brighter than those further away

- **Elevation/Relative height**: Objects further away from you appear to be higher in the visual field; if you asked a child to draw her house and then asked her to draw her grandmother's house, she would likely place it higher in the picture to signify its distance from her own home

- **Interposition/Overlap**: Objects nearer to you appear in between you and objects which are further away

- **Linear perspective**: Parallel lines seem to converge as they move off into the distance; think of how a railroad track would appear to you as it recedes into the horizon, or simply look at how the tiles on the floor below you seem to narrow and come together as distance from you increases

- **Motion parallax**: Objects near you appear to move more quickly than objects further away from you; think of how slowly an airplane seems to move in the sky when it is far away but then how speedy it is as you view it landing from an airport window

- **Texture gradient**: Objects further away from you are not as precise and detailed in their appearance, while objects closer to you are more distinct; again, look at the floor or perhaps at the ceiling and you can see this distance cue at work

- **Relative size:** When viewing a scene with two objects that you know to be roughly the same size you will perceive the larger object as being nearer to you

The following are **binocular depth cues** - you need both eyes for these:

- **Convergence**: As an object moves closer to you, your two eyes converge on it, and you feel tension in the ciliary muscles of the eye

- **Retinal disparity** (also known as **binocular disparity**): Each eye actually receives a slightly different image of any object you are viewing, and the two are put together in the visual cortex. Your brain figures out the distance of an object based on the amount of disparity between the two images. Research in the 1990's demonstrated that there are cells in the visual cortex that respond specifically to binocular disparity. The nearer an object is to you, the more difficult it is to combine the two images, which might account for why you "see double" as you view your own finger while you move it closer and closer to your face.

In the past, you might have been exposed to **reversible figures** like the well known "Old Lady/Young Lady" image or **reversible figure-ground images** like the equally well-known "Vase or Faces?" example and other perceptual illusions and phenomena. We include examples below. However, it is unlikely that you would have to specifically recall the name of an illusion on the AP Exam.

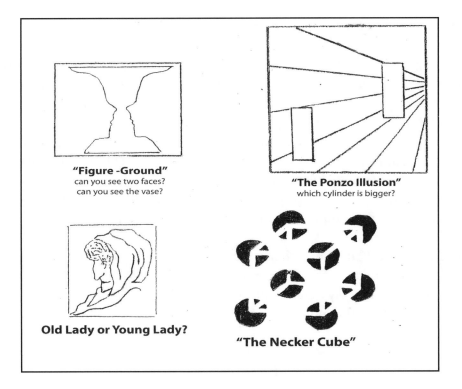

"Figure -Ground"
can you see two faces?
can you see the vase?

"The Ponzo Illusion"
which cylinder is bigger?

Old Lady or Young Lady?

"The Necker Cube"

There are also a few illusions of motion that you will want to be familiar with. If you've ever watched a movie, you've experienced **stroboscopic movement.** This occurs when slightly different still frames are projected in rapid succession giving the appearance of smooth movement. A similar illusion is the **phi phenomenon.** A series of lights switched on one after another creates an illusion of a single moving light. Another fascinating illusion of apparent motion is the **autokinetic effect**. In this illusion a stationary beam of light is projected on a wall in an otherwise completely dark room. If you stare at the projection long enough, the light appears to move.

**Name Hall of Fame**

Just as many colleges have their own sports halls of fame, populated by standouts from that particular school who might or might not be part of a *national* hall of fame, so too with names from this unit. Specialists in sensation and perception might consider recognition of them indispensable, but, for an introductory college psychology course and for the authors of the Advanced Placement Exam, they probably are not. It is possible that you could encounter a multiple-choice item on the history of psychology that refers to names like **Wilhelm Wundt, Gustav Fechner, Edward Titchener or Ernst Weber**. Each of them was an early researcher in psychophysics, but their names would likely be used simply as another cue for you in responding to a question of greater breadth.

**David Hubel** and **Thorsten Wiesel** won a Nobel Prize for identification of feature detector cells in the brain, so that makes them pretty important, but, again, no AP Exam question would be completely dependent on simply recalling their names. The concept of *feature analysis* would be the more likely focus.

**Essay Themes**

The concepts of **perceptual set, expectancy** and **schemas** are very important. They overlap with other units (you will encounter them for sure in the Memory unit in the context of eyewitness recall, in Thought and Language in terms of *mental sets* in problem solving and in Social Psychology under the umbrella of prejudice and stereotyping) and they form the foundation of the entire 'perception' portion of this unit. If you don't understand them, go back and review!

The omnipresent "nature, nurture or both?" debate in psychology is relevant in this unit. Do we *learn* about size and shape constancy, or are we in some way born, perhaps for some evolutionary reasons, to "get" such things? You could ask the same question about our mastery of depth and distance cues, and probably most anything else in this unit. You may also want to consider: To what extent is human sensory and perceptual experience learned, and to what extent is it "hard wired"? To what extent are the human brain and sensory system "plastic" and adaptable, even in the case of extreme loss or deprivation?

# Sensation and Perception

|  |  |
|---|---|
| <ul><li>absolute threshold</li><li>difference threshold/J.N.D.</li></ul><br><ul><li>signal detection theory:<br>(hits, misses, false<br>alarms, correct rejections)</li></ul><br>• "Psychophysics"<br><br>## Introduction To 'Sensation'<br><br><ul><li>transduction</li></ul><br><ul><li>selective attention</li><li>divided attention</li><li>cocktail party effect</li><li>dichotic listening</li><li>dichotic viewing</li></ul><br>• Weber's Law<br><br>• subliminals<br><br>• intattentional blindness; change blindness | <ul><li>motion detector cells</li><li>feature detector cells</li></ul><br><ul><li>rods</li><li>cones</li></ul><br>• summation<br><br>## Vision<br><br><ul><li>the fovea</li><li>the blind spot</li><li>retinal/binocular disparity</li><li>the visual cortex</li><li>sensory adaptation</li><li>dark adaptation</li><li>perceptual adaptation</li><li>habituation</li></ul><br><ul><li>color vision theories<br> - opponent-process<br> - trichromatic</li><li>color "blindness"</li></ul> |
| <ul><li>cochlea</li><li>hair cells</li><li>ossicles & tympanic membrane</li></ul><br>• the auditory cortex<br><br>• sound localization<br><br>## Hearing<br><br><ul><li>place theory</li><li>frequency theory<br> - the volley<br>  principle</li></ul><br><ul><li>conduction deafness</li><li>sensorineural/nerve deafness</li></ul> | <ul><li>the sense of touch</li><li>the somatosensory cortex</li></ul><br><ul><li>phantom pain</li><li>gate control theory</li></ul><br>## The "Other" Senses<br><br><ul><li>vestibular sense</li><li>kinesthetic sense</li></ul><br><ul><li>olfactory sense<br> - anosmia<br> - pheromones</li><li>gustatory sense<br> - taste cells<br> - supertasters/<br>  non-tasters</li></ul><br><ul><li>synesthesia</li><li>redintegration</li></ul> |

# Sensation and Perception (continued)

## Introduction To 'Perception'

- Sensation vs. Perception
- top-down processing (a.k.a. 'organismic variables')
- bottom-up processing (a.k.a. 'stimulus variables')
- context
- frame of reference

- perceptual set
- schemas

## 'Depth' And 'Constancy'

- size & shape constancy
  - distal stimulus
  - proximal stimulus

- depth/distance cues:
- binocular or retinal disparity
  - convergence

  - accommodation
  - linear perspective
    - relative size
    - interposition
  - elevation, brightness
    - texture gradient
    - motion parallax

## Organizing Our Perceptions

- Gestalt principles
  - closure
  - inference
  - similarity and proximity

- feature analysis/parts-based object recognition
- prototype matching/image-based object recognition

- reversible figures
- figure-ground images
- color afterimages

- impossible figures

## Illusions And Other Phenomena

- illusions of apparent motion:
  - autokinetic effect
  - phi phenomenon
  - stroboscopic movement

- The Muller-Lyer Illusion
  - The Ponzo Illusion

## Practice Items

- **Time yourself** on this section, and record how long it takes you. This information will be useful to you later on

- If you work at the pace you will need on the actual AP Exam, this section should take you no more than 10 minutes and 30 seconds

- If it takes you only three minutes and you get them all correct, more power to you! If you are done in less than seven minutes and you make 3 or more errors, then you ought to consider slowing down a bit

- THESE SECTION ITEMS ARE **NOT** IN ORDER OF DIFFICULTY!

1. Place theory states that

   (A) the accuracy of recall of a particular event is very much dependent on the physical location in which one attempts to retrieve the memory
   (B) hair cells at particular locations on the basilar membrane respond to incoming sound waves, and the auditory cortex interprets those locations to identify the pitch of a sound
   (C) humans determine depth and distance almost exclusively in terms of the placement of one object in relation to all other objects in the visual field
   (D) humans determine depth and distance almost exclusively in terms of the elevated location of a particular object in the visual field
   (E) rods and cones are located at the back of the retina to increase visual acuity

2. As a depth and distance cue, texture gradient is characterized by

   (A) varying levels of brightness of distant objects
   (B) reduced clarity of the distant image(s) in the visual field
   (C) differences in the images received by each retina
   (D) parallel lines receding into one single line in the visual field
   (E) recognition of proximal stimuli

3. Viewing a computer screen, a man identifies the letter 'R' even though it is in a highly unusual and unfamiliar font, because he judges that the letter most resembles the models for an 'R' the man has in his head. This is most consistent with

   (A) feature analysis theory
   (B) perceptual constancy
   (C) accommodation
   (D) prototype matching theory
   (E) closure

4.  Damage to the tympanic membrane and ossicles would likely result in

(A) redintegration
(B) synethesia
(C) aphasia
(D) conduction deafness
(E) sensorineural deafness

5.  The ability to accurately perceive common images even when there are slight gaps in those figures is best accounted for by

(A) the autokinetic effect
(B) the phi phenomenon
(C) the distinction between distal and proximal stimuli
(D) habituation
(E) gestalt

6.  The visual acuity of the human retina is best

(A) on the periphery of vision
(B) in the fovea
(C) where the optic nerve exits the eye
(D) at the level of bipolar cells
(E) at the level of ganglion cells

7.  In a book review, you read the title of a new novel called "Paris in the the Spring" and fail to notice that the title has two 'the's' in it, largely because you'd quite logically assumed it would be a correct sentence. This oversight illustrates the effect of _____ on our experience of the world.

(A) dichotic viewing
(B) controlled processing
(C) accommodation
(D) habituation
(E) perceptual set

8.  Which of the following senses respond directly to chemical energy rather than physical energy?

(A) Gustatory and Olfactory
(B) Vestibular and Gustatory
(C) Olfactory and Auditory
(D) Touch and Visual
(E) Kinesthetic and Visual

9. One classic measure of the minimum amount of sound the typical human can detect at least half the time it is present is the tick of a watch under quiet conditions at a distance of 20 feet. This is an example of

   (A) volley principle
   (B) assimilation
   (C) absolute threshold
   (D) the J.N.D.
   (E) gate control

10. Which of the following is the correct progression of visual processing in the human eye?

    (A) Rods and cones; bipolar cells; ganglion cells; optic nerve
    (B) Rods and cones; ganglion cells; bipolar cells; optic nerve
    (C) Bipolar cells; ganglion cells; rods; cones
    (D) Bipolar cells; rods and cones; ganglion cells; optic nerve
    (E) Optic nerve; rods and cones; ganglion cells; bipolar cells

11. You and your friend are on a five-day hiking trip. Your friend decides each day to remove one light item from his 30-pound backpack and secretly place it in your similar backpack. At the end of the trip you have not yet detected a difference in the weight of your pack. Which of the following best accounts for this?

    (A) Perceptual habituation
    (B) Change blindness
    (C) Weber's Law
    (D) Stroboscopic movement
    (E) Size constancy

12. Two college roommates are studying in their dorm room when one asks "Is that a phone ringing next door?". Her roommate responds "No, I don't think so, but I'll go check". She returns with the news that there was no phone ringing in the next room. In signal detection theory, the first roommate's perception is called

    (A) a hit
    (B) a miss
    (C) a false alarm
    (D) a correct rejection
    (E) an illusory correlation

13. When you first walk into a loud rock concert, the noise might seem unbearable. However, after a short time hair cells in your cochlea stop responding to that unchanging stimulus. Which of the following accounts for this?

    (A) Inattentional blindness
    (B) Signal detection theory
    (C) Sensory adaptation
    (D) Sensory interaction
    (E) Opponent process theory

14. Damage to the semicircular canals located deep in the inner ear would likely result in

    (A) trouble maintaining balance
    (B) difficulty moving individual body parts
    (C) an inability to distinguish between different high pitched sounds
    (D) difficulty in overall visual perception
    (E) anosmia

15. The process by which sound waves are transformed into electrochemical messages is known as

    (A) sensory assimilation
    (B) sensory migration
    (C) energy gradient
    (D) amelioration
    (E) transduction

# Chapter 4
# *States of Consciousness*

### Introduction

- Why do human babies sleep for as much as twenty hours a day, while you sleep (perhaps reluctantly) far less? For that matter, what accounts for the fact that deer and giraffes sleep perhaps two hours per day, while brown bats or lions might sleep twenty? Why is it that humans tend to sleep in one large chunk, at night?

- How valid are the various sleep and dream theories? What causes sleep disorders?

- To what extent do dreams have meaning? What purpose, if any, does dreaming serve? What, if anything, can we ever really *know* about dreaming?

- Just what is hypnosis anyway? Is it an "altered state of consciousness" or merely a "relaxed state of suggestibility"? To what extent does willingness play a role in an individual's "hypnotizability"?

- To what degree is the effect of psychoactive drugs largely a placebo effect?

These are the kinds of questions you will address in this relatively brief chapter on consciousness. This unit carries the least weight of all in the advanced placement curriculum. Only three or four of the 100 multiple-choice items on the AP Exam will be from this area. Many students think that's unfortunate, because this is often one of the most popular topics in introductory psychology. People enjoy learning about sleeping, dream interpretation, the nature of hypnosis and the influence of psychoactive drugs. It's quite stimulating to really *think* about these things as well.

### Sleep

There are various theories about how and why humans sleep, many of which overlap with other topics in the AP Psychology course. We'll point out some of those connections as we go, and you will undoubtedly identify several of your own. In order to understand theories as to why we sleep when we sleep we must first understand how a typical night's sleep progresses. There are five stages of sleep, four of them conveniently numbered one through four and the fifth called **REM** (an acronym for '**rapid eye movement**'). Stages one through four progress from light to deep sleep and are collectively referred to as non-REM

(**NREM**) sleep. Students, and some teachers, often assume that the REM period immediately follows the deep sleep of stages three and four, but that is not how it works. The sleeper climbs back up, from stage four to three to two and then enters the REM period. Following this, the sleeper begins a second sleep cycle. Each sleep cycle lasts approximately 90 to 110 minutes. As the night's sleep goes on, the sleeper spends progressively less time in slow-wave, deep sleep and more time in stage 2 and REM, although the complete cycle itself remains about 90 to 110 minutes. In a typical night the sleeper will stop entering stage four after the second full sleep cycle, and will spend progressively more time in the REM stage.

Stage one sleep, light sleep, is characterized by fairly rapid brain wave activity as recorded on an electroencaphalogram, or **EEG**. Stage one is a brief transitional stage that is sometimes marked by *hypnagogic* hallucinations and the feeling that one is falling or floating. Stage two sleep, in which the largest percentage of your total sleep time is spent, is characterized by **sleep spindles**, small jumbles of very rapid electrical activity. It's still an open question what these mean or what purpose they serve. Stages three and four are thought of as deep sleep. This is called **delta sleep**, as the longer, slower electrical waves present during these stages are labeled **delta waves**. For this reason, the period is also referred to as **slow wave sleep**. In this deeply relaxed state, the sleeper's breathing rate, body temperature and heart rate decrease, and he or she is very difficult to rouse.

The individual then retreats back through stages three, two, and then enters REM. This segment of the sleep cycle, so-called because during it the eyes actually do move beneath the eyelids, is often called active sleep or **paradoxical sleep**. It is *paradoxical* because while the brain is quite active and heart rate and blood pressure are elevated, the major muscle groups of the body are essentially paralyzed. Your motor cortex actively sends messages, but your brainstem stops those messages from traveling to the body's muscles resulting in the inability to move. Blood and glucose rush to the brain to facilitate neural activity, and the EEG readout in REM therefore resembles that of a person who is awake or very lightly asleep, but a naive observer would judge the sleeper to be in a deep slumber. Generally speaking, REM is marked by characteristics of sympathetic nervous system activation, while deep or slow wave sleep is characterized by parasympathetic activation.

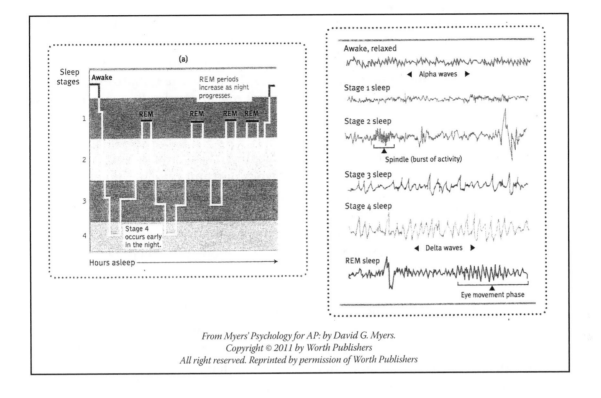

It is in the REM period that the majority of **dreaming** occurs. In fact, 80% of participants in sleep studies vividly recall dreams when awakened during or shortly after REM sleep. If, in a **REM deprivation** study, an individual is intentionally awakened at the onset of each REM period for some time, and then later is allowed to sleep normally, the sleeper tends to have longer REM periods. This is called **REM rebound**, and suggests that our bodies really need REM and will do what is necessary to get it. It's also worth noting that people deprived of stage 3 or 4 sleep experience a *NREM rebound.* The need for REM is supported by the fact that during key periods of development early in life, we need and get significantly more sleep and more REM. Babies, for instance will spend nearly 50% of their sleep in REM, which has led many to believe that it plays a major role in development, perhaps by facilitating the growth of new neural pathways. Across the lifespan there are differences in the amount of time spent sleeping and the percentage of time spent in each stage. For example, we seem to have a reduced need for REM and slow-wave sleep as we age.

It seems obvious that we need sleep. Even individuals who go remarkably long periods without sleep probably do get what are called **microsleeps**, which are tiny, seconds long periods of sleep that are not necessarily *psychologically* satisfying but do seem to help the person "get through". How much sleep we need and *why* we get it *when* we get it are questions researchers have frequently investigated. Each of us is governed by an internal biological clock that runs our **circadian rhythms** (in Latin, 'circa' means *about*, and 'dies' means *day*). The sleep-wake cycle is a clear example of a circadian rhythm but your body has many other 24-hour rhythms. For example, body temperature fluctuates daily, reaching a peak at 4:00 pm and bottoming out at 4:00 am. Activity in a part of the hypothalamus called **the suprachiasmatic nucleus (SCN***)* seems to govern our 24-hour clock. The *SCN directly influences* **the pineal gland,** which secretes the hormone **melatonin.** As darkness falls the *SCN* sends signals to increase production of melatonin, leading to drowsiness. By morning melatonin production is almost non-existent.

Nowadays, some people who have trouble sleeping take synthetic forms of melatonin to deal with the problem. You may also recall (from our unit on The Biological Bases of Behavior) that **serotonin** is a major neurotransmitter involved in sleep, although it is difficult to say exactly how. One characteristic of major depression, which is often linked to lower-than-normal levels of serotonin activity, is sleep disturbance. But for some that translates into an inability to sleep, while for others the problem is sleeping too much. Why is it that reduced serotonin activity has such divergent effects?

Of course, there are other questions about the need for sleep in general Do we sleep simply to rejuvenate ourselves, to rest and recuperate, as the **restorative theory** of sleep suggests? Or, do we sleep in order to dream? Supporters of **memory consolidation theory** (also called **information-processing theory)** contend that we need to sleep and dream in order to sift through the day's events, filing and processing memories that we wish to keep and disposing of those we want to discard. Indeed, Nobel Prize winner Francis Crick once wrote, "We dream to forget."

As we asked at the start of this chapter, why do humans tend to sleep in one big chunk (monophasically) at night (nocturnally)? One theory as to why we sleep *at night* is called **adaptive** or **evolutionary theory.** Proponents of this theory contend that, in evolutionary terms, it has always been safer and more functional for humans to sleep at night. In the distant past, for example, it was adaptive (good for one's survival) to bed down for the evening once it was dark, since going out was likely to lead to trouble with unseen tar pits and unfriendly nocturnal creatures. This view suggests that sleeping in one chunk at night preserves and protects our species.

"Evolutionary lessons"

There are some **sleep disorders** with which you must familiarize yourself. Those you are most likely to encounter on the Advanced Placement Examination are summarized below:

- **Insomnia**: An inability to fall asleep, or stay asleep, or at least the subjective sense of such an impairment. Some people who complain of having insomnia actually have pretty normal sleep patterns, but don't perceive them as such.

- **Hypersomnia**: Getting or needing too much sleep, perhaps to the point of impairing day to day functioning.

- **Narcolepsy**: A sudden, involuntary drop into sleep. In many cases, the sufferer quickly enters REM, which makes the condition even more problematic because of the loss of major muscle functioning that accompanies REM. Although the exact cause of narcolepsy is not known, there appear to be significant biological bases for the disorder. Specifically, there is a shortage or absence of hypocretins, a class of neurotransmitters that help maintain wakefulness.

- **Apnea**: The sufferer frequently stops breathing during the night and must "restart" themselves, "awakening" to some degree to do so but often without complete awareness, which makes this a disorder that sometimes goes undiagnosed. Thus, the individual may feel fatigue and sluggishness during the day even though they believe they're sleeping through the night. In fact, they may not be proceeding through all the stages of sleep, including REM.

- **Night terrors**: Not the same as nightmares; most common in children, although also occurring in adults, night terrors are characterized by a frightened "awakening", with high physiological arousal (sweating, increased heart and respiration rates, and so on), but little or no recall of the event in the morning. These are non-REM occurrences. Unlike the typical nightmares all of us experience they seem to occur during the deepest part of sleep, in stage four, and thus early in the night's sleep, for as you may recall, most stage three and four "delta sleep" occurs during the first two ninety minute sleep cycles of the night.

- **Somnambulism**: Walking in one's sleep. This too tends to happen during stage 4 sleep. This may be a result of dreaming in a non-REM period, when one's body *is* able to "act out" parts of a dream

- **Somniloquy**: Talking in one's sleep with no subsequent recollection of doing so.

- **REM sleep behavior disorder:** This happens when a sleeper is not "paralyzed" during REM. This allows them to physically act out their dreams, which at times results in injury.


### Dreams

*"A dream which is not interpreted is like a letter which is not read"*
*(from the Talmud)*

*"Dreams are only thoughts you didn't have time to think about during the day"*
*(unknown source)*

With which of the preceding quotes do you most agree? Each reflects, to some degree, a different theory of dreaming. There are several "dream theories," many of which are also linked to other topics in this course.  Do you find your dream life is more emotional than your real-life? If so, why would that be? Why is it that your dreams are often so illogical, and why is it that, in the course of the dream, you generally "roll with" that illogic? Are your dreams in first person, or are you watching yourself? Sleep studies using *fMRI* technology indicate activation of the visual cortex during REM (are you thus really "seeing" your dream?). The amygdala, a key component of the emotional limbic system, is also active. Meanwhile, the prefrontal cortex is largely offline. Could the latter two observations account for the highly emotional element of dreaming? Addressing these questions requires some spiraling back to your earlier study of The Biological Bases of Behavior, while also foreshadowing a later unit on Motivation and Emotion. In a moment, we'll also draw a parallel between one sleep theory and your previous unit on Sensation and Perception. It's likely you'll see more connections when you study Memory and Personality Theory.

In the course of an average night of sleep you may spend ninety total minutes in the REM state. Much of that period is spent dreaming. What is going on during that time? As we saw above, **memory consolidation theory** of sleep is also essentially a **dream theory**. The theory envisions dreams as a kind of **information processing mechanism**. Research indicates that there is a correlation between REM sleep and memory, thereby supporting this view. J. Allan Hobson and Robert McCarley developed the **activation-synthesis theory** of dreams. They recognize how active the brain is during REM periods when the majority of dreaming takes place. They postulate that random neural stimulation from brainstem regions activates other brain regions involved in memory, perception, and emotion. The brain combines these elements and we then try to make sense of it by superimposing a story line onto it. We synthesize all of the details into a "dream". You may see a connection here to Gestalt psychology, which we looked at in the unit on Sensation and Perception. Recall that this school of thought is based on the notion that humans have a strong tendency to try to organize information into meaningful wholes.

**Memory Consolidation Theory-
the evidence**

(Sullivan/Raczynski)

The most well-known dream theory comes from the **Freudian psychoanalytic school of thought**. In 1900, Sigmund Freud proposed that "Dreams (are) the royal road to a knowledge of the unconscious activities of the mind," and that statement reveals the core of the theory, which postulates that dreaming is a form of wish fulfillment. Freud argued that dreams have **manifest content**, the obvious, superficial "plot" of the dream, and the more important **latent content**, which he deemed to be the unconscious symbolic underlying meaning of the dream. As we will see later in our study of Personality Theory, Freud believed that the unconscious mind was a storehouse of wishes and desires which we were not willing or able to express in the real world but which might come out in various behaviors or in our dreams. Freud's theory remains controversial, and it warrants critical discussion in class and critical analysis in your own head. There are many popular books on dream interpretation that are interesting to explore but should be read with a healthy skepticism. Even Freud himself was known for warning people not to overanalyze dream content, especially without training.

One final area of interest in regard to dreams is the concept of **lucid dreaming**. If you've ever been dreaming and had a sense that you were indeed in a dream, then you recognize the roots of lucid dreaming. In some cases, people who have awareness that they are in a dream report being able to control many aspects of the dream. Research has indicated that individuals can teach themselves to influence events in their dreams - some small children have even learned to do so in order to control or even stop recurring nightmares.

## Hypnosis

Yet another topic from this unit that requires critical analysis is **hypnosis**. There are at least two competing interpretations as to just what hypnosis is. One argues that it is a **very relaxed state** in which the subject is highly suggestible and merely playing the role of a "good subject," while others contend it is truly an **altered or dissociated state of consciousness**. The successful use of hypnosis in pain management supports that latter hypothesis to an extent, but the debate continues.

**Ernest Hilgard**, the name you should probably most associate with the "altered state" side of the debate in preparation for the AP Exam, identified what he called the **hidden observer** in hypnotic subjects. If an individual was hypnotized and told to *dissociate* from some painful stimulus, a highly hypnotizable subject could do so and report low or nonexistent levels of pain, but a second part of their consciousness (a hidden observer) can report that there was pain. It's as if part of the subject is hypnotized while another part watches over the hypnosis session. But the mere idea of some people being "highly hypnotizable" while others are not is a point of interest to those who support the "hypnosis is merely a relaxed state of suggestibility" school of thought; if someone is "highly hypnotizable," maybe that just means they're "highly suggestible" whether they are hypnotized or not. Clark Hull is one respected psychologist who pointed out that anyone volunteering for hypnosis has essentially already agreed to play along with the hypnotist.

You may remember the concept of demand characteristic from the first chapter on Statistics and Research Methodology. In that context we explored how survey respondents might sometimes figure out and then deliver the answers the survey administrator wants to hear. How much is hypnosis a matter of social demand characteristics?

Hypnosis has many different uses, but one of the most striking is the ability of hypnotized subjects to manage their experience of pain. People have successfully used hypnosis during childbirth and even major surgeries as an alternative to pain killing medication. How is this possible? PET scans reveal that some pain processing areas become less active during hypnosis. It's also possible that hypnosis is a form of amplified selective attention and that hypnotized people are so focused that they are able to dissociate from the painful sensations. For people with addictions, a hypnotist will often give a **posthypnotic suggestion**, an instruction that is to be carried out after the hypnotic session is concluded. While the evidence for using hypnosis to successfully treat addictions is mixed, many studies suggest it is a useful tool in treating obesity. Research does <u>not</u>, however, support the idea that hypnosis can be used for age regression (hypnotically taking one back to an earlier time) to recover buried memories.

## Psychoactive Drugs

A **psychoactive or psychotropic drug** is a chemical substance that impacts behavior, perceptions, moods or mental processes. In order for a drug to have an effect, its chemical molecules must cross the **blood-brain barrier**. This barrier blocks certain material in the blood from entering brain tissues. Once across this barrier, the effect of the drug is largely determined by which neurotransmitter systems it influences. You may recall from the BioPsych chapter that some drugs are *agonists*, which <u>enhance</u> the effect of a neurotransmitter and other drugs are *antagonists*, which <u>inhibit</u> the effect of a neurotransmitter. A single drug may influence many neurotransmitters, but most of the drugs we discuss here influence the dopamine-sensitive "pleasure centers" in the brain.

With repeated use of most *psychoactive* drugs one builds a **tolerance**, which results in the need for greater and greater amounts of the drug to experience the original effects. This can lead to **physical dependence** on the drug, meaning that a user has intense cravings and a physiological need for the drug. And, if one suddenly stops taking a substance after long-term usage, there can be distressing, even painful side effects collectively referred to as **withdrawal** symptoms. You may find it interesting to discuss in your class the effect that *perceptual set* has on the effect of a drug. Another intriguing discussion topic might revolve around cultural differences in drug use.

You will also want to familiarize yourself with the different categories of drugs and gain a general understanding of the physiological effects of the following:

- **Depressants** slow nervous system activity. Alcohol is a depressant that stimulates GABA activity. Recall that GABA works much like the brakes of your nervous system. Its increased activity results in slower physical and mental reaction times and also impairs judgment and memory. Barbiturates (tranquilizers) and benzodiazepines (anti-anxiety drugs) are other examples of depressants.

- **Opiates** such as opium, morphine, oxycodone, and heroin suppress pain and induce sleep while also inducing states of euphoria. These powerful and highly addictive drugs tend to be agonists for endorphins. With repeated use the brain stops producing its own endorphins leading to severe (in some cases deadly) withdrawal symptoms when the user tries to quit.

• **Hallucinogens** such as LSD, mushrooms and peyote alter one's perceptions, often causing very dramatic hallucinations. LSD greatly disrupts the transmission of serotonin along with other brain chemicals. It is chemically very similar to serotonin, so the molecules of LSD often lock into serotonin receptor sites. As evidence of this, when a hallucinating subject is given a serotonin antagonist, hallucinations are greatly diminished. THC (tetrahydrocannabinol), the active ingredient of marijuana, is also classified as a mild hallucinogen. After exposure to THC, vivid visual hallucinations are unlikely, but one may experience dramatic differences in taste and other sensory experiences. Some of the drugs discussed in this section stay in your system for a very short time, but THC remains in your bloodstream for as long as a month. Because it stays in your bloodstream for so long, people may not build tolerance, and it may take less of the drug to experience a high.

• **Stimulants** stimulate or activate the nervous system and essentially speed up levels of arousal and activity and suppress appetite. Nicotine, the active ingredient of tobacco, is a commonly used stimulant. Another stimulant, caffeine, is the most widely used psychoactive drug in the world. Other powerful stimulants such as cocaine and amphetamines increase dopamine and norepinephrine activity in the brain resulting in elevated mood and increased energy. Repeated use of these drugs can cause long-lasting structural damage to dopamine neurons in the brain's reward system making normally pleasurable activities less enjoyable.

### Name Hall of Fame

On the exam you may well see names like **J. Allan Hobson and Robert McCarley**, in reference to activation-synthesis dream theory, and **Ernest Hilgard's** name is a good bet to show up amongst the multiple-choice items, but in both cases they will be given to you and will serve as cues in the stem of an item. It is very unlikely that you would have to identify any of their names as the answer to a question.

**Sigmund Freud** is a 'Babe Ruth' sort of name in psychology - that is, everyone would have him in the hall of fame, even the many psychologists who don't think his work is psychology. Some would label it as an interesting 'philosophy' but would not consider it 'science'. If nothing else, he is one of the most recognizable names in the <u>history</u> of psychology, and his ideas have had a profound impact on the way humans think about and talk about themselves. His is a name you have to know or you can't say you know psychology.

**Wilhelm Wundt** is often thought of as the founder of 'experimental psychology', as he set up the first psych lab in Germany in the late 1870's. He's considered a **structuralist**, and that fits in with this unit on States of Consciousness. Structuralists examined the *mental structures* of consciousness, so their name cues you as to their focus. They hoped to identify and understand the basic building blocks of the mind. They often used **introspection** to do their work - simply stated, they asked subjects to look inside themselves and report on their cognitive experiences. Another early area of exploration into human consciousness came to be called **functionalism**. There's no surprise here - functionalists were more interested in what our consciousness and cognitions were *for*. They wondered about the *uses* of our sensations and mental processes. Their focus was on how our minds adapt to the environment. **William James**, usually considered the first great American psychologist, was a functionalist. Functionalism is a dominant perspective in philosophy of mind nowadays, but how does functionalism account for subjective consciousness? How does it explain what each of us actually experiences? If someone late in life saw the color 'orange' for the first time, would there be any way to quantify or put into words what she had 'learned'? She might say "So *that's* orange!", But could she do more? At that point, would we know any more about her experience of 'orange'?

**Essay Themes**

Remember that the percentages given to you by the College Board for each unit in the Advanced Placement Psychology curriculum refer to the multiple-choice only. In this case, that percentage is 2-4 %, which means two to four items of the 100 multiple-choice questions will involve states of consciousness. The percentage doesn't say anything about essay coverage, but it is very unlikely that an essay would focus on this unit. The more you know about **Freud and psychoanalysis** the better, as that *is* a prime candidate for at least part of an essay, and this is your first of several exposures to it in the curriculum, but otherwise you needn't worry about an essay asking you to trace the development of a typical night's sleep or to expound on two or three sleep and dream theories. Such an essay proposal would probably be rejected as too narrow in terms of content coverage.

There are topics in this unit that naturally invite critical thinking. For example: What is the evidence regarding hypnosis? What is the evidence about the purposes of sleep? Of dreams? What do we make of the fact that people sleep less, with less REM, as they age? Babies spend huge amounts of time in REM sleep - are they dreaming at that time? If not, why not? If yes, what form do their dreams take? Reflecting on these issues in class or on your own will deepen your grasp of any specific related concept that might show up on the examination.

# States of Consciousness

## Sleep

- melatonin and the pineal gland
- circadian rhythms
- stages of sleep 1 to 4
- delta waves/ delta sleep
- REM– paradoxical sleep
- REM Rebound
- sleep & aging
- sleep deprivation
- microsleeps
- Theories: why sleep?
  - restorative theory
  - memory consolidation theory
  - adaptive/evolutionary theory
- Sleep disorders:
insomnia, hypersomnia, narcolepsy, apnea, night terrors, somnambulism, somniloquy, REM sleep behavior disorder

## Dreams

- Theories: why dream?
  - memory consolidation theory
  - activation synthesis theory
  - psychoanalytic theory
- Freud
  - manifest content
  - latent content
  - dream interpretation
- lucid dreaming
- Common recurring themes: why?
- Nightmares vs. Night Terrors

## Hypnosis

- What is it? 2 views:
1)
2)
- professional applications
- Hilgard's "hidden observer"
- post-hypnotic suggestion
- Links to other units:
  - perceptual set
  - placeboes
  - demand characteristic

## More On States Of Consciousness

- What is consciousness?
  - structuralism
  - functionalism
  - introspection
- Psychoactive/Psychotropic Drugs
  - stimulants
  - depressants
  - hallucinogens
  - opiates
- The blood-brain barrier
- Recall: agonists, antagonists
- tolerance
- withdrawal
- physical dependence

**Practice Items**

- **Time yourself** on this section, and record how long it takes you. This information will be useful to you later on

- If you work at the pace you will need on the actual AP Exam, this section should take you no more than 10 minutes and 30 seconds

- If it takes you only three minutes and you get them all correct, more power to you! If you are done in less than seven minutes and you make 3 or more errors, then you ought to consider slowing down a bit

- THESE SECTION ITEMS ARE **NOT** IN ORDER OF DIFFICULTY!


1. After her bridal shower, a young woman dreamed that she was dining with her parents when a young male grabbed her wallet containing her driver's license, credit cards, cash, and family pictures. She awoke in a cold sweat. After discussing the dream with a friend, her friend suggests that she is anxious about losing her identity in her approaching marriage. This explanation of her dream represents what Freud would refer to as

   (A) manifest content
   (B) latent content
   (C) semantic content
   (D) structuralism
   (E) functionalism


2. Which theory of sleep proposes that we sleep in order to allow our brains to sort through events of the day, filing away what needs to be kept and throwing out information that is no longer useful?

   (A) Adaptive theory
   (B) Evolutionary theory
   (C) Freudian wish-fulfillment theory
   (D) Activation-synthesis theory
   (E) Memory consolidation theory

3. Which of the following would best support Ernest Hilgard's view of hypnosis as a dissociated state?

   (A) A hypnotized subject reports that he felt unusually open to suggestion during the hypnotic session
   (B) A hypnotized subject reports awareness of an intensely unpleasant smell but is not directly responsive to it
   (C) A hypnotized subject voluntarily discontinues participation in a hypnotic session
   (D) For some time a hypnotist is unable to rouse a subject from a hypnotic state
   (E) A long-term cigarette smoker stops smoking after a series of hypnotic sessions

4. An agonist is a psychoactive drug that

   (A) produces tolerance without withdrawal
   (B) blocks the effect of a hormone
   (C) mimics and enhances the effect of a neurotransmitter
   (D) inhibits the effect of neurotransmitters
   (E) makes recovery from physical addiction more difficult

5. Which stage of sleep is characterized by erratic brain waves called sleep spindles?

   (A) Stage 1
   (B) Stage 2
   (C) Stage 3
   (D) Stage 4
   (E) REM

6. The "paradox" of REM sleep is that

   (A) during it the brain is quite active but the major muscle groups are essentially paralyzed
   (B) the sleeper is not actually "asleep" for most of it, but is in a hynopompic state
   (C) adults experience it, but newborns do not
   (D) newborns experience it, but the elderly do not
   (E) there is no evidence suggesting it has a purpose

7.  Which of the following is most affected by opiates?

    (A) Endorphins
    (B) Melatonin
    (C) Hypocretin
    (D) GABA
    (E) Acetylcholine

8.  The phenomenon of REM rebound supports the notion that

    (A) we require more REM sleep as we age
    (B) human infants are not yet developed enough to experience REM sleep
    (C) REM sleep is essential for growth and functioning
    (D) the latent content of dreams is meaningful
    (E) the latent content of dreams is not meaningful

9.  The sleep disorder characterized by spontaneous, involuntary drops into REM sleep is called

    (A) somnambulism
    (B) apnea
    (C) maintenance insomnia
    (D) REM sleep behavior disorder
    (E) narcolepsy

10. Felicia finds she consistently awakens only seconds before her alarm sounds each morning. This is evidence for the existence of

    (A) REM rebound
    (B)  REM sleep disorder
    (C) the hidden observer
    (D) circadian rhythms
    (E) adaptive theory

# Chapter 5
# *Learning Theory*

### Introduction

You will undoubtedly find much that is relevant to your own life experience in this unit, which outlines how we learn through conditioning, observation and cognition. We can readily break this unit down into four sub-topics: classical conditioning, operant conditioning, observational or social learning and cognitive learning. In this unit you will consider questions like: How much does human learning involve deliberate thought and how much is essentially reflexive in nature? Under what circumstances and conditions do humans learn through observation; what ramifications does this kind of learning have on society at large and individuals in particular? To what extent are human behavior, motivation and personality explained by learning theory? You will also want to reflect on how you might apply your knowledge of learning theory in your future as a student, as a parent, as a professional, and as a citizen.

### Classical Conditioning

**Classical conditioning** is a form of reflexive learning based on making new **associations**. If you ever got excited upon hearing the music of an ice cream truck as a child (or now!), you know about classical conditioning. If you have a pet that comes running out to the kitchen as soon as he or she hears the can opener or the rustling of the bag of food, you know about classical conditioning. Learning the labels used in classical conditioning can be a struggle, but the basic mechanism is familiar to most of us. Simply speaking, the learner associates something that naturally leads to a response with something new that didn't previously lead to that response. The sound of a can opener doesn't at first mean anything to a kitten. However, when she comes to associate that particular sound with the imminent arrival of food (which *does* naturally interest the kitten), she will respond to that sound. The sound of the can opener must have reliably predicted the arrival of food, or the kitten would be unlikely to make a strong connection between the two events. In a learning theory course, you would learn more about the *Rescorla-Wagner Model*, a mathematical formula which demonstrates this concept of **contingency**, but for the AP Exam you need only know that the **conditioned stimulus** (in this case, the sound of the can opener), must reliably predict the presentation of the **unconditioned stimulus** (in this case, the cat food) in order for strong conditioning to occur.

**Ivan Pavlov** is one name you'll want to associate with classical conditioning in psychology, although he was a not a psychologist and there had been work with such conditioning mechanisms done before his time. Pavlov, a Nobel Prize winning physiologist, was studying the digestive systems of dogs when he made note of how the animals seemed to respond to previously neutral stimuli in much the same way as the kitten we spoke of above. To test this, Pavlov began to pair the presentation of meat powder, which naturally makes a dog salivate, with a previously neutral stimulus. Most people remember this as a bell, but Pavlov actually used metronomes and other tones at first. He presented the sound of a metronome, followed immediately by the arrival of the meat powder, which led to a salivation response in the dogs. After repeated pairings of the metronome and the meat powder the dogs began to salivate at the sound of the metronome. When the dogs salivated at the sound of the metronome, without the presentation of the food, Pavlov said there'd been **acquisition** of conditioning. In essence, they had *learned* to respond to the new stimulus. If the dogs were to then salivate upon hearing similar, but not identical tones we would say the dogs had **generalized**. If the dogs salivated only to the metronome and did *not* generalize, we'd say they had **discriminated**.

Pavlov argued that as long as the sound of the metronome and the presentation of the food were paired together in the same rough space and time, that the dogs would make the association and conditioning to the metronome would occur. But why wouldn't the dogs connect the color of the walls or the size of the food bowl with the presentation of food? Clearly, they didn't make the connection with just anything that happened to be around. It was in questioning this idea of **contiguity** that Robert Rescorla and Allan Wagner revised Pavlovian theory with their concept of contingency, mentioned above. Learning theorists today favor Rescorla's model, which clearly adds a <u>cognitive</u> (thinking) component to classical conditioning.

Students sometimes struggle with the terminology of Pavlov's classical conditioning, but it's not so difficult to reason most of it out from the terms themselves (although the English versions of those terms are somewhat different than what Pavlov intended in his Russian language descriptions of them). As you review these terms it may be useful to substitute the word 'conditioned' with 'learned'. To say a response is *unconditioned* means that it is a natural, unlearned response. A *conditioned stimulus* refers to something the subject has learned to respond to. A summary of the terminology follows:

•   **The unconditioned stimulus (US or UCS)** is the thing the organism naturally, reflexively responds to. In trying to break down a classical conditioning example into the appropriate terms, it may be useful to start with the UCS by simply asking yourself, "What naturally caused a response in the learner, without any apparent need for learning?" That's the UCS. In the kitten example above, the UCS is the cat food and in the case of Pavlov's dogs, it was the meat powder.

- **The conditioned stimulus (or CS)** starts as a **neutral stimulus (NS)** because at first it elicits no response from the subject. After repeated pairings with the *UCS*, however, it becomes learned; hence the term *conditioned stimulus*. In identifying this, ask yourself "What is the learner now responding to that they did not previously respond to in this way?" or "What have we now conditioned the learner to respond to?" or even simply, "What did the organism learn?" In the kitten example above, the kitten learned to respond to the sound of the can opener, which is therefore the CS. In the Pavlov example, the dogs were conditioned to salivate upon hearing the metronome, the sound of which (the CS) had not originally elicited any such response.

- **The unconditioned response (UR or UCR)** is the natural, unlearned, largely reflexive response to the UCS. In the kitten example, it is excitement at the presentation of cat food (as manifested by the cat's running into the kitchen), while with Pavlov's dogs it was salivation at the presentation of meat powder.

- **The conditioned response (or CR)** is the new, learned response to the CS. For the kitten, it is running into the kitchen in response to the can opener, while for Pavlov's dogs it is salivation at the sound of the metronome

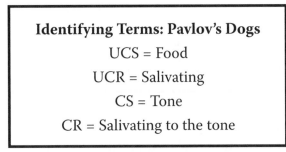

**Identifying Terms: Pavlov's Dogs**
UCS = Food
UCR = Salivating
CS = Tone
CR = Salivating to the tone

**John B. Watson** is another famous researcher in the study of classical conditioning. Watson is sometimes referred to as the "father" of **behaviorism,** a major psychological perspective focused on studying observable behavior, rather than the subjective *introspective* techniques used by his predecessors. He believed that psychologists should study only objective, measurable phenomena and that subjective mental processes are immeasurable and therefore a waste of time. Behaviorists believe that our actions are a direct result of past conditioning and environmental influences. The following quote from Watson is representative of this way of thinking:

*"Give me a dozen healthy infants, well-formed, and my own specified world to bring them up and I'll guarantee to take any one at random and train him to become any type of specialist I might select- doctor, lawyer, artist, merchant-chief, and yes, even beggar-man and thief, regardless of his talents, penchants, tendencies, abilities, vocations, and race of his ancestors..."*

In 1920, Watson set out to test the notion that **phobias** resulted from classical conditioning using an orphan who has come to be known as **Little Albert**. Albert was around a year old when Watson introduced him to a white rat, which Albert liked. He then paired the arrival of the rat with the striking of a very loud gong near Albert's ear, which, quite naturally, Albert did *not* enjoy. Indeed, he cried and tried to escape from the area. After a very few such pairings (**white rat - loud noise = fearful response**), Albert began to exhibit signs of aversion immediately upon seeing the white rat. Remember, he had originally frolicked happily in the company of the rat, but was now classically conditioned to fear it. Further, Watson argued that Albert then *generalized* his fear to all white, furry things. Worst of all, later Watson apparently lost track of Albert and never **de-conditioned** him. In order to **extinguish** the classically conditioned response, Watson would have repeatedly presented the CS (again, in this case, it was the white rat) alone. Its presence would not again be paired with the sound of the loud gong. After several **extinction** trials, the CR would weaken and eventually disappear. After these trials are conducted, there are sometimes cases of **spontaneous recovery**, a kind of flashback to the previous conditioning even after it had been de-conditioned. This is usually only a brief recurrence however.

---

**Identifying Terms: Little Albert**

UCS = Loud noise

UCR = Fear response

CS = Fluffy white rat

CR = Fear response to the fluffy white rat

---

Watson's research provided one possible explanation about how we develop phobias, but his failure to conduct extinction trials with Little Albert is considered highly unethical today. This sad ending to the story therefore serves as a link to the **ethical principles** in psychological research that you studied in the first unit of this course. It also makes learning theorists wonder if Albert's conditioning would have been extinguished over time on its own. In effect, later in life, anytime Albert was exposed to a white furry object and it was <u>not</u> paired with an aversive stimulus such as a loud noise, that would serve as a kind of naturalistic extinction trial.

If you've ever eaten a food and become sick later you may have experienced a classically conditioned **taste aversion** (meaning you've learned to avoid that food). It can sometimes be a bit trickier to identify the UCR and the CR in the case of such learning. In the earlier examples, the UCR and the CR were actually identical, but not so in the example of taste aversions. For example, if you had contracted a virus that had not yet manifested itself at lunchtime, you would likely eat a normal meal at that time. Let's say that at around 6 p.m., you begin to vomit, as a result of this virus. You might very well associate the illness with something you had eaten at noontime. Although it was <u>the virus</u> that caused the illness, you might well connect that unpleasant outcome with the fried clams you had at lunch, and avoid them in the future. In this case, the unconditioned response is vomiting. You didn't learn or become conditioned to vomit in response to a virus (the unconditioned stimulus) - it just happened! The conditioned response (to the conditioned stimulus of fried clams) is *aversion*. You probably won't actually vomit at the idea of eating fried clams, but you will avoid eating them because you have come to associate them with vomiting. *Taste aversions* are unique in our discussion of classical conditioning in that learning can result after only one pairing of the CS and UCS and, the UCR is not necessarily immediate. In fact sometimes hours pass before one gets ill.

**John Garcia** is the researcher most associated with conditioned *taste aversions*. He and others argue that this learning demonstrates **biological preparedness**, meaning we have a *predisposition* to make such a connection, as it would be useful for our survival to be able to identify foods that might be harmful to us. This evolutionary mechanism may also help explain why phobias of snakes and heights are much more common than phobias of books or bicycles. The former have historically been a potential threat to our survival.

You might encounter a couple of other classical conditioning concepts on the AP Exam, although it is unlikely. Just in case, they are summarized below:

**Blocking**: If your kitten was classically conditioned to come running when she heard the can opener, that learning could then interfere with conditioning to some other stimulus. For example, if you switched to a hand-held can opener that made a distinctly different sound from the first opener, it may take even longer than before for the kitten to connect the sound of it with dinnertime. In essence, the first CS blocks the learning of a new CS, or at least slows it down.

**Second or higher order conditioning**: Assume Pavlov's dogs are now salivating at the sound of a metronome, which serves as the conditioned stimulus. Could we now pair the sound of the metronome with some new stimulus, say a red light, and get conditioning to *it*? The red light would *not* be paired with the original unconditioned stimulus, the meat powder. The answer seems to be yes, although the conditioning is generally weaker and requires more trials. Researchers trying to go to a *third* level of conditioning have not been successful.

**First order conditioning**
CS (metronome) + UCS (food) ▸▸ UCR (salivation)
CS (metronome) ▸▸ CR (salivation)

**Second order conditioning**
CS (red light) + CS (the metronome) ▸▸ CR (salivation)
CS (red light) ▸▸ CR (salivation)

"Classical" Conditioning

## Operant Conditioning

**Operant conditioning** also involves making associations, but in this case it is a matter of **connecting behaviors with their consequences**. The learner performs a behavior, and that action is either reinforced or punished. According to early theorist **Edward Thorndike**, if the result of some behavior is pleasant or desirable, the organism is likely to repeat that behavior. If the consequence of some act is undesirable, the organism is less likely to act in that way again. This simple principle is called the **law of effect**, and it is the basis of what Thorndike called **instrumental conditioning. B. F. Skinner**, a leading behaviorist, furthered Thorndike's work but preferred the label operant conditioning because it emphasized that a subject is actively "operating on" its environment. Skinner is considered a 'radical behaviorist' for arguing that thinking and other inner states were inaccessible to science and irrelevant to our study of behavior. A learner's actions, he believed were the product of that learner's history of reinforcement and punishment. He argued that free will is a myth and our actions are best explained and predicted by the consequences that we have received.

**The Law of Effect...**

**"No longer so curious"**

(Sullivan)

The important types of consequences used in *operant conditioning* are summarized below. It may be helpful while you are learning these to keep in mind that reinforcement leads to favorable outcomes and increases the likelihood of the reinforced behavior. Punishment, on the other hand, leads to unfavorable outcomes and theoretically decreases the punished behavior.

- **Positive reinforcement** encourages a behavior. It involves a pleasurable consequence (such as getting a food reward), which is delivered upon completion of some desirable action by the subject. A researcher might **shape** a complex behavior in an animal by positively reinforcing it for each successive step it took toward the goal behavior. Animal trainers often use **chaining** in which they *shape* a sequence of behaviors. Once learned, the animal is positively reinforced only upon completion of the chain of desired behaviors.

- **Negative reinforcement** also encourages a behavior. Think of 'negative' in terms of <u>subtraction</u>, in that an unpleasant condition is <u>removed</u> when a desired behavior is completed. The taking of aspirin is negatively reinforcing in that the behavior removes the pain of a headache making one more likely to take aspirin in such a situation in the future. Be careful - this is *not* the same as punishment, although you will sometimes wrongly hear them used as if they are identical. Psychologists identify two types of negative reinforcement; **escape learning and avoidance learning**. A person who feels extreme anxiety in social environments may engage in *escape* behaviors. For example, when they start to feel anxiety they remove themselves from that setting, which in turn relieves their anxiety. In avoidance learning, that same subject learns to avoid the aversive setting completely. This avoidant behavior is strengthened because they no longer experience the anxiety they associate with socializing.

- **Punishment** (sometimes called **positive punishment**) discourages a behavior. It is an unpleasant (aversive) consequence that is delivered when a subject does what you do <u>not</u> want him to do.

- **Omission Training**, (sometimes called **negative punishment**) also discourages a behavior as something the learner likes is taken away. For example, if you break your curfew and your parents take your car away for a week, they are technically using *omission training*.

To prepare for the AP exam you should know the difference between primary and secondary reinforcers. **Primary reinforcers** are unlearned and are inherently reinforcing to most if not all members of a species. The list of them is short - food and water are definitely on the list, and some would say that adequate shelter, love, and sex are primary reinforcers too. Intuitively, some students in our culture think of money as a primary reinforcer, because it has become so much desired and in many ways is <u>the</u> reinforcer for industrialized westerners, but its value as a reinforcer is still learned and is largely (though not exclusively at this point) a result of its role as the currency with which you obtain primary reinforcers.

**Secondary reinforcers** (also called **conditioned reinforcers**) are those we learn to value. For example, an animal could be trained to value a poker chip as a reinforcer if poker chips could be used to trade for food. The poker chip has no inherent value to most animals, just as money has no inherent value to human infants. Secondary reinforcers are often used in **token economies**, where a learner is given tokens upon completion of a task and they can later trade those tokens for prizes or other reinforcers that they desire.

You'll also need to understand some basic approaches as to how and when consequences are delivered in operant conditioning. In **continuous schedules** of reinforcement the consequence is delivered after every instance of the goal behavior. In **intermittent (or partial) schedules** of reinforcement a learner may have to perform a goal behavior multiple times before being reinforced. The most rapid learning occurs with continuous reinforcement, but intermittent schedules are much more resistant to de-conditioning or extinction because the learner does not know when the next reinforcement is coming. The four specific types of intermittent schedules are summarized below:

- **A fixed ratio schedule (FR):** Reinforcement will be delivered after a specified number of desired <u>responses</u>. Examples include receiving frequent flyer rewards for some set amount of miles already flown or being paid by your employer for every 7 toys you assemble (an FR = 7 schedule).

- **A variable ratio schedule (VR):** Reinforcement will be delivered after some number of <u>responses</u>, but the amount is not specified for the learner. A VR = 5 schedule means that <u>on the average</u> of every fifth response would be reinforced, but not necessarily every five. Examples include playing the lottery or selling magazines door-to-door. In each case there <u>will</u> be a payoff but you don't know how many times you'll have to perform the behavior to receive one.

- **A fixed interval schedule (FI):** Reinforcement is delivered based on a specified <u>passage of time</u>. The first desired response after that passage of time is reinforced. If you are anxiously awaiting a piece of mail due on Friday and you know what time the mail carrier always arrives, you will check for the mail then but not before; your checking is then reinforced when you find the desired piece of mail.

- **A variable interval schedule (VI):** Reinforcement is delivered after some established <u>period of time</u> but that interval changes from one trial to the next. If you are awaiting an important piece of mail due on Friday but the daily delivery time is highly variable, you might be likely to check more often to see if it has arrived, since you do not know exactly when it might get there.

Much of Skinner's work with these schedules was done with rats and pigeons in an apparatus called an operant chamber or a Skinner box. He used different consequences and delivery routines to mold some pretty remarkable behaviors in these animals.

But, not surprisingly there are limitations in such conditioning. Many researchers have identified an **instinctual drift**. When in doubt, animals revert to behaviors that come naturally. Rats are not inherently disposed to push levers, so when presented with a lever they may revert to biting, scratching, or sniffing. Thus, their innate tendencies may interfere with their conditioning.

What is desirable or reinforcing to one potential learner is not necessarily reinforcing to another. Indeed, something that serves as a reinforcer for one individual could actually be a punishment to another. This helps us understand what is called the **Premack Principle**, named after David Premack. It states that one ought to identify what is reinforcing for a subject and then use it to reinforce desired behaviors that the subject is not so likely to perform on his or her own. In Premack's words, "a preferred activity can be used to reinforce a non-preferred activity." It is sometimes thought of as **the grandmother clause**, because a grandmother may apply such a principle when she promises her grandchild that he can play in the sandbox if he finishes his asparagus. This would be a successful ploy, of course, only if the grandson enjoys playing in the sandbox. If playing there inevitably leads to painful interactions with his older sister, he may actually be *less* likely to eat his asparagus. Here, a behaviorist would argue not that operant conditioning doesn't work, but that one must choose reinforcers and punishers carefully and deliver them consistently so the learner can make the connection between the behavior and an individually meaningful consequence. This is an example of **contingency in operant conditioning**, in that the performance of the behavior must reliably predict that the consequence <u>will</u> occur in order for learning to take place. In general, it is also best to deliver consequences as quickly as possible. Otherwise, the learner may be less likely to connect the behavior with the outcome.

Another important point in the application of consequences involves **overjustification**. This predicts that if you begin to reinforce a behavior that the individual is already predisposed to perform, it may actually discourage the subject from continuing to do it. There is some evidence, for example, that reading programs for schoolchildren can have this effect. If students are promised a reward for reading a certain number of books, they will indeed read more to earn the reward, but often will stop completely once the reward is discontinued. Further, those who already read a lot before the reinforcement program often *read less* while the promise of the reward is in force (although they may still read enough to obtain the reward) and then *continue* to read less after the reward is discontinued. Dan Ariely recently conducted a study at Duke University demonstrating that small and medium sized bonuses helped performances on various workplace tasks, but high bonuses seemed to lead to too much stress. The performance level of the "high bonus" recipients was the worst of the three groups. Did the added pressure of the big bonus cause them to "choke"?

## Cognitive Learning

Some kinds of learning are placed under the heading of **cognitive learning**, even though classical and operant conditioning and observational learning all involve their share of cognitions (that is, thinking and mental processes) as well. Three types you should know about are summarized below:

- **Insight learning**: Sometimes an organism ruminates on a problem and then has a relatively sudden solution come to mind; picture old cartoons in which a light bulb would turn on over the head of a character who suddenly came upon an idea. Wolfgang Kohler noticed such insights in chimps in the 1920's - he placed bananas in a variety of hard-to-reach locations and watched how the chimps got at them. After a period of simple trial and error, Kohler argued that the chimps would stop and reflect on the problem and then appear to just "get" a solution.

- **Latent learning**: Edward Tolman coined this term for learning that has been acquired but is not demonstrated until the subject is reinforced for doing so. Tolman's landmark experiment involved three different groups of rats attempting to learn a maze. When Group A ran the maze, they were rewarded with food each time they reached the end. It should not surprise you to learn that after repeated trials they made fewer errors and reached the food more quickly. Group B never received food for reaching the end and as you might suspect, they did not improve at completing the maze. Group C wandered the maze for the first ten days without reinforcement for finishing the maze and showed no improvement, but on day eleven they began receiving food whenever they did successfully navigate the maze. Behaviorists would have predicted that the rats would now follow the same trend as Group A, slowly improving with each reinforced trial. Instead the rats in Group C immediately performed as well as or better than Group A. This indicated that the rats in Group C had indeed learned the route prior to being reinforced, but up to then had no reason to demonstrate that knowledge. Tolman argued that the rats had developed a **cognitive map** or mental representation of the maze and could call it up if there was an incentive to do so.

- **Learned helplessness**: **Martin Seligman** coined this term for a process in which one tries to do something, continually fails, and then quits trying altogether. If an individual believes that, no matter what they do, they cannot control outcomes, they will conclude that they are helpless to effect change. They've learned that they are helpless. It's possible that you or some of your classmates have experienced learned helplessness in one or more subjects in school. Perhaps in middle school you gave your best effort in math, but continually failed and now in high school you find that you don't really put much effort into that subject because you truly believe it won't matter. Learned helplessness is a major foundation of cognitive explanations for depression, and has other applications in psychology, which you will encounter in the unit on Personality Theory.

## Observational Learning

**Albert Bandura** and others would contend that much of what we learn comes from observation. For instance, if a mother **models** a behavior for her son, that child is likely to imitate what she has done, especially if the adult's behavior is **reinforced** in some way. The child would also have to have a sense that they could successfully and safely carry out the act and control its outcomes to some extent. Bandura called this a sense of **self-efficacy**.

Bandura's famous 1963 study in **observational** or **social learning** involved the use of adult models, who were videotaped punching and kicking a doll named Bobo. Children who first watched the video were then placed in the same room as depicted in the video, with the same array of toy choices, and promptly imitated the adult models, beating on Bobo. Further, they tended to assault the doll in very specific ways, mirroring the adult behavior of pinning Bobo to the floor, using a hammer to strike him and tossing him in the air. Children in a control group, who did not first view the video and were given a chance to play in the same environment did not behave in such ways. It may be interesting to debate in your classes whether the results would be similar if we replicated Bandura's work today, and if kids are just as likely to imitate *pro-social* behavior (that is, kind, helping acts) as hurtful behavior. You might also want to discuss the extent to which television, video games, and popular culture depictions of sexual behavior and drug use influence our behavior. This topic also presents an opportunity to refer back to the unit on The Biological Bases of Behavior and revisit the role of mirror neurons. These neurons may well form the biological basis for observational learning.

## Transfer of Learning

If you were asked to learn one musical instrument that would prepare you best to learn other instruments, which would you choose? Would knowing how to play the piano help you in learning the flute, or the guitar? If you are a good skier, would that skill transfer well to snowboarding? If you can throw a baseball or softball, is it likely you can throw a javelin as well? How about psychology - does learning about it help you in learning other things? These are all questions about **positive and negative transfer of learning**. If knowing how to play the piano aids you in learning the flute, that would be an example of positive transfer. If knowing how to play the piano actually impedes your mastery of the flute, we would call this negative transfer. You can see how negative transfer of learning is a form of blocking which we mentioned in our treatment of classical conditioning. You'll also see connections to these concepts in the next unit on memory.

**Name Hall of Fame**

**Ivan Pavlov** and **B.F. Skinner** are first ballot inductees into the psychology name hall of fame. Even though there is a lot of evidence that something like classical conditioning had been done before, Pavlov is still considered its father. Likewise, **Edward Thorndike's** Law of Effect came well before Skinner did his work, and it is the basis of operant conditioning, but Skinner's is the name to know for the AP Exam. **John B. Watson** would also probably get into the hall without much argument from anyone. He is usually considered the founder of behaviorism, although many introductory psychology students seem to remember him most for questionable ethical practices in his work with **Little Albert** and for losing his university teaching position because of an affair with a research assistant.

Many students of psychology would also have **Albert Bandura's** name on a "top ten list" of who ought to be in the hall of fame. You need to recognize his work in observational learning and modeling, particularly in the context of his Bobo experiment. **Martin Seligman** is very well known and still quite active, but you would not likely have to regurgitate his name on its own, although you may well see it linked with the concept of learned helplessness or with cognitive explanations for depression on the examination. **John Garcia's** name might be linked in a question stem or in a response choice to study of classically conditioned taste aversions, and you might have similar cues in regard to latent learning (The name: **Edward Tolman**), insight learning (The name: **Wolfgang Kohler**) and contingency in classical conditioning (The name: **Robert Rescorla**). However, you should not worry about having to pull the names Garcia, Tolman, Kohler or Rescorla by themselves out of your memory. You might also see **David Premack's** name, but it would be in relation to the Premack Principle in operant conditioning, so that's more a matter of concept recognition than name recognition.

**Essay Themes**

The very first free response question ever used on an Advanced Placement Psychology Examination was on the **similarities and differences between classical conditioning and operant conditioning**. Such a question is less likely to make it onto the exam nowadays as it might be ruled out as being too narrowly focused on just one unit. Still, it does tell you that this stuff is pretty important in the minds of those who create the test. If you don't have a pretty good grip on what classical and operant conditioning are, you don't really know learning theory.

A solid critical thinking question in this unit revolves around observational learning. Specifically, what is the evidence regarding violence in the media and its impact on human behavior? If you explore this issue in a lively class discussion, it will deepen your grasp of the fundamental concepts in social learning, and learning theory in general.

The bulk of this unit is about **behaviorism**, and that school of thought has made a frequent showing on free response AP Exam items. By the end of the advanced placement course, you ought to be able to write a succinct paragraph or so outlining the core ideas of each of the major schools of thought in psychology (Behaviorist, psychoanalytic/psychodynamic, cognitive, biomedical, humanist). That by itself would have gotten you through more than one essay on previous AP tests. As the course progresses, **you will see much overlap between this unit and others** (Like Development, Motivation, Personality, Abnormal Psych and Treatment), so, while it isn't particularly large, it is quite important.

# Learning Theory

## Classical Conditioning

- CS
- UCS
- UCR
- CR

- contingency
- blocking

- 2nd or higher order conditioning

- classically conditioned taste aversions

> "BEHAVIORISM" focusing on observable behaviors and how they're learned is more important than guessing about inner experiences or mental processes

- Acquisition
- Generalization
- Discrimination
- Extinction
- Spontaneous Recovery

- Biological Predispositions?
- Instinctual drift?

## Operant Conditioning

- Pavlov's dogs
- Watson & Little Albert

- Thorndike's "law of effect"
  - B.F. Skinner
    - contingency
    - immediacy
    - the Premack Principle
    - overjustification

- shaping: chaining

- positive reinforcement
- negative reinforcement
  - escape, avoidance learning
  - punishment/aversion
  - primary reinforcers
  - secondary reinforcers

- Schedules of reinforcement
  - continuous vs. intermittent
    - fixed ratio (F.R.)
    - variable ratio (V.R.)
    - fixed interval (F.I.)
    - variable interval (V.I.)

## Social Learning

Also known as:
- observational learning
- "modeling"

- Bandura and "Bobo"

- role of self-efficacy

- role of reinforcement

## Cognitive Learning

- Kohler, chimps and insight learning

- Tolman, rats & mazes
  - latent learning
  - cognitive maps

- Seligman and learned helplessness

- positive and negative transfer of learning

## Practice Items

- **Time yourself** on this section, and record how long it takes you. This information will be useful to you later on

- If you work at the pace you will need on the actual AP Exam, this section should take you no more than 10 minutes and 30 seconds

- If it takes you only three minutes and you get them all correct, more power to you! If you are done in less than seven minutes and you make 3 or more errors, then you ought to consider slowing down a bit

- THESE SECTION ITEMS ARE **NOT** IN ORDER OF DIFFICULTY!

1.  A child who is deeply afraid of spiders sees a large spider on her lawn, and is now afraid of grassy areas. Her newly acquired fear of grassy areas demonstrates

    (A) social learning
    (B) second order conditioning
    (C) classical conditioning
    (D) extinction
    (E) discrimination

2.  People who repeatedly buy lottery tickets believing that if they play often enough they will eventually win, are reinforced on which of the following schedules?

    (A) Fixed interval schedule of reinforcement
    (B) Fixed ratio schedule of reinforcement
    (C) Variable interval schedule of reinforcement
    (D) Variable ratio schedule of reinforcement
    (E) Continuous schedule of reinforcement

3.  According to Edward Tolman, a rat might assimilate the details of a maze through passive exposure to it, although it may not demonstrate that knowledge in the absence of reinforcement. He called this

    (A) backward conditioning
    (B) the overjustification effect
    (C) self efficacy
    (D) latent learning
    (E) insight learning

4. A week ago a child was attacked and bitten by a big dog, and he now shows a fear response around all dogs. This illustrates the concept of

   (A) generalization
   (B) discrimination
   (C) social learning
   (D) insight learning
   (E) instinctual drift

5. In a language laboratory, a language teacher checks in on her students at varying, unpredictable times and awards bonus points if a student is continuing to engage in the oral lesson. This is an example of a

   (A) fixed interval schedule of reinforcement
   (B) fixed ratio schedule of reinforcement
   (C) variable interval schedule of reinforcement
   (D) variable ratio schedule of reinforcement
   (E) continuous schedule of reinforcement

6. How would Ivan Pavlov have conducted extinction trials after his classical conditioning of a salivation response in dogs?

   (A) By repeatedly presenting the CS without ever again pairing it with the UCS
   (B) By reinforcing the behavior he wished to extinguish
   (C) Through the use of temporal conditioning
   (D) By administering a placebo to the dogs immediately after conditioning
   (E) Through modeling the target behavior

7. In operant conditioning, reinforcement refers to anything that

   (A) gives the organism an intrinsic desire to succeed
   (B) increases the likelihood that a behavior will occur again in the future
   (C) immediately follows an undesired response
   (D) results in latent learning
   (E) decreases a target behavior

8.  A rat learns to escape an electric shock as soon as it is administered by running through a small opening in an operant chamber. This is an example of

    (A) primary reinforcement
    (B) secondary reinforcement
    (C) negative reinforcement
    (D) omission training
    (E) positive punishment

9.  B.F. Skinner would most likely agree with which of the following explanations for a superstitious behavior such as a player wearing the same pair of socks for every game of the football season?

    (A) The player saw successful teammates wearing the same socks each game.
    (B) The player was punished in the past for wearing those socks.
    (C) The first time the player wore those socks during a game his team won.
    (D) The player was classically conditioned to associate the socks with football.
    (E) Humans have an instinctual drift to associate clothing with the environment.

10. According to Robert Rescorla, the strength of a classically conditioned response decreases as the predictive value of the CS-UCS pairing decreases. He argued that this is so because classical conditioning requires

    (A) contiguity
    (B) contingency
    (C) acquisition
    (D) shaping
    (E) chaining

11. In operant conditioning, the Premack Principle states that

    (A) primary reinforcers have more intrinsic reinforcing value than secondary reinforcers
    (B) a previously learned response can block the learning of a later, similar response
    (C) one can pair a conditioned stimulus with a second conditioned stimulus and acquire conditioning to that second stimulus
    (D) a desired behavior for a particular individual can be effectively used as a reinforcer for another, less preferred activity
    (E) punishment is an ineffective consequence because the subject does not learn the appropriate behavior

12. According to research on overjustification, offering a child an external reward for reading, something they already enjoy, will likely

    (A) increase their overall satisfaction with reading
    (B) increase their enjoyment of the external reward
    (C) decrease their interest in both reading and the reward
    (D) result in reading more in the future, even when there is no external reward being offered
    (E) result in less enjoyment in reading and reduced likelihood of choosing it in the future when there is no external reward associated with it

13. A supervisor has difficulty when her company switches from one type of computer to another. She works more slowly because she continues to seek applications that were available on her old computer but are not present on the new system. This is an example of

    (A) positive transfer of learning
    (B) negative transfer of learning
    (C) behavior chaining
    (D) second order conditioning
    (E) insight learning

• The next two items (# 14 and #15) refer to the following scenario:

Jordan has been a coffee drinker for the past ten years. He has noticed recently that just the sight of his coffee cup seems to elicit more alertness and wakefulness from him.

14. In this example of classical conditioning, what is the conditioned stimulus (CS)?

    (A) The coffee cup
    (B) The coffee
    (C) The caffeine in the coffee
    (D) The heightened level of alertness
    (E) In this scenario there is no conditioned stimulus

15. If Jordan felt more alert only upon seeing his own coffee cup and not other cups in his house, he would be demonstrating

    (A) higher order conditioning
    (B) trace conditioning
    (C) stimulus discrimination
    (D) stimulus generalization
    (E) blocking

# Chapter 6
# *Cognition, Part 1: Memory*

*"You have to begin to lose your memory, if only in bits and pieces,*
*to realize that memory is what makes our lives. Life without memory is no life at all...*
*Our memory is our coherence, our reason, our feeling, even our action.*
*Without it, we are nothing."*
*(Luis Bunuel)*

**Introduction**

According to psychologist Ulric Neisser cognition can be defined as, "How people learn, structure, store and use knowledge." Seven to nine of the one hundred multiple choice items on the AP Psychology Exam will involve Cognition, which in turn is broken into two parts: Memory and Thought and Language. Many of the concepts you will encounter in studying Memory can be demonstrated for you, and they'll thus be easy to retain. This topic also contains reference to the use of **mnemonic devices**. Learning about such memory aids will help you in this unit and also in retaining information from future chapters and other courses.

In this chapter we will explore questions like: To what extent can memory be relied upon? Under what conditions is it most and least reliable? Is it a benefit to remember everything, or are there some things that are desirable to forget? What accounts for forgetting trivial or even important information? Lastly, how can we apply our understanding of the basics of human memory function to facilitate recall and recognition of information, events, people and places?

What if you were given the option of taking a "memory improvement drug", would you do it? Or would you fear unforeseen side effects? If such a drug worked on the hippocampus, how might it affect the hippocampus in performing its numerous other functions? Also, would such a drug leave you overwhelmed by information?

Consider the flip side. What if you were offered a drug that erased memory? You might well want such a medication if you were tortured by memories of a romantic relationship gone wrong, or a terrible accident, or a wartime trauma. Would erasing such memories be desirable in the short, medium and long term?

You might wish to ponder questions such as these as you explore human memory.

## Information Processing

The **information-processing model of memory** is built on a three-phase flow in human memory. First, we **encode** information, then we must **store** it, and finally we must be able to **retrieve** what we have stored. Some liken this model to the operations of a library. When a librarian receives a new book, he first identifies and catalogues it (encoding) and then he places it on a shelf (storage), from which it can be readily retrieved. Books, like memories, can be "lost" at any step along the way. If, for example, a catalogued book was borrowed and returned but then replaced on the wrong shelf, it would essentially be lost even though it is in the library. This would be especially true in a library with a very large capacity; a book that ought to have been placed on shelf number one on the first floor of the library which was instead placed on shelf number five on the seventh floor of the library might just as well have been burned, as its retrieval would require a book-by-book review of the entire inventory.

A more commonly used analogy for this information-processing model is drawn with computers. You could not pass in the research paper you have typed on your word processor (encoding) unless you have saved your work (storage) and also remembered its file name so that you can retrieve it.

## Encoding

The first step of memory according to the *information-processing* view is encoding, which involves entering information into memory. While learning new concepts in psychology, you are paying attention and giving thought, which is called **effortful processing**. There are also many stimuli in your environment that you encode without any effort through **automatic processing**. Generally speaking, our brain does not engage in slow, step-by-step encoding. Instead it uses **parallel processing**, allowing us to encode multiple elements simultaneously.

It's pretty clear that **the more deeply you process incoming information**, the more likely it is that you will retain it for future reference. **Deep processing** refers to consciously adding meaning or making connections with information we are taking in. We can attribute much of our inability to remember to **shallow processing** when we first encountered the material. In school, for instance, we often use **maintenance rehearsal**, which involves simple repetition as a means to encode what we are taught. It is a relatively shallow way to encode the information because we fail to attach any **meaning** to it or place it in some relevant **context**. **Elaborative rehearsal** is a superior studying technique because it requires thinking about the meanings or uses of some concept. It's interesting to note that many students who claim they cannot remember, say, the last ten U.S. presidents, can remember numerous details about the last ten CD'S put out by their favorite musical group. They may even spend more time rehearsing the list of presidents in preparation for a test than they ever spent "rehearsing" the names of the CD titles or band members, but the latter has meaning to them and is thus more readily stored and retrieved.

Phone numbers, social security numbers and bank card numbers are all examples of how encoding can be facilitated through **chunking**. Rather than remembering 11 digits in a string, we can group the digits into more manageable segments. Thus, 14325581212 becomes 1-432-558-1212; 1776186519181945 can be chunked into 1776, 1865, 1918, 1945, and NFLCIAFBINASA can be read as NFL, CIA, FBI, NASA. In the latter two examples, the chunking method is combined with the attachment of meaning or context to the groupings, which increases ease of recall.

Encoding is also greatly influenced by our **schemas**, which impact our memory for people, places and situations. A schema is a cognitive framework based on our previous experience. This set of expectations help us fill in the gaps in our memories. Of course, such schemas can also lead us to build things into memories that fit our expectations but not the reality of the circumstance. This is called **constructive memory** or **confabulation**. For example, earlier in this chapter we made mention of a librarian. Many students, if later tested on the details of the chapter may erroneously recall a female librarian in the example. Our use of a male librarian may have gone undetected because people tend to have a female schema for a librarian.

Have you ever had difficulty recalling a specific word but had a sense that it was a long word? Perhaps you could even recall exactly where it was on the page. If so, it may be that when you first learned the word you encoded it **visually**, which involves memorizing the information by making it into a mental picture. If you cannot pull the word out of your memory but you do remember that it rhymes with something else or have a feel for the rhythm or sound of the word, it could be because you encoded it **acoustically**. If you can recall that a word is synonymous with another word, even though you cannot at the moment recall the actual word, this might be attributed to earlier **semantic encoding**. A commonly used illustration of these types of encoding involves analyzing the errors individuals make in attempting to recall the names of the seven dwarfs from the "Snow White" fairy tale.

An example of a *semantic encoding error* might be remembering a dwarf who was "really smart" without specific name recall; there was an intelligent character named Doc. Remembering a character called Dumpy or Bumpy instead of the actual character, Grumpy is an example of an *acoustic encoding error*. If one was more reliant on *visual encoding*, he or she might remember the physical appearance of the characters - that most have beards although one (Dopey) did not, and so on.

**Mnemonic devices** rely on our ability to make mental images like some of those above. In order to remember something using mnemonics, one links some part of it (a visual image, the way the word or a part of the word sounds, etc.) to something one already knows. Some mnemonic techniques for name recall work by making a connection between the name you hear and the face you see. For instance, if introduced to a man named Cliff you might picture his face or head as a high, steep cliff. Later, upon seeing his face, the image of a cliff comes back to you. The key is to first attend to and hear the name. Many people who argue that they're "not good with names" probably never really encode the name when introduced to someone.

In other mnemonic approaches, you tie a set of images of the things that you are trying to remember to a familiar place (like your bedroom) and then simply mentally walk your way through that familiar scene, retrieving the images as you go. This is called the **method of loci**. Or you create an image using "peg words" which you have memorized; you then simply recall the already memorized peg words and the image you associated with it comes back to you. The classic *peg word mnemonic* requires that you memorize the number one as a bun, two as a shoe, three as a tree, four as a door, five as a hive, six as sticks, seven as heaven, eight as gate, nine as line and ten as hen. Each peg word rhymes with its corresponding number. If you wish to remember a list of things to get at the store, you "hang an image" on those pegs, imagining biting into a hamburger *bun* which is filled with MILK, then picturing a *shoe* with a huge head of LETTUCE stuffed into it, etc. It's certainly fine to use outlandish imagery, but it is just as important to add action to your mental pictures. This seems to aid later retrieval. Many memory experts would contend that the images or techniques one uses are less important than the effort it takes in even trying to use a mnemonic. That effort alone encourages deeper, more meaningful processing.

---

**Effective Encoding Strategies**

• Utilize the **spacing effect**. When you prepare for a test, distributed rehearsal will lead to better retention than massed rehearsal or cramming.

• Engage in elaborative rehearsal by using vivid imagery and creating mnemonics.

• Try to make connections between your life and the information you are trying to encode. This is called **self-referencing.**

• Even after you feel you have mastered a topic, long-term retention is improved with continued rehearsal, also known as **overlearning**.

---

**Storage**

Another model for memory, the *Atkinson-Shiffrin model*, overlaps in many ways with the information-processing model. It does, however, differentiate between different types of storage mechanisms, postulating the existence of a **sensory register, short-term memory (STM) and long-term memory (LTM).** The sensory register, or simply **sensory memory**, allows us to take in the plethora of sensory inputs that are available at any moment. Its functioning is very brief - most of what "hits" the sensory register receives no further attention or processing from the observer. In effect, such information is not encoded and is then lost.

Each of the major senses has a sensory register that allows us to hold a representation of incoming sensory information if only for a brief period. Most of that sensory information fades within one second unless more attention is given to it. George Sperling conducted a famous study to test visual sensory memory, which is also called **iconic memory**. He flashed three rows of three letters on a screen for one-twentieth of a second and then asked subjects to recall the letters. He found that people remembered only about half of the entire array of letters, but if he instead asked subjects to recall any single row they remembered the line without any problem.  He surmised that all the letters were still in their memory for a fleeting moment, but by the time they started to recite them, many had faded. This research reveals that for a few tenths of a second we can recall any part of a scene that we have just looked at. We have a similar sensory mechanism for auditory information, called **echoic memory**. Things that we hear, even if we aren't paying attention, register and linger for three to four seconds.

When we try to store information that enters our sensory memory in short-term memory, it quickly becomes apparent that **STM has a rather limited capacity**. In general, STM is deemed to last less than **20 seconds** and hold about 7 +/- **2 unrelated items** (the latter was identified by researcher George Miller and is often called the **"magic number"** of short-term memory capacity). If no deeper processing is done in order to enter material into longer term storage, it will fade pretty rapidly, and, if we try to hold more than 8 or 9 items in STM, we tend to start knocking out earlier items. Often, you will hear STM linked to a term called working memory, as if they are synonymous, but that's not exactly true. **Working memory** draws on both STM and LTM. It allows for information that is already stored to be brought to conscious awareness, while also juggling new material as it enters short-term memory. Some people think of working memory as a desktop, on which you array the files you already have and the newer material you're being exposed to. From there, you sort and process it all.

**Long-term memory** is thought by many to have no limits in terms of capacity. Theoretically, we cannot run out of room in LTM. If we "do something" with incoming material through rehearsal, chunking, mnemonic elaboration or some other processing strategy, it can enter relatively permanent storage. Later, we'll look at how we still manage to forget things that are in LTM.

There are a few other types of memory you should know about for the advanced placement course. They are summarized below:

- **Episodic memory** refers to memory for a specific event or period of time in one's life. These memories essentially provide a way for us to re-experience the things that have happened in our lives. One vivid type of episodic memory is a **flashbulb memory**. Flashbulb memories are detailed memories of emotionally charged events for which we have vivid recollections. In a prototypical flashbulb memory individuals feel they can recall exactly what they were doing when a major event happened. Research, however, indicates that our confidence and the vividness of the memory do not necessarily predict well for our accuracy. These memories are often shared among people of a generation. For example, your parents may have detailed memories of the day that President Kennedy was assassinated. Others may clearly remember the day that Princess Diana was killed in an accident. More recently, memories of the events of September 11, 2001 have undoubtedly become classic examples of flashbulb memory.

- **Semantic memory** involves memory for information. The facts and ideas that you typically learn in school are largely a matter of semantic memory. You probably know that the first President of the United States was George Washington – that is an example of semantic memory.

- **Procedural memory** includes memory for specific actions, such as riding a bicycle, tying one's shoes, or swimming. These are the most enduring types of memories; it is essentially true that once you learn to ride a bike you never forget.

Although our long-term retention of memories is far from perfect, there are many things in our environment that prime us to more accurately remember the past. According to the **encoding specificity principle**, we retrieve information best when we can re-create the original conditions in which we learned the information. Research on **context dependent memory** indicates that one is more likely to recall information if one is in the same physical space or a similar physical context as when one encountered the material. Theoretically, the best place to be tested on your knowledge of Advanced Placement Psychology would be in the room where you were taught the material. The use of context cues has also been used in some legal proceedings to facilitate more accurate eyewitness recall.

The concept of **state dependent memory** proposes that one is more likely to recall details of something if one is in a similar emotional and physical state as when exposed to the events one is trying to recall. A person who witnessed a scenario during a fight or flight response would recall details of that scenario better if in a similarly aroused state.

Moods also serve as powerful retrieval cues for information. The concept of **mood congruent memory** is demonstrated by our tendency when feeling down to vividly recall other sad episodes in our lives and when happy to recall more positive times in our lives. Our moods seem to prime us to re-experience past times when we have felt that particular mood.

Another fascinating topic to explore is that of **eidetic imagery/memory**. This is the official term for photographic memory, which in its true form is quite rare. It involves very precise and long lasting memory as if one has stored an actual photograph to "look at" in their head.

### Retrieval

Many of the memory problems we have involve **retrieval issues**. We have the sense that the memory is "in there" but we just can't seem to pull it out. This common retrieval problem is known as the **tip of the tongue phenomenon**. Also, while we sometimes cannot precisely <u>recall</u> details stored in our memories, we can <u>recognize</u> them when cued in some way. An item on a test that asked you to give a definition of a term is assessing your **recall** of that concept, while a multiple choice item is assessing **recognition**. Further, at times it appears we "remember" something without knowing that we do. This is called **implicit memory**, as opposed to **explicit memories**, which you can consciously declare (explicit memory is sometimes referred to as *declarative memory*). An implicit memory may need to be *primed* or cued in order for you to recall it. For example, in research done with patients who had damage to the hippocampus, the patients were unable to declare any explicit recall of items in a word list they were shown. However, if cued by, say, letter combinations like 'ch' and asked to think of the first word that came to mind beginning with 'ch', they were more likely to come up with words that they had seen on the list they'd been shown earlier (in this example, perhaps the word 'charter'), even though they had no conscious recollection of having seen the words. The procedural memories discussed earlier are also examples of implicit memories. Both implicit and explicit memories are part of long-term memory storage. The graphic below will help you keep the types of LTM straight.

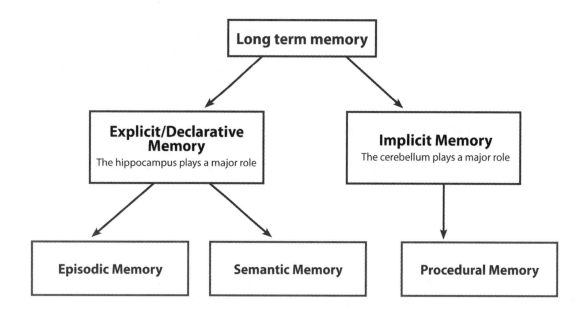

When individuals with healthy memory systems are given a list of words to remember, we often see evidence of an interesting set of phenomena known collectively as the **serial position effect**. If given a series of fifteen words describing behaviors in a baseball game (such as hit, pitch, bunt, and so on), individuals are more likely to recall items presented at the beginning of the list (called the **primacy effect**) and the end of the list (the **recency effect**). Recall is also better for words that stand out for their **semantic distinctiveness.** That is, they have meanings that catch one's attention or do not fit the schema of the list. Further, some individuals might "remember" words that in fact were never presented. This is a result of their attempts to reconstruct the list and to then confabulate items that meet their expectancy of what *might* be on such a list.

Expectancy or set can also greatly influence one's **eyewitness recall**. An eyewitness to a crime might unknowingly apply gender, racial or place schemas in trying to reconstruct the events they witnessed. Thus, it is possible to add details to a memory just as it is easy to forget (or **level**) details. Researcher Elizabeth Loftus has also discovered that the way one is asked to recall events (the **framing** of the questions) can influence how those events are then recalled. This is similar to the idea of posing "leading questions" in a courtroom. If a witness to a robbery is asked, "Which hand was the gun in?" before it is even established that there *was* a gun; this can elicit responses quite different from more open-ended questioning techniques.

Loftus conducted a now famous experiment on eyewitness recall by having subjects watch a brief video of a car accident. Later the subjects were asked a series of very detailed questions about the accident. The participants were asked identical questions, except for one critical variation. One group was asked, "How fast were the cars going when they bumped into each other?" and another group was asked "How fast were the cars going when they smashed into each other?" As you might predict, the "smashed" question led to significantly higher estimates of speed, but it also spawned other inaccuracies. A week later subjects were re-interviewed. All subjects were asked, "Did you see any broken glass?" In the video there had been no broken glass, yet nearly all of the people that had been asked how fast the cars were going when they "smashed" into each other clearly remembered seeing broken glass. Loftus has also repeatedly demonstrated that memories are highly vulnerable to the **misinformation effect**, in which you can alter one's memories by supplying them with misleading or inaccurate information.

In other studies, participants do an intake survey about many situations they may or may not have experienced as a child. Let's say that one subject has no recollection of having once fallen off her bike, resulting in an injury that required a hospital visit. The experimenter later asks that subject to imagine that very situation happening to them. The research suggests that asking people to vividly and repeatedly recall such events actually leads some to later believe that they did indeed experience the event. This phenomenon, called **imagination inflation**, has been reported in as many as 25% of subjects in such experiments. Over time, such false memories can seem as real to us as "legitimate" memories.

*"Just because someone thinks they remember something in detail,*
*with confidence and with emotion, does not mean that it actually happened.*
*False memories have these characteristics too."*
*(Elizabeth Loftus)*

### Memory and The Brain

Much remains unknown about how exactly memories are encoded, stored, and later retrieved but psychologists have discovered some specific brain regions that are directly involved in memory. Finding the location of specific memories has been elusive and many experiments demonstrate that complex memories are not stored in any one location. Most neuroscientists believe that stimuli trigger neural networks to fire, thereby recreating the memory. The memory is not simply replayed as if it were an exact recording but rather reconstructed each time we remember. The following is a quick summary of the physiological components of memory that you are most likely to see on the AP Exam:

- **Long-term potentiation (LTP)** provides a neural explanation of how memories form and endure. You may recall from The Biological Bases of Behavior that when a group of neurons fire together repeatedly, the synaptic connections strengthen. New dendrites and synapses form, allowing for more efficient communication between these neurons. Much of what we know about LTP comes from the Nobel Prize winning work of Eric Kandel. For the past 30 years Kandel has worked with *Aplysia*, a sea snail, to map out neurological changes as the snail is classically conditioned to respond to one stimulus or another. The neurons activated in a new response show changes in structure and function, which allow quicker communication in those networks.

- **The hippocampus,** considered part of the limbic system, seems responsible for the formation of new memories. Damage to the neurons in the hippocampus which release acetylcholine (you may recall our discussion of that neurotransmitter's role in memory in our unit on the Biological Bases of Behavior) would likely not effect retrieval of previously stored memories but might prevent storage of any new material.

- **The cerebellum,** located in the hindbrain, seems involved in memory for conditioned responses, such as a classically conditioned eye blink response. Procedural memories may also be processed and stored here.

- **The prefrontal cortex** seems at least partly involved in "habit" learning; a person with damage to the hippocampus might well retain the ability to perform some "habit-based" behavior even though he or she has no explicit memory of having learned that behavior because of the hippocampal damage. Another part of the limbic system, the caudate nucleus, also appears to play a role in storage of habit memories; the entire cortex, especially the temporal and frontal lobes, seem involved in the retrieval of various types of memories

- **The amygdala,** an important structure in the emotional limbic system, appears to play a big role in encoding the emotionally-charged elements of memory especially those involving anger and fear. When stress hormones are released our amygdala becomes active causing increased activity in regions of the brain associated with memory, mainly the hippocampus. Input from the amygdala appears to strengthen or even sear these memories into the brain. This could explain why flashbulb memories and traumatic memories are so enduring.

*"Hermann had trouble remembering where his new psychology class was held..."*

## Forgetting

There are many theories about why we forget. Perhaps forgetting some things may serve an adaptive purpose in that it keeps us from becoming overwhelmed by useless information. Famed psychologist William James agreed saying, "If we remembered everything, we should on most occasions be as ill off as if we remembered nothing." Forgetting can result from a breakdown in encoding, storage, or retrieval. Some memories are omitted simply because they never get beyond the limitations of short-term memory or because they are not deeply processed. Others may be forgotten because they **decay** over time with diminishing reference to them.

In exploring the concept of forgetting, early memory researcher **Hermann Ebbinghaus** taught himself thousands of lists of nonsense syllables (such as QUH, WAB, XOT, FOJ) and then tested his recall of those lists at various intervals. He graphed the findings and developed what he called a **forgetting curve**. This curve shows that in the first few hours there was a rapid drop in recall, but over time he still retained between 20-30% of the list. Even a month later he still maintained this baseline. You may have already found in your learning that much of the content from, lets say, your middle school history class has faded, but there is still a sizable amount that you will likely never forget. It should also be noted that Ebbinghaus was learning nonsense material, which is incredibly difficult to encode. Most of the information you are trying to memorize is hopefully more meaningful and thus the forgetting curve might be less steep.

Some memories are forgotten because of interference from other information. In **proactive interference**, something from the past inhibits your attempts to recall more recent material. For instance, your locker combination from sophomore year is still in your mind the first few times you try to open your new locker in junior year. Soon, you will see evidence of **retroactive interference**, in which new information works backward to erase or inhibit older memories - your junior year combination now interferes with recall of the previous year's combination. If you have ever changed your email password you likely experienced proactive interference. The first few times you try to sign in you may try to use your old password rather than the new one. Of course, months after the change you may struggle to recall the old password, which demonstrates retroactive interference. The concepts (from the chapter on Learning) of positive and negative transfer may help you understand the interferences. If you did well in biology last year, will that help you in chemistry this year? That is, will the previous learning help you with the new learning, or might it actually hinder your performance on the new task, at least at first? The later example would be proactive interference.

The interferences above may help you in sorting out two labels for different types of memory dysfunction: Retrograde amnesia and anterograde amnesia. In retroactive interference, new information <u>works backward</u> (just as a "retro fashion trend" moves us backward in time to an earlier style), interfering with recall of older information. In **retrograde amnesia**, some trauma or damage <u>works backward</u>, erasing memories from the period before the damage occurred. If you were in a car accident and suffered retrograde amnesia, you would have memory loss for events that came *before* the accident. Knowing that, you can then reason out **anterograde amnesia**. If you were in a car accident and suffered from anterograde amnesia, you would have memory loss for information *since* the accident. Damage to the hippocampus would likely lead to anterograde amnesia. Memories stored before the damage occurred would remain in place, but you would be unable to form new memories.

We may at times be motivated to forget. Indeed, few of us would choose to have the capability to remember all of the embarrassing or traumatic things that happen to us. Sigmund Freud proposed that we bury these types of distressing thoughts so deeply in our unconscious mind that we are no longer aware of their existence. He referred to this motivated forgetting as **repression**, and it has long been one of the most hotly debated topics in the study of memory, partly because it is an elusive concept to demonstrate scientifically. Repression is also controversial because it directly contradicts the idea that highly emotional events persist and are etched into our memory. Although there have been many accounts of recovered memories of abuse and other traumas through therapy and hypnosis, many psychologists question the validity of these claims.

### Name Hall of Fame

You don't have much to worry about in terms of name recall in this unit. **Elizabeth Loftus** would easily make it into a psychology hall of fame, but you still probably will not have to know her name in order to get a multiple choice item correct. However, you certainly ought to know about her work in eyewitness recall and constructive memory. It's possible you will encounter the name **Hermann Ebbinghaus**, although it would more likely appear in an item about the history of psychology. Your grasp of his forgetting curve is much more likely to be assessed than is recall of his name. **Endel Tulving** is credited with coining the terms procedural, semantic and episodic memory, but, again, his name would be supplied for you on the exam. Likewise with **Richard Atkinson** and **Richard Shiffrin** of the Atkinson-Shiffrin model.

### Essay Themes

**Eyewitness recall** is a major area of study in this unit, and exploration of it covers a lot of other ground in memory, so it may be a valuable focus point for you in your preparation. You certainly must have a basic understanding of the workings of **short-term memory** and **long-term memory**. Finally, it is relatively easy to envision an essay item that asks about phenomena in **forgetting** while overlapping with **Freudian theory** in terms of repression, cognitive changes in **development over the lifespan**, and perhaps units on **Testing and Individual Differences** and **thought/language**. Remember, the Advanced Placement Psychology test development committee tries hard to come up with free response questions that cut across multiple content areas.

# Memory

## Encoding

- Shallow vs. deep processing
- Mnemonic devices (ex: peg word, method of loci)
- Memory and the brain
  - The hippocampus
  - The cerebellum
  - The amygdala
    - Acetylcholine
- Long term potentiation (LTP)
- Visual encoding
- Semantic encoding
- Acoustic encoding
- Elaborative rehearsal
- Maintenance rehearsal
- Chunking
- Schemas

## Storage

- The sensory register
  - Iconic and echoic memory
- STM
  - Capacity?
  - Duration?
- LTM
  - Capacity?
  - Duration?
- Eidetic memory
- Episodic memory
  - Flashbulb memory
- Procedural memory
- Semantic memory
- The encoding specificity principle
- Context-dependent memory
- State-dependent memory

## Retrieval

- The serial position effect
  - The primacy effect
  - The recency effect
- Semantic distinctiveness
- Recall vs. recognition
- The tip of the tongue phenomenon (T.O.T.)
- Explicit/declarative memory
- Implicit memory
- Eyewitness Memory:
  - Framing
  - Constructive memory
  - The Misinformation Effect

## Forgetting

- Ebbinghaus and "the forgetting curve"
- Decay
- Leveling
- Motivated forgetting
  - Repression
- Constructive memory
- Imagination inflation
- Proactive interference
- Retroactive interference
- Anterograde amnesia
- Retrograde amnesia

120

### Practice Items

- **Time yourself** on this section, and record how long it takes you. This information will be useful to you later on

- If you work at the pace you will need on the actual AP Exam, this section should take you no more than 10 minutes and 30 seconds

- If it takes you only three minutes and you get them all correct, more power to you! If you are done in less than seven minutes and you make 3 or more errors, then you ought to consider slowing down a bit

- THESE SECTION ITEMS ARE **NOT** IN ORDER OF DIFFICULTY!

1. A rat is injected with adrenaline and then is trained to perform a novel task. Later, it is found that he performs the same task best when again given a dose of adrenaline. This finding is consistent with research on

   (A) explicit memory
   (B) semantic memory
   (C) mood-congruent memory
   (D) context-dependent memory
   (E) state-dependent memory

2. Which of the following is the best illustration of the effect of framing in memory?

   (A) Subjects report different speeds of the cars involved in a videotaped automobile accident depending on whether they were asked how fast the cars were traveling when they "made contact" with each other vs. "smashed into" each other
   (B) An eyewitness to a crime "fills in the gaps" of his account by relying on his expectations of what might typically have happened in such a case
   (C) An individual can only recall details which match the frame of reference he had prior to exposure to those details
   (D) Police officers choose members of a line-up who bear no physical resemblance to their suspect
   (E) An eyewitness to a crime recalls fewer and fewer details of the events as time passes

3. In a fictional study on memory, researchers briefly present a photo of a teacher's desk and workspace to volunteers, and then ask those participants to recall everything they can about the picture. They find that 71% of the respondents remember seeing a stapler on the desk, even though there is no stapler in the actual photograph. This tendency to wrongly add on to a memory based on one's schemas or expectations of what "ought to" have occurred is called

   (A) constructive memory
   (B) retrograde amnesia
   (C) working memory
   (D) decay
   (E) explicit memory

4. Which of the following is the best argument to account for the primacy effect in recalling a series of items?

   (A) The items you recall were presented more recently than other items
   (B) You tend to recall the most important items on a list
   (C) The first items on the list are likely to be more effectively rehearsed than other items
   (D) There has not been adequate time for retroactive interference to occur
   (E) You tend to recall items that stand out as having unique or surprising meanings

5. A runner's recollection of the day that she completed her first marathon is most clearly an example of which of the following types of memory?

   (A) Semantic
   (B) Procedural
   (C) Episodic
   (D) Working
   (E) Sensory

6. Charlotte was daydreaming when her teacher called on her and asked her to repeat what was just said in class. She was clearly not paying attention, but much to her surprise she found that she could indeed repeat the very last thing that was said. This was most likely the result of

   (A) shallow processing
   (B) semantic memory
   (C) iconic memory
   (D) echoic memory
   (E) long-term potentiation

7. Fifty volunteers in a memory experiment are asked to learn a list of words, and are then tested on their recall of the list. Next, they are asked to learn a second list of words and are tested on that list as well. A second set of 50 volunteers is asked to learn only the second list. They score significantly better than group #1 on recall of the second list.

   This significant difference in scores is likely due to

   (A) the misinformation effect
   (B) retrograde amnesia
   (C) the encoding specificity principle
   (D) proactive interference
   (E) retroactive interference

8. Which of the following lists most accurately represents the progression of memory according to the information-processing theory?

   (A) Sensory memory, short-term memory, long-term memory
   (B) Visual encoding, acoustic encoding, semantic encoding
   (C) Encoding, storage, retrieval
   (D) Shallow processing, deep processing, implicit memory
   (E) Primacy, constructive memory, forgetting

9. In the late 19th century, Hermann Ebbinghaus tested his own recall of lists of nonsense syllables he had previously learned through rehearsal. From this work, he proposed the concept of a forgetting curve, which suggests

   (A) recall of meaningless items drops very quickly after initial learning but then tapers and levels off
   (B) material already stored in long term memory takes precedence over new material, especially if that material is relatively meaningless
   (C) there is no long term retention of nonsensical information
   (D) new material will quickly interfere with recall of old material
   (E) memory for nonsensical information is explicit but not implicit

10. Which of the following is the best example of context dependent memory?

   (A) A potential eyewitness to a crime tells two different stories to two different questioners
   (B) Students who learn a vocabulary list while in a particular classroom do better at recalling the words when in that same room
   (C) A man who learned several complicated definitions while in a joyful mood does better in recalling the definitions when again in a joyful mood
   (D) A rat cannot retain memory of a learned response when it is learned in an unfamiliar environment
   (E) Individuals with damage to the cerebellum are unable to form short-term memories

NO TESTING MATERIAL ON THIS PAGE

GO ON TO THE NEXT PAGE

# Chapter 7
# *Cognition, Part 2: Thought and Language*

## Introduction

In part two of our study of cognition we explore thinking, problem solving and language acquisition. This topic also has clear connections to Developmental Psychology, which is coming up next, and to the later chapter on Testing and Individual Differences.

We will begin with a look at how humans solve problems, followed by an examination of some of the typical mistakes people make in thinking and decision-making. Next, we will explore the basics of language acquisition and some general theories about how we so readily learn language at an early age and how language interacts with thought and culture. As you study this intriguing topic you may want to consider some of the following questions:

- What common errors do people commit when making judgments and reaching decisions?

- To what extent does learning about the typical traps in human thinking and judgment actually facilitate improvement in those areas?

- Are there developmental "windows" of time in which one is pre-programmed to acquire skills such as language? If so, does this suggest that when such a window closes for a particular individual that he or she can never fully compensate for the lost opportunity?

- How much of human language acquisition is based on imitation of models and how much will essentially unfold on its own as long as one is in a reasonably supportive environment?

- To what extent is there an interaction between the *language* of a culture and the *thinking* of individuals in that culture?

## Thinking and Problem Solving

Experts on thinking and problem solving make frequent reference to 'concepts' and 'prototypes', so to start with you need to know what psychologists mean when they use those terms. **Concepts** are ideas that we group together because of some shared properties or characteristics. Husky, collie and poodle are examples of the concept category 'dog'. There are three different types of such categories: superordinate categories, basic categories and subordinate categories. Here is an example:

| If the superordinate category is ▶▶ ▶▶ | *Vehicle* |
|---|---|
| A basic category might be ▶▶ ▶▶ | *Car* |
| And a subordinate category might be ▶▶ ▶▶ | *Honda* |

| If the superordinate category is ▶▶ ▶▶ | *Car* |
|---|---|
| A basic category might be ▶▶ ▶▶ | *Honda* |
| And a subordinate category might be ▶▶ ▶▶ | *Honda Accord* |

As you can see from the above table, *superordinate* categories are broad and overarching, *basic* categories include specific examples of the superordinate category, and *subordinate* categories refer to examples of the basic level category.

Many of our ideas are considered **formal concepts**, meaning that the concept has very specific rules that define it. A 'square' is a formal concept because its shape is defined by certain physical rules. We also create **natural concepts**, which we form out of our everyday experiences. Natural concepts do not have a fixed set of defining features, but do have typical characteristics and are often based on prototypes. A **prototype** is a model, or best example of a particular thing. If you were asked to think of the prototypical bird, you'd be more likely to mention robin or eagle or sparrow than penguin or pterodactyl.

### Problem Solving: Strategies and Obstacles

On the other hand, if you were being tested on your ability to think divergently, you would want to generate answers like 'warbler' and 'thrush' to the question "Can you supply me with the names of as many birds as you can?" Most of your thinking in school is **convergent thinking**; that is, there is a particular answer the teacher is seeking and he or she wants the students to converge on it, just as cars converge at a four-way stop sign. The "right answer" is in the intersection. In **divergent thinking**, you are asked to think creatively, to generate as many possible answers to a question or problem as you can. True "brainstorming" sessions utilize divergent thinking by encouraging participants to offer any possible solution to a problem that comes to mind. No editing or judgment is allowed during this period. Sometimes participants find it useful to stop when creativity has seemingly been exhausted to allow **incubation** to occur. They leave the problem for a time, allowing their minds to work on it without conscious effort. Sometimes this can lead to further insights when they return to the problem. Only <u>after</u> such steps are taken does the creative thinking group edit or eliminate some ideas, while many are combined and recombined with others.

Humans seem to be unique among animals in that they can take part in a thinking process like that described above, and then reflect on their thoughts and methods. This thinking about one's own problem-solving strategies is called **metacognition**. It allows people to evaluate the success of their approach in solving problems.

In our everyday lives, when confronted with problems we rely on various strategies to arrive at a solution. On some occasions we may struggle with a problem and then have a flash of **insight** in which a correct solution suddenly comes to us. In other cases we solve problems by using a basic **trial and error** approach. We try many possible solutions and then discard those that do not help us.

In attempting to solve problems, humans are sometimes limited by **functional fixedness**; that is, they are trapped in seeing only certain prescribed uses for some object. They believe a potato is for eating, not to be used as a temporary emergency gas cap. A paper clip is for attaching things to each other, not for making earrings or chains. This in turn is related to the concept of **mental set**, which is a kind of fixation on one particular way to solve a problem. The best teachers of mathematics are able to teach students to understand a problem and to see solutions from perspectives the student can handle. Often, students can solve problems using certain formulaic methods, but then are trapped into approaching <u>all</u> problems in that one way, even when that strategy simply won't work any longer.

We often fall victim to **implicit assumptions** in problem solving. That is, we assume there are rules limiting what we can do even when such rules do not exist. The classic example of this, contained in most introductory psychology textbooks, is the "nine dot problem". Problem solvers are asked to connect nine dots, arranged in three rows of three, without picking up pen or pencil, using four lines (or fewer) which must be straight. Because the dots are arranged in a box-like configuration, people assume

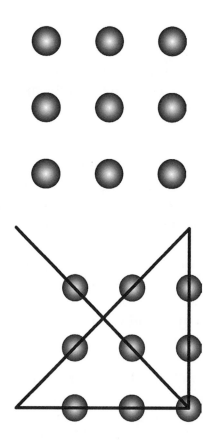

that they must work "within the box" which is suggested by the dots. In fact, avoiding this implicit assumption is the key to solving the problem, as one must "break out of the box" in order to reach a solution.

The way a question is framed can sometimes affect our ability to solve a problem. Take no more than 5 seconds to respond to the following:

*"What is 8 times 7 times 6 times 5 times 4 times 3 times 2 times 1?"*

The answer is 40,320. Few people get that in five seconds of course, but they DO give higher estimates than those asked

*"What is 1 times 2 times 3 times 4 times 5 times 6 times 7 times 8?"*

The questions are the same, but the **framing** of them influences responses, as is often true in problem solving.

Humans do have some useful approaches that help us problem solve and make decisions. An **algorithm** is a step-by-step method that guarantees a solution as long as each step is properly executed. **Heuristics** are short cuts in problem solving. You will sometimes see them referred to as "rules of thumb". Each has strengths and weaknesses. If you instantly know the answer to the question, "What is 79 times 10?" then you see the potential value of heuristics. Long ago you probably learned the heuristic that suggests you simply add a zero to any number that is multiplied by ten. This saves you the trouble of doing it all the way out algorithmically. If you went to an unfamiliar store to buy cheese and used an algorithmic approach to find some, you would have to carefully look on every single shelf in each aisle until you found the cheese you wanted. Doing this guarantees that you would (eventually) find what you are looking for. You are probably better off, however, using a heuristic and going directly to the dairy section or refrigerated section where cheeses are typically found.

### Errors and Biases in Thinking

Heuristics make some of our decisions easier, but they can also lead to some predictable errors. In the 1970's, researchers Daniel Kahneman and Amos Tversky identified two common heuristic errors that you must know for this course- the **availability heuristic** and the **representativeness heuristic**. In the case of the former, we judge the probability of some event based on what comes most readily to mind (what is most readily <u>available</u> in the mind). The example Kahneman and Tversky used involved the dangers of airplane travel vs. roadway travel. While any individual is statistically much more likely to be hurt or killed in a car accident than in a plane crash, participants in their research often predicted the reverse, because the relatively rare plane crashes get so much attention and thus come more easily to mind than the all too common car crashes which occur every day. The *availability heuristic* is also easily seen when you ask people, "Is 'k' more commonly the first letter in a word, or the third letter in a word?" A majority of people answer that 'k' is more likely to be the first letter of the word, because those are the words that come to mind more quickly. In reality, 'k' is almost three times more likely to be the third letter in a word. Once you think of words like 'cake' and 'bike', you realize just how common such words are.

Researchers in the field of cognition suggest that the availability heuristic may lead us to be fearful of things that are in reality quite improbable. Emotionally laden information comes to mind quickly, causing us, at times, to reason emotionally rather than logically. The events of September 11, 2001 demonstrate this reasoning. After 9/11 there was a sharp decrease in the number of people using air travel but driving throughout the US greatly increased. Because 9/11 was such a vivid, emotional and highly publicized event people turned to driving as a safer means of travel. The sad irony is that traffic deaths greatly increased during this post-9/11 period.

In the **representativeness heuristic** we judge the probability of some event based on how well it matches some *prototype* or *schema* we already have in our minds. Kahneman and Tversky asked questions like this: Is the following individual more likely to be an Ivy League psychology professor or a truck driver?

-   *A man, 5' 7", 155 pounds, who wears glasses, attends poetry readings and enjoys classical music*

Most people reported that such a person was more likely to be an Ivy League professor, even though Kahneman and Tversky argued that he is far more likely to be a truck driver, if only because there are hundreds of thousands of truck drivers and probably only 100 to 200 Ivy League psychology professors. Even if fully 50% of those professors fit the *schema* they described, it'd still be far more likely statistically that such a man was a truck driver.

Although using heuristics makes us prone to errors, this type of thinking may have an evolutionary advantage. Historically, it has benefited humans to "trust their gut" in order to assess possible danger in their surroundings. If something comes to mind quickly, that's probably because it's important. Heuristics allow for fast decision-making, which is often very valuable in a threat-filled world.

One thing that quite commonly hinders humans in thinking and problem solving is **confirmation bias**. Individuals tend to look for and attend to evidence that supports what they already believe, and disregard or "explain away" evidence to the contrary. Once a person becomes convinced that most UFO sightings are indeed cases of extraterrestrial visitation, they are less likely to pay attention to arguments that offer alternative hypotheses. They will, however, latch onto stories that might confirm their previous conviction.

A closely related concept, **belief perseverance,** states that once we have formed an initial belief we are slow to change our minds even if there is direct evidence that the belief is wrong. This is especially true when we have made our belief public to others. Let's say you campaigned for and supported the winning candidate for President of the United States. That president later repeatedly demonstrates poor judgment and is even accused of breaking the law. According to belief perseverance, you'll be resistant to altering your original view of that person.

Part of that resistance may stem from **cognitive dissonance**. We feel cognitive dissonance when our thoughts or behaviors don't match. In the example above, you might realize on some level that the president has done a less-than-stellar job, yet you *did* openly support him or her in the past. These two conflicting notions cause tension. To reduce that tension, we ignore the poor performance and convince ourselves that the president is still doing a good job. We will circle back to this idea in the upcoming unit on Motivation and Emotion.

We're also sometimes guilty of committing the **self-serving bias**, in which we take credit for successes and blame circumstances for things that don't go as well. If you do well on a test you are more likely to think that it was because of something you did, but when you do poorly in some class you are much more likely to blame your performance on bad teaching or some other situational factor. This may also be linked to the tendency of people to be **overconfident** in their judgments and decisions, a consistent finding among researchers. We tend to want to be "right," and to believe that we already *are*!

In the 1990's, David Dunning and Justin Kruger conducted research on a concept now labeled **The Dunning-Kruger Effect**, or *illusory superiority*. They found that some people who are bad at a particular thing often believe they are quite good at it. In fact, their incompetence may be what keeps them from *realizing* they are incompetent. For example - the obliviousness that makes some people bad drivers will also ensure that they remain oblivious to how bad they are.

Dunning and Kruger asked some people to tell a joke and then rate themselves on how well they delivered it. Next, the researchers asked others to judge the joke-teller's ability to put the humor across. Dunning and Kruger reported that the worst aspiring comedians were more likely to overrate their humorous abilities, even after being told they had been given *low* scores by their listeners.

Finally, when people learn the outcome of an event or solution to a problem, they are often convinced that the answer was really quite obvious and they "knew it all along." This is called **hindsight bias**. On Monday morning, fans of professional football are often adamant that they clearly saw the error of their favorite team's ways during their game the day before. But did those fans really detect those problems as the game was actually unfolding? We do tend to be smarter about things after they've already occurred.

## Language

*"Human language appears to be a unique phenomenon,*
*without significant analogue in the animal world"*
*(Noam Chomsky)*

The study of language, how we acquire it and how it interacts with behavior and cognition is sometimes called **psycholinguistics**. There is ongoing discussion as to just how much we are preprogrammed at birth to acquire language. Case studies of children living in extreme social isolation for the first years of their lives, as in **The Genie case study** and the case of **The Wild Child of Aveyron**, add complexity to this debate. Genie was discovered in 1971 living in what appeared to be a "normal" middle class home in California. In fact, her parents had essentially imprisoned her in her bedroom for most of the first 13 years of her life, for reasons that remain unclear. She had little sensory input in the room, no appropriate social interaction and was apparently punished for making sounds. When she was removed from this wretched situation, she made some significant strides at first in acquiring spoken language, but then pretty much stopped progressing. Some contend she could have continued to develop if the people who worked with her had a more systematic approach to helping her. Indeed, there was a fair amount of competition between various people involved with her case, and some would say the tensions that arose as a result might have blocked Genie's potential. Another question that arose early on: were Genie's language deficits a result of Genie's social isolation, or had she been born mentally handicapped? Remarkably, Genie was quite engaging socially, and she demonstrated awareness of what had happened to her, and that further complicated the "was she born mentally retarded?" issue. Genie is still living in California but authorities are now very protective of her privacy. It does seem clear that she made no dramatic improvement since the "Genie Project" was discontinued.

Some of these same themes permeated the case of "Victor", who was discovered living in the woods near Aveyron, France around 1800. It appeared he was about the same age as Genie had been when she was discovered. He too was brought into civilized society and efforts were made to teach him language. He too stopped progressing after some early success, and the project to help him learn was abandoned. He died some 20 years later, possessing only rudimentary language skills.

There has long been a debate about how humans acquire language. Most of this debate has centered on the *nature versus nurture* issue. Some believe the acquisition of language is mostly a matter of inborn ability, while others believe that environmental factors are responsible for our linguistic development. Behaviorists like B.F. Skinner strongly adhere to the latter view. Skinner argued that we learn language primarily through reinforcement provided by siblings, parents and other caregivers. He saw that when a child spoke a word accurately, people around that child often heap praise on the speaker. In fact, if a girl is attempting to say "cookie", her parents may reward her for uttering anything that sounds remotely close to the word. As the child grows, the parents may stop reinforcing close approximations to the word, and will only reward her when she says "cookie" clearly. Her parents may later only reinforce her for making a grammatically correct request such as, "May I have a cookie?" The basic idea of such *shaping* is that each step on the path to proper word usage is reinforced, while incorrect speech is less likely to be rewarded, thus extinguishing that speech pattern.

Linguist Noam Chomsky disagrees with the Behaviorist's view and argues that language acquisition is **native** or inborn to humans, given a reasonable environment. Because kids seem to learn language so quickly and effortlessly, he theorized that we must have a kind of **language acquisition device** (or LAD) in our brains that allows us to soak up language, especially during **critical periods** in early childhood. If we miss those critical periods, it might be too late to make up for the loss (others prefer to think of these as *sensitive*, rather than *critical* periods; this suggests that the "window" for learning is not completely closed at any particular time). This natural predisposition to learn language helps to explain, he argues, why we can understand the many different possible **deep structures** of a sentence drawn from one basic arrangement of words (its **surface structure**). No one ever teaches us that the sentence, "The artist painted me on his front porch," which has a simple eight-word surface structure, has many different potential meanings (deep structures), yet we somehow know it anyway. Chomsky also argued that language is a creative enterprise.

Children frequently put together new combinations of words even though they've never been reinforced for that particular construction, and they've never heard another person speak that identical sentence. Clearly, he concludes, they are not simply parroting others, as some behaviorists might contend.

Today, many psycholinguists have combined the theories of Skinner and Chomsky and favor an **interactionist** model, which postulates that we may indeed have a biological predisposition to soak up language, but it is triggered and nurtured through social interaction. Further evidence for such a predisposition was discussed in the chapter on The Biological Bases of Behavior. In that chapter, we identified areas in the left hemisphere of the brain (although for a few it is in the right hemisphere) heavily involved in speech. You may recall the role Broca's Area and Wernicke's Area play in our ability to express ourselves and understand others. While their functions appear to overlap, Broca's Area is most associated with expression of language, while Wernicke's Area facilitates the comprehension of language.

A child's brain also seems remarkably *plastic* when it comes to learning language. Children are remarkable in their ability to pick up many languages. As we get older it becomes more difficult to produce some sounds in languages that we weren't exposed to early in life. Our brains have pruned away the pathways that would facilitate such learning.

## The Progression of Language Acquisition

Children generally progress from cooing and vocal play to a **babbling** stage. At the beginning of the babbling stage, babies are capable of producing the **phonemes** (basic sounds) of any language. In fact, if you were listening to a six month old babble, you would not be able to determine which language(s) the child had been exposed to. At about nine months old babies start to babble only in the phonemes of the language to which they have been exposed. In a sense, the brain is becoming specialized to understand that particular set of sounds. Babbling then becomes more complex and soon the baby is using sounds like "ma" or "da" to communicate. Next, they enter a **holophrastic** stage in which a child essentially expresses complete thoughts with one word, as in saying "juice" to mean, "Pardon me, I would very much like something to drink if you don't mind." Children often move to the use of single words around the age of one. At about 18 months old, children experience a dramatic increase in their vocabulary and move to a stage of **telegraphic speech** (the two or three word sentence stage, as in "me walk" or "mommy give toy"). At this point, it is clear that children have a grasp of **semantics**, a term that refers to the study of the meaning and interpretation of words. Lastly, children begin to acquire proper **syntax** - appropriate word order and grammatical structure.

Very generally speaking, a child will be cooing, gurgling and squealing at around two months old, and then babble at around six months. These early vocalizations are sometimes thought of as *pre-linguistic stages*. Soon the child begins to use the sounds of the language, phonemes, to form **morphemes**, which are the smallest linguistic units that carry meaning. To remember this you might think 'm' for 'morpheme', 'm' for meaning. A morpheme can be a word or a piece of a word, as long as it adds meaning. For instance, 'ch' is a phoneme, a sound of the English language, while 'ed' is both a phoneme and a morpheme, as 'ed' at the end of a word adds the concept of past tense to that word.

Estimates are that the typical child may have 50 or so words in their vocabulary by 18 months of age, 13,000 words by age six and 40,000 words by the fifth grade. You might wonder how such calculations are made, and frankly, so do we. In any case, it is clear that a child's vocabulary increases at a remarkable rate.

In forming sentences, children often make mistakes such as **overregularization**. An example is "Yesterday, I goed to the store." Apparently, they have learned that 'ed' adds past tense to a word but have not yet learned the exceptions to that rule. They are thus overusing the regulation (you may see this referred to as **overgeneralization** as well). This tendency is often used to refute the Behaviorist view of language described earlier. If a child learns language solely through reinforcement or imitation of models, why would they create sentences like that?

Even though a child may wrongly say "Yesterday I goed to the store", she has still gotten her point across, even though the grammar is incorrect. This illustrates the distinction between **descriptive grammar** and **prescriptive grammar**. If an adult has ever corrected you for saying something like "I ain't going" and you replied "Oh, you know what I meant", you are basically arguing for descriptive grammar, while the adult is holding you to the proper, prescribed way of expressing yourself.

**Ape language** is a fascinating subject. There are a few cases in which primates have successfully mastered sign language allowing them to quite eloquently express themselves. It is unlikely that you will encounter the topic on the Advanced Placement Examination, but this is an area worth exploring, especially in regards to the major questions that arise from it, such as: What *is* 'language'? Do apes use words and sentences in the same way that humans use them? Do they understand that a word is essentially a symbol for something else? If apes have difficulty with syntax, and research suggests they do, is that evidence that they really aren't using 'language' but have merely been conditioned to respond in certain ways to certain sounds, much as they might to a bell or horn?

Finally, you should familiarize yourself with the **Whorfian Hypothesis** or the **Linguistic Relativity Theory** (you may also see this called the **Whorf-Sapir Hypothesis**). The most extreme reading of this theory states that one's language determines the ways one thinks. The classic example, which was once very commonly used, refers to Alaskan Inuit words for 'snow'. Allegedly, the Inuit have far more such words than do other, less snow-laden cultures, and this leads them to think differently about their world. This "fact" by itself is in debate, as is the question of whether language influences cognition or vice versa. Recent research further clouds this picture as psycholinguists uncover evidence indicating other cross-cultural differences in the kind and number of words used to express certain ideas.

### Name Hall of Fame

**Noam Chomsky** is likely to show up on a typical AP Exam, although the item would be more along the lines of a "Chomsky's theory of the LAD refers to _____" type question than a "Who forwarded the theory of the LAD?" type question. In other words, you will probably not have to recall his name specifically in order to get an item correct. **Daniel Kahneman** and **Amos Tversky** are leading researchers in problem-solving and decision-making, but they too would not likely be "the answer" to a question. The "**Genie**" case study and the case of **Victor, The Wild Child of Aveyron** are both important and could be used by your teacher to highlight issues of language acquisition in this unit or in a discussion of nature vs. nurture and critical period debates in developmental psychology, so you should have a basic familiarity with one or both of those stories.

### Essay Themes

The "**nature, nurture or false dichotomy?**" argument lends itself to free response formats, although it may fall more neatly into the units on the Biological Bases of Behavior, Developmental Psychology and Personality Theory. **Critical period theory** proposes a window of time during which a child is especially ready to learn language. It further suggests that if that opportunity is missed that it might be very difficult to catch up. This is clearly intertwined with nature/nurture themes, and could therefore be a point of emphasis in a "Nature vs. Nurture" essay, as could the behaviorist perspective on language acquisition.

Any proposed free response item asking you to summarize the flow and timetable of typical language acquisition in children would likely be rejected as too narrowly confined to one unit. An essay proposal focusing exclusively on problem solving strategies and common errors would probably meet the same fate during the test development process.

# Thought and Language

## (top-left quadrant)

- mental sets; functional fixedness
- the effect of framing on decisions
  - hindsight bias
  - the self-serving bias
  - confirmation bias; belief perseverance

### Traps and Errors in Thinking and Problem Solving

- the availability heuristic
- the representativeness heuristic

## (bottom-left quadrant)

- concepts, prototypes
- divergent vs. convergent thinking
- Categories:
  superordinate
  basic
  subordinate

### Problem Solving, Decision Making

- algorithms
- heuristics
- incubation
- metacognition

## (top-right quadrant)

- Chomsky and "nativism"
  - The L.A.D.
- surface and deep structure of language

- Broca's Area
- Wernicke's Area

### More on Language

- The Interactionist Model
- The Whorf-Sapir Hypothesis
  - linguistic relativity, linguistic determinism
- Links to other units:
  Skinner and Bandura: How do we acquire language?

## (bottom-right quadrant)

cooing -> babbling -> holophrastic speech -> telegraphic speech -> proper syntax
- phonemes
- morphemes
- descriptive vs. prescriptive grammar
- overregularization

### Language Acquisition

- semantic networks
- Critical/Sensitive Period Theory

137

**Practice Items**

- **Time yourself** on this section, and record how long it takes you. This information will be useful to you later on

- If you work at the pace you will need on the actual AP Exam, this section should take you no more than 10 minutes and 30 seconds

- If it takes you only three minutes and you get them all correct, more power to you! If you are done in less than seven minutes and you make 3 or more errors, then you ought to consider slowing down a bit

- THESE SECTION ITEMS ARE **NOT** IN ORDER OF DIFFICULTY!


1. In our judgments and assessments, we sometimes rely too much on the first examples that come to our minds. This is called

   (A) the representativeness heuristic
   (B) the availability heuristic
   (C) insight
   (D) convergent thinking
   (E) overregularization


2. The three-word sentence "Eat your food" can have three different underlying meanings, depending on which of the words you emphasize. This example illustrates the

   (A) linguistic relativity hypothesis
   (B) role of descriptive grammar in human expression
   (C) varieties of syntax in speech production
   (D) surface structure of language
   (E) deep structure of language


3. "Anything seems commonplace, once explained." This statement by the fictional detective Sherlock Holmes illustrates what common cognitive error?
   (A) Confirmation bias
   (B) Hindsight bias
   (C) The self-serving bias
   (D) Cognitive dissonance
   (E) Metacognition

4. A woman on a long car trip uses a potato as a radiator cap when her car overheats and the original radiator cap is lost. She has overcome which of the following traps in thinking and problem solving?

   (A) Belief perseverance
   (B) Functional Fixedness
   (C) The Representativeness Heuristic
   (D) The Availability Heuristic
   (E) The Overconfidence Bias

5. Which of the following would serve as the best argument AGAINST the Whorf-Sapir Linguistic Relativity Theory?

   (A) The fact that a culture has different specific words to express the same thing doesn't necessarily mean that those who use such words think differently about that thing
   (B) There is cross-cultural evidence that supports the idea that few cultural differences exist in terms of when children acquire language
   (C) There is evidence to support the idea that there is such a thing as an inborn tendency to absorb language
   (D) There is evidence to suggest that holophrastic speech develops before telegraphic speech in nearly all cultural environments
   (E) The fact that apes seem able to learn sign language does not mean that they *use* language as humans do

6. A college student is struggling with a very challenging mathematical problem. Rather than continue with it, she decides to leave the problem and return to it later, in the hope that she'll then have a useful insight into the solution. She is demonstrating an understanding of the value of

   (A) trial and error learning
   (B) generativity
   (C) heuristics
   (D) algorithms
   (E) incubation

7. The fundamental sounds of a language are called

   (A) syntactical utterances
   (B) morphemes
   (C) phonemes
   (D) holophrases
   (E) linguistic elaborations

8. Which of the following statements best represents Noam Chomsky's view of language acquisition?

   (A) Language develops as a result of positive reinforcement from our caretakers
   (B) Most of our language is acquired from watching and imitating the language of others
   (C) Language is acquired differently in different cultural settings
   (D) Language is an inborn ability that will flourish if given an appropriate environment
   (E) Our patterns of thought dictate the rate at which we acquire language

9. Telegraphic speech

   (A) begins in the first six months of childhood
   (B) only develops as children reach the fourth year of life
   (C) serves as evidence for Behaviorists that children learn to speak through imitation of others
   (D) refers to the stage in language acquisition in which children express themselves in two-word sentences
   (E) is rarely seen in children who have been consistently exposed to more than one language from birth

10. Two friends attribute their excellent math test scores to their high level of ability and effort, and their low scores in science class to their teacher's favoritism and unfair grading. These students are exhibiting

    (A) belief perseverance
    (B) algorithmic thinking
    (C) the self-serving bias
    (D) cognitive mapping
    (E) prototypical thought

# Chapter 8
# *Developmental Psychology*

### Introduction

Although this unit will comprise seven to nine percent of the multiple-choice items on the AP Exam, there is more than the typical amount of information in it. In fact, developmental psychology may be the most expansive field in all of psychology. It covers a broad range of material, examining physical, cognitive, social, emotional and moral development from birth until death. Although most early research in the field focused on children, there has been significant interest in recent years in studying **development across the life span**. As you read about this fascinating topic, you will undoubtedly make connections to your own life and reflect upon how you progressed through the stages being discussed. There are also a multitude of connections with other units, such as Statistics and Research Methodology, The Biological Bases of Behavior, Sensation and Perception, Learning Theory, Thought and Language and Testing and Individual Differences. That makes this a very valuable topic in your overall test preparation.

One basic question developmental psychologists explore is, "Do all healthy humans progress through development in the same order and at the same ages?" In researching this question psychologists often employ the use of longitudinal and cross-sectional studies. In the former, you study the development of a specific group of subjects over a long period of time. In the latter, you might compare subjects from different age groups as a more immediate way of determining the age at which kids reach certain developmental landmarks. Cross-sectional studies have great value, but occasionally comparing one **cohort** (a group of people around the same age that have experienced most of the same historical changes) to another can be misleading. For example, people raised in different time periods will not possess the same abilities to use new technology. Those disparities are not likely a result of differing cognitive abilities but rather a **cohort effect** based on the generation in which they grew up.

### Themes in Development

In general, developmental theories can be broken into two categories: continuous and discontinuous. **Continuity theories** propose that development is very gradual and it is difficult at any one time to notice the changes that are occurring. **Discontinuity theories** are more stage-like, in that changes occur more dramatically and obviously; one "makes a jump" to another level. Such theories also suggest that development through the stages is largely **unchanging and universal**, implying that everyone goes through the same steps in the same order. As you look at various stage theories in this chapter, you will see this is a stimulating topic for discussion and critique.

You've already encountered the famed **nature vs. nurture debate** earlier in this book. Most developmental psychologists would argue that it is a *false dichotomy*; that is, genetics and environmental factors interact so much with each other that they are inextricably intertwined. Even if certain characteristics "run in families," so too does environment. It is impossible to completely isolate the individual contributions of biology and environment on human development.

**Twin studies** are a powerful and fascinating way to explore the question of what makes us develop as we do. The most dramatic of these involve monozygotic (identical) twins separated at birth or soon after. When reunited decades later, they often display remarkable similarities in habit, lifestyle, intelligence and personality. This seems to support those who favor "nature" in the nature/nurture debate, although some critics argue that we need to focus as much on possible differences between reunited identical twins as we do on whether they smoke the same brand of cigarette or work in similar occupations.

As part of the nature vs. nurture issue, it's important to recognize the terms maturation and socialization. **Maturation** refers to development that largely unfolds on its own, as if according to a biological program, as long as the individual is in a reasonably supportive environment. Most children will simply progress to walking when they're ready, and they don't require intensive training to do so. Maturation is supported by cross-cultural studies showing that kids around the world tend to walk, talk and master toilet training at very similar ages. If you recall the **Genie** and **Wild Child of Aveyron** case studies from the unit on Thought and Language, you will remember that in both cases the child was in such a restrictive environment that maturation in many ways was blocked. Of course, it remains a mystery as to whether the two children were cognitively and physically healthy to begin with – could it be both were born mentally retarded? That is still an open question. In any case, while being raised in what was certainly a less than supportive environment, they missed the theoretical **critical period** for language acquisition, and could therefore never fully gain the skills a healthy child in a healthy setting would have acquired.

**Socialization** refers to the impact of the social environment on development. It is an ongoing process in which culturally desirable skills, attitudes, and behaviors are shaped by society. A child may begin to babble as a result of simple maturation, but then is socialized into the particular language of the society in which he or she lives.

## Prenatal Development and Early Physical Development

*"Environment does not begin at birth."*
*(Robert Sapolsky)*

With Sapolsky's quote in mind, let us take a look at the prenatal environment. While in the womb, a child-to-be progresses through *the germinal or zygotic stage* (the first two weeks or so) to *the embryonic stage* (from 2 weeks to about 8 weeks) to the *fetal stage*. Throughout much of this period cell growth occurs at an astonishing rate - by some estimates, ¼ million cells per minute. Each organ, limb and body system has a critical period for development. If problems arise during these periods, significant developmental issues may result.

At any point along the prenatal journey, exposure to **teratogens** can impair normal development. A teratogen is anything that harms an organism before birth. Exposure of a human fetus to x-rays, lead and mercury can all hurt the developing child. Tobacco can also serve as a teratogen. Cigarette smoking increases the risk of miscarriage, premature birth and low birth weight. If the mother drinks alcohol during pregnancy, it may lead to **fetal alcohol syndrome (FAS)**. Children born with FAS have distinctive facial features such as a wider than normal set of the eyes, a narrower eye opening, and a thin upper lip. They may suffer from serious behavioral impairments and, in some cases, serious mental retardation. Indeed, FAS is a leading cause of mental retardation in the United States.

You might encounter **imprinting** on the AP Exam, even though it is questionable whether it applies to human infants. The term refers to a newborn's tendency to respond to an active stimulus in its environment as if it is its mother. In most natural cases, such a stimulus *is* the mother, and it would be a healthy, adaptive response for the newborn to attach to the mom quickly. Critical period theory may apply to imprinting as well; the time immediately after birth seems particularly important for such attachment in many animals. In the 1930's, **Konrad Lorenz** tinkered with this natural mechanism by replacing a mother duck with a surrogate parent - namely, Konrad Lorenz. The baby ducklings imprinted on him, and followed him around as if he were their mother. It is generally believed that *human* attachment is more complex and ongoing, and is not subject to a single critical period as described above.

While human newborns may not attach, literally or figuratively, to whatever stimulus presents itself immediately after birth, it is clear that human newborns and infants do need physical touch and nurturance. **Harry Harlow** refers to this as **contact comfort**. He conducted research with infant monkeys who were separated from their biological mothers and placed with artificial, surrogate parents. Harlow found that the baby monkeys sought comfort and support from soft, terry cloth "mothers" rather than hard, wire "mothers," even when it was the wire mother that had provided the child nourishment through a bottle attached to the surrogate's body. Since then research has shown that premature human babies grow faster and healthier if given daily massages, and it has become accepted wisdom that frequent, nurturing physical touch is essential for healthy development in all humans. If, as a youngster, you had a favorite blanket or doll to which you were attached, it may be that this **transitional object** gave you some of that desired physical contact.

For centuries, many people accepted philosopher John Locke's idea of '**tabula rasa.**' He argued that a newborn's mind is a blank slate, in that children are born without built-in concepts or knowledge. According to Locke, children acquire knowledge only through life experience.

Yet, the evidence is strong that babies do arrive with some innate *reflexes*. Those you might encounter on the AP Examination are summarized below:

- **The rooting reflex**: Touch a newborn (or *neonate*) on the cheek and he or she will turn the head in that direction, "rooting" for a food source.

- **The sucking reflex**: Just what you would think it is - put something in the mouth of a newborn and he or she will reflexively suck on it.

- **The grasping reflex**: This is also self-explanatory. Place your finger in the palm of a newborn and his or her tiny hand will close around it.

- **The Babinski reflex:** If you stroke the bottom of a newborn's foot the toes fan out and then curl back in.

- **The stepping reflex**: Support a newborn under the arms and it will simulate walking strides. This reflex disappears around 2 months old.

- **The Moro reflex**: This is sometimes called *the startle reflex*. An unexpected stimulus such as a loud noise usually elicits a response in which the child throws her arms and legs out then pulls them back into the body, often accompanied by a quivering or shaking of the body.

Are breathing, blinking, crying, swallowing and smiling truly reflexes? Some would place them in the category and others would not, although all manifest themselves very early in neonates. If reflexes are an intuitive, programmed, involuntary response to a stimulus, then blinking and swallowing seem to qualify. Breathing isn't a response to a stimulus per se, but it probably belongs on the list as well. Do babies cry and smile directly in response to stimuli? Perhaps not, but crying and smiling too are included on many lists of inborn reflexes.

Of course, it's difficult to know what's *really* going on in the mind of an infant. You learned about habituation in the chapter on Sensation and Perception, and that tendency in humans to stop attending to something after repetitive exposure to it is often used by developmental psychologists to explore what pre-linguistic children are experiencing. Theoretically, we can guess that a child who has stopped looking at something has lost interest in it, but that remains only an educated guess. Still, using habituation tests, psychologists have inferred that newborn babies demonstrate preferences for their mother's face, voice and scent.

Babies are born with functioning, though limited, sensory equipment. A newborn's vision is strongest for stimuli at a distance of 8-12 inches from their face (perhaps the distance of a mother's face). While neonates typically begin with 20/300 vision (meaning that they can see at 20 feet what those with perfect vision can see at 300 feet) they are clearly capable of visually tracking moving objects.

One thing human babies certainly do very early on is imitate. It is entertaining to view photos and videos depicting babies just a few days old **mimicking facial expressions**. The fact that most infants can imitate multiple facial expressions by twelve days old may serve as evidence that mirror neurons (the cells in the brain that respond when an individual is performing a behavior but also when one is *watching another* perform that behavior) are already at work. Babies also seem pre-wired to have a fondness for faces. They stare much longer at a circle containing face-like features than a circle filled with other shapes.

There is evidence that while human babies are not born with **depth perception** they acquire some degree of it fairly early in life. Eleanor Gibson and her colleagues used a **visual cliff apparatus** to study the depth perception of children before they could walk. A baby was placed on a surface and encouraged to crawl across what appeared to be a rather large drop. Even with their own mothers coaxing them, babies as young as six months old would not cross the drop. It is important to note that they were safe at all times; the "cliff" was merely an illusion created by a checkerboard pattern under a glass surface. Gibson concluded that even these very young babies could indeed perceive that there was a potentially dangerous drop.

**Cognitive Development**

How do children develop their understanding of the world? How can we meaningfully examine the cognitive development of young children who are unable to communicate their feelings and thoughts directly to us? There aren't easy answers to these questions, but they are essential for psychologists investigating cognitive development.

The big theory in cognitive development is that of Swiss psychologist **Jean Piaget.** He studied the thinking of youngsters, paying special attention to the errors that they made. From his observations, he developed a stage theory of cognitive development that is still very much embraced today. Further studies from around the world indicate that Piaget had the general sequence of cognitive milestones correct, but many argue that Piaget underestimated the abilities of children at different points in their growth.

Piaget argued that babies' minds were not miniature versions of adult minds - they reason quite differently than grownups when they encounter problems in the world. Piaget believed that children handled the new information they constantly encountered by means of **assimilation and accommodation**. In the former, the child attempts to fit new experiences into the cognitive frameworks, or *schemas*, they already possess. In *accommodation*, they actually adjust their schemas or behaviors to incorporate the new information. A classic example used by many teachers involves a child's identification of animals: a youngster who has learned the word 'doggie' sees a coyote at the zoo and identifies it as 'doggie'; the child is attempting to *assimilate* this new thing, a coyote, into a previously formed 'doggie' schema. Soon, the child will *accommodate* by creating a new, 'coyote' schema.

Piaget argued that we all progress through four stages of cognitive development, assimilating and accommodating as we go. A summary of those stages follows:

- **The sensorimotor stage** (birth to around 2 years old): The cognitive task of the child here is to explore and learn about the environment, through the use of the senses and one's developing motor abilities. Between the ages of four and eight months, a child begins to grasp the concept of **object permanence** (understanding that a ball that rolls out of sight into a closet still exists, even though unseen).

- **The preoperational stage** (two to around seven years old): In this stage, children begin pretend play, which demonstrates that they are beginning to be able to **think symbolically** - that is, that one thing can represent something else. The child's language development is a striking illustration of this development. In essence, using words to refer to objects and events *is* symbolic thinking.

Preoperational children also tend to believe that inanimate objects have feelings and intentions. When they trip over a toy they may proclaim that the toy is mean or was mad at them. This personification is called **animism**.

At the beginning of this stage children are highly **egocentric**. For Piaget, this meant they were cognitively unable to take the perspective of another. Later in this stage, usually around age four, children gain the ability to take the perspective of others and start to understand that other people have their own thoughts and motives, which may be drastically different from their own. Psychologists refer to this newly gained knowledge as a **theory of mind**. This new cognitive ability may account for a child's ability to experience empathy and respond with comfort or help when others are distressed.

- **The concrete operational stage** (about 7 to 11 years old): This is often identified as the stage in which the child becomes capable of **logical thinking**, although this may be an area in which Piaget underestimated kids - many would say preoperational children think logically as well. While children in this period are not yet able to think abstractly they are quite comfortable with **use of mental representations**. One key Piagetian milestone in this stage involves mastery of **conservation**, the idea that the amount of something doesn't change with changes in its appearance or arrangement. You may have observed children who are disappointed because they wanted dad to cut the pizza into eight pieces and he only cut it into four; they feel he's cheated them out of a substantial amount of pizza! Some theorists argue that mastery of conservation of number comes earlier than mastery of conservation of volume and mass, but the AP Examination will not assess you on such a distinction. In general, children master conservation by six to eight years of age.

- **The formal operational stage** (11 years of age or so onward): One critique of Piaget's theory is that he focused only on younger children and then inappropriately lumped everyone over the age of twelve together into one cognitive group. It is in this stage that people **think abstractly and hypothetically** and are thus able to consider future possibilities and imaginary scenarios.

The work of Russian theorist **Lev Vygotsky** has recently garnered renewed interest. Vygotsky passed away in 1934 but his views on the impact of the **social context** on a child's cognitive growth were revisited beginning in the 1970's. Vygotsky differs from Piaget in that he clearly believed that cognitive development was less a matter of biological maturation than of social interaction. Vygotsky believed that a child's mind wouldn't develop much more than an animal's mind without help and guidance from adult mentors. He argued that children internalize the instructions and warnings of those around them into *inner speech*. The child thus develops the ability to have internal conversations with him or herself which help to govern behavior. Vygotsky also proposed the idea of a **zone of proximal development**, or **ZPD.** This describes the divide between what a child knows and can do on their own and what they *might have the potential to do* given a supportive enough environment. Children who regularly interact and receive instruction from a teacher or caregiver are more likely to reach the top of this range.

### Social Development

It is unlikely that you will run into items on **birth order theory** on the Advanced Placement Exam, but you might find it interesting to consider the possible effect of your birth order on the development of your personality. **Alfred Adler** was the first to theorize that birth order may have such effects (arguing, for example, that a first born child may be more achievement-oriented than a child born later). His name will come up again in your study of personality theory, so his theory is certainly worth a look. In your own experience for example, you might have felt a sense of **dethronement** as a child when a new sibling arrived in the household. Adler believed that the arrival of a new sibling meant that you would be receiving less of your parent's attention and affection and that loss may lead you to harbor resentment toward your new sibling. Your parents might have some interesting stories about your reactions to losing some of the attention you had become used to receiving!

You should expect to encounter questions on attachment styles and parenting styles under the umbrella of social development. **Mary Ainsworth** placed young children in "**strange situations**," separated for a time from their mothers, and then monitored the children when the mother returned. Ainsworth evaluated their behaviors to measure the level of security and insecurity in the bond between mother and child. A summary of her **attachment styles** follows:

- **Secure**: The child is somewhat distressed when the mother leaves but is relatively easy to calm and greets the mother warmly upon her return, using her, in Ainsworth's words, as a "secure base of operations." Nearly two-thirds of children tested demonstrated this attachment style.

- **Avoidant**: The child generally ignores the mother when she returns; in this style the child often appears to "attach" just as much to a stranger as to the mother.

- **Resistant/Ambivalent**: The child sends mixed messages to the mother upon her return, seemingly wanting to be held but then resisting attempts by the mother to do so.

- **Disorganized**: A newer category (identified by Ainsworth's colleagues) in which children appear confused, disoriented and even fearful with their mothers; some postulate a correlation with this style and abusive home environments.

Many developmental psychologists agree that these early attachment styles *can predict well for future social functioning*. Longitudinal studies indicate securely attached children have longer lasting, healthier relationships while avoidant and resistant attachment styles are correlated with deviant behavior later in life. There is, however, conflicting evidence as to whether the attachment style an individual has at one age remains stable over time and across situations.

Separation anxiety and stranger anxiety are two related terms you need to know, first discussed in detail in the 1950's and 60's by **John Bowlby**. **Separation anxiety**, which often begins at between six and nine months old, is characterized by distress at being separated from parents or a familiar caregiver. Some theorists would contend that there is a correlation between the end of the most intense levels of separation anxiety and mastery of object permanence, which would allow the child to know that dad is not "gone" even though he may temporarily be out of sight. Many theorists believe that by about eight months of age children have begun to form schemas for faces that are familiar to them, and can therefore recognize when faces are *not* familiar. This can lead to **stranger anxiety**, which is characterized by distress upon encountering new, unfamiliar people. There is evidence that separation and stranger anxiety unfold in about the same ways and at about the same times cross culturally, with separation anxiety peaking at between 13- and 15 months old, and stranger anxiety peaking sometime late in the first year of life.

In the early 1970's, **Diana Baumrind** described a set of **parenting styles** that undoubtedly have an impact on a child's social development. A summary of those follows:

- **Authoritarian**: This is a top-down parenting approach in which the parents establish the rules, expect obedience and strictly punish transgressions. These parents are very demanding of the child and tend not to be particularly warm or responsive to their children's needs.

- **Authoritative**: These parents are the authority figures but they are willing to listen to input from the children, respecting their basic rights and explaining the rules and decisions they set down. This is often seen as the most "successful" style as the parents set high standards for the child but are also caring and responsive to the youngster's needs.

- **Permissive**: These parents give children considerable freedom to make their own decisions, either because they are more tolerant and trusting of their children's abilities or because they are less engaged in the upbringing of the children. They tend not to be demanding of their children but are generally warm and responsive.

- **Uninvolved** or **Neglectful**: The parents have essentially abrogated responsibility for the raising and control of their children. They do not set limits for the child and tend to reject or ignore the child's needs.

Baumrind believed that over ¾ of families operated in one of the first three styles. Many parents, however, may not fit perfectly into one category but instead combine elements from each. Longitudinal studies indicate authoritative parenting styles tend to correlate with positive outcomes for children. Children raised in these homes tend to be more self-reliant, have higher rates of self-esteem, and also demonstrate higher levels of social competence. It is of course important to note that these are only correlational studies and we should not necessarily infer causation from these findings.

The development of gender identity and roles is a highly engaging discussion topic, but before you spark such a discussion in your class it is important to specify some gender-related terms that people often wrongly use interchangeably:

- **Sex** is biologically determined (you are biologically a male or a female).

- **Gender** refers to culturally acquired behaviors and attitudes associated with one's biological sex.

- **Gender identity** refers to the sense of being a boy or a girl.

- **Gender constancy** is the sense that one is a boy or a girl and, barring very dramatic intervention, will remain so.

- **Gender role** refers to the behaviors considered appropriate for males and females in a given social setting.

- **Gender typing** refers to the process of acquiring the traditional roles associated with the distinctions between males and females in a culture.

- **Gender schemas** are mental constructs or generalizations about which toys, activities, and jobs are most associated with males and females.

- **Androgyny** refers to the presence of both male and female behaviors or characteristics in the same person.

### Development Over the Lifespan: Erikson's Psychosocial Stage Theory

**Erik Erikson** created a stage theory of **psychosocial development across the life span**. He proposed that people face various psychological and social crises at different ages that they must resolve in order to continue healthy development. He broke these periods of crisis into eight stages:

- **Trust vs. mistrust** (birth to approximately 18 months): The child learns what to trust in the environment, and gains a "fundamental sense of one's own trustworthiness."

- **Autonomy vs. shame and doubt** (approximately 18 months to 3 years old): This period is marked by dramatic gains in physical and cognitive skills, which the child actively attempts to utilize. The child begins to seek a sense of internal control and independence, but feels regret and even shame at losses of self-control.

- **Initiative vs. guilt** (about 3 to 6 years old): A child's self-esteem begins to emerge from their rapidly growing abilities and they are now able to set goals and work to achieve them. This period is critical for developing a **self-concept** in which children gain insight into who they are in terms of appearance, personality, and ability. The child takes pride in the tasks he initiates and feels guilt rather than shame when he comes up short.

- **Industry vs. inferiority** (about 6 to 12 years old): The child seeks to master the cognitive and social skills required for successful participation in society. Success with these skills makes them feel industrious and competent while failures can lead to deep feelings of inferiority and inadequacy.

- **Identity vs. role confusion** (adolescence): The teenager seeks to answer the questions "Who am I?" and "What do I want to do and be?" For Erikson this was the critical time to gain a core understanding of who one is and what roles one should play as an adult.

- **Intimacy vs. isolation** (early adulthood): The young adult either successfully establishes strong, committed relationships or faces the task of dealing with some level of isolation.

- **Generativity vs. stagnation** (middle adulthood): Adults, now in their 40's or 50's, strive to be productive in a meaningful way (usually through work or parenthood) to create an lasting legacy for future generations. Erikson believed a failure to be generative led to feelings of emptiness and purposelessness. This could also contribute to a feeling of resentment toward younger generations.

- **Integrity vs. despair** (late adulthood): The older adult reflects back on his or her life, feeling either a sense of accomplishment and pride or a sense of missed opportunities and thus, sadness.

These stages have been the focus of much research and are subject to much debate. Many people see significant overlap between stages two, three and four, while others argue that the adolescent identity crisis is not specific to adolescence and recurs throughout the life span. The stages have also been criticized for being too vague and subjective to be tested scientifically. Erikson's theory is also nearly three decades old, and the simple fact of increased life expectancy changes how people view different periods of life, not to mention the vast number of sociocultural phenomena that would affect this hierarchy of stages as time passes.

## Development Over the Lifespan:
### Adolescence

When individuals enter **puberty**, the point at which they are sexually mature and can reproduce, they acquire primary and secondary sex characteristics. **Primary sex characteristics** are directly involved with reproduction. Females mark the start of puberty with their first menstrual cycle, which is called **menarche**. At that point they are able to conceive and bear a child. Meanwhile, puberty is a time of astonishing sperm production in males. Some estimates indicate that males produce upwards of 1,000 sperm per second in this period. Examples of **secondary sex characteristics** include the deepening of the voice and growth of pubic and body hair in males, and breast and pubic hair development in females.

In regard to adolescence, you may find it interesting and relevant to learn about theories of the personal fable and the imaginary audience. **David Elkind** argued that adolescents tend to create a story of "specialness" about themselves, a **personal fable** in which the teenager feels a sense of invulnerability, believing that the rules of safety don't really apply to them. This is why teenagers seem so much more likely than others to engage in high risk, potentially destructive behaviors.

One might interpret the personal fable as a form of egocentrism. Some make the same connection to the adolescent sense of an **imaginary audience**, which was also proposed by David Elkind. It reflects the teen's belief that others are constantly monitoring the adolescent, watching for mistakes, moments of embarrassment, and so on. Of course, many would argue that this phenomenon is not exclusive to the teenage years.

During adolescence the frontal lobes of the brain continue to develop. Throughout the teens and early twenties, the axons of neurons in the prefrontal lobes are being wrapped in myelin, allowing for faster neural communication. Importantly, adolescence is also a key period for the pruning of unused synaptic connections. This may account for differences between teenagers and adults in their judgments, inhibitions, level of social awareness, and ability to understand how decisions in the short-term can have lasting long-term consequences.

In the past, developmental theories have transitioned from adolescence directly into adulthood, but there has been significant research in recent years on an intermediate stage that psychologists are terming **emerging adulthood**. Turning eighteen once meant that one was expected to take on the responsibilities of an adult, but as more and more teenagers go to college there has been a noticeable change in the length of time "twenty-something's" remain reliant on their parents. Likewise, people generally get married later than they typically did in the past. The transition to 'adulthood' is thus less abrupt than it once was. You may find it interesting to discuss with your classmates the extent to which *emerging adulthood* is occurring across cultures.

## Development Over the Lifespan:
## Adulthood and Aging

The **social clock** is an intriguing concept in development that definitely cuts across age group lines. If you feel there is a strong expectation for you to go to college immediately after high school and that taking a year off to find out more about yourself would be discouraged, then you have a sense of social clock expectations. If you are 35 years old and single and people consistently ask you why you are not yet married, you will have another sense of the social clock. If you are 35 and married, there may be *social clock* pressure to have children.

The **empty nest syndrome** refers to the adjustments parents make to the last of their children leaving home. For some parents this can be a liberating experience, for others a period of establishing re-acquaintance with each other, for still others a time to find another focus for their efforts and attentions. The next major life event for many is retiring from a longstanding career. Much like the empty nest, retirement may stir both positive and negative sentiments among the retirees. In recent years, psychologists have given more and more attention to the field of **positive psychology**, which in part studies the factors that are correlated with happiness at different points in the lifespan. We look more at positive psychology in our next chapter on Motivation and Emotion.

While one's first impulse might be to believe that contemplation of death and dying is reserved for Erikson's "late adulthood," in fact any of us can face loss, grief and imminent death at any time. **Elisabeth Kubler-Ross** formulated a stage theory addressing our encounters with grief. She argued that we go through five stages (you may see variations and additions to this theory elsewhere, but for the purposes of the AP Exam these five stages are the key) in dealing with loss: **denial, anger, bargaining, depression and acceptance**. Kubler-Ross did not envision this as strictly hierarchical. In your own experience with loss you might have found that you revisit certain stages repeatedly and don't necessarily progress in an orderly fashion through the steps from start to finish. Most psychologists would agree that although these may be typical experiences during grieving, the progression of the stages is fluid and unpredictable.

**The hospice movement** is heavily influenced by work like that of Kubler-Ross, in that it is essentially a philosophy of treatment of the dying that is warm, personalized and informed about the psychological processes which impact those facing relatively imminent death.

## Development of Moral Reasoning

*"Conscience: the inner voice that warns us that someone may be looking"*
*(H.L. Mencken)*

Finally, we need to take a quick look at the development of a moral sense. The most well known work in this area was conducted by **Lawrence Kohlberg**, who used a fictional story called **"The Heinz Dilemma"** to evaluate levels of **moral reasoning** in children. The dilemma posed the basic question, "Would you steal a drug in order to save a life?" Based on his evaluations of the responses children offered to this question, Kohlberg devised yet another stage theory, this with **three levels of moral reasoning**:

- **The preconventional level** (characteristic of children aged 4 to about 10) in which the focus is reward and punishment; the responses are self interested ("I wouldn't steal the drug because I would get into trouble")

- **The conventional level** (characteristic of children aged about 10 to 13) which, as its name suggests, focuses on social conventions; responses center on issues like "What will others think of me?" and "What are the rules we've all agreed to follow?"

- **The postconventional level** (not typically reached until age 13, if it is reached at all) in which moral decisions are based on personal, internal judgments of right and wrong; thus, this is sometimes referred to as *the principled level*

In some ways Kohlberg's theory became most famous when it was criticized, especially by **Carol Gilligan**. She argued that Kohlberg generalized a theory of moral reasoning for all people even though his original participants were all males. She thought that Kohlberg missed the fact that males and females tend to view moral dilemmas differently; men look at such judgments in a more absolute and *justice-based* way, women with a more relative, relationship-based, *caring* orientation. More recent evidence, however, indicates that Kohlberg's first two levels seem to be universal, with little gender or cross-cultural variation.

One useful way to review your grasp of some key concepts in this unit while also exploring an intriguing line of thought is to discuss the relationship between cognitive development and moral development. As one becomes more cognitively advanced, does moral reasoning deepen as well? If so, does that translate into more advanced moral *behavior*? Or is there relatively little connection between intellect and morality?

## Name Hall of Fame

**Jean Piaget** would be a lock for inclusion in anyone's psychology name hall of fame. After him, things get a little more complicated. There are several names in this unit that almost certainly will show up on the AP Exam, but will you have to "know" *the name* of these individuals who have contributed so much to the field but may not be definite candidates for the hall of fame? To be safe, answer 'yes' to this question and look again at **Mary Ainsworth** and her theory of attachment, **Lev Vygotsky** and the influence of socialization on development, **Erik Erikson** and his eight stage theory of psychosocial development across the life span, and **Lawrence Kohlberg** and **Carol Gilligan** in regard to moral development.

You may also see the names, **Diana Baumrind, Harry Harlow, Eleanor Gibson, Alfred Adler, John Bowlby, Elisabeth Kubler-Ross** and **David Elkind**, but those would likely appear only in connection with another cue in a multiple-choice stem.

## Essay Themes

The **nature vs. nurture debate** seems to be a natural candidate for a free response item that could cut across content areas. In the AP Psychology program there has yet to be a free response question on a **specific stage theory** or on **stage theories in general**. Such discontinuity theories play a big role in this chapter. Piaget's theory of cognitive development might be the most likely candidate for an essay. It is even more likely that the test development committee would target stage theories as a whole, again attempting to incorporate elements of other units in the question as well. There are some important **links between this unit and others**, as suggested by the "test prep" graphic organizer that follows. Revisit those in your mind when you begin final preparations for the AP Exam.

# Developmental Psychology

- Nature vs. nurture
- Continuity vs. discontinuity
- Genetic determinism or predisposition?
- Twin studies
- Maturation vs. socialization

## Themes In Development

- Genie & the Wild Child
- Critical/sensitive period theory
- Vygotsky & "socio-cultural" factors: zone of proximal development

## Pre-natal Development, Reflexes And Physical Development

- Stages of pregnancy
- Teratogens
- Fetal alcohol syndrome
- Imprinting
- Harlow's monkeys and contact comfort
- Transitional objects

- Reflexes:
  - rooting
  - sucking
  - grasping
  - moro/startle
  - Babinski
  - stepping

- The visual cliff
- Infant imitation

## Cognitive Development

- Piaget:
  1)
  2)
- Assimilation
- Accommodation
- Object permanence
- Animism
- Egocentrism
- Conservation
  3)
  4)

CRITICISMS:

## Social Development

- Ainsworth's "strange situations" and "attachment styles"
  1)
  2)
  3)
  4)
- Stranger anxiety
- Separation anxiety

- Parenting Styles
  1)
  2)
  3)
  4)
- Birth Order Theory

- Gender identity
- Gender constancy
- Gender role
- Gender typing
- Gender schema
- Androgyny

157

# Developmental Psychology (continued)

- Erikson's Psychosocial
  Stages of Development:

  1)

  2)

  3)

  4)

  5)

  6)

  7)

  8)

- Puberty

- Menarche

- Primary sex characteristics
  Secondary sex characteristics

- Egocentrism?

- The Personal Fable
- The Imaginary Audience

- The Identity Crisis?

## Adolescence, Etc.

- Emerging adulthood

- The social clock

- The empty nest

- Kubler-Ross on
  death, grieving:
  "D.A.B.D.A."

## Adulthood And Aging

- Kohlberg and the "Heinz Dilemma"

Level One:
Level Two:
Level Three:

- Gilligan's criticisms of Kohlberg

## Development Of Moral Reasoning

- "Stats & Research"
  - Longitudinal studies
  - Cross-sectional studies
  - Cohort effect

- "Learning Theory"
  - Skinner
  - Bandura

## Links To Other Units

- "Thought & Language"
  - Language acquisition

- "Sensation and Perception"
  - A baby's senses
  - The visual cliff

- "BioPsych"
  - Genetic
    predispositions
  - Genetic
    abnormalities
  - Arousal levels

158

## Practice Items

• If you work at the pace you will need on the actual AP Exam, this section should take you no more than 10 minutes and 30 seconds

• THESE SECTION ITEMS ARE **NOT** IN ORDER OF DIFFICULTY!

1. Lawrence Kohlberg used the fictional "Heinz Dilemma" to assess the development of moral reasoning in children. If a child is asked "Would you steal a drug in order to save a life?" and she responds "Yes, because a person's life is even more important than following the rules," where would Kohlberg likely place such an answer in his theoretical framework?

   (A) Level one: Preconventional
   (B) Level two: Conventional
   (C) Level three: Postconventional
   (D) Level four: Formal Operational
   (E) Level five: Abstract Reasoning

2. Maturation

   (A) is a less powerful mechanism in humans than in other primates
   (B) differs significantly from culture to culture
   (C) is governed by adult agents of socialization
   (D) refers to the systematic development of cognitive and physical abilities that unfolds naturally if a child is in a reasonably supportive environment
   (E) is the direct result of influences such as social learning, classical and operant conditioning, latent learning and insight learning

3. Which of the following would be most likely to act as a teratogen?

   (A) Exercise
   (B) Physical nurturance
   (C) Music
   (D) Alcohol
   (E) Anger

4. Two-year old Abby insists on dressing herself and putting her shoes on by herself. If her parents intervene to help she gets very frustrated. According to Erikson's psychosocial theory of development, Abby is likely facing which developmental crisis?

    (A) Generativity vs. stagnation
    (B) Identity vs. role confusion
    (C) Intimacy vs. isolation
    (D) Integrity vs. despair
    (E) Autonomy vs. shame and doubt

5. According to Jean Piaget, which of the following would have been mastered by the end of the "sensorimotor" period of cognitive development?

    (A) An understanding of categorical thinking
    (B) The ability to reverse mathematical operations
    (C) The knowledge that inanimate objects like chairs do not have feelings or thoughts
    (D) The knowledge that even though a toy is currently out of sight it still exists
    (E) The knowledge that the amount of something does not change simply because of a change in its appearance

6. High levels of self-esteem, self-reliance and social competence have been most closely linked to

    (A) children with secure attachments raised by authoritative parents
    (B) teenagers who quickly establish a strong identity
    (C) babies with low levels of stranger or separation anxiety
    (D) adolescents who reach the conventional stage of moral development
    (E) infants who attach to transitional objects early in life

7. Which of the following is a central criticism of Jean Piaget's stage theory of cognitive development?

    (A) Piaget failed to include clear age delineations for each of his stages
    (B) Piaget misidentified many cognitive differences between children and adults
    (C) Piaget chose a test sample that was too large to examine appropriately
    (D) Piaget often overestimated the cognitive abilities of children
    (E) Piaget often underestimated the cognitive abilities of children

8. When touched lightly on one side of the mouth, a healthy human newborn will automatically turn its head in that direction, searching with its mouth for a food source. This is called

    (A) the Babinski reflex
    (B) the rooting reflex
    (C) the Moro reflex
    (D) the grasping reflex
    (E) habituation

9. In Mary Ainsworth's "strange situations" study, some children basically ignored their mother's return and continued to do what they were already doing. Ainsworth labeled this as

    (A) an avoidant attachment style
    (B) a resistant/ambivalent attachment style
    (C) a secure attachment style
    (D) an authoritative attachment style
    (E) a disorganized attachment style

10. With which of the following statements would Lev Vygotsky have most agreed?

    (A) Moral development happens in predictable stages that are the same across cultures
    (B) There is nothing more important to a child than receiving contact comfort from a caregiver
    (C) Cognitive abilities are biologically predisposed and will unfold as a simple matter of maturation
    (D) A child's optimal cognitive development requires interaction with and guidance from parents or other adult mentors
    (E) Birth order determines one's personality and cognitive abilities more than any other factor

11. Conservation and hypothetical, abstract thinking are typically mastered in which two of Jean Piaget's stages of cognitive development, respectively?

    (A) Formal operational; concrete operational
    (B) Concrete operational; preoperational
    (C) Concrete operational; formal operational
    (D) Sensorimotor; formal operational
    (E) Sensorimotor; preoperational

12. Which of the following is not a typical characteristic of development during adolescence?

    (A) The belief that others are always monitoring them, watching for mistakes and moments of embarrassment
    (B) The feeling that one needs to be meaningfully productive in work or family life with an accompanying sense of 'stagnation' if unsuccessful
    (C) The continued development of the frontal lobes
    (D) Cognitive development marked by Piaget's formal operational stage
    (E) The development of secondary sex characteristics

13. Harry Harlow's work with infant monkeys and surrogate mothers suggests that

    (A) infants seek not only a food source but also a source of contact comfort
    (B) inborn reflexes in primates are more limited than was once thought
    (C) when distressed, an infant will turn reflexively to a caregiver that has to that point been its primary food source
    (D) even the simplest primates learn through observation if they see the model being reinforced for the behavior
    (E) infants tend to avoid attachment to surrogate parents

14. David Elkind proposes that adolescents tend to have an exaggerated sense of their own uniqueness and invulnerability. He called this

    (A) preoperational thinking
    (B) concrete operational thinking
    (C) the personal fable
    (D) the social clock
    (E) emerging adulthood

15. Which of the following best summarizes Carol Gilligan's central criticism of Lawrence Kohlberg's theory of moral development?

    (A) Kohlberg proposed three primary levels of moral reasoning while Gilligan argued for a fourth which Kohlberg had not accounted for
    (B) Responses from a large percentage of volunteers indicated a lack of understanding of the questions they were being asked
    (C) Males and females tend to view moral situations in different ways
    (D) Kohlberg's theory was based only on the responses of females
    (E) Kohlberg's levels of moral development were too broadly defined

# Chapter 9
# *Motivation and Emotion*

### Introduction

In 1984, Arvind Pandya ran backwards from Los Angeles to New York City, a distance of over 3,100 miles, in 107 days – he covered an average of nearly 30 miles per day. In 1986, Pat Bower lived in a barrel on top of an 18-foot flagpole for 40 days and one hour. In 1997, Elaine Davidson established the record for total number of body piercings – four hundred sixty two. One hundred and ninety two of those were on her head. In 1998, Shridar Chillal had the fingernails on his left hand measured at 20 feet, 2 1/4 inches. And in 1998, Mike Howard walked on an aluminum bar between two hot air balloons at a height of over three miles, using no safety ropes.

The Guinness Book of World Records, from which each of these facts was drawn, presents a smorgasbord of oddities, most of which invite the question, "Why do people do what they do?" That question is at the core of this unit.

(Sullivan, Olney)

Material from this unit will account for six to eight multiple-choice questions on the AP Exam. In the official AP Psychology curriculum progression, this unit comes <u>before</u> the unit on Development, but the order used in this book is easily defensible as well. Many textbooks also break this topic into two separate chapters, one specifically on motivation and the other focusing on emotion. In a sense, then, this is another "two in one" chapter, but you probably won't find it overwhelming in terms of total volume of material.

## Motivation

As with most elements of human behavior described in this book, motivation is influenced by biological, psychological and social factors. As you will see, many of our behaviors are **intrinsically** motivated, meaning we do them for their own sake – for the simple pleasure of doing them. Other motives are **extrinsic** - we do some things in order to receive some external reward. Some high school students take AP Psychology because they want to challenge themselves academically (*intrinsic motivation*) while others may be mostly motivated by the possibility of gaining college credit (*extrinsic motivation*).

Many of the findings in the field of motivation serve as the foundation of **industrial and organizational (I-O)** psychology. This branch of psychology applies motivational principles to boost the efficiency, productivity, and well being of workers and the companies that employ them. An I-O psychologist may look at modes of communication within a company, assess the effectiveness of the leadership within a certain institution, or develop ways to screen applicants to find the best people for a particular kind of work. They may also work on ways to keep employees satisfied and engaged with their jobs.

Let us delve deeper into the study of motivation by looking at a summary of some major perspectives that attempt to explain why we do what we do.

**Ethologists** study animal behavior in the natural setting. They have proposed various **instinct theories** to explain such behaviors. To an ethologist, an **instinct** is an innate, preprogrammed behavior that is released in response to some stimulus. A true instinct is unlearned and is present in most all healthy members of the species. These instincts (also called **fixed action patterns**) manifest themselves in response to some particular environmental event (**a trigger feature or sign stimulus**). For example, some types of small birds instinctively hide from hawks; they appear to recognize the hawk as a dangerous predator by the hawk's eyes. The eyes are thus the trigger feature initiating the fixed action pattern of flight. Migration patterns and hibernation are fixed action patterns triggered by changes in the animals' environment.

Some people don't like the term 'instinct' partly because in the past it has been used in a kind of circular argument describing behavior ("He did what he did out of instinct"...

"But why does he have this instinct?"... "Well, he was born with it"). Today, instinct theories have lost favor partly because they don't provide a clear explanation for why we behave as we do.

**Sociobiology** also focuses on the role of basic biological mechanisms in motivation. This controversial perspective is based on the contention that people behave in ways that are most likely to **perpetuate their own genes**. A once classic example of this referred to nomadic extended family groups of indigenous peoples. When such a group faced especially difficult environmental conditions and short supplies, older members of the band might voluntarily leave the group and die, apparently committing a kind of *altruistic suicide* in order to assure the survival of the others. A sociobiologist would argue that this was not so much a pro-social act as an attempt to keep one's own genes alive through the survival of one's offspring. Some have questioned just how often such events actually occur, and many wonder in any case just how well this theory explains more mundane human motivations.

**Evolutionary psychology (EP)** draws from both sociobiology and ethology, maintaining the basic premise that many human behaviors are genetically influenced. This perspective applies many of Charles Darwin's principles of evolution and natural selection to explain psychological phenomena. Broadly speaking, EP proposes that behaviors serve an adaptive purpose, helping us survive, reproduce and pass those behaviors on through our offspring. This may account for sex differences in mate selection. According to this view, men seek out females that are younger, as youth suggests health and fertility. When females look for mates, they are drawn to slightly older males (suggesting the ability to survive!) with the resources necessary to help provide for the offspring that they produce. You can see why these are controversial arguments that are difficult to definitively verify.

Clark Hull proposed **drive theory** (you may also see this referred to as **drive-reduction theory**), which is based on the notion that we all have fundamental needs that must be fulfilled. If we are deprived of them we will be driven to act in ways to meet those needs and return to **homeostasis**, an ideal internal state of balance or equilibrium. If an individual is exceptionally cold, he will feel driven to seek warmth in order to become internally steady again. The same might be said about hunger. Your body has a *need* for nutrients - if you haven't consumed any for a while, you will experience tension, producing a *drive* to eat. Eating returns you to homeostasis, eliminating the discomfort you had been feeling. This theory is often criticized because it doesn't account for the wide spectrum of human behaviors. It "works" in explaining thirst or sex drive, but does it explain the motivation to run marathons or parachute out of airplanes? The theory implies that humans are always doing things to *reduce* tension, but it seems clear that sometimes people go out of their way to seek stimulation.

**Arousal Theory** helps to account for that tendency to engage in sensation seeking behaviors. The argument here is that we each have a preferred, optimal level of arousal and we act in ways to remain at that level. For some people, a lazy Saturday on the couch in front of the television is perfectly stimulating, while others would find such a day intensely uncomfortable and would be motivated to do more. Some individuals are highly motivated to seek stimulation; others feel comfortably stimulated even when relatively inactive. Historically, some individuals have looked out at the ocean from a safe harbor and felt a great pull to explore what was out there, while someone else standing right by their side might have had no such feeling. **Yerkes-Dodson Law** provides a prediction about the relationship between arousal levels and performance. It suggests that there is an interaction between aroused states, the difficulty of the task to be carried out, and eventual performance on that task. For example, a moderate level of stimulation (in the form of nervousness, anxiety, etc.) is best for performance on a difficult task, such as taking the AP Psychology Exam, while one might be able to handle a much higher level of arousal in performing a well-learned or "easy" task.

The theories that we've discussed up to this point all focus on internal processes that influence motivation. **Incentive Theory** looks at how external factors drive us. This theory suggests that **we are pulled toward behaviors by extrinsic rewards** or incentives. In our society, we often entice people to perform certain behaviors by offering them some desired outcome in return, as in the payment of cash bonuses to employees who do exceptional work. Incentives could also be negative; an individual may be motivated to behave in a certain way to **avoid an unpleasant outcome**. You can see the obvious connection here between incentive theory and **behavioral** concepts of positive and negative reinforcement and punishment, which you studied in the unit on Learning Theory.

As proposed by Leon Festinger, **cognitive dissonance theory** states that we strive to bring our thoughts, attitudes and behaviors into agreement with each other. In a sense, we are thus seeking a kind of cognitive homeostasis, more commonly referred to as **cognitive consistency**. If you belong to a group in school that speaks out against drunk driving but then drink heavily at a party and attempt to drive home (please do not do such a dangerous thing), you will undoubtedly feel tension and anxiety. This dissonance between your previously stated attitude and your current behavior will motivate you to either modify your attitude or adjust your behavior in order to return to a comfortable internal state. For instance, you may decide to quit the club. Or, you might reduce the cognitive tension by rationalizing that you had no other ride home and thus "had to do it." At times, we can perform rather elaborate cognitive contortions to reduce the disequilibrium we feel when confronted with a disparity between our thoughts and our behaviors.

**Humanists** like **Abraham Maslow** are very optimistic about human nature and motivation. Maslow proposed the existence of a **hierarchy of needs**. He theorized that we all have needs, which we are motivated to satisfy. Some are fundamental survival needs (we require food and water for example), while others are more ambitious, such as the desire to realize one's full potential as a human. Maslow called this the need for **self-actualization**; for him it is the highest goal to which individuals aspire. It is characterized by self-acceptance, a willingness and desire to consider the needs and wants of others, creativity, spontaneity and non-conformity. In order to reach self-actualization one must first meet lower level needs in his hierarchy - in order, they are the **physiological needs** for food and water, the need for **shelter and safety**, the need for **belonging and companionship** and the need for **self esteem**. In Maslow's paradigm, if you were starving, your focus would be on food, not on the search for meaningful companionship.

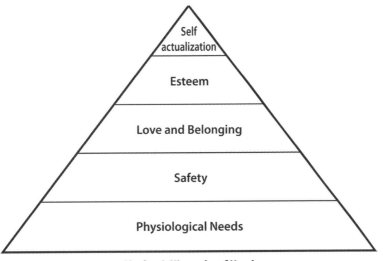

***Maslow's Hierorchy of Needs***

Maslow's theory is very popular, although it's worth discussing whether you think it is strictly hierarchical - that is, do all people follow this same flow in the same order? What about hunger strikers who deprive themselves of food, one of the most basic physiological needs, in order to meet other goals? What of individuals who seem to value social needs for belonging above a need for self-esteem? Also, Maslow himself acknowledged that many people do not even attempt to reach true self-actualization. Is the humanistic assumption that all people are striving to reach their fullest potential inherently flawed?

A more recent perspective on motivation, **self-determination theory**, has many parallels with Maslow's positive view on human motivation. This theory postulates that humans have "inherent growth tendencies" and do most things out of intrinsic motivation. They argue that humans intuitively seek autonomy, competence and relatedness. Self-determination theory is typically seen as a part of **positive psychology**, which focuses on how positive emotions and attributes such as happiness, optimism and resilience contribute to our overall health and well being. Led by **Martin Seligman**, among many others, positive psychology focuses on understanding human strengths, well-being and contentment. Positive psychologists note, for example, that when people are happy, they are much more likely to help others. This is sometimes called the **feel-good, do-good phenomenon**.

So what is it that contributes to happiness? Research in this area indicates that some of the strongest predictors of happiness are being in a loving relationship, having work that you enjoy, and having an extroverted (outgoing, upbeat, sociable) personality. Moderate predictors of happiness include good health, religious affiliation and a solid social support network. The variables that are statistically unrelated to happiness may surprise you. Age doesn't seem to matter much, and neither does one's intelligence level. Having children doesn't by itself make people happier, nor does having money. Once people have enough money to meet their basic needs, getting more of it does not appear to make people happier.

## Some Specific Motivations

There are many different types of specific motivations that psychologists examine, and it is difficult to predict which are most likely to show up on the Advanced Placement Examination. It is safe to say, however, that you should know a bit about the motivations behind *eating*, *aggression* and *achievement*.

## Hunger/Eating

There are many factors that contribute to our drive to eat – the topic deserves a book all its own. For the purposes of the AP Exam, you should know that the hypothalamus, in the limbic system of the brain, plays a central role in the regulation of appetite and satisfaction. **The lateral hypothalamus (the LH)** is most involved in "hunger" messages, while **the ventromedial hypothalamus (the VMH)** sends "stop, I think you've had just about enough!" messages. Thus, some think of the LH as the hunger center of the brain, and the VMH as the satiety center. However, those are not the only physiological mechanisms involved in hunger. Several hormones in the endocrine system play a role in eating and satiation. Insulin, which is secreted by the pancreas, controls blood glucose levels. Increases in insulin diminish blood glucose causing you to experience hunger. The sight or smell of food can actually stimulate insulin production, thereby increasing your appetite. Ghrelin is secreted by an empty stomach and cues your brain that food is needed. Leptin is secreted by fat cells and acts to reduce appetite.

A related theory is based on the concept of a **set point**. This states that our brain and endocrine system essentially act just as a thermostat does in a home. If the thermostat is set at 68 degrees, the furnace turns itself on when the temperature drops below that level and turns itself off when the temperature climbs above 68 degrees. In the same way, our body has an individual set point for body weight and adjusts metabolically to keep you at that level. This may help to explain why dieting by itself is often frustratingly unsuccessful in keeping you at some goal weight - your body is apparently battling to get you back to your set point. Some psychologists, however, no longer accept the deterministic set point theory and instead prefer a *settling point theory*. Their contention is that slow and gradual shifts in eating habits can alter the body fat percentage at which your body feels most comfortable.

You can see that there is a mix of physiological factors telling us when to eat and to stop eating. But there are also a number of other influences on appetite. Culture influences the foods to which one is exposed and therefore likely to prefer. Advertising, television and the film industry do much to instill in us certain "ideals" of beauty, and those heavily influence our individual self-image. Self-image in turn affects our eating habits. There are a variety of other **external cues** that influence eating. Among them are:

- Time of day

- The availability and appearance of food

- The fact that those around you are eating

- Involvement in a social event that is built around a meal

On the AP Exam you may encounter specific references to eating disorders. **Anorexia nervosa** is a condition characterized by self-starvation. One commonly used threshold for diagnosing it is the failure to maintain at least 85% of what is considered the normal body weight for that individual's height and age. Even at such low body weights, sufferers still believe themselves to be fat, and are often obsessed with the fear of gaining weight. **Bulimia nervosa** is more prevalent than anorexia. Bulimia is characterized by compulsive binge eating, followed by purging through either vomiting or taking laxatives. Bulimics may have weight fluctuations but are usually within or above the normal weight range. *Bulimia* and *anorexia* affect women at a much higher rate than men, and there are cross-cultural differences as well. Westernized countries tend to have higher rates of both. In these cultures, women may be more disposed to link their self-concept with body image, which in both disorders is often quite distorted.

## Aggression

You could probably take an entire college course on aggression. It's a big and highly relevant topic, but, in terms of the AP Exam, you only need to know a bit about it. You may recall one of the central functions of the amygdala from our study of The Biological Bases of Behavior. This limbic system structure sizes up emotional situations, especially in terms of "high arousal" emotions like anger and aggression. Of course, there are also other biological factors related to aggression. For example, males tend to be significantly more aggressive than females, perhaps because they produce more of the hormone testosterone. Many correlational studies indicate that in men, the higher their testosterone levels, the higher their aggression level.

On the exam, you may also encounter a distinction between **hostile and instrumental aggression**. *Hostile aggression* is carried out for its own sake, while *instrumental aggression* at least theoretically is aggression that is working toward some other goal besides the aggression itself. Bumping someone out of the way to get possession of the ball in soccer would be deemed instrumental aggression, while bumping someone into the wall in the school corridor would likely be viewed as hostile aggression. You could likely have a stimulating discussion in class about other examples: Is stepping on an ant hostile or instrumental aggression? Punching an opponent in a boxing match? Yelling out the window at a driver who has just cut you off in traffic?

The **frustration-aggression principle**, proposes that when we are unable to reach an objective we become frustrated, which may lead us to act out in an aggressive manner. Further, for people who are already prone to aggression, heat, overcrowding, a painful experience, or being under the influence of alcohol all serve to amplify aggressive tendencies.

Some theorists argue that aggression can be **cathartic**. They contend that the American fondness for football or professional wrestling or violent movies serves as a safety valve for aggression - if people can "get their aggressions out" in such settings, they won't actually act them out in more dangerous ways. Freudian psychoanalytic theory is often associated with this view, which is not surprising when you know that it is based on the importance of the unconscious mind and its influence on behavior. The concept of catharsis is controversial. Many argue that while it may provide temporary relief, it actually magnifies aggressive tendencies over time. This may be a rich topic for classroom discussion and analysis.

### Achievement

The drive to achieve has been a much-studied topic. Various methods have been used to attempt to measure **achievement motivation**. One is called the **Thematic Apperception Test, or TAT**. Used by researchers like David McClelland, this **projective test** (so called because of the expectation that one might "project" something about themselves onto an otherwise ambiguous stimulus) involves presenting a photograph or picture to a volunteer and asking them to tell a story about it. The stories are then rated for levels of achievement motivation. In general, McClelland and others have reported, after analysis of their TAT results, that there is a link between a *desire to achieve* and a *fear of failure*. Individuals with a high drive to succeed and a relatively low fear of failure are most likely to seek challenges that are worthy of their efforts but also reasonably attainable, whereas a person with a high fear of failure might choose to pursue very "safe" paths or nearly impossible ones. In the latter case, they are thus allowed to fail, since no one, including themselves, really expected success in the first place.

Another kind of projective test is a "Finish the Story" test used by Matina Horner in 1970. She supplied the first line of a possible story and asked volunteers to take it from there. One such first line was, "John has just finished his first year of medical school and is first in his class..." while another read "Alice has just finished her first year of medical school and is first in her class..." Like McClelland, Horner too rated the volunteer's answers to determine their level of achievement motivation. One of her conclusions was that some women feared success - they had a "will to fail." It may be interesting to discuss in class what the results would be if her work was replicated today.

### Emotion

In the AP Psychology curriculum, the emotion section of this unit is relatively light on content, and much of it is linked with other units, especially The Biological Bases of Behavior. The one difficult area involves the basic theories of emotional response. Exactly how does an emotion unfold? There are a few major attempts to explain this, and it can be hard to sort them out, especially since they are usually referred to by names that do not cue you as to their meaning.

According to **James-Lange Theory**, in a potentially emotional situation, we first recognize physiological changes, such as an increased heart rate – only then do we identify the "emotion." In this theory, autonomic nervous system activation is seen as the root of an emotional experience. As we veer off the highway in an attempt to avoid an accident, we first feel our hearts pounding and our palms sweating and then, when we finally come to a stop on the shoulder of the road, we say, "I was afraid." The labeling of the emotion follows the bodily responses. It's almost as if the physical *creates* the emotional.

In **Cannon-Bard Theory** (sometimes called **Thalamic Theory**, after the thalamus, the relay station in the brain), the recognition of physiological changes and the awareness of the emotion are processed simultaneously by the thalamus. When sensory information arrives at the thalamus that message activates the sympathetic nervous system and alerts the cerebral cortex at the same time. If you were hiking in the woods and saw a bear, that visual stimulus would trigger a "fight or flight" response and the "emotion of fear" simultaneously.

The **Schachter-Singer Theory** (also called **Two-Factor Theory**) adds a cognitive component to emotion. It proposes that one can interpret identical physical sensations differently according to the context in which they occur. The same feeling of butterflies in your stomach would tell you that you are *nervous* before a big game, but might tell you that you are *happily excited* as you open a huge birthday present. There are thus two factors at work – physiological arousal and cognitive interpretation of that arousal, which sounds suspiciously like James-Lange Theory except that specific *situational* cues are taken into account prior to experiencing the emotion. That is one way to help you to remember this theory: think 'S' for Schacter-Singer and 'S' for situations.

In the earlier unit on Sensation and Perception, you studied opponent process theory as it relates to color afterimages. Some experts contend that opponent processes help to explain emotions as well. You may recall that drive theory suggests we are driven to satisfy needs in order to return to homeostasis. **Opponent process theories** make a similar argument, which has been used to account for why some individuals enjoy bungee jumping or rock climbing or become addicted to certain drugs. When you do your first dangerous rock climb, your initial emotional response will likely be fear and anxiety. After completing the climb, you do not merely return to a homeostatic baseline but instead have an opposing feeling of happiness, even euphoria. The next time you go climbing, according to the theory, the primary emotion of fear is reduced, but the opposing process of elation can be just as great or greater than the first time around. You can see how such a process might also trap you in a pattern of drug abuse. If the primary "high" of taking a drug is less intense on repeated administration, and the opposing "crash" is just as unpleasant as it was originally, sometimes a user falls into taking more of the drug to escape the crash, thus beginning a perilous cycle.

### Emotional Expression

In your review of the biological bases of emotional response, you might also consider how polygraphs (lie detectors) theoretically work. Basically, their job is to measure sympathetic nervous system responses, which might be indicative of lying (such as elevated heart rate, increased sweating and so on). You might have fun in class discussing the validity of this approach. Many people believe that lying is easily seen in the facial expressions that people make when answering questions, but although many claim to be excellent intuitive lie detectors, scientific studies indicate that few people do better than chance at identifying lies.

Psychologist Paul Ekman has proposed that when we lie, there are *microexpressions* on our face that indicate deceit. These are often so fleeting that the human eye might miss them, but new research indicates that computer software may be able to analyze those expressions, thereby identifying lies. Functional magnetic resonance imaging (fMRI) technology also holds promise for lie detection. This brain scanning technique has revealed that when people lie, certain areas of their brain become active that are not active when that individual is telling the truth.

While Ekman has done significant work in the study of lying, he is even more well known for his **cross cultural research into the facial expression of emotions**. He found that individuals in all cultures tend to recognize and express basic emotions in the same way in terms of facial expression. It is now widely accepted that the facial expressions for the emotions fear, anger, happiness, surprise, disgust, sadness and contempt are truly universal. This suggests that some fundamental kinds of emotional responses are inborn in humans.

Although facial expressions for certain emotions may be biologically pre-wired, there are cultural influences determining the extent to which we display those emotions. Ekman and others argue that we learn cultural **display rules** early in life that govern how and when we display certain emotions. Other studies on facial expression indicate that we are quicker to recognize negative emotions on someone's face than positive emotions. Perhaps this is an adaptive trait that allows us to respond quickly to possible threats.

We can also apparently induce some emotions through simple physical manipulations. The **facial feedback hypothesis** states that if one forces a smile, it really is more likely that individual will feel happier. Try it - make yourself look sad and then see how you feel! This finding lends support to the James-Lange Theory discussed earlier. Perhaps bodily responses do indeed alter your subjective experience of emotion.

### Stress

The growing field of *health psychology* has garnered much interest in recent years, and one topic receiving much attention is that of **stress**. Hans Selye did the first extensive research on this topic. He argued that we all experience stress in much the same way. Selye proposed the **general adaptation syndrome (GAS)** in which people go through three basic stages- alarm, resistance and exhaustion. **Alarm** essentially involves a 'fight or flight' reaction in response to the threat. During **resistance** you attempt to fight off or cope with the **stressor** while your body maintains the physiological state it reached in the *alarm* stage. To Selye, if the stressor is not removed, this will eventually give way to **exhaustion**. You can remember this theory with the mnemonic *G.A.S. is A.R.E.*

More recent work by theorists such as Richard Lazarus suggests that an individual's cognitive appraisal of the situation is the key in responding to stress. According to Lazarus, we first evaluate whether or not this is a stressful event *to us* (our **primary appraisal**), and we then judge whether and how we can cope with the stressor (our **secondary appraisal**). Much of the effect that stress has on our body is influenced by our assessment of our ability to cope with the stressor. As you will see in the coming chapters, *cognitive psychologists* propose that restructuring the way we think about situations in our lives can greatly reduce stress and anxiety.

There are some types of stress inducing "conflicts", identified by Kurt Lewin, which you must learn about to prepare for the AP Exam. One is called an approach-approach conflict. If you have ever had two equally attractive options on a Saturday night and couldn't decide which one to choose, then you have experienced an **approach-approach conflict**. Both choices are desirable, but you can only opt for one of them. In an **avoidance-avoidance conflict**, you are compelled to choose between two equally *unattractive* options. A trip to the dentist is an oft-used example. Do you make an appointment even though you'd rather not out of fear and anxiety, or do you allow your teeth to rot out of your head? Neither choice tops your list of priorities, but you must do one or the other. In an **approach-avoidance conflict**, a certain situation has both attractive and unattractive elements that make it difficult for you to decide what to do. For example: you very much like the programs at a certain college that has accepted you, but it is very expensive. Or, you are in love with a person but also fear losing your freedom if you commit to him or her. Or you're playing a sport that you love but the coach drives you crazy. Each of these examples could also become **multiple approach-avoidance conflicts**. You are in love with someone but fear commitment; so far, simple approach-avoidance. That someone also has a lot of money, which would be advantageous, but you know it would make you feel guilty. Further, your parents love your partner and have really "adopted" him or her, but your partner's parents don't like *you*, and so on.

### Name Hall of Fame

**Abraham Maslow** is one of the better-known names in psychology, and you must recognize his connection to the humanistic school of thought and to his hierarchy of needs. You might see **Clark Hull's** name when drive theory is mentioned, and **Konrad Lorenz** is a name to associate with ethology; likewise with **Leon Festinger** and cognitive dissonance theory. Of those, only Maslow's is a name that you might have to know in order to answer a question correctly. In the content outline you saw the names of **David McClelland** and **Matina Horner** in reference to their studies on achievement, but you will not be directly tested on recall of those people, and the same almost certainly applies to **Paul Ekman, Richard Lazarus, Kurt Lewin or Hans Selye;** they would be named only in connection to their particular theories and it would be your knowledge of the *theory* that would be assessed.

### Essay Themes

In this unit you've seen another reference to **opponent process theory**, echoing work you did in the unit on sensation and perception. You could also look at the inhibitory and excitatory action of neurotransmitters, from the chapter on the biology of behavior, as a kind of opposing process. Obviously then, this is the kind of theme that can cut across content areas and is thus a rich area for a possible free response question. Even if it never comes up as an essay item, it will help you across the board on the multiple-choice section to know opponent process theories well.

Although such an item may be dismissed by the test development committee as too specific to one unit, it isn't hard to imagine a free response item which asked you to **account for some particular human behavior** from the perspective of an ethologist, sociobiologist, drive theorist, etc. See the upper left quadrant on side one of the "test prep" scheme to remind yourself of those major schools of thought.

## Some Specific Drives and Motivations

- Hunger/Appetite:
  - Genetic predispositions
  - Endocrine system
  - Set/settling point theory
  - Self image; culture
  - External cues
  - Eating disorders
- Achievement Motivation
  - The T.A.T.
- Aggression: hostile vs. instrumental

## Links to Other Units

- I-O Psych
- Freud on motivation
- Skinner on motivation
  (Review overjustification and Premack Principle)
- Bandura on motivation

## Theories of Motivation

- Ethology:
  - What's an 'instinct'?
  - Fixed action patterns
  - Sign stimuli, trigger features
- Sociobiology/Evolutionary Psychology
- Drive Theory and homeostasis
- Self-determination theory
- Incentive Theory
  - Extrinsic motivation
- Cognitive Dissonance
- Arousal Theory (note: Yerkes-Dodson Law)
- Maslow's Hierarchy of Needs

## Conflicts

- Approach-Approach conflicts
- Avoidance-Avoidance conflicts
- Approach-Avoidance conflicts
- Multiple Variations of each

# Motivation and Emotion (Continued)

## Theories of Emotional Response

- James-Lange Theory
- The role of the limbic system
- Schachter-Singer "Two Factor" Theory
- Opponent-Process Theory
- Cannon-Bard "Thalamic" Theory

## The Physiology of Emotions

- Review: The Sympathetic Nervous System:
  - The "fight or flight" response
  - Epinephrine release, etc.
  - The parasympathetic system and return to homeostasis

## Stress and Coping

- Lazarus and Folkman on cognitive appraisal and coping with stress
- Selye and the G.A.S.
  1) A
  2) R
  3) E
- Positive Psychology

## More on Emotions

- Ekman on facial expressions of emotions
- Cultural display rules
- Facial-Feedback Hypothesis
- Frustration-Aggression Hypothesis

**177**

**Practice Items**

• Time yourself on this section, and record how long it takes you. This information will be useful to you later on

• If you work at the pace you will need on the actual AP Exam, this section should take you no more than 10 minutes and 30 seconds

• If it takes you only three minutes and you get them all correct, more power to you! If you are done in less than seven minutes and you make 3 or more errors, then you ought to consider slowing down a bit

• THESE SECTION ITEMS ARE NOT IN ORDER OF DIFFICULTY!

1. According to Abraham Maslow's hierarchy of needs, which of the following statements is true?

   (A) Physiological needs must be met before an individual achieves self-actualization
   (B) The fundamental need for social affiliation is the first step in the hierarchy
   (C) There are significant cultural differences in the rate at which individuals attain self-actualization
   (D) In western, industrialized cultures, women tend to rely on men to satisfy their safety and esteem needs
   (E) Individuals who fail to reach self-actualization inevitably feel a sense of despair in later life

2. A Viking explorer sets out on a journey to unexplored new lands hoping to acquire wealth and admiration from his peers. Which of the following theories of motivation best explains this particular explorer's voyage?

   (A) Incentive theory
   (B) Drive theory
   (C) Sociobiological theory
   (D) Cognitive dissonance theory
   (E) Ethological theory

3. Anorexia nervosa is a disorder marked by

   (A) major changes in serotonin and insulin levels
   (B) self starvation and a failure to maintain at least 85% of normal body weight
   (C) cycles of binge eating followed by purging
   (D) frequent binge eating episodes followed by normal caloric consumption
   (E) significant weight fluctuations at or slightly above the normal range

4. Which field of psychology most strongly emphasizes human strengths, happiness and optimism?

   (A) Industrial and Organizational (I-O) psychology
   (B) Positive psychology
   (C) Evolutionary psychology
   (D) Ethology
   (E) Behavioral psychology

5. Which of the following are most responsible for triggering our appetite and cuing us that we are full, respectively?

   (A) The pancreas; The hypothalamus
   (B) The hypothalamus; The amygdala
   (C) Insulin; Ghrelin
   (D) The lateral hypothalamus; The ventromedial hypothalamus
   (E) The ventromedial hypothalamus; The lateral hypothalamus

6. According to the Yerkes-Dodson law

   (A) to succeed on a difficult task it is best to have a moderate level of arousal
   (B) to succeed on a difficult task it is best to have a high level of arousal
   (C) it is best to have no arousal when performing easy tasks
   (D) each person has an optimal level of arousal that they seek to maintain
   (E) we choose challenging tasks if we have a high level of achievement motivation

7. Which of the following would be the strongest piece of evidence in support of Paul Ekman's research findings into facial expressions of emotions?

   (A) A boy who was born blind displays a universally recognized look of disgust, even though he has never seen someone else display that facial expression
   (B) A criminology student is confident that she can "read" the facial expressions of suspected criminals
   (C) A criminology student is convinced that it is impossible to "read" the facial expressions of suspected criminals
   (D) A newborn does not appear to utilize a social smile in response to others
   (E) Adults in different cultures appear to express disgust very differently

8. Which motivational theory would most support the premise that humans seek affiliation with others because traditionally those bonds have supplied protection from threats to their survival?

    (A) Arousal Theory
    (B) Maslow's hierarchy of needs
    (C) Self-determination theory
    (D) Evolutionary theory
    (E) Ethology

9. Which of the following is the most accurate criticism of drive theory?

    (A) It does not account for the motivation to satisfy hunger or thirst
    (B) It does not account for the motivation to satisfy the sex drive
    (C) It does not give sufficient attention to homeostatic regulation
    (D) Often, humans seek to increase rather than decrease their levels of stimulation
    (E) Individual motivations vary cross-culturally

10. "To think is easy. To act is difficult. To act as one thinks is the most difficult of all." This statement, attributed to Johann Wolfgang von Goethe is most reflective of which of the following theories?

    (A) Appraisal theory
    (B) Cognitive dissonance theory
    (C) Drive-reduction theory
    (D) James-Lange theory
    (E) Sociobiological theory

11. "We feel sorry because we cry, angry because we strike, afraid because we tremble." This quote summarizes which of the following theories of emotional response?

    (A) Drive-reduction theory
    (B) Opponent process theory
    (C) Two Factor Theory
    (D) James-Lange Theory
    (E) Cannon-Bard Thalamic Theory

12. Which of the following theorists supported the idea that humans have a general stress response in which exhaustion eventually results if the stressor is not removed?

    (A) Abraham Maslow
    (B) Clark Hull
    (C) Hans Selye
    (D) Richard Lazarus
    (E) Walter Cannon

13. Which of the following best demonstrates Kurt Lewin's concept of an approach-avoidance conflict?

    (A) Choosing between ice cream and apple pie for dessert
    (B) Choosing between your two favorite movies to watch on a Saturday
    (C) Scheduling a potentially painful dentist visit rather than risk tooth decay
    (D) Wanting a great looking car that has very poor gas mileage
    (E) Going to a college that has weak academics because you lack confidence in your intellectual abilities

14. Homeostatic theories of motivation argue that

    (A) most motivation is instinct driven
    (B) humans are motivated to seek an internal physiological balance
    (C) motives tend to be static and always changing
    (D) we must meet our basic physiological needs before we can self-actualize
    (E) we are mostly motivated by external incentives

15. David McClelland would argue that individuals with a high need to achieve and a low fear of failure would tend to choose tasks

    (A) based on how others are likely to view their choice
    (B) that insure success
    (C) that appear nearly impossible, in order to avoid responsibility for potential failure
    (D) from which it would be relatively easy to extricate oneself
    (E) that supply a reasonable but still challenging chance for success

NO TESTING MATERIAL ON THIS PAGE

GO ON TO THE NEXT PAGE

# Chapter 10
## *Personality*

---

### Introduction

If someone wanted to learn about your personality which of the following would most inform their inquiry?

- Viewing your Facebook profile
- Listening to the music on your iPod
- Noting how you decorate your bedroom
- Seeing the clothes you wear on a daily basis
- Scanning the books on your bookshelf
- Looking through the inside of your car
- Knowing your preference of musical instrument
- Knowing your preference for a pet
- Reading a teacher's assessment of your personality
- Reading a peer's assessment of your personality

Probably none of these would fully capture the complexity of your personality. **Personality** can be described as an enduring pattern of thoughts, feelings and behaviors that makes each of us unique. As you progress through this unit, keep in mind the following questions.

- To what extent do nature or nurture account for personality development?
- Is any one theory of personality development sufficient in terms of understanding such a complex phenomenon?
- To what extent is personality merely a response to the demands of the situation?
- How stable is personality across situations?
- How stable is personality longitudinally?

You can expect to encounter five to seven multiple-choice items from this unit on the AP Exam. One could argue that Personality Theory may be the most important unit in terms of your success on the AP Exam, because it has substantial overlap with other topics in the AP course, and it also describes the major schools of thought in present-day psychology. If you don't know about those perspectives in some detail, you simply do not "know" college level introductory psychology.

Before summarizing those major perspectives, we will consider some significant themes that are essential to the study of personality. One of those is the **nature vs. nurture** debate, which we last touched upon in Development. There, we learned about **twin studies** and reflected back even further on the concept of **genetic predispositions**, first mentioned in the chapter on Biopsychology. Many would argue there is evidence of personality as soon as a child is born, which indicates a significant genetic influence. Some babies can appear to their parents as being inherently calm and content, while others are irritable, fussy and hard to control.

A child's typical mood, emotionality and preferred activity level are collectively referred to as **temperament**. Psychologist Jerome Kagan classifies temperament patterns in terms of *reactivity. High-reactive* infants tend to be apprehensive and react in an intense, even fearful manner when introduced to new experiences or people. *Low-reactive* infants tend to be sociable and calm when exposed to new situations. Longitudinal studies investigating temperament indicate these patterns remain fairly stable across the lifespan. While these tendencies may be inborn, it is also generally accepted that environmental influences can pull children from either end of the spectrum to more of a middle ground.

Another piece of evidence to support the biological basis of personality comes from adoption studies. This research compares the results of personality tests from adopted children with their biological parents and their adoptive parents. Results consistently show that the child is much more similar in personality to their biological parents than to their adoptive parents. Findings such as this have raised questions about just how much of a role parenting and environment play in personality development.

Many students, when asked to take sides in the nature vs. nurture controversy, are reluctant to do so. They argue that personality and development in general involves "a little bit of both." You might think of that as taking the easy way out, but this is a case where straddling the fence might indeed be the best approach to the problem. Once again, many theorists contend that the nature vs. nurture debate is a false dichotomy; that is, we humans cannot attribute our growth solely to either nature or nurture.

Another central theme in this unit is that of the **stability of personality across situations**. Does each of us have personality characteristics that are consistent no matter what the circumstance, or is the situation the major determinant in how we behave? Theorists like **Walter Mischel** have argued for the latter, and are thus sometimes called **situationists**.

Many theorists also wonder about the **stability of personality over time**. If we were to conduct a longitudinal study on a group of individuals deemed to be "shy" at age six, would we discover that they are still "shy" at fifty-six? This question invites others: How do we operationally define 'shyness'? What measures do we use to assess levels of shyness? How do we control for variability in situations over time? We will explore some of that in this chapter, and in the next unit on Testing and Individual Differences.

It's possible that the AP exam will make reference to nomothetic vs. idiographic approaches to the study of personality. **Idiographic methods** involve the evaluation of case studies *individually* (that word sounds enough like 'idiographic' to perhaps cue your recall if you encounter the term on an examination). That definition may make more sense to you when you compare it to **nomothetic approaches**. Researchers taking that approach assume that all people share pretty much the same basic traits, but to differing degrees. Therefore, they essentially look at each individual in comparison to others - to some sense of a 'norm' amongst all people. The word 'norm' might sound enough like 'nomothetic' to help you with recall of it in the future.

## Trait and Type Theory

The first personality theory we'll look at is **Trait Theory**. Supporters of this view focus on describing the individual characteristics that define a person. For them, a **trait** is a tendency toward certain behaviors or emotions, no matter what the situation. Trait theorists believe that these tendencies are stable and predictable over time. There are several different theories as to which traits are most basic in humans. **Gordon Allport** was the first to try to list and describe fundamental human personality traits. He proposed that a small number of people have a **cardinal trait**, or a single defining personality characteristic that is dominant in all situations. More importantly, Allport believed that each of us has five to ten **central traits,** which are the significant characteristics that form the core of our personality. We also have **secondary traits** that are often present in an individual but are not nearly as defining of that individual. Allport undertook the time-consuming task of identifying words used to describe personality by conducting an exhaustive search of the English dictionary. At first, he identified 18,000 words that could be used to describe human personality. By eliminating synonyms, he then reduced the list to 171.

In 1950, **Raymond Cattell** reduced Allport's list even further by using a complex statistical analysis of abilities or characteristics that seem to go together, called **factor analysis**. This method identified 16 underlying factors that Cattell believed were fundamental in describing all people. These core traits are known as the sixteen personality factors (**16 PF**). He argued that you could describe anyone using these 16 factors (such as assertiveness, conscientiousness and self sufficiency), although the degree to which each is present differs from person to person.

In 1967, **Hans Eysenck** contended that there were three essential components of personality: psychoticism, extroversion and neuroticism (you might associate Eysenck's name with the mnemonic **PEN** to help you recall this). Psychoticism refers to the general level of emotional caring and empathy one has (or doesn't have); extroversion (you may also see this spelled as *'extraversion'*) refers to how outgoing, friendly and social a person is; and neuroticism is linked to the level of basic emotional stability one possesses, as measured in terms of self esteem, feelings of guilt and so on.

The most popular trait theory at present is called **the Big Five**, or **the Five-Factor Model**. Those five personality traits, used to describe everyone to some greater or lesser degree, are openness, conscientiousness, extroversion (perhaps the most studied of all these traits), agreeableness and neuroticism. These are summarized below:

- **Openness**: The degree to which one is open to new experiences and learning
- **Conscientiousness**: The degree to which one is responsible, hard working and reliable; this is sometimes thought of as *dependability*
- **Extroversion/extraversion**: The degree to which one is outgoing, expressive, active and social
- **Agreeableness**: The degree to which one is honest, considerate, likable and tolerant
- **Neuroticism**: The degree to which one is anxious, self conscious or impulsive; it might be easier to think of this as *emotionality*

Cross-cultural studies on the *Big Five* suggest that these may well be the core characteristics of personality in most cultures, although you would see significant differences in the degree to which each culture exhibits the five traits. It has also been found that these traits are stable in individuals, especially after the age of thirty.

To assess and to deepen your grasp of this theory and the others in this unit, it is useful to critique them in classroom discussion. Ask yourself what *you* see as weaknesses of each theory. For example, a central argument against trait theory is that it does not take the power of the *situation* into account. In fact, it's based on the idea that a trait is only a trait if it is consistent no matter what the situation. Trait theorists are also criticized for stopping at mere description of personality traits; they offer little in the way of explanation as to where those characteristics come from.

Other theories categorize personalities into specific *types*. One well-known theory attempts to distill the list of core human characteristics and manages to cut the number to two: **Type A** personalities and **Type B** personalities. Type A's are driven, competitive, rigid, hostile and intense, while Type B's, well, aren't. They're viewed as more calm, laid back and easy going. The theory was derived from the uncovering of a statistical correlation between the presence of what came to be called Type A characteristics and stress-related illness such as heart disease. The elements of Type A personalities that seem most connected to these health issues are hostility, negative affect and anger. Critics of this theory point out that placing all people into one of two categories is just not very realistic.

### Freudian Psychoanalytic Theory

A long-standing but much criticized perspective on personality is **Sigmund Freud's psychoanalytic theory**. Its primary focus is on uncovering and understanding the influence of **unconscious conflicts, needs and wishes, especially those rooted in early childhood**. Today, theories that adhere to this notion that unconscious processes determine thoughts, feelings, and behavior are more typically labeled **psychodynamic**. Because it is based on the existence of something, the unconscious mind, that is impossible to observe or test, many scientists dismiss psychoanalysis as a set of interesting ideas and nothing more. Still, it has had a huge cultural and historical impact, in part because of its emphasis on sexual conflict. This focus simultaneously catches the attention of the public and disillusions many psychologists who think Freud went overboard with his sex-based interpretations of personality development.

A commonly used metaphor for Freud's conception of the psyche is that of *an iceberg*. Upon viewing an iceberg, some may see it as a slab of ice floating on the surface of the water. They fail to realize that there is a much larger foundation of ice below the water line, without which the tip of the iceberg that we can see would not exist. According to Freud, that tip represents the **conscious mind**, while the submerged portion is the **unconscious mind**. He also postulated the existence of a **preconscious mind**. This is the part of the iceberg that is immediately below the surface, out of sight for the moment but easy to see if one looks for it. You may recall reference to the unconscious mind in our earlier study of Freudian dream interpretation. Freud claimed that dreams were the "royal road to the unconscious," telling us things we might not be willing to tell ourselves consciously. Sometimes, according to Freud, we also tell others things that we don't consciously wish to tell them but which come out anyway, as in a **Freudian Slip** like "That's a nice mess...uh...I mean *dress*, you're wearing."

(Sullivan, Levitre)

Freud believed that we have an instinctual life drive (**eros**) which is directed by a sexual energy called **libido**. We also have a death drive (**thanatos**) that accounts for some of our aggressive, self-destructive thoughts and behaviors. He also proposed the existence of three components of the psyche, the terms for which have become part of everyday language: id, ego and superego. **The id** is all below the water line, if we may continue with the iceberg metaphor. It is based on **the pleasure principle**, essentially looking to meet needs without restriction. It is like a little child who wants what she wants when she wants it. **The ego**, mostly but not entirely situated above the water line, develops as the child learns they cannot simply act on every impulse they have. The *ego* operates on **the reality principle**, working to balance the id's desire for immediate gratification with **the superego's** harsh judgment of how one ought to behave, while remaining mindful of the demands of the external world. The superego, the last of the three to develop (between the ages of three and six), is mostly under the surface and is often referred to as an internalized mother's voice. It is as demanding, unreasonable and relentless in its pursuits for perfection as the id is in its quest for gratification. Thus the id and superego are constantly battling each other leaving the ego to perform the delicate job of referee, keeping them both in balance.

According to Freud, the ego protects itself from pain and anxiety through the use of unconscious **defense mechanisms**. These often help us through difficult or traumatic periods in our lives, although they can be maladaptive (damaging to your survival or happiness) if carried to excess, because they often distort reality. Below is a summary of the defense mechanisms you are most likely to encounter on the AP Exam:

- **Denial**: Rejecting the truth of a painful reality, as in a person's refusal to accept a frightening medical diagnosis.

- **Displacement**: "Taking out" an emotion on a safe or more accessible target than the actual source of the emotion, as in punching a wall rather than confronting the boss who has angered you.

- **Projection**: Attributing something that we don't like about ourselves to someone else, as in accusing your best friends of being controlling and rigid when it is you who unconsciously fear your own tendencies toward such behavior.

- **Rationalization**: This is basically excuse making, as in telling yourself that you had to cheat on the exam because everyone else was probably going to do it as well.

- **Reaction formation**: Associating the word 'opposite' with this may help in your recall of it. Sometimes we unconsciously protect ourselves from undesirable emotions by behaving in ways that are exactly opposite of how we truly feel, as in showering a person with affection when we really, at heart, resent them.

- **Regression**: Figuratively going back in time to a safer, simpler way of being, as in assuming childlike behaviors when facing stress or trauma.

- **Repression**: This is essentially unconscious forgetting; something painful is buried so deeply that we no longer even know it is part of us, as sometimes occurs when an individual must deal with physical or sexual abuse in childhood.

- **Sublimation**: One way to help your recall of this is to associate the term with 'substitution'; an undesirable emotion or drive is unconsciously replaced by a socially acceptable one. Some Freudians might argue, for instance, that a surgeon is sublimating aggressive tendencies - making incisions is a socially acceptable and even heroic way to be aggressive.

- **Suppression**: This is essentially conscious forgetting, a conscious attempt to push something out of your mind. If you are asked about job prospects for the summer and at the moment you have none despite repeated efforts, you might say, "I'm trying not to think about that." In a sense, this is different from a "true" defense mechanism in that it is conscious.

Another part of Freud's theory is that of the five **psychosexual stages** of development: oral, anal, phallic, latency and genital. In each stage, the child's sexual energy (libido) is focused on a different area of the body. As development unfolds, an individual faces certain conflicts. If those conflicts are appropriately resolved, all is well and good. If, however, the individual remains **fixated** on a certain stage, it could have far-reaching, lifelong implications.

In the **oral stage** of development (birth to about 18 months), pleasure is derived from the mouth. If a child becomes fixated in this stage it may lead to behaviors in adulthood such as smoking, drinking, excessive eating, or a dependent personality.

In the **anal stage** (18 months to 3 years old), the focus is on the anus and defecation, especially as regards the ability to withhold or expel feces. If the parents were too harsh on the child during this stage, the child may become *anal retentive* which in later years might lead to excessive neatness, or being uptight, stingy and controlling. At the other extreme, overindulgent parenting may lead to *anally expulsive* behaviors such as messiness or impulsiveness in the adult. Here is an example of where Freud's theory has had influence on popular culture. If you have ever heard someone referred to as "anal", you have heard a Freudian reference. An "anal" person is basically Type A - uptight, time bound, driven. A Freudian would argue that such a person did not successfully resolve the anal stage of psychosexual development and is thus fixated on the control issues inherent in that stage.

During the **phallic stage**, the three to six year old learns that he can derive pleasure from stimulation of the genitals. It is at this time that the child faces the **Oedipus Complex** (you may also see this labeled Oedipal Complex). Freud theorized that boys at this stage unconsciously feel romantic attraction to their mothers and thus feel in competition with their fathers. This period creates tremendous anxiety, as the father is seen as an ever-present threat. In fact, Freud proposed that the boy's obsession with his mother stirs up fears that his father may castrate him if his desires are discovered. For girls, this period is marked by Freud's conception of **penis envy**, the phallic stage phenomenon in which girls notice and are jealous of a boy's penis. Some Freudians contend that this unconscious penis envy contributes to a fundamental sense of inferiority in females. There is also a version of the Oedipus Complex for females, usually called the **Electra Complex**. In it, the young girl is in unconscious competition with her mother for the father's affection and attention.

A child resolves this conflict in the phallic stage by **identifying** with their parent of the same sex, taking on many of that parent's characteristics and *internalizing* that parent's beliefs and morality. This period of *identification* plays an important role in the child's development of a superego, and it also greatly contributes to a child's gender identity or sense of being male or female. Freud believed that by the end of the phallic period the child's personality is essentially fully formed.

The child next sublimates his Oedipal urges, channeling them into socially acceptable activities, which leads him into a long **latency period**, in which sexual energy is submerged ('latent' essentially means 'hidden'). This lasts through the middle of childhood up to adolescence. The final stage of mature adult sexuality begins at that point – it is called the **genital stage**.

One critique of Freud's theory is that it is too male-centered. Others argue that the theory is built upon the study of a small number of patient case studies, and those patients are not a representative sample of the population. Still others point to a lack of scientific validity. Freud's ideas are not testable or *falsifiable* – it's hard to imagine how one could disprove the theory. For example, much of his theory rests on the notion of repression. But how would one test that it occurs? A Freudian must rely on a kind of circular argument – the evidence of unconscious conflict is that it is unconscious!

While there is plenty to criticize, most people accept the concept of an unconscious mind. This by itself is a major contribution. Freudian defense mechanisms also have a powerful resonance, although the degree to which they happen *unconsciously* is unclear.

## Neo-Freudians

Many of Freud's followers agreed with parts of his psychoanalytic theory but offered their own revisions. Some broke with Freud in arguing that culture and society play a more central role in our development, while others questioned the importance of unconscious sexual and aggressive drives. The **Neo-Freudians** led the way in the revision of pure Freudian theory.

One leading neo-Freudian, **Carl Jung**, was a staunch follower of Freud at one point but broke with Freud, at least in part, because he had a different conceptualization of the unconscious. Jung altered Freudian theory by postulating the existence of the **collective unconscious**. This is a set of common themes, or archetypes, inherited from the wealth of human experience and shared by all people. These **archetypes** include a sense of "femaleness" in males (**anima**) and a sense of "maleness" in females (**animus**). Jung also introduced archetypes like "the shadow" (the dark side we all have deep inside us), "the hero," "the wise old man" and "the nurturing mother." These archetypes are often expressed through a culture's mythology and folk tales.

Jung was much more positive about human nature than Freud, and he is also notable for being the first to describe extraversion and introversion as essential elements of personality.

**Karen Horney**, another neo-Freudian, was a leader in adding a female perspective to psychodynamic theory. She countered Freud's notion of penis envy by arguing that, while women were understandably envious of the status that males have in most societies, that this need not have anything to do with the possession of a penis. Horney also proposed that males may well be jealous, on an unconscious level, of the female ability to have children. This came to be called **womb envy**. Horney also theorized that we are all driven by an instinctual sense of **basic anxiety**, a kind of unease in a dangerous world, and she argued that **social and cultural factors** play a much larger role in the growth of personality than Freud had believed.

**Alfred Adler** was another psychoanalyst who eventually broke with Freud. We made brief reference to his birth order theory in the chapter on Developmental Psychology. He, like Freud, believed that personality is basically determined by age five, but he differed from Freud in his belief that social factors play a primary role in personality development. Adler may be best known for his conception of the **inferiority complex**. Adler contended that we all have a drive to be competent, but as children we develop a deep sense of inferiority. As we go through life we are thus *striving for superiority* to compensate for what we deem to be our inadequacies.

## Behaviorist Theory

You may recall from your study of Learning Theory that behaviorists (such as John Watson and B.F. Skinner) argued that the study of human phenomena should be limited to observable behaviors and how those behaviors have been shaped and reinforced through our environment. In the context of personality, radical behaviorists might argue that you aren't really born with specific traits. Rather, you have been conditioned through reinforcement to act certain ways in certain situations. You may act one way with your parents and a completely different way with your friends because your friends reinforce behaviors that your parents frown upon. If you are significantly different from your siblings in terms of personality, a behaviorist might note that the difference is because each person is exposed to different environments throughout life and those differing environments inevitably deliver significantly different reinforcements or punishments.

## Social-Cognitive Theory

Next we turn to **Social-Cognitive Theory**, which blends elements of the cognitive perspective, the behaviorist perspective and the sociocultural perspective. The focus here is on how the interlocking effects of thoughts, behaviors and environment influence your personality. Thus, you might see them referred to separately or in different combinations, such as *Cognitive-Behavioral Theory* or *Social Learning Theory*. Later, in the unit on Treatment of Psychological Disorders, you will learn about the cognitive-behavioral therapeutic approach, which will be easy for you to understand after you've finished this section.

**Albert Bandura's** theories may best exemplify this **combination of cognitive, social and behavioral elements**. You may remember his "Bobo Doll" study of observational/social learning in the unit on learning theory. Bandura believed that we learn and develop through active interaction with the environment. Thus, he went further than the radical behaviorists who would argue that our personalities are *solely* the result of conditioning. Bandura disagreed with the radical behaviorists in recognizing that there is a role for human thought processes and decision-making in learning. We develop through watching others in our surroundings, yes, but we also choose which environments to be in, which in turn exposes us to certain types of individuals and situations, which in turn leads us to make other choices, which in turn afford us specific types of experiences which <u>again</u> lead us toward particular choices, and so on. Bandura called this ongoing interaction **reciprocal determinism** and believed that our personality largely emerges from this process. Bandura also thought that an essential piece of this interaction involved **self-efficacy**, the sense that one can control outcomes in one's environment.

**Julian Rotter's** concepts of **internal and external locus of control** are related to the sense of self-efficacy. Rotter was a behavioral researcher, but he was not a radical behaviorist like Skinner. He acknowledged that human cognitions *were* involved in learning. Individuals with an internal locus of control, for example, have the feeling that to a large extent they can control the consequences of their behaviors. People with an external locus of control tend to see outcomes as being out of their control. A man with such a perspective might view his failure to get a job he desired as "just bad luck" or "all politics", rather than evaluating what he can do to effect a desired outcome in future situations. Rotter is basically talking about the difference between people who believe they can control their own fate and those who believe that there is little they can do to influence what happens to them. People who believe they have some control over most aspects of life tend to have better overall health and lower rates of depression. They also tend to be better at delaying gratification, and achieve more in school and at work.

Rotter's proposals are in turn linked to **Fritz Heider's attribution theory**. In it, Heider describes how individuals account for their behavior and the behavior of others - To what do they attribute their success or failure? A student who does poorly on an exam is making an internal, **dispositional attribution** if she says, "I could have and should have tried harder", and is making a **situational attribution** if she says, "The classroom was so noisy and the teacher is so bad I couldn't possibly do well." Later, in Social Psychology, we will explore the **fundamental attribution error (FAE)**, in which people tend to make dispositional attributions for negative behavior by others ("He cut me off in traffic because he's a loser!"), while ignoring *situational* factors ("Maybe he cut me off because he was about to miss his exit").

Another cognitive view of personality comes from **George Kelly**. He proposed the concept of **personal constructs**, which are individual views of good and bad, right and wrong, selfish and unselfish etc. that each of us builds ('constructs') for ourselves. According to Kelly, our personality is built from a collection of cognitive interpretations of life events. Just as several of us could watch the same movie and have starkly different views about it, we build very different interpretations of the world around us. For example – for some of us, silence is wonderful, while for others it can be quite unsettling.

In the unit on Learning Theory, you read about **Martin Seligman's** conception of **learned helplessness**. Seligman argues that if a person tries hard to affect some outcome and continually meets with failure, the individual will soon stop trying altogether. In a sense, they've made a cognitive judgment that they are helpless. Seligman also developed a theory of **explanatory styles**, which will play a role in your study of psychological disorders and treatment as well. According to Seligman, an individual with an **optimistic explanatory style** is more likely to tell herself that bad times are not likely to last and needn't effect one's entire life. The person tends not to blame themselves for unfortunate events that occur. People with a **pessimistic explanatory style** see bad times as stable and unlikely to change.

They also see painful events as impacting their entire lives and are more likely to blame themselves for the traumas they experience. It is therefore not surprising that Seligman and others have suggested a correlation between negative explanatory styles and the presence of depression while other research indicates a link between optimism, a boosted immune system and a longer life span.

### Humanistic Theory

The **Humanistic perspective** is the most upbeat and optimistic of all the personality theories. Opponents of it, in fact, argue that the theory is unrealistically positive about human motivations and ignores the human capacity for evil. They also contend that it, like psychoanalysis, is difficult to explore empirically; it's hard to measure humanistic concepts and phenomena. While critics remain, the growing domain of Positive Psychology has drawn heavily from the humanistic perspective, and researchers in this field are starting to develop reliable empirical tools to measure some of the elements that form the foundation of happiness and human striving.

Humanism is *person-centered* (later, you will learn about *client-centered therapy*, a humanistic approach to treatment of psychological disorders). It explores our inner capacity for growth and self-fulfillment with a focus on individual human potential. It has been called "The Third Force" in psychology, developing as a kind of response to the rather pessimistic psychoanalytic and behavioral perspectives. Humanists contend that those perspectives were far too deterministic, and underestimated (or denied) the importance of free will. Humanists such as **Carl Rogers** and **Abraham Maslow** believe that people generally strive to reach their fullest potential. As you saw in the last unit on Motivation and Emotion, Maslow called this **self-actualization**.

Rogers felt that a person could reach that goal through relationships characterized by **unconditional positive regard,** or **UPR**. Unfortunately, many relationships are built instead on **conditions of worth**, in which one "loves" another only as long as they meet certain requirements and expectations. Rogers also emphasized the role of one's **self-concept** (how one thinks of oneself) in being happy. He believed that the most contented individuals were those who had the smallest gap between their **ideal self** and their **real self**. Those who have much incongruence between how they would like to be and how they actually are tend to have a sense of dissatisfaction with their lives. Relationships with UPR help to close the gap between the real and ideal selves, giving us a stronger self-concept and helping us to become fully functioning adults.

## Culture and Personality

To what extent does society and culture shape our behavior and personality? It won't surprise you to learn that much of how people respond to the question, "Who are you?" is greatly influenced by the culture(s) to which they have been exposed. Cultures vary greatly in the degree to which they value **collectivism** versus **individualism**. *Individualistic* societies such as those in North America and Western Europe tend to emphasize individual achievement, and focus on giving priority to personal goals. Independence, leadership and self-fulfillment are highly valued in such cultures. *Collectivist* societies (such as China, Japan and many others) are more likely to value group goals over individual pursuits, and often define themselves in terms of their role in the context of the group. They may place more emphasis on group harmony and obligation rather than uniqueness and individualism. These environmental factors influence the type of personality traits that are encouraged and expressed.

## Name Hall of Fame

There are quite a few names in this unit, and many of them would be certain inductees in any psychologist's name hall of fame. Even those who see psychoanalysis only as an interesting *philosophy* that is not scientifically rigorous enough to be accepted by psychologists would likely still vote **Sigmund Freud** into the hall of fame for his historical and cultural importance. As we saw in learning theory, **B.F. Skinner** easily makes it into the hall of fame as well. You also learned about **Albert Bandura** in that unit. He's a tougher call in terms of hall membership, but here he is in a second unit in the course, so it's best to know his name and not just his theories of observational learning, self-efficacy and reciprocal determinism. **Carl Jung** probably makes it into the hall too, especially since Jungian psychoanalytic approaches are more popular now than strict Freudian methods. It's a good bet that you'll meet the other major neo-Freudians, **Karen Horney** and **Alfred Adler**, on the AP Exam, but it's doubtful that you will have to directly recall their names in order to get an item correct.

Humanists **Abraham Maslow** and **Carl Rogers** would get a majority of votes on the hall of fame ballot. Their names come up in more than one unit of the course, which is reason enough to familiarize yourself with them. Then things get a bit trickier; is **Martin Seligman** in? If he is, then **Fritz Heider** may make it too. You're safe if you only remember personal constructs and locus of control and not the names **George Kelly** and **Julian Rotter**, but what about all the trait theorists - **Gordon Allport**, **Hans Eysenck** and **Raymond Cattell**? In those cases too, you almost certainly do not need to know their names in order to answer questions correctly.

## Essay Themes

As you saw in the chapter on development, the '**Nature, nurture or false dichotomy?**' theme is a big one. Since 1992, the first year of the AP Psychology Exam, one of the more popular types of free response item has been along the lines of **"Explain anxiety/ depression/ etc. from each of the following perspectives: psychoanalytic, behavioral, etc."** Having a sound grasp of each of these major schools of psychological thought will serve you very well on the AP Exam and in any psychology course you take in the future. On side two of the test prep graphic organizer for this unit, you can see many links to other units. (Some of which you have not yet studied - for example, in the next unit we will explore various tests that are used to measure personality). That quadrant of the test prep will be useful to you in preparing for free response items on the AP Exam.

## Themes in Personality Theory

- Nature, Nurture or False Dichotomy?
- Personality – stable over time?
- Temperament
- Which predominates – Personality or Situation?

## Trait Theory

- FOCUS: Largely inborn characteristics and tendencies
- "The Big Five" O.C.E.A.N.
- Allport and
  - Cardinal traits
  - Central traits
  - Secondary traits
- Cattell and "The 16 P.F."
  - Note 'factor analysis'
- Eysenck and P.E.N.
- Type A and Type B Theory
- CRITICISMS?

## Freudian Psychoanalytic Theory

- FOCUS: Unconscious conflict, esp. from early childhood
- Freudian Slips
- Eros, Thanatos, Libido
- The Iceberg Analogy
- Id, Ego, Superego
- Psychosexual Stages:
  - Oral
  - Anal
  - Phallic
  - Latency
  - Genital
- Defense Mechanisms:
  - Denial   - Displacement
  - Repression   - Projection
  - Identification
  - Sublimation
  - Regression
  - Reaction formation
  - Rationalization
- CRITICISMS?

## The Neo-Freudians

- Karen Horney
  - Basic anxiety
  - Womb envy
- Carl Jung
  - Archetypes in the collective unconscious
- Alfred Adler
  - The inferiority complex
- CRITICISMS?

# Personality *(Continued)*

## Behaviorist Theory

- FOCUS:
  We "learn" our personalities through conditioning and observation

- Bandura and social learning

- Skinner and "Radical Behaviorism"

- CRITICISMS?

## Social-Cognitive Theory

- FOCUS:
  Our thinking judgments, self perceptions; social /environmental impact

- Heider and attribution theory

- Rotter and "locus of control"

- Bandura and social learning
  - Self-efficacy
  - Reciprocal determinism

- Kelly's personal constructs

- Seligman and learned helplessness; explanatory styles

- CRITICISMS?

## Humanistic Theory

- FOCUS:
  Optimistic outlook on human aspirations and potential

- Abraham Maslow
  - Free will; human potential
  - Goal: self actualization

- Carl Rogers
  - The value of U.P.R., vs. conditions of worth

- CRITICISMS?

## Links to Other Units

- "Testing and Indiv. Differ.":
  - Projective tests
  - The MMPI, etc.
  - Reliability, Validity

- "BioPsych":
  - Genetic predispositions
  - Arousal levels

- "Consciousness":
  - Freud on dreams

- "Learning Theory":
  - Skinner, Bandura

- "Development":
  - Twin studies

198

## Practice Items

•    THESE SECTION ITEMS ARE **NOT** IN ORDER OF DIFFICULTY!

1. "Aggression is a human instinct; society may be able to control it to some extent, but we will never eliminate it, since we all have an unconscious pull toward it." This statement would most likely come from a proponent of which of the following perspectives?

   (A) Psychoanalytic
   (B) Behaviorist
   (C) Humanist
   (D) Social-cognitive
   (E) Trait Theory

2. Reaction formation

   (A) results from an internalization of the ways significant others view you
   (B) helps to account for why many individuals develop a positive explanatory style
   (C) is a predictable response to frustrated attempts at self-actualization
   (D) is a response that individuals consciously generate in order to respond to the external demands of a challenging situation
   (E) is a defense mechanism that unconsciously protects one from unpleasant feelings or cognitions

3. With which of the following would a humanist most likely agree?

   (A) "A musician must make music, an artist must paint, a poet must write, if he is to be ultimately at peace with himself."
   (B) "Give me a child and I'll shape him into anything."
   (C) "A man who has been the indisputable favorite of his mother keeps for life the feeling of a conqueror."
   (D) "Once established, reputations do not easily change."
   (E) "I don't sing because I'm happy. I'm happy because I sing."

4.  A man who is wrestling with guilt over unethical practices he must carry out in his work speaks loudly and often about the unethical practices of those in other professions. Sigmund Freud would likely characterize this as

    (A) sublimation
    (B) projection
    (C) suppression
    (D) identification
    (E) passive aggressiveness

5.  "General laws of behavior and experience that apply to all individuals are not very useful; people are simply a collection of largely inborn characteristics that are stable across situations." This statement best summarizes which of the following personality perspectives?

    (A) Behaviorist
    (B) Neo-Freudian
    (C) Freudian
    (D) Social Learning Theory
    (E) Trait Theory

6.  Which of the following would serve as the best evidence in support of Gordon Allport's concept of cardinal traits?

    (A) Respondents to a survey indicate internal tension between their life goals and the activities they are currently engaged in
    (B) Results from an experiment support the notion that an individual's self perception tends to match the perception of those around them
    (C) Evidence from several naturalistic observations suggests that individual personality characteristics vary substantially from situation to situation
    (D) A longitudinal study suggests that personality characteristics can be significantly affected by major life events
    (E) A statistically significant percentage of volunteers score identically on two different tests for extraversion administered twenty years apart

7. Riley has a large piece of pastry at breakfast, even though he has promised himself to follow a stricter diet. He has two more large slices of the same pastry later in the day, telling himself, "I already messed up my diet, I may as well enjoy myself today and start fresh tomorrow." This is an example of which Freudian defense mechanism?

    (A) Rationalization
    (B) Sublimation
    (C) Repression
    (D) Projection
    (E) Displacement

8. In Albert Bandura's conception of personality, reciprocal determinism

    (A) leads inevitably to a sense of superiority
    (B) influences one's sense of the ideal self
    (C) contributes to an exaggerated sense of hostility
    (D) is marked by a constant interaction between basic elements of personality, the behaviors one chooses, and environmental influences
    (E) implies that one's personality is determined by a mixture of unconscious motives and the drive for self-actualization

9. An individual who believes that they essentially have control over occurrences and outcomes in their lives are said to have

    (A) a reactive temperament
    (B) an internal locus of control
    (C) a psychosexual fixation
    (D) a pessimistic explanatory style
    (E) a highly developed superego

10. One major criticism of Freudian psychoanalytic theory is that it

    (A) describes individual personality characteristics but not their origins
    (B) focuses too much on sexual conflict in adulthood
    (C) assumes that all behaviors are learned through conditioning
    (D) is excessively optimistic about human nature
    (E) is essentially untestable and unmeasurable

11. The "Big Five" personality characteristics are

    (A) outgoingness, concern, excitability, anxiety, naturalness
    (B) openness, conscientiousness, neuroticism, psychoticism and stability
    (C) openness, conscientiousness, extroversion, agreeableness and neuroticism
    (D) extroversion, neuroticism, psychoticism, anxiety, hostility
    (E) anxiety, hostility, sociability, dependability, emotionality

12. According to Sigmund Freud, deciding whether to return an extra $100 a bank teller accidentally gave you is a conflict between

    (A) conscious and preconscious
    (B) libido and latency
    (C) id and superego
    (D) psychoticism and neuroticism
    (E) prototypes and archetypes

13. "The goal of the human soul is conquest, perfection, security, superiority." This statement is most illustrative of

    (A) Carl Jung's theory of animus in the collective unconscious
    (B) Albert Bandura's reciprocal determinism
    (C) Karen Horney's concept of basic anxiety
    (D) B.F. Skinner's radical behaviorism
    (E) Alfred Adler's inferiority complex

14. "The real problem is not whether machines think but whether men do." This quote illustrates a fundamental difference between the

    (A) real self and the ideal self
    (B) cognitive and behavioral perspectives
    (C) id and superego
    (D) Freudian view and the Neo-Freudian view
    (E) situationists and trait theorists

15. According to a psychoanalyst, which of the following would be a probable result of fixation in the anal stage of psychosexual development?

    (A) Extreme narcissism
    (B) Excessive neatness and obsessiveness
    (C) Compulsive eating behaviors
    (D) Confusion about one's gender identity
    (E) Feelings of inferiority

# Chapter 11
# *Testing and Individual Differences*

### Introduction

This topic is treated differently from textbook to textbook and from course to course. Sometimes, theories about intelligence, which are a large part of this unit, are handled within the chapter on Thought and Language. In other cases, intelligence is given a separate treatment along with a look at assessments of that elusive concept and other types of assessments used in psychology. Occasionally, part of that assessment section is incorporated into the unit on Personality Theory, as there is much overlap between the two subjects. Here, we will try to tell you what you need to know about all psychological assessments and the many attempts to define 'intelligence' under the Advanced Placement Psychology curriculum umbrella of Testing and Individual Differences. You can expect to encounter five to seven questions from this unit on the AP Exam.

Developmental psychologist Jean Piaget once said, "Intelligence is what you do when you don't know what to do." Some high school psychology students dispute that, placing more emphasis on the acquisition and retention of information in their attempts to define 'intelligence'. How much of intelligence involves memory? How much is it about planning strategies to solve new problems? How much of it is not about thinking, per se, at all? For example - the great American psychologist William James defined 'genius' as, "little more than the faculty of perceiving in an unhabitual way." Here are some more questions you might consider as you embark on this unit:

- Can we come up with one definition of intelligence, or is it so multifaceted that three or four lines in a textbook simply cannot capture its complexity? Since 'intelligence' is a social construct, many question whether any one definition of it could ever be meaningful cross-culturally.

- Are **savants** (individuals with serious cognitive limitations such as mental retardation or autism who possess a remarkable talent in, for example, art or music) intelligent? If not, would you say they are unintelligent? Or does the term not apply at all in such cases?

- Is intelligence genetically transmitted, or is it more the result of socialization and learning?

These issues form the crux of the first portion of this unit, while the second part focuses on how we assess things like intelligence, personality and learning.

## What is Intelligence?

In 1904, **Charles Spearman** postulated that there is such a thing as **general intelligence**, or *g*, that can be empirically assessed. He noticed that people who excelled in one area of mental ability tended to do well on most other cognitive tasks. He concluded that one common mental factor must underlie the ability to perform well on other more specific tests such as verbal, analytical and spatial tasks. Thus, specific abilities (which Spearman referred to as 's') such as mathematical computation, problem solving and reading and writing are supported by a learner's overall general intelligence. Spearman utilized **factor analysis** to support his theory. Factor analysis is a statistical technique that looks at correlations between two (or more) variables. This measures the extent to which there are common factors that are present in something like *g*. For example, if we find that scores for several subtests are highly correlated, we might assume they are each measuring a common underlying factor or ability.

In the middle of the 20th century, **Raymond Cattell** proposed a view that many still accept today. Cattell believed that there were two factors of general intelligence - crystallized intelligence and fluid intelligence. **Crystallized intelligence** is the ability to absorb, retain and access information, while **fluid intelligence** refers to the ability to process information quickly and solve problems one has not seen before. Fluid intelligence involves speed and flexibility in problem solving. Longitudinal research indicates that crystallized intelligence generally increases over time, while fluid intelligence declines with age. Similarly, over time physical flexibility and speed inevitably decline, even though the older person still knows *how* to do the things they could do as a younger person.

Other early researchers broadened the scope of the concept by postulating the existence of a wider range of components in intelligence. **Louis Thurstone** contended that there were seven **primary mental abilities**. He, like Spearman, used factor analysis to identify these seven clusters of intelligence. **J.P. Guilford** offered a **cube model** that included over 120 features of intelligence; his cube resembled a Rubik's Cube that was segmented into blocks, each of which represented a type of intellectual ability.

Contemporary views of intelligence have tended toward theories of multiple intelligences, as opposed to defining intelligence as one general ability. **Robert Sternberg's triarchic theory** features three kinds of intelligence: *creative*, *practical* and *analytical*. *Analytical intelligence* includes abstract reasoning, evaluation, verbal abilities and most of the basic skills you associate with success in school. Most intelligence tests tend to focus on measurement of this type of intelligence. *Creative intelligence* involves one's ability to generate new ideas and effectively solve novel problems. *Practical intelligence* includes being able to effectively manage situations in everyday life and solve real world problems. Sternberg believes that each of these intelligences can be empirically assessed. He also notes that each is independent of the others. For example, one could score very high on practical intelligence, but that score may not significantly correlate with the other two types of intelligence.

Another contemporary theory also suggests the existence of many types of intelligence. **Howard Gardner's theory of multiple intelligences** (often abbreviated as **MI**) has become enormously popular, especially amongst educators. Gardner proposes eight different types of intelligence:

- *Linguistic* (This is sometimes simply referred to as "word smart")
- *Logical-mathematical* (You guessed it – "number smart", or "reasoning smart")
- *Musical* (This is marked by sensitivity towards sounds, pitch and rhythms. People with musical intelligence would be skilled at performing, writing and appreciating music)
- *Spatial* (The ability to accurately perceive, understand and reconstruct visual images - an architect or an interior designer would likely have good spatial intelligence)
- *Bodily-kinesthetic* (Accomplished dancers, gymnasts and rock climbers would score well here)
- *Interpersonal* (Understanding and empathizing with others)
- *Intrapersonal* (The capacity and willingness to look inside and understand one's own feelings and motivations)
- *Naturalistic* (The capacity to understand and categorize different elements of the natural world - a farmer or an archeologist would likely possess naturalistic intelligence).

Gardner argues that public education's tendency to focus most on verbal and mathematical intelligence does not do justice to other equally valuable kinds of intelligence. He also notes that each type of intelligence is independent of the others - it is quite possible to excel in one but not the others. One might ask if high school grade point averages and other such "report card" measures take that claim into account.

Critics of Gardner's theory question his use of the term 'intelligence'. Many ask if the bodily-kinesthetic intelligence of an athlete or craftsman is really a kind of intelligence in the same way verbal reasoning is. Some critics claim that Gardner's intelligences are more aptly labeled 'talents', and are too broad to measure empirically. Others believe that theories like Gardner's have broadened the definition of intelligence so much that it now wrongly encompasses any valued ability.

Recently, researchers have also focused much attention on **emotional intelligence (EI)**. In many ways, EI (tests for which measure **EQ**, short for emotional quotient, as compared to intelligence quotient, or IQ) builds on Gardner's concepts of interpersonal and intrapersonal intelligence. For Gardner, interpersonal intelligence involves awareness of and sensitivity towards others. Intrapersonal intelligence features the disposition to look inside oneself, to explore one's own emotions and insights, and to appropriately govern one's feelings. In combination, that's a fair definition of EI. Some psychologists believe that emotional intelligence is more valuable and adaptive in our present-day world than traditional cognitive views of intelligence. Peter Salovey and John Mayer have identified four major components to EI. First, one needs to be able to accurately identify emotions in themselves and others. Second, one needs an awareness of how emotions shape thinking and decision-making. Next, one must be able to understand and analyze the emotions they are experiencing. Finally, one needs the self-control to regulate ones' emotions. Researchers studying EI continue to refine tests to measure this construct. Thus far, they have provided some evidence that high levels of EI are positively correlated with success in marriage, education, careers and parenting.

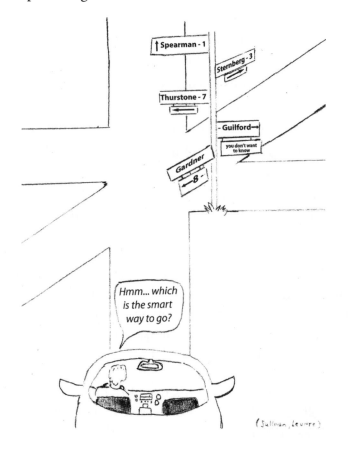

**Intelligence Testing**

As a student, you know all too well the role that testing can play in one's life. **Psychometrics** is a field that studies the measurement of many human characteristics, including cognitive abilities and personality traits. In this section, we focus on the evolution of intelligence testing. Later, we briefly look at some psychometric measures of personality.

It is obviously difficult to measure intelligence, in light of the many competing interpretations of what it is. Further, many fear the implications of attempting to assess such an elusive concept. Does a single score on any intelligence test tell us something valuable? If it does, how should the score be used? Should a child who has scored poorly on an IQ test be told his or her score? How about a child who has scored exceptionally well? Should a schoolteacher have access to a student's IQ score? What about the danger of **the self-fulfilling prophecy**, in which a teacher's expectations for a student, whatever they may be, actually influences that student's self-image and performance? If teachers and students are not given access to IQ scores, who is, and why?

French psychologist **Alfred Binet** is usually considered the father of intelligence testing. He was the first person, working with Theodore Simon, to develop tests to assess one's ability to learn, which some would say is a nice shorthand definition of intelligence. Binet and Simon were working to build a test that could help French officials identify children who might struggle in the public schools. Binet hoped these tests would identify students with special needs - he did not believe they necessarily measured intelligence. Binet's test created normed scores (averages) for children of different ages. Then the scores of each student who took the test were compared to the pre-established norms to see if the child was progressing at the rate of a "normal" child of that age.

Binet's tests were later translated into English and amended by **Lewis Terman** at Stanford University. **The Stanford-Binet Test** became the first widely used intelligence test. It yielded an individual's **IQ**, or intelligence quotient, which was built on the concept of **mental age**. This was a comparison of a child's chronological age to the previously determined average mental ability for that age (the **norm**). For example, a child of seven years old who scored like the typical seven-year-old on the intelligence test was said to have a mental age of seven. Since 100 had been normed as the average score for intelligence, this would give the child an IQ of one hundred. The formula for the intelligence quotient was *mental age divided by chronological age, multiplied by one hundred* - you can now see why it is called IQ, if you recall what a quotient is in mathematics. Thus, a 10-year-old child who demonstrated a mental age of 13 on the Stanford-Binet had an IQ of 130 and a 10-year-old child with a mental age of 6 had an IQ of 60.

As you might already have surmised, the concept of mental age soon was viewed as one of the flaws in these early attempts to measure intelligence. It worked well enough for young people, but what happened when you tried to evaluate a 17-year-old's intelligence as compared to other 17-year-olds? Is there a significant and measurable difference between the mental age of a 17-year-old and an 18-year-old, for example? The problem only intensifies as the years pass; it seems almost silly to speak of the typical difference in mental ability between a 43-year-old and a 45-year-old. To remedy this, a more sophisticated statistical attempt to compare one's performance and ability with others developed. This is called the **standard age score, or SAS**.

The Stanford-Binet Intelligence Test has been revised and re-normed many times and is still in use today, but an even more commonly used set of intelligence tests is named after their developer, David Wechsler. In the 1930's, Wechsler began to try to address some of the weaknesses in the Stanford-Binet. One of those was the Stanford-Binet's dependence on language. This returns us to the question, "What is intelligence?" While most people would agree that intelligence, at least in part, does involve the ability to communicate, to understand vocabulary and to respond to questions verbally, Wechsler saw that intelligence was more than that as well. He developed performance tasks, which were not dependent on the understanding of the language of the tester, or of any language at all. The Wechsler assessments include two types of subtest - performance tasks and verbal tasks. The performance scale involves picture completion, picture arrangement, object assembly, mazes and more. The verbal scale includes tests on general information, digit span, vocabulary, comprehension and more. The Wechsler tests provide separate scores for different clusters of ability, which can help identify areas of significant cognitive strengths or weaknesses. This test also yields one composite score that reflects your overall performance.

Wechsler is also credited with being the first to create intelligence tests specific to different age groups. Early versions of the Stanford-Binet fell into the "one size fits all" category. Today, the Wechsler Preschool and Primary Scale of Intelligence (**WPPSI**), the Wechsler Intelligence Scale for Children (**WISC**) and the Wechsler Adult Intelligence Scale (**WAIS**) are the most widely used IQ tests.

Early on, individuals deemed to have very high and very low IQ scores were seen as exceptional. We now use the term "**gifted**" for those who score very well (the IQ cutoff today is usually a minimum of 135) and "**retarded**" for those who score on the low end of the scale. The American Psychiatric Association has established the following IQ ranges for various levels of retardation: 55-70 is *mild* retardation, 40 to 55 is *moderate* retardation, 25 to 40 is *severe* retardation and below 25 is *profound* retardation. In addition to low IQ, mental retardation is also marked by significant trouble adapting to the normal demands of living independently. The term 'retarded' has acquired strongly negative connotations in modern society. It has sadly been used in everyday language as a term of derision, which makes many uncomfortable with its use in any context, but it is still the accepted label in psychology for individuals who have substantial cognitive limitations. Early attempts at similar labeling had met the same fate - *idiot*, *imbecile* and *moron* are still commonly used words of insult, but they were originally used to identify different levels of what we now call retardation. Efforts are underway to change this label, and today it is not uncommon to see mental retardation instead labeled *intellectual disability*.

In the field of education, some attention has been given to **exceptional children** at both extremes, with more emphasis historically placed on those who were judged to be retarded or disabled. Some psychologists have argued that gifted children are as "different" in their way as mentally retarded children are in theirs and advocate a strong and perhaps equal commitment to both groups. This might serve as an energizing discussion topic in your class. As you may recall from the chapter on Statistics and Research Methodology, Lewis Terman and his colleagues conducted a notable study of gifted children beginning in 1921. Terman looked longitudinally (spanning over 80 years!) at a group of 1,500 children with IQ scores above 135. Contrary to the stereotypical belief that gifted children were socially inept and maladjusted, Terman found that these high scorers were quite well adjusted. In comparison with the general population, they attained higher levels of education and employment, and were happier, healthier and more emotionally stable.

You may recall the description of a **normal distribution** in the unit on statistics and research methodology. Below we provide a look at a **perfect normal curve** with percentile distributions and the theoretical example of a perfectly symmetrical curve of IQ scores. Some theorists would argue that if we could somehow assess the IQ of every human being and then plot each score, we *would* have a perfectly symmetrical distribution, with the largest percentage of individuals (a little over 68%) falling within one standard deviation away from the mean in either direction (the standard deviation for intelligence scores has been calculated at 15 points, and, as you saw above, the mean IQ score is one hundred; thus, one standard deviation below the mean is 100 - 15, or 85, two standard deviations below the mean would be 85 - 15, or 70, and so on). Only a very small percentage of scores on a perfect normal curve would fall at either extreme.

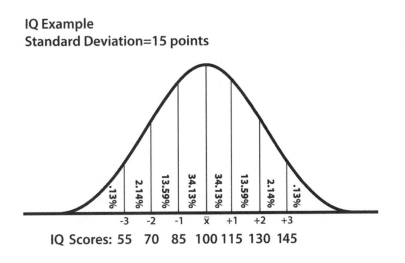

IQ Example
Standard Deviation=15 points

A quick quiz on the above visual representation:

  A. If someone scores three standard deviations above the mean in this IQ distribution, what is her score?

  B. If someone scores at the 97th percentile in this distribution, what is his score?

  C. If someone's IQ score is 85, what approximate percentile is she at?

*Answers: A. 145, B. 130, C. 16ᵗʰ*

### Issues and Controversies in the Study of Intelligence

In previous units, we've discussed the famed nature vs. nurture debate, and that issue confronts us once again in this unit. Discussion of intelligence continues to spark vigorous arguments about the extent to which intelligence is fixed at birth, and how much environment contributes to one's intelligence. Some support a *fixed model* for intelligence, arguing that it is mostly innate and unchanging across the lifespan. Others subscribe to a *growth model*. They believe environmental interventions can strongly impact the development of intelligence.

*"I have no patience with the hypothesis... that babies are born pretty much alike."*
*(Francis Galton)*

Francis Galton of Great Britain was a multi-talented geographer and meteorologist who is also credited with proposing the first fingerprint identification system, and recognizing the value of systematic twin studies. But he is most remembered for his view that many human talents (such as intelligence) are inborn, and tend to fall on a normal curve. In the 1880's, Galton first used the term 'eugenics' in reference to selective breeding of humans. Like many others, he believed it might be advantageous to encourage certain people to breed together (*positive eugenics*), while discouraging others from doing so (*negative eugenics*). While Galton himself warned against the possible excesses of such a program, numerous eugenics societies emerged across the globe in the 20th century. You won't see it in many history textbooks, but an American Eugenics Society functioned in the United States for fifty years, folding only in 1973. Today, many theorists still argue about the genetic origins of intelligence, and the extent to which that general characteristic (if there even is a general characteristic we can rightly call 'intelligence') is normally distributed in society. Obviously, there are significant social implications inherent in such issues.

Many researchers have concluded that intelligence is 50-60% a matter of **heritability**; that is, that 50 to 60 percent of the *difference between individuals* in intelligence is due to genetics. This does not say that 50-60% of your IQ is a matter of genetics. Rather, it means that 50-60% of the IQ differences between you and your classmates can be attributed to heredity.

Twin studies lend support to the nature side of this argument, especially studies of identical twins that were separated at birth and raised in different environments. When you compare the IQ scores of such twins years later they are nearly identical, even though they experienced different "nurturance" growing up. Adoption studies also support a strong genetic influence on intelligence. In longitudinal studies, adopted children's IQ scores correlate much more strongly with their biological parents than with their adoptive parents. This trend tends to strengthen as the child gets older.

Those on the nurture side of the debate point out that *even if* heredity accounts for 50% of individual differences in IQ, intelligence is clearly not cast in stone. That still leaves a significant amount of variability unaccounted for, and those differences are likely the result of environmental influences. Even height, a trait that would seem almost exclusively attributable to heredity, can be affected by environment. Increases in average height over the last century have happened too quickly to be attributed to evolution. Most contend that people are taller today because of better nutrition and overall improvements in health management. This demonstrates the potential power of environment in influencing our genetic blueprint.

Supporters of the nurture view often point to the **Flynn Effect**. James Flynn found that IQ scores in America (and 19 other nations) have steadily risen in the last half-century. He noticed that each time modern intelligence tests have been re-normed, a test-taker needed to get more items correct to obtain the average score of 100. Today, if a representative sample of people took an intelligence test from 1950, their average would be well over 100 - as high as 120 by some estimates. Though the cause of this phenomenon is not clearly understood, many speculate that the rising scores are due to a host of environmental factors. They cite better nutrition, more stimulating surroundings, increased access to schooling and increased cultural focus on testing as possible reasons for the Flynn Effect.

To bridge the divide between the nature and nurture viewpoints, some have proposed that perhaps we are genetically endowed with a specific range for intelligence. Our environment determines whether we reach the high or low end of that range. Some researchers call this genetically determined limit a *reaction range*, and have further postulated that it applies to other traits, not only intelligence.

Another area of controversy stems from the differences in performance between different racial groups on intelligence tests. Within the US, average differences between groups have been as high as 15 points. Some have used this argument as evidence that certain races are indeed different in terms of cognitive capabilities. Others reject that notion and note that similar trends in IQ scores emerge when we compare groups of different socioeconomic status. It is also important to note that intelligence **differences within groups** far exceed the **differences between groups**. For example, while whites may score 10-15 points higher on intelligence tests than blacks, the difference *within* each group is significantly larger than the variability between the groups.

Recent discoveries on **stereotype threat** have complicated this discussion. Stereotype threat refers to a self-fulfilling prophecy in which minority groups, well aware of negative stereotypes about their group's performance on a given test, feel apprehension and anxiety that lead them to perform poorly on the test. Perhaps they are worried that a poor performance will confirm pre-existing stereotypes, and that concern actually inhibits their performance. For example, in tests of mathematical and engineering ability, women tend to do less well than men when they take the test in a mixed gender environment. However, if women take the tests without the presence of males, their scores actually match those of men. Researchers argue that women have been made aware of the notion that males are more gifted in math and engineering, and that knowledge hurts their performance while taking the test side-by-side with men. While no single factor accounts for group differences in testing, it seems likely that stereotype threat contributes to that variability.

You might discuss with your classmates the concept of **test bias**. You may focus on intelligence tests, but could also easily diverge into biases inherent in the SAT, the ACT and other assessments with which you are familiar. Do assessments favor those of certain cultures? Are any commonly used assessments biased against some racial and ethnic groups? Are there gender biases in such standardized tests? Does the language alone in a test create a biased assessment? Is there, for example, a bias in favor of those who speak certain kinds or dialects of English?

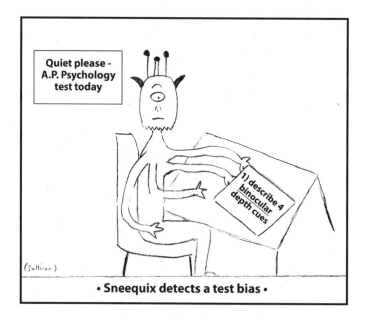

### Other Assessments

Some tests are designed to measure **achievement** - that is, mastery of some body of knowledge or skills. Most exams you take in school, including the AP Psychology Exam, fall into this category. Other tests purport to measure **aptitude** - the ability to do or learn something in the future. The SAT is designed to test your aptitude for college. Vocational tests that high school and college students sometimes take supposedly measure your ability to do well in specific jobs. Some assessments strictly rely on **paper and pencil** items, with which you've become so familiar in the course of your schooling. Other assessments are more **performance based.** You would probably agree that a paper and pencil test for a driver's license is a necessary but not complete method of evaluating whether one should receive a license. One still needs to actually demonstrate the ability to drive a car; in this case, actual *performance* matters most of all in assessing that ability.

Some assessments in psychology are **group tests**, while others are **individual tests**. Group tests, like the SAT and the ACT, are given to many people at once. Individual tests are proctored in a one-on-one setting; both the Stanford-Binet and Wechsler intelligence tests fit this category. You'll also want to know the differences between **speed** and **power tests**. A speed test is timed and usually consists of more items than the typical person can finish in the allotted time. This type of test relies heavily on fluid intelligence, which we described earlier. Power tests present items that become increasingly difficult as the test goes on. They are designed to measure the upper limit of your ability in the area being tested.

Two personality assessments you should be familiar with in preparation for the AP Exam are **The MMPI** (The Minnesota Multiphasic Personality Inventory) and **The Myers-Briggs Inventory**. Both are called *self-report inventories* because the subjects are reporting on their own tendencies. The MMPI was originally designed to diagnose mental disorders, and it is still the most widely used assessment tool among clinicians. It has over 500 true or false items designed to identify characteristics of personality and behavior. The Myers-Briggs Inventory is a "forced choice" test; this means you are asked to choose which of two statements is most representative of your thoughts, feelings or behaviors. While the Myers-Briggs test remains quite popular (over one million people take it each year), the results from the test are unreliable. According to one study, if you took the Myers-Briggs test today and then took it one month later, your results would differ more than 50% of the time, which would indicate that you possess significantly different personality traits from one month to another.

You may also recall earlier references to **projective tests** of personality, so called because the subject's impression of ambiguous stimuli (such as a set of ink blots) is thought to "say something" about that individual. The theory is that subjects "project" truths about themselves onto the picture, photograph or ink blot they are shown. **The Rorschach Test** offers an array of inkblots for the subject to identify or describe. **The TAT** (Thematic Apperception Test) requires subjects to tell stories about photographs or drawings. Other projective assessments ask subjects to complete unfinished stories and sentences, or to draw pictures of, for example, themselves or their homes. Such tests have detailed systems for evaluation of responses; it is a misconception to think that those who administer projective tests simply offer a subjective "feel" about what responses represent. Still, questions remain as to their validity - Do they really measure what they claim to measure? Might the interpreter of the responses project their *own* feelings onto the interpretations? Can we predict anything meaningful about one's behavior or personality from these tests?

(Sullivan, Lewistre)

### Characteristics of All Sound Assessments

Good tests share three basic characteristics; they are standardized, reliable and valid. All of the intelligence tests we've discussed are **standardized**. This means that they are given in the same manner, under the same time limitations and with the identical instructions from administration to administration. Standardized tests also have protocols to ensure that scoring is uniform. Without such standardization, the issue of possible confounding variables would arise (you may remember this concept from our first unit on research methodology). If, for example, there were no standardized instructions for the SAT, one group of students might outperform another not because they were superior on the test but because they were given more extensive directions or more time to complete the assessment.

The establishment of **norms** is another component of standardization. Norms are established by administering an assessment to a representative sample of individuals similar to the population for whom the test is designed. The scores from that sample become the standard to which later test takers can compare their own scores. If there were no norms, you would have no sense of what a 500 on the SAT math section or a 22 on the ACT meant.

All legitimate assessments must also be reliable and valid. **Reliability** refers to the extent to which a test yields consistent results. Some types of reliability may also refer to the consistency of the scoring procedures. **Validity** refers to whether or not the test actually assesses what it claims to assess. For the purposes of the AP Exam, it is probably enough for you to know the basic difference between those two concepts, but a summary of some specific types of reliability and validity follows.

## Reliability

- **Test/retest reliability:** Does the score you received on a test correlate with your later performance on the same test? For example, your score at age 18 on the *WAIS* would likely be highly correlated with your score if you took the test at age twenty-five, thirty-five and so on. The higher the correlation between these scores, the stronger the test/retest reliability.

- **Equivalent form reliability:** Does the score you receive on a test correlate with the score you receive on another test of the same material? For example, if you try the SAT in October and then again in November, you would not take the exact same test, but an equivalent form. The authors of the SAT contend that in that short period of time your scores on both assessments should be pretty much the same.

- **Split-half reliability:** Does your score on the first half of a test correlate with your score on the second half of the test? This measure of reliability would not be relevant to the AP Psychology Exam, since the multiple-choice section on that assessment is arranged in order of difficulty. However, on a unit test in your course, this information might tell the teacher a lot about how he or she constructed the test, whether it may be too long, and so on. Another way to calculate split-half reliability would be to score odd numbered and even numbered items separately and then compare the scores to see if they were similar.

- **Inter-rater reliability:** Does the score one grader assigns to your assessment correlate with the score another grader gives on that test? For example, when your AP Psychology free response essays are graded, it is often the case that more than one "reader" scores each of your answers - both readers are "blind" to the score the other gave your work. This is to ensure that all readers are scoring similarly according to the rigorous scoring guidelines established at the beginning of the reading session.

- **Intra-rater reliability:** Does the score a grader gives on a test match the score they give to the same test when they unknowingly grade it again? Many of your teachers would probably admit that the order in which they read essays, for example, could influence their scoring, even if they have the best intentions regarding fairness. If a teacher read your paper first when starting on a set of 100 essays, would that score correlate with the score the teacher gives if the essay is reinserted into the pile at the very bottom? If, of course, the teacher suspected that they had already scored this essay then you couldn't learn much in terms of intra-rater reliability, but if the scorer graded it anew, as a new essay (which is not an unreasonable expectation in a stack of 100), fatigue and the influence of all the other papers already read might well yield a different score than the first time around.

### Validity

- **Face validity:** With a quick perusal of the assessment, does the test seem to evaluate what it claims to evaluate? If you were given a test supposedly designed to measure your musical ability and the entire first page of the document asked questions about your favorite foods and beverages, you might well question the face validity of the assessment.

- **Content validity:** Does the assessment test the body of material (the content) it is supposed to test? If a psychology exam were deemed to have content validity, that would mean that the exam asked questions that were relevant to the topic and represented the material that was covered in the course. On the other hand, if your history teacher tells you to prepare for a test on the American Revolution and then gives you an exam containing several items on the writing of the Constitution, you might well argue that the test does not have content validity.

- **Construct validity:** This represents the broadest and perhaps most important aspect of validity. It essentially looks at the question, "Does the assessment accurately test what you have defined as the characteristics you wish to assess?" For example, if you developed a test to measure levels of hyperactivity in children, you would have to build (or "construct") an operational definition (recall our unit on research methodology) of 'hyperactivity' that your test would be designed to evaluate.

- **Criterion validity:** Do the results from the assessment correlate with results from *other* measures designed to assess similar or related things? If we construct a test to measure intelligence, we would need to show that scores on our test are highly correlated to some other valid measurement of intelligence. If results from our assessment paralleled those from other measurements such as the Wechsler Adult Intelligence Scale (WAIS), we could say that our test had criterion validity.

- **Predictive validity:** Does the test accurately forecast the level of some future performance? For example: Does performance on the SAT correlate with later college achievement? The authors of the SAT offer much statistical evidence that the test does have predictive validity - you might have an interesting discussion in class as to whether the exam predicts future performance or actually *influences* future performance.

### Name Hall of Fame

Because it is difficult to write multiple-choice items about the many theories of intelligence without reliance on the test taker's recall of specific proper names, you are not likely to encounter a lot of items on this topic on the cumulative Advanced Placement Examination. Psychology teachers differ on how much direct recall of proper names should be measured on a test, and so do members of the AP Psychology Test Development Committee. This unit brings that issue to the forefront, because so many of the theories covered here are directly associated with the name of the theorist.

With that said, the names **Howard Gardner** and **Robert Sternberg** are two in this unit that are most likely to be important in and of themselves on the AP Exam. Later you'll encounter Sternberg's triangular theory of love, which we look at in the unit on Social Psychology. The mere fact that his name arises in more than one unit makes him a solid candidate for induction into our name hall of fame. Gardner's theory of multiple intelligences has had such a broad cultural impact that you can't really claim to have a good grasp of introductory psychology without recognizing his contributions.

Don't fret too much about the many theories of intelligence and the names of those who forwarded them. The authors of the AP Psychology Exam do not conspire to try to trip students up; they do not wish to confuse you as to whether this item refers to Thurstone's or Guilford's theory for example. The exam will surely assess your knowledge of fluid and crystallized intelligence before it will ask you merely to recall Raymond Cattell's last name.

**Alfred Binet's** name is an important one in the history of psychology, but his name is associated with his test, which makes things easier for you. The same can be said about **David Wechsler**.

### Essay Themes

It would be a very difficult task in the time allotted for the AP Psychology Exam to write a free response essay on the different theories of intelligence. For that reason, the test development committee is unlikely to include one. This is not to say that those theories are not worth your study time. Reference to one or two of them could well show up on a free response question, but it's pretty certain that you would not have to deal with more than that.

In the AP Psychology curriculum this unit is entitled "Testing and Individual Differences", and the theme of "difference" (between groups and individuals) is an important one in our ever-shrinking world. It would be hard to construct a free response item on the subject that would be manageable for students and "score-able" for exam readers, but the concepts of **test bias** and **culture-fair testing** surely deserve reflection on your part.

# Testing and Individual Differences

## Intelligence Tests

- Mental age
- S.A.S.

- Alfred Binet:" The Father of Intelligence Testing"
- Bias: race, culture, language, sex
- Differences between groups vs. differences within groups?

- Wechsler's IQ tests
  - The WISC
  - The WAIS

- The Stanford-Binet IQ Test
- Terman's longitudinal study
- Stereotype Threat
- The Flynn Effect

## Reliability, Validity … and more

- Test/Re-test Reliability
- Equivalent Form Reliability
- Split Half Reliability

- Predictive Validity
- Content Validity

- Inter-Rater Reliability
- Intra-Rater Reliability

- Construct Validity
- Criterion Validity

- Factor Analysis
- Norming an assessment
- Standardization of assessments

## What is 'Intelligence'?

- Spearman: "G" and "S"
- Cattell: fluid and crystallized intelligence
- Galton and the normal curve
- Mental retardation/intellectual disability
- Savants

- Gardner's Theory of "M.I."
- Emotional Intelligence

- Sternberg's Triarchic Theory of Intelligence

- Intelligence – a 'growth' model or a 'fixed' model?
- Genetic Predispositions for intelligence?; Heritability

## Other Assessments in Psychology

- Psychometrics

- The M.M.P.I
- The Myers–Briggs

- The S.A.T. – Reliable? Valid?

- Projective Tests:
  - The T.A.T.
  - The Rorschach
  - more …

- Achievement Tests vs. Aptitude Tests
- Performance Tests vs. Paper and Pencil Tests

**Practice Items**

• THESE SECTION ITEMS ARE **NOT** IN ORDER OF DIFFICULTY!


1.  A major difference between the earliest intelligence tests and Wechsler intelligence tests like the WISC and the WAIS was

    (A) the earliest assessments did not use the concept of mental age
    (B) the earliest assessments were not appropriate for children
    (C) the Wechsler tests were the first English language assessments
    (D) the Wechsler tests were the first to be adequately normed and standardized using appropriate psychometric measures
    (E) the Wechsler tests had more performance-based rather than purely language-based items


2.  Which of the following, if true, would reflect the concept of heritability?

    (A) Your individual height is 90% genetic
    (B) Height is entirely inherited
    (C) Environment is a big factor in height
    (D) 90% of the difference in height between individuals is the result of genetics
    (E) There are significant cultural differences in average height


3.  Which of the following best illustrates the concept of stereotype threat?

    (A) An assessment uses slang vocabulary that is unfamiliar to one group of test-takers
    (B) Hispanics and Asians score differently on the same assessment
    (C) Hispanics and Asians score similarly on the same assessment
    (D) A Caucasian student does less well on a standardized math examination after reading in a test preparation manual that Asians typically outperform whites on such tests
    (E) African-American students perform less well because their standardized test is proctored by someone who has never administered such an examination


4.  Which of the following best illustrates the concept of content validity?

    (A) An assessment predicts how well you will perform in college
    (B) Your performance on the SAT positively correlates with your performance on the Wechsler Intelligence Scale for Children (WISC)
    (C) Results on the first half of a unit test are almost identical to results on the second half of the test
    (D) A test is determined to accurately assess the learning of material in a particular course
    (E) A test is appropriately administered and confidentiality is maintained

5.  Robert Sternberg and Howard Gardner would likely agree that

    (A) emotional intelligence is the single best predictor of future success in life
    (B) a "general intelligence" factor is the primary component of intelligence
    (C) self-report inventories are the most objective way to measure intelligence
    (D) there are multiple types of intelligence, and talent in one area does not necessarily predict how someone would perform in another area
    (E) intelligence testing can and should be used as a way of identifying and helping students with cognitive limitations

6.  If you wanted to evaluate the test/retest reliability of the scale in the science laboratory, you would

    (A) weigh a target object on it, then weigh that same object on a scale that you know to be accurate, and compare the results
    (B) weigh a target object on it several times in succession and compare the results
    (C) weigh a container on it, once with material inside and once with no material inside
    (D) have an engineer examine a schematic drawing of the scale to determine its reliability
    (E) weigh a target object on it and have a neutral observer record the result

7.  On a normal distribution of IQ test scores, with a mean of 100 and a standard deviation of 15 points, a score of 70 would place you in approximately what percentile of the population?

    (A) 3rd
    (B) 16th
    (C) 50th
    (D) 84th
    (E) 97th

8.  Two history teachers independently grade the same exam, and each assigns the exam a nearly identical score. This suggests strong

    (A) split-half reliability
    (B) intra-rater reliability
    (C) inter-rater reliability
    (D) content validity
    (E) criterion-related validity

9. Longitudinal research suggests that _____ is most likely to decline as we age.

   (A) Verbal/linguistic ability
   (B) Fluid intelligence
   (C) Crystallized intelligence
   (D) Emotional intelligence
   (E) Performance on recognition tasks

10. Upon taking the original Stanford-Binet intelligence test, ten-year old Sam is judged to have a mental age of a nine-year old. At the time, Sam would therefore have been assigned an IQ of

    (A) 70
    (B) 90
    (C) 100
    (D) 115
    (E) 190

NO TESTING MATERIAL ON THIS PAGE

GO ON TO THE NEXT PAGE

# Chapter 12
# *Abnormal Psychology*

### Introduction

Our focus here is to describe psychological disorders and discuss possible reasons for how they develop. In the next chapter, we turn our attention to possible methods of treating such disorders. You can expect to encounter seven to nine questions from Abnormal Psychology on the AP Exam.

Movies and television regularly highlight some of the disorders you will encounter in this chapter. Unfortunately, these popular culture references often simplify and even misidentify psychological disorders. After reading this chapter, you will be much better able to discriminate between the accurate and the inaccurate.

As you read you will see many links to previous chapters. Your foundation in the chapters on The Biological Bases of Behavior and Personality Theory will be especially useful in your study of Abnormal Psychology.

Throughout human history, individuals have suffered from mental illness. In earlier times, those who suffered from what we now call 'disorders' were thought to be **possessed**

**by witches, demons or evil spirits**. For a very long period, such people were often simply locked away, out of sight of the "healthy" masses. Today, we have adopted a **medical model** to explain psychological disorders. This model is devoted to the study of the causes, characteristics and treatments of psychological disorders. While many experts disagree on the exact causes of each disorder, the **biopsychosocial model** has gained popularity in recent years. People who adhere to this approach believe that most disorders are not caused by any single factor; they instead result from a combination of biological, psychological and social factors. This **eclectic** view borrows from many of the major psychological perspectives that we've discussed throughout this book (i.e. behavioral, cognitive, sociocultural).

The sometimes controversial but widely used book that helps clinicians to identify mental disorders is called the **Diagnostic and Statistical Manual of Mental Disorders**, or **DSM**. The first edition of this book, published in 1952, contained descriptions of nearly 100 different disorders. The most recent edition describes nearly three times that many. There have been many revisions of this book. As of this writing, the **DSM-IV-TR** was still in use. This text revision (TR) of the 4th edition was published in 2000. Work on a new edition has been underway for years, and the *DSM-V* is due out in 2013.

The authors of the DSM endeavor to write **operational definitions of each disorder**, describing their characteristics and the frequency and duration of the associated symptoms. The DSM uses a *multiaxial* system for diagnosing disorders. On *Axis I*, clinicians report anxiety disorders, mood disorders, somatoform disorders, dissociative disorders, developmental disorders and the schizophrenias. *Axis II* is for reporting personality disorders and mental retardation. *Axis III* is for reporting medical conditions that may impact the sufferer's mental disorder. *Axis IV* provides the opportunity to record environmental factors that may be contributing to the patient's mental state. Finally, clinician's make a "global assessment" of the overall functioning of a patient on *Axis V*.

While the DSM describes the symptoms of each disorder, the book *does not* include any discussion of the causes or possible treatments of disorders. This is largely because each psychological perspective views causes and treatments differently.

Some agree with **Thomas Szasz** that such a book serves only to provide us with labels for behaviors that are not "disorders" at all. Szasz argued that such labels could cause as many problems as they solve, in that they demean the individual to whom the tag is applied and that individual might actually feel compelled to live up to the expectations which accompany the "disease" (another example in psychology of the *self-fulfilling prophecy*).

In a famous study of the 1970's, **David Rosenhan** explored the effects of such labels. He and several colleagues visited different mental institutions and reported that they were hearing voices. They did not report any other symptoms, but, not surprisingly, they were each admitted, most with a preliminary diagnosis of schizophrenia (one of the general symptoms of schizophrenia is auditory or visual hallucinations). One was thought to be possibly suffering from bipolar disorder (once known as manic-depression, this affective disorder is characterized by dramatic shifts in mood). Of course, any responsible physician, nurse or aide would take such symptoms seriously, but it is what happened after these pseudo-patients were admitted that gets at the heart of the "labeling" debate. Once inside the institution, the pseudo-patients returned to their normal behavior, and never again reported experiencing auditory hallucinations. Although they remained as patients for an average of nearly three weeks, no member of the professional staff ever "caught on" that they were really healthy. Rosenhan wrote that several actual patients expressed doubt about the pseudo-patients' mental illness, but it seems for most of us that applying a label like 'schizophrenia' to a person influences how each of their subsequent behaviors is perceived. Imagine, for instance, how *you as a doctor* would react to this scenario: you ask a patient you believe suffers from schizophrenia why they seem to be taking notes on a daily basis, and the patient responds that he is conducting psychological research on institutionalization. In Rosenhan's study, encounters like these only seemed to confirm the doctor's belief that the patient indeed suffered from schizophrenia.

All of the participants in Rosenhan's study were eventually released, of course, but all were told that their condition was "in remission," not cured, or absent altogether. Clearly, these psychological labels do tend to stick.

But it would be nearly impossible to talk about, recognize and diagnose psychological disorders if we didn't have a commonly agreed upon way of doing so, and the DSM serves that purpose. One primary goal in creating that systematic process of defining and diagnosing disorders is to establish inter-rater reliability between diagnosticians. The precise definitions of the DSM help because it is often quite difficult to distinguish between "unusual" behavior and "disordered" behavior. Of course, one of the criteria for psychological abnormality is that the behavior in question is **unusual or atypical**; that is, most people don't do it. But, we all probably do or think things that are atypical without being disordered. So, psychologists and psychiatrists use some **other criteria** to help draw that line more clearly:

- The behavior is **disturbing to others**

- The behavior **violates cultural standards**

- The behavior is **disturbing to self**

- The behavior is **irrational, indefensible or unjustifiable**

- The behavior is **maladaptive** - that is, it greatly impairs one's daily functioning or even one's survival

It isn't necessary for all of these to exist in order to label behavior as 'disordered'. For example, it may be hard to tell in many serious mental illnesses whether or not the patient himself is disturbed by his behaviors. As you will see, some personality disorders are in part marked by the individual's unwillingness or inability to acknowledge that anything is "wrong" with them.

The "cultural standards" criterion is a complicated one. For one thing, some psychological disorders common in one culture or region may be nearly nonexistent in others. Eating disorders are sadly quite common in some western societies but are almost unheard of in many other parts of the world. Dissociative identity disorder, once known as multiple personality disorder, also seems peculiar to western cultures. Also, cultural standards are always subject to debate and change. Homosexuality was once listed in the DSM, but is no longer. That is one striking example of how our societal view of "illness" doesn't necessarily remain constant.

In class, you might further examine that issue in a discussion of **the insanity defense.** While 'insanity' is a legal term and not a formal clinical label, a healthy debate as to when an individual is no longer fully responsible for their behaviors because of mental defect can deepen your understanding of what is considered 'abnormal' in clinical psychology. In the courtroom that line has changed somewhat over time, and the same can be said in psychology as well.

Throughout the rest of this chapter, please keep **"the intern's syndrome"** in mind. As you learn more about different disorders, you might discover a tendency to diagnose yourself or those around you. Try to resist that temptation. As you read about obsessive-compulsive disorder, for example, please remember the above criteria for abnormality; the fact that you might be somewhat ritualistic in preparing for a big game, or an important recital, or in taking your morning shower does not necessarily mean you suffer from OCD.

There are many different categories of psychological disorders described in the DSM. We will not attempt to cover them all. Instead, we give you a sampling of those that are a part of the AP curriculum.

### Mood Disorders

The mood disorders (you may hear some refer to these as affective disorders – 'affect' refers to feelings or emotion) that you are likely to encounter on the AP Examination are outlined below:

- The symptoms of **major depression** include deep sadness, feelings of hopelessness or worthlessness, loss of energy, loss of interest in pleasurable activities, changes in appetite and sleep patterns and suicidal thoughts. More people seek mental health services for depression than any other disorder, which is why it is sometimes labeled the 'common cold' of psychological disorders. You may also see this called **clinical depression** or **unipolar depression** ('uni' means one, so this term refers to the patient's being trapped at one end of the mood spectrum). **Dysthymia** is a mood disorder similar to depression, but with less severe symptoms. A diagnosis of dysthymia requires that symptoms be present for at least two years.

- **Seasonal affective disorder** is characterized by symptoms similar to major depression but is triggered specifically by changes in the seasons. Reduced light exposure during the winter months seems to be the main cause; indeed, intensive exposure to artificial light is one treatment approach for **SAD**.

- **Bipolar disorder** (you might also hear it referred to by its previous name, **manic-depression**) is characterized by extreme shifts in mood, from deep depression and listlessness to **mania**, which is marked by extreme euphoria, inflated self esteem, a "flight" of ideas and speech and marked distractibility. Other maladaptive symptoms include a drastic increase in impulsivity and a tendency to engage in high-risk behaviors. Some sufferers cycle through such changes much more quickly and unexpectedly than others; some often return to a kind of baseline state with relatively no symptoms, while others are either manic or depressed pretty much all the time. *Rapid cycling* is a term that is sometimes used to describe bipolar subjects that experience four or more episodes of mania and depression within a year. **Cyclothymia**, a disorder similar to bipolar, involves less severe bouts of mania and depression that persist over at least a two-year period.

Establishing the line between "normal" and "clinically abnormal" levels of depression can be quite challenging. All of us have been depressed at some point or another, perhaps as the result of a trauma or loss, but was it *clinical depression*? One of the criteria for major depression is that it is not necessarily directly associated with a particular event; another is that it has persisted for at least two weeks. Likewise, many people feel "down" in wintertime, because the days are shorter, or perhaps because the weather precludes involvement in some outdoor activities, but they do not suffer the more serious levels of depression which accompany SAD.

The point where extremes of mood are pervasive and damage healthy functioning is certainly important, and so is the self-evaluation of the individual. Most clinicians would probably consider a person's sense of their own unhappiness as sufficient justification for intervention.

**Etiology of Mood Disorders:**

The term **etiology** refers to the history and possible causes of a disorder. There seems to be a genetic predisposition for mood disorders (bipolar disorder even more so than depression) as evidenced in studies of mood disorders within families and especially identical twin pairs. Those who approach this from the **biomedical perspective** would also focus on brain chemistry, especially in regard to levels of serotonin and epinephrine or norepinephrine. There is a correlation between lower than normal activity levels of those neurotransmitters and the presence of depression. Drugs such as Prozac, Paxil and Zoloft, which all increase serotonin in the brain, are often effective in treating depression. Bipolar disorder also seems linked to neurotransmitter activity. One common treatment for bipolar disorder, lithium, seems to help by operating on the norepinephrine system.

There's growing evidence that depression is linked to the stress response, specifically in regard to cortisol, a stress hormone secreted by the adrenal gland. It seems as if the brain can become trapped in a kind of stress loop, which can contribute to impaired function in the hippocampus. This in turn may be connected to a breakdown in communication between the prefrontal cortex of the brain and the entire limbic system. Further, some who suffer with depression have been found to have lower than normal activity levels in parts of the frontal lobes.

**Psychoanalytic and psychodynamic theorists** might trace the roots of depression to unresolved unconscious anger, perhaps toward a lost loved one, turned inward. **Cognitive psychologists** propose that individuals who suffer from depression habitually explain bad events as being *internal, stable* and *global*. They tend to blame themselves (*internal*) for bad things that occur, they believe that such things are more likely to last (*stable*) and will impact every facet of their lives (*global*). Depressed people tend to have pessimistic explanatory styles. They may *ruminate*, or constantly think about the negative aspects of their lives. Some studies indicate that women are more likely to do this, which may be why they are more likely to suffer from depression. **Aaron Beck**, a famed cognitive psychologist, proposed the **cognitive triad**, which states that negative views about the self, the world and the future, all contribute to depression. Along this same line, it's also worthwhile to review Martin Seligman's concept of *learned helplessness* as a possible cause of depression. You may recall his proposal that when we consistently fail at tasks, it creates a sense that we have no control over outcomes, and as a result we stop trying. Such a cycle may greatly contribute to the onset and perpetuation of depression.

**Behaviorists** might argue that the symptoms of depression are reinforced in some way, perhaps by getting attention from others. **Humanists** would likely focus on a possible lack of loving interactions and an absence of unconditional acceptance from others in the life of the sufferer. A humanist might also view depression from an *existential perspective* - a depressed individual might be having difficulty finding meaning or purpose in life. A

**sociocultural theorist** might note that depression is statistically more common in females (women are two times more likely to suffer from it) and investigate whether there are societal or environmental factors that lead to this. However, the fact that depression is more prevalent in females across cultures might lead us back to a biomedical explanation - could there be something about female physiology that makes them more vulnerable to depression? Or, is it that there are similarities in the ways women are viewed and treated in most cultures? Or, does depression result from a complex *interaction* of biological, cultural, cognitive and emotional factors?

## Anxiety Disorders

Anxiety disorders are relatively common, but it is important to keep the intern's syndrome in mind here. All of us have fears, but are we "phobic"? All of us feel anxious or apprehensive or agitated at times, but do we suffer from generalized anxiety disorder? All of us may occasionally have unwanted thoughts in our head that we can't dismiss, but does that make us obsessive? At what point does an individual cross over into disordered behavior?

The anxiety disorders you are most likely to see on the AP Exam are summarized below:

- **Generalized anxiety disorder (GAD):** This is marked by chronic, high levels of anxiety with ongoing tension, apprehension and nervousness that does not seem to be linked to any specific trigger or stimulus. This may also be referred to by the Freudian term "free floating" anxiety.

- **Panic disorder:** This disorder is marked by "recurrent, unexpected panic attacks". People who suffer from this experience intense fear accompanied by significant sympathetic nervous system activation, which is not necessarily triggered by any particular event, object or situation. The severe chest pain, muscle tightness, numbness and dizziness that accompany a panic attack are often misinterpreted as signs of a heart attack. The disorder can also be marked by the fear that one might have another panic attack, or by a general feeling of impending danger.

- **Phobia:** This is not simply a fear. The term refers to a deep-seated, irrational fear; irrational in the sense that one may feel intense terror even in seemingly safe conditions. The DSM breaks 'phobia' into three basic categories. Some are **specific phobias** (such as fear triggered by certain animals, or by heights or enclosed spaces), some are **social phobias** (marked by extreme shyness and a fear of being scrutinized and criticized by others) and a third type is **agoraphobia**, an intense fear of public settings or any setting from which there is no ready means of escape in case of a panic attack. Some think of this in terms of it's literal meaning, "fear of the marketplace," while others think of it more as fear of fear - that is, that a sufferer is frightened at the possibility of experiencing panic in an unfamiliar or unsafe setting.

- **Obsessive-compulsive disorder:** Obsessions are persistent, undesirable *thoughts*, while compulsions are *actions* that one feels driven to carry out. One especially disturbing characteristic of this condition is that the sufferer usually recognizes that the obsessions and/or compulsions are irrational or maladaptive, and does not want to have them, but cannot control them. One common example of this disorder revolves around an obsessive fear of germs, which may lead the sufferer to compulsively wash his or her hands.

- **Post-traumatic stress disorder (PTSD):** Occurring after a deeply troubling event (such as natural disaster, assault or wartime experiences), this is a condition marked by restlessness, irritability, sleep impairment, loss of concentration, nightmares and flashbacks to the traumatic event.

The maladaptive criterion is important here. If a compulsion for order has led you to take two or three hours every morning arranging your desk before you can begin work, this will obviously interfere with your functioning on the job. You may well consider yourself an orderly person, but not to such a degree. The "indefensible, irrational or unjustifiable" criterion certainly applies as well. It would be perfectly normal, even healthy, to fear being trapped on the ledge of a tall building. An individual who is phobic about heights might feel genuine agitation, even panic, when merely looking at a photograph of window washers working on a high-rise office complex, even though he or she is quite safe.

### Etiology of Anxiety Disorders:

**Behaviorists** offer a powerful learning theory argument for the causes of phobias. They argue such fears are conditioned, perhaps very early in life. Recall the case of Little Albert in the learning theory unit; that is an example of how phobias could be classically conditioned. Such deep-seated fears might be operantly conditioned as well - if you innocently approached a dog as a toddler and were bitten, that basic "response resulting in unpleasant consequence" formula might well lead to a life-long fear of dogs. Phobias may also result from observational learning. If your parents or grandparents demonstrated a powerful fear of mice, you might well imitate that model. Theoretically, compulsive behavior might be operantly reinforced, in that it relieves the anxiety that would come if the behavior was *not* carried out. In fact, some victims of OCD say that, while they do not want to do what they do, it feels better to do it than *not* to do it.

From the **biomedical viewpoint**, some would argue that we are biologically prepared to fear things that have been threats to our survival in the past. This may account for the frequency of height or snake phobias. There is also pretty strong evidence to support a genetic predisposition for panic disorder, phobias and OCD. You may remember from our work on the biological bases of behavior that GABA is the major inhibitory neurotransmitter - think of it as functioning something like the brakes on a car. There is a correlation between the presence of anxiety disorders and lower-than-normal levels of GABA. It's as if the brakes in the car are not working properly. Drugs in the benzodiazepine family (such as Valium and Xanax) boost GABA activity and are often successful in treating anxiety disorders. Some anti-depressants that stimulate serotonin activity also help people with OCD, so it's reasonable to assume that malfunctions in the serotonin system play some role in that disorder. Research also suggests that a part of the brain called the caudate nucleus may be different in people suffering from OCD. The amygdala, in the limbic system, is very much involved in fear and aggression, and dysfunction in it may well play a role in the development of phobias and PTSD.

**Cognitive psychologists** contend that panic disorder can result from a misinterpretation of bodily sensations. They argue that sufferers may view relatively normal physiological responses to stress as more dangerous and alarming than others do. In general, cognitive theorists would contend that anxiety disorders are rooted in cycles of self-defeating and maladaptive thoughts. They may also contend that those who develop anxiety disorders have not found healthy ways of mentally coping with the inevitable stresses of life.

For **a psychoanalyst**, the object of a phobia might symbolically represent an unconscious conflict, perhaps sexual in nature. A *person or client centered therapist*, from the **humanistic** school of thought (recall the unit on Personality Theory) might trace the origins of anxiety to a gap between one's real self and one's ideal self.

## Dissociative Disorders

These rare disorders are marked by a loss of identity or the sense of self. In a sense, a victim is disconnected ("dissociated") from who they are and what has happened to them. Each of the three disorders presented below also involve significant memory loss, often of important events. While the memory loss is usually temporary, it is quite puzzling because there do not seem to be any physical causes for the memory disruption.

The dissociative disorders you should know for the AP test are summarized below.

- **Dissociative identity disorder** (formerly known as multiple personality disorder): This rare condition involves the existence of two or more separate personalities housed in one body. The separate personalities may demonstrate dramatic differences in the behaviors and emotions they display. Some reportedly have differences in handwriting, speaking (including speaking other languages) and handedness.

In many cases the personalities are not aware of each other. It's important not to confuse this with schizophrenia, although many in popular culture and the media do exactly that. You may also see this disorder abbreviated as **DID**.

- **Dissociative amnesia** is characterized by a large-scale loss of memory for important events or one's own identity. It can be very sudden in onset and in recovery, and is often associated with a highly upsetting or traumatic incident.

- **Dissociative fugue** is sometimes called "traveling amnesia", because it is marked by amnesia and physical relocation. In many instances, the fugue is preceded by a highly upsetting or stressful event. It is a rare condition, but you may have read of cases in which a person ends up hundreds of miles away from home, unaware of who they are and how they got there. The fugue may last hours, days or even months. In most cases, all of the past memories come back, but interestingly, once they recover the memories they may have no recollection of the fugue period. Both dissociative amnesia and dissociative fugue are generally temporary conditions, which subside as the sufferer becomes more able to deal with the stressful events confronting them.

These disorders are rare and quite dramatic, so it is easier to see a clear line between "normality" and "abnormality" in these cases. But it may be interesting for you to discuss in class how much any or all of us "dissociate" from time to time. Some psychologists argue that all people can be placed somewhere on a spectrum of dissociation, without calling any of us "disordered". Many of us have "different personalities" in different situations, although we do not think of ourselves as suffering from DID. Think of how you behave around your parents as compared to your peers, or how you are at soccer practice as compared to drama rehearsal, or what comes out in you during a conversation with a teacher as compared to a conversation with a boyfriend or girlfriend.

Dissociative identity disorder is one of the more controversial clinical labels today. It's very hard to wrap one's mind around just what it *is*, and there are some who say it doesn't really exist. Skeptics contend that therapists may unintentionally produce symptoms by subtly suggesting the existence of altered personalities to the patient. Practitioners who use hypnosis have been especially scrutinized for explicitly asking subjects to produce other personalities while in that highly suggestible state. This is not to say that there's nothing troubling the patient, but perhaps their symptoms are a response to the therapist's expectations as much as anything else.

**Etiology of Dissociative Disorders:**

**The psychoanalytic or psychodynamic school of thought** offers intriguing explanations for the causes of dissociative disorders. They might view all three of the disorders described above as powerful defense mechanisms, unconsciously built to protect oneself from a painful memory. Amnesia and fugue could be seen as extreme kinds of repression. Dissociative identity disorder is highly correlated with severe physical or sexual abuse early in childhood, and psychoanalysts contend that the condition is a complex attempt to escape the pain of that trauma.

### Somatoform Disorders

These are disorders with physical symptoms but no apparent physical cause. The causes seem to be *psychological*, but the symptoms are "real" and are not the result of malingering or faking.

The somatoform disorders you should know for the AP test are summarized below:

- **Conversion disorder** is so-called because the sufferer is essentially converting *psychological* stress into *physical* symptoms, as in a soldier who becomes paralyzed under the stress of battle and truly cannot move, even though no underlying physiological problem can be found.

- **Hypochondriasis** involves a preoccupation with the persistent fear that one has an illness, even in the face of medical evidence to the contrary. Sufferers frequently misinterpret minor bodily symptoms as signs of serious illness.

- **Body dysmorphic disorder** is characterized by intense anxiety about a perceived physical deformity or defect. It might be interesting for you to discuss possible cultural contributions to the incidence of body dysmorphic disorder. In cultures overrun by images of how one is "supposed" to look, is it more likely that individuals will be unable to see themselves accurately and affectionately?

Conversion disorder is dramatic, clear-cut and pretty nearly impossible to "fake", so the "normal vs. abnormal" line is clear. But hypochondriasis may present a diagnostic problem. Many people casually use the term "hypochondriac" in everyday conversation, but when is it clinically appropriate? Certainly, if a preoccupation with one's health is causing significant personal distress, that is one signal of a serious problem. The sufferer's behavior may also be disturbing to co-workers or family members, which is another of the psychological criteria for abnormality.

### Etiology of Somatoform Disorders:

A **psychoanalyst** would certainly focus on unconscious defenses against trauma in explaining conversion disorder. Some **behaviorists** argue that such a condition might actually be a cry for attention, which if given would reinforce the presence of symptoms. This argument might also apply to those with hypochondriasis. A **cognitive** therapist might explore a hypochondriac's exaggerated ways of thinking about and explaining bodily sensations that others might judge to be routine.

## The Schizophrenias

It's fairly common to hear this called the most serious of all mental illnesses. While symptoms of schizophrenia typically do not manifest themselves until the late teens or early twenties, they are often quite severe and seriously impact one's ability to function in society. Worldwide, about one percent of people will suffer from schizophrenia at some point in their life. Some will experience one episode and the disorder will go away completely. Others will experience episodes on and off for the rest of their lives, and some will experience chronic symptoms that never fully subside.

It is very common to confuse this with dissociative identity disorder, perhaps because the term 'schizophrenia' suggests "split personality" to people. The label refers instead to a split *from reality. Psychosis* is a synonymous but somewhat outmoded term for such a split.

The major symptoms of schizophrenia include:

- **Hallucinations**: Sufferers may see, hear or otherwise sense things that do not actually exist. While hallucinations can occur with any sense, auditory hallucinations are the most common in schizophrenia.

- **Delusions**: These refer to false beliefs, such as **delusions of grandeur** (believing one is a significant figure in history, a religious prophet or some other person of major importance) or **paranoid delusions** ("Law enforcement officials have me under constant surveillance").

- **Inappropriate or flattened affect**: Flat affect refers to an apathetic or emotionless state. Some sufferers may demonstrate emotions that are highly inappropriate for the given situation.

- **Disorganized speech**: The victim's speech is very loosely connected, and words can be thrown together in odd, nonsensical ways - this is sometimes called "word salad".

- **Catatonic** (also called psychomotor) **behaviors**: Some schizophrenics display physical peculiarities, which may include remaining motionless for hours (this is called *catatonic stupor*). Others may exhibit *catatonic excitement* in which one engages in a repetitive, aimless behavior for long periods of time.

It's important to note that most people with schizophrenia do not experience all of these symptoms. The DSM requires that at least two of the above symptoms be present for at least one month in order to make a diagnosis.

You may see the major characteristics of schizophrenia categorized into **positive and negative symptoms**. Don't think of these as value judgments (i.e. good or bad), but rather in terms of *adding* or *subtracting*. Positive symptoms are those that a sufferer *has* that a healthy person does *not* (such as hallucinations, false beliefs or disorganized speech), while negative symptoms refer to something the sufferer *lacks* that a healthy person *has*. Negative symptoms include flattened affect, decreased speech and social withdrawal.

The DSM categorizes schizophrenia into specific types, which are summarized below:

- **Paranoid schizophrenia:** The central symptom here involves delusions, although the victim may also suffer from hallucinations etc. The delusions are usually of the paranoid kind, although they may be intermingled with delusions of grandeur.

- **Disorganized schizophrenia:** The central symptoms here are cognitive and emotional. Speech and thought are very confused, and emotions can be highly childlike or inappropriate.

- **Catatonic schizophrenia:** This type is relatively rare in comparison with the others. The central symptom here involves motor disturbances, which may take the form of immobility or excessive motor activity. In some cases, the patient will strike a pose and freeze in that position for hours at a time. During these episodes, the sufferer may go hours without speaking or responding in any way to stimuli in their environment.

- **Undifferentiated schizophrenia:** This is sometimes thought of as a kind of "wastebasket" category, in that it describes schizophrenia that does not fit neatly into the other subtypes.

Because this too is such a serious disorder the line identifying 'abnormality' is clearer than in other categories. Often, the victim has lived a normal childhood and adolescence and onset of the disease is sudden and frighteningly dramatic.

**Etiology of Schizophrenia:**

The **biomedical model** predominates in uncovering the possible roots of schizophrenia.

Twin studies support the notion of a genetic predisposition for schizophrenia, as do studies of parents with schizophrenia and the rates of the disease in their biological children. You may recall that the prevalence rate of schizophrenia in the population is one percent. However, if you have one biological parent with the illness you are six times more likely to get it. If both parents have it, you are 46 times more likely to develop it, and if you have an identical twin with the disorder, you are 48 times more likely. Clearly, there is some biological vulnerability for the disorder, but these data also suggest environmental factors must also play a role – otherwise the agreement rate between identical twins, for example, would be even higher.

Researchers who support the **dopamine hypothesis** stress the relationship between schizophrenia and heightened dopamine activity in the brain, which may reflect an excess of that neurotransmitter or an oversensitivity of dopamine receptors. **Antipsychotic drugs**, which inhibit dopamine activity, are often successful in treating most positive symptoms of schizophrenia. Brain imaging techniques reveal that many individuals with schizophrenia have enlarged ventricles (fluid filled openings) in the brain. It's possible that these openings reflect a loss of tissue in the frontal lobes (the higher level "command center" of the human brain) and the temporal lobes (which may account for some of the language dysfunction of schizophrenia). There's video evidence supporting the idea that individuals who develop schizophrenia often demonstrated unusual motor development and function as little children. This too may involve frontal lobe problems. Extensive research also shows that a mother who has a virus during pregnancy is statistically more likely to bear a child who will develop schizophrenia. You can see there are a lot of possibilities here. As yet, there is no definitive biological answer to the question, "What causes schizophrenia?"

The **sociocultural perspective** might focus on the income levels and home environments of schizophrenia sufferers. There is a statistical correlation between the presence of schizophrenia and low socioeconomic status. Still, just as with the biomedical examples above, we must remain mindful of the dangers of inferring *causation* from correlation. Investigators have also looked at communication styles in the homes of those who develop schizophrenia, and some subscribe to a theory that suggests a relationship between distorted or inconsistent communication in the home and schizophrenia.

**The diathesis-stress model** is an attempt to tie some of these perspectives together. It suggests that biological predispositions (a diathesis) interact with stressful environmental triggers in the development of some disorders, such as schizophrenia. For example, an individual with no genetic "push" toward schizophrenia may not be harmfully impacted by unpredictable or erratic communication patterns in a household, while someone with a genetic predisposition could be. This model has been proposed as a possible explanation for many disorders.

## Developmental Disorders

This category refers to disorders that are "usually first diagnosed in infancy, childhood or adolescence". The major developmental disorders are summarized below.

- **Autism:** This falls under the sub-category of "pervasive developmental disorders". It is characterized by a lack of appropriate social responsiveness and highly impaired communication. Those with autism may sit alone, seemingly disconnected from their surroundings for very long periods of time. They may rock back and forth or engage in other repetitive, seemingly aimless, sometimes self-abusive behaviors. They often fail to use appropriate non-verbal communication such as eye contact or facial expression. It's very difficult to summarize the constellation of possible symptoms in this disorder, and it can look very different from case to case.

- **Attention deficit/hyperactivity disorder:** Like autism, this disorder is more common amongst boys, which is obviously a point of interest to researchers. It is characterized by impulsivity, sustained inattention and limited ability to focus on tasks. You might see it abbreviated as ADHD.

- **Conduct disorder:** Some think of this as a childhood version of adult anti-social personality disorder, which we examine in a later section. Both are marked by frequent lying, stealing, manipulation and cruelty accompanied by a relative lack of remorse for such actions or empathy for those hurt by their transgressions.

- **Tourette's Disorder** (also referred to as Tourette's *Syndrome*): Individuals with Tourette's display consistent vocal or motor 'tics', defined in the DSM as "sudden, rapid, recurrent, non-rhythmic, stereotyped motor movement or vocalization." Many suggest that Tourette's is a relative of obsessive-compulsive disorder.

It appears likely that the next edition of the DSM will modify some of the designations that currently fall under the category of 'pervasive developmental disorders'. For example, **Asperger's Disorder** (characterized by "impairments in social interaction" accompanied by abnormally intense engagement in a narrow area of interest and/or repetition of idiosyncratic rituals or routines) may well be redefined or re-categorized in the future. There will undoubtedly be ongoing attempts to clarify all of the diagnostic criteria for disorders along the so-called "autism spectrum."

In many public schools today there is a debate about whether ADHD is over-diagnosed. Some ask for a clearer line to be drawn between "normal" childhood and adolescent behaviors and "hyperactivity." Once again, the maladaptive criterion is important in diagnosing developmental disorders. Likewise, many children at some time or another engage in lying or stealing, but it is when such behavior is chronic and a consistent impediment to normal functioning for the child that a diagnosis of conduct disorder becomes a consideration.

## Etiology of Developmental Disorders:

The roots of autism are still poorly understood. However, the cognitive perspective proposes that children with autism fail to develop a *theory of mind*. This inability to understand that others have different perceptions, intentions, motivations and beliefs from their own may greatly hinder their ability to succeed socially.

Biomedical studies suggest that genetics play a role in autism. Other research suggests that children with autism show brain differences in the cerebellum. It may also be that the mirror neurons in the brains of autistic people do not function normally. This might account for the lack of empathy in those individuals. Recent research using MRI brain imaging at McLean Hospital in Massachusetts provides some tentative hope for better diagnosis of autism, focusing on areas of the brain responsible for language and social functioning.

Attention deficit/hyperactivity disorder is often successfully treated with medication, which suggests a biomedical basis for that condition, perhaps in terms of reduced inhibitory neurotransmitter activity. If conduct disorder is indeed a relative of anti-social personality disorder, it too may be linked to lower than normal levels of physiological arousal, which is one theoretical explanation for sociopathic behavior.

## Eating Disorders

From our discussion in the Motivation and Emotion chapter, you may recall the basic symptoms of **anorexia nervosa** (marked by an intense fear of gaining weight or being fat which in turn leads to eating habits that result in substantially below normal body weight) and **bulimia nervosa** (characterized by an eating pattern of binging and purging).

Of those two conditions, bulimia nervosa can be more difficult to diagnose because those who are bulimic are often not as obviously underweight as those with anorexia. The DSM sets a threshold for an anorexic diagnosis at a body weight that is less than 85% of what would typically be expected for that individual.

## Etiology of Eating Disorders:

A **behaviorist** might focus here on contingencies of reinforcement that may in the past have rewarded control. Certainly, many would argue that "control" plays a role in the development of eating disorders, in the sense of being able to choose what, how and whether one eats. A proponent of **cognitive theory** might attribute eating disorders to the distorted self-image that so many sufferers seem to have. Others link eating disorders to obsessive-compulsive disorder, and some medications for the latter condition help with eating disorders as well. Those most interested in **biomedical** explanations might also look at why eating disorders are so much more common in females than in males. Of course, that fact also requires **sociocultural** consideration, as does the fact that there are significant cultural differences in the rates of diagnosis of eating disorders. What, after all, does it mean to be "too thin"? How do we define terms like 'attractive' and 'unattractive'? The media and society at large both regularly transmit messages about such things, and it is difficult to pin down exactly what influence those messages have on self-image and eating habits.

## Personality Disorders

Up to this point, we've discussed only *Axis I* disorders from the DSM. Personality disorders are categorized as *Axis II* disorders. People with personality disorders show extremes of certain personality traits that undermine their daily social and emotional functioning. While some of these are quite dramatic, they are typically seen as less debilitating than the disorders we've previously discussed. There has been much controversy over the current system of diagnosing this group of disorders. It can be difficult to tell them apart. The DSM-V will likely usher in major changes to the diagnostic criteria for this category of disorders and may well eliminate some types altogether. Personality disorders are also notoriously hard to treat successfully, partly because the sufferer may not see their maladaptive personality characteristics as a problem.

The essential personality disorders for AP Exam preparation are summarized below:

- **Anti-social personality disorder:** This is *not* a reference to someone who is shy or socially withdrawn; rather, it refers to an individual who is rebellious, deceitful, and manipulative, with no apparent sense of remorse or empathy for those they may hurt.

- **Narcissistic personality disorder:** The primary symptom here is a dramatically exaggerated sense of one's own value and importance.

- **Histrionic personality disorder:** This is marked by an insatiable need and search for attention and a tendency toward highly emotional behavior.

- **Borderline personality disorder:** The key word that dominates this diagnosis is 'instability'. It can be marked by sudden and intense rages, deep insecurity and fear of abandonment and general instability in relationships and emotional interaction.

- **Paranoid personality disorder:** This disorder involves persistent suspiciousness marked by a chronic sense of being observed and persecuted.

+ **Dependent personality disorder:** As you may suspect from its name, this is marked by an over-reliance on others, pronounced fear of separation from loved ones and an inability to initiate activities on one's own.

This is a good category for classroom discussion on the labeling issue. We all can think of people we know who are somewhat narcissistic, but do they meet the criteria for narcissistic personality disorder? We all know of cases in which a person was deeply hurt by the loss of a relationship and acted in somewhat irrational ways in response, but is that borderline personality disorder? Are these actually disorders, or merely extremes within the "normal" range of human behavior?

### Etiology of Personality Disorders:

The most research in this area has been done on anti-social personality disorder. Findings indicate that those with the disorder have physiological differences, including lower autonomic nervous system arousal and significantly less activity in the frontal lobes. Such individuals do not seem to respond to arousing or anxiety-provoking stimuli in the same way as those without the disorder. **Behaviorists** and **sociocultural theorists** might examine the home environments of those with anti-social personality disorder, to see if and how limitations on inappropriate actions were imposed during childhood. Behaviorists might also propose that those with personality disorders are somehow reinforced in their actions. Adherents to any one of the psychological schools of thought would certainly be interested in uncovering why narcissistic and anti-social personality disorders affect males more frequently, while borderline, histrionic and dependent personality disorders are much more common in females.

**Name Hall of Fame**

**David Rosenhan's** important study of institutions and diagnostic labels is often referred to simply as "The Rosenhan Study", so it is imperative that you know his name. Many more names of importance will surface in the next chapter on Treatment, which is sometimes linked with this unit under the umbrella of Clinical Psychology.

**Essay Themes**

This is a unit you should emphasize in your studying. Several free response items in the past have focused on descriptions and treatments of psychological disorders. The major schools of psychological thought emerge again here, and you already know how important it is to be conversant with them. Even though the creators of the AP Psychology Exam are very careful about the distribution of items on the multiple choice section of the test (this unit is another that is allotted 7 to 9 of those 100 questions), students have been known to report that "it seemed to be all about Abnormal Psych!" That may be because there is so much overlap between this unit and others, making it difficult to determine where one unit begins and another ends. This should further convince you to give Abnormal Psychology your full attention.

# Abnormal Psychology

## What Is 'Abnormal'?

- Thomas Szasz
- Criteria for 'abnormality'
- Historical Views of Abnormality
- The 'insanity' defense
- Rosenhan & institutions
- The DSM
- Etiology
- The Diathesis-Stress Model
- The Biopsychosocial Model

## Mood Disorders

- Bipolar Disorder
- Major Depression
- CAUSES?
- SAD
- Cyclothymia
- Dysthymia

## Anxiety Disorders

- OCD
- GAD
- Phobias
- Panic Disorder
- PTSD
- CAUSES?

## Dissociative Disorders

- Dissociative Amnesia
- Dissociative Fugue
- DID
- CAUSES?

242

# Abnormal Psychology (Continued)

## Developmental Disorders

- Autism
- Types of Schizophrenia
  - Paranoid
  - Disorganized
  - Catatonic
  - Undifferentiated
- Tourette's Disorder
- Conduct Disorder
- CAUSES?
- ADD
  ADHD

## The Schizophrenias

- Schizophrenia: general symptoms
- 'Positive' and 'Negative' Symptoms
- CAUSES?

## Somatoform Disorders

- Body Dysmorphic Disorder
- Conversion Disorder
- Hypochondriasis
- CAUSES?

## Personality Disorders

- Anti-Social
- Dependent
- Narcissistic
- Borderline
- Paranoid
- Histrionic
- CAUSES?

243

**Practice Items**

- **Time yourself** on this section, and record how long it takes you. This section should take you no more than 10 minutes and 30 seconds

- THESE SECTION ITEMS ARE **NOT** IN ORDER OF DIFFICULTY!

1. A disoriented 37-year-old woman is discovered wandering in a park. She reports no recollection of her identity or of how she got there. After an investigation the police learn she actually has a husband and child and lives over 200 miles away. This woman most likely suffers from

   (A) dissociative fugue
   (B) dissociative amnesia
   (C) conversion disorder
   (D) borderline personality disorder
   (E) histrionic personality disorder

2. Enlarged ventricles in the brain, an excess of dopamine activity and frontal lobe dysfunction are all correlated with the presence of

   (A) eating disorders
   (B) bipolar disorder
   (C) schizophrenia
   (D) dissociative identity disorder
   (E) unipolar depression

3. Negative symptoms of schizophrenia include

   (A) auditory and visual hallucinations
   (B) paranoid delusions
   (C) delusions of grandeur
   (D) grossly disorganized thought patterns
   (E) social withdrawal and lack of emotion

4.  The presence of dissociative identity disorder is

    (A) strongly correlated with physical or sexual abuse in childhood
    (B) strongly correlated with the presence of disorganized schizophrenia
    (C) strongly correlated with the presence of catatonic schizophrenia
    (D) typically associated with abnormalities in the limbic system of the brain
    (E) linked to malfunctions in the dopamine circuit

5.  The diathesis-stress model of psychological disorders is most synonymous with which of the following perspectives in psychology?

    (A) The cognitive perspective
    (B) The humanist perspective
    (C) The biopsychosocial perspective
    (D) The psychoanalytic perspective
    (E) The sociocultural perspective

6.  Which of the following is most consistent with the presence of depression?

    (A) Occasional periods of mania
    (B) Disorganized thought and speech
    (C) Abnormally low levels of serotonin and epinephrine
    (D) Loss of memory for important life events
    (E) Extreme episodes of panic

7.  Which of the following categories of disorders involve psychological stressors which translate into physical symptoms?

    (A) Anxiety disorders
    (B) Somatoform disorders
    (C) Adjustment disorders
    (D) Affective disorders
    (E) Psychotic disorders

8. You are a behavioral psychologist. A person you know has such a fear of horses that he refuses to go anywhere near a neighboring farm where several horses are stabled. If asked to explain this phobia, you would most likely argue that

   (A) horses are symbolic of the man's unconscious fear of his father
   (B) the man was born with a genetic predisposition for anxiety and fear
   (C) the man was likely deprived of loving interaction in early childhood
   (D) the man needs to be shown that his perception that horses are to be feared is distorted and unreasonable
   (E) the man is being reinforced for not going near the farm by a reduction in anxiety when he steers clear of it

9. Cognitive theories of depression would most emphasize

   (A) brain structure abnormalities
   (B) chemical abnormalities in the central nervous system
   (C) unconscious early childhood experiences
   (D) the sufferer's history of reinforcements and punishments
   (E) self-defeating, maladaptive thought processes

10. A woman reports she feels disgustingly dirty unless she bathes and changes clothes at least four times a day, and that her house is not acceptable for visitors unless she cleans every room in the house at least twice a day. These characteristics are symptomatic of

   (A) tardive dyskinesia
   (B) obsessive-compulsive disorder
   (C) disorganized schizophrenia
   (D) conduct disorder
   (E) SAD

11. Months after surviving a hurricane that destroyed his home, Louis feels persistent anxiety and irritability and experiences recurring nightmares about the disaster. These symptoms are consistent with

   (A) generalized anxiety disorder
   (B) conversion disorder
   (C) tardive dyskinesia
   (D) posttraumatic stress disorder
   (E) borderline personality disorder

12. Which of the following disorders is <u>not</u> listed as an *Axis I* disorder in the DSM?

    (A) Histrionic personality disorder
    (B) Dissociative amnesia
    (C) Bipolar disorder
    (D) Autism
    (E) Hypochondriasis

13. An individual has periods of relative calm repeatedly shattered by intense anxiety, accompanied by a dramatic increase in respiration, heart rate and sweating, all of which seem to have no obvious environmental trigger. These characteristics are most consistent with

    (A) generalized anxiety disorder
    (B) schizoaffective disorder
    (C) social phobia
    (D) panic disorder
    (E) bipolar disorder

14. Twenty-eight-year-old Jake's behavior is characterized by lack of self-control, impulsiveness, consistent defiance of authority and a lack of empathy or remorse. These characteristics are most consistent with

    (A) conversion disorder
    (B) anti-social personality disorder
    (C) histrionic personality disorder
    (D) post-traumatic stress disorder
    (E) dysthymic disorder

15. The DSM-IV-TR

    (A) provides explanations about the causes of abnormal behavior
    (B) categorizes psychological disorders and lists the specific symptoms of each disorder
    (C) has been shown to provide little inter-rater reliability between psychologists
    (D) outlines a clear plan for the treatment of each psychological disorder
    (E) focuses predominantly on the cognitive and psychoanalytic perspectives

GO ON TO THE NEXT PAGE

# Chapter 13
# Treatment of Psychological Disorders

### Introduction

In many ways, this chapter is a continuation of the chapter on abnormal psychology. Your teacher may even combine the two topics, under the umbrella of "Clinical Psychology." In this section, we turn our focus to the ways in which professionals attempt to treat various psychological conditions. In your study, you will want to consider the following questions: How would we operationally define "success" in therapy? How do we measure the effectiveness of various treatment approaches? Are the principles of any particular treatment approach less relevant than the basic relationship between therapist and client/patient? What are the criticisms of each treatment approach, and how valid are those criticisms?

Five to seven questions on the multiple-choice segment of the AP Exam will be about Treatment.

### Treatment – An Overview

If you ever have the chance, take a course on the history of psychology. It is an often overlooked topic, but it's quite interesting. The history of the treatment of "psychological" disorders is fascinating, and tells us much about the times in which such therapies were used. We place the word psychological in quotation marks because some psychological conditions were thought at one time to be the work of demons or evil spirits who had possessed the body of the victim. Indeed, one historical treatment technique, called *trephining*, involved drilling a hole in the skull of the patient in an attempt to show such spirits the door.

The institutions which housed mental patients in the past were often frightening places. In some of them the public could pay to view institutionalized patients, much as one might visit a zoo. Reformers like **Philipe Pinel** in early 19th century France, his contemporary, **Dorothea Dix** in 19th century America, along with many others, tried with some success to invite society to see that those suffering from mental illness required nurturance and treatment, not incarceration.

In the late 20th century there was a widespread movement toward **deinstitutionalization**. This was founded, at least in part, on the view that those with mental disorders could be helped and sometimes completely cured. Much of the deinstitutionalization movement was spurred by the advent of antipsychotic drugs, which helped many people with schizophrenia function in society. The plan was to have a wide array of community health services available to those patients released from mental hospitals. However, as funding decreased, these services became less and less available, leaving many severely impaired individuals without the care they needed. One unintended result of deinstitutionalization is that many seriously ill people have ended up homeless due to the lack of space in shelters and other care facilities, and the inability of community programs to keep up with the high demand for mental health interventions.

There are many different professionals who are qualified to treat psychological disorders. **A psychiatrist** is a medical doctor with a specialty in mental health. Because he or she is an M.D., a psychiatrist can prescribe medications. **A clinical psychologist** may also be a 'doctor', but has a PhD rather than an M.D. Thus, if such a professional suggested medication as part of your treatment, he or she would have to refer you to a psychiatrist or other medical doctor to obtain a prescription. In recent years, clinical psychologists have fought to obtain the ability to prescribe drugs, and as of this writing psychologists in New Mexico and Louisiana have secured that right. **A counselor or counseling psychologist** is another professional licensed to practice psychotherapy. It's likely that individual would have a master's degree or doctorate in clinical psychology or a related discipline.

In the last chapter you learned that there are many competing theories on the causes of disorders. In this chapter, you'll find an even greater number of approaches to treat those disorders. While there may be hundreds of treatments, they can be broken down into two general categories- *psychotherapies* and *biomedical treatments*. Psychotherapies are sometimes called *talking cures*, as they rely on discussion between the patient and therapist. Biomedical treatments involve the use of medical interventions to treat disorders.

As we turn now to the major therapeutic schools of thought, please keep in mind that many therapists today are actually **eclectic** in their approach. They rely on many different techniques, borrowed from many different models, in their attempt to tailor treatment specifically to the individual patient at hand. In fact, research suggests that the key to a successful therapeutic experience depends most on the level of **warmth and trust in the relationship** between patient and therapist, not on the particular orientation of the psychologist. The therapist's ability to **offer an objective, caring and professional view** of the patient's life and issues seems to be of greatest importance.

### The Psychoanalytic and Psychodynamic Models

The label 'psychoanalyst' is *not* a catch-all term for any type of therapist, even though it is sometimes used as such in everyday language. A psychoanalyst is a particular kind of clinician, whose techniques are based on Sigmund Freud's and Carl Jung's theories of the unconscious mind. A psychoanalyst is usually a medical doctor. As part of a psychoanalyst's training, he or she would actually undergo analysis themselves. Psychoanalysis focuses on **the achievement of insight through the uncovering of unconscious internal conflict**. Freud believed most of our problems stem from traumatic early childhood events that have since been buried in the unconscious. For example, fixation in the oral or anal stages (recall Freud's psychosexual stages from our study of Personality Theory) may create conflict that leads to disorder later in life. Freudian psychoanalysis often involves use of techniques like:

- **Free association:** In classical psychoanalysis, the patient lies on a couch or sits on a chair while the analyst sits out of the sight line of the patient. This theoretically facilitates free association, in which the patient lets their mind roam freely from topic to topic, emotion to emotion. The idea is that the patient expresses whatever comes to mind and at some point reveals important matters that might be at the heart of one's troubles. The idea is to say the first thing that comes to mind, without editing. Delays in responding could imply **resistance**, which suggests the patient is fighting what he or she really wants to say. Resistance is an indication that the therapist may be getting close to uncovering a meaningful conflict - the unconscious counters by hindering the progress of therapy. Theoretically, exposing these issues provides insight into the source of the problem and thus a release of emotions, which can be **cathartic** for the patient.

- **Dream interpretation:** As you know, Freud referred to dreams as "the royal road to the unconscious" and many analysts today still rely on interpretation of the latent content of dreams (the underlying, hidden themes in a dream), analyzing details that may be symbolic of issues in the patient's life. It is important to note that they look for recurring *patterns* in dream content, not merely on single dream reports.

Over the long-term of analysis, a psychoanalyst would likely expect, and perhaps encourage to some extent, a phenomenon known as **transference**. Transference is a form of displacement in which the patient begins to express feelings for the analyst that actually represent feelings they have toward a significant person in their life, such as a parent. There are obvious dangers in this, but if handled appropriately by the analyst it can offer insights into the patient's genuine emotions and conflicts.

Psychoanalysis is often criticized because much of it is built on a kind of circular argument. For example, if an analyst contends that the patient is repressing a painful early childhood trauma, and the patient denies it, it's possible for the analyst to argue that the patient's resistance is proof of the repression. Since the unconscious mind is not observable, any conjectures as to what is going on in there must remain conjectures and cannot be proven or disproven.

The more modern **psychodynamic** therapy is essentially a condensed version of the traditional psychoanalytic approach. One criticism of the latter is that it involves multiple weekly sessions, which might continue for many years, making it prohibitively expensive for all but the wealthy. The psychodynamic approach attempts to address this issue by focusing a bit more on how the patient's present life is impacted by unconscious issues. The patient usually has once weekly sessions, and therapy is less long-term than traditional analysis.

## The Humanistic Model

*"To my mind, empathy is in itself a healing agent."*
*(Carl Rogers)*

You may recall from previous chapters that humanists believe people are innately good, and can exercise free will to change the course of their lives. The humanistic approach to therapy is usually viewed as the most optimistic and life-affirming of the talking cures. Indeed, one criticism of the model is that it is naively positive about human motives and desires. Like the psychodynamic therapies discussed above, humanistic therapies are often referred to as *insight therapies* because they aim to enhance self-knowledge, which in turn promotes healthy growth.

Humanists believe that the client is in charge of his or her own therapeutic advancement. They tend to prefer the term 'client' over 'patient' to emphasize this focus on the individual's need (and desire) to help him or herself. The humanistic therapist hopes to support the client in their quest for happiness by offering what **Carl Rogers** called **unconditional positive regard (UPR).** Rogers feared that most relationships in life were marked by **conditions of worth** (as in when someone seems to "love" you only because you're wealthy, or physically attractive), and that a healthy therapeutic situation would provide empathy and help with no strings attached and no judgments offered. Roger's **client-centered** or **person-centered therapy** is the hallmark humanistic treatment. The therapist's role here is to provide genuine, non-judgmental acceptance and empathy as the client works toward self-acceptance. Humanistic therapy is *non-directive*, meaning that the therapist does not tell the client what to do, but rather actively listens, reflecting and echoing what has been said.

Humanist **Abraham Maslow** contended that most people want to become **self-actualized**, to reach their fullest potential as human beings. Carl Rogers also believed that people had a sense of their **ideal self**, which most individuals aspired to reach. Humanists like Rogers and Maslow would likely argue that the cause of most unhappiness is the knowledge that there is *incongruence* between one's **real self** (another Rogerian term) and one's ideal self. The goal of therapy is for the client to take on the task of closing that gap.

**Existential therapy** is a humanistic method that strives to help the client find meaning and purpose in life. They emphasize free will, and encourage the client to take responsibility for their choices and the situations they find themselves in.

**Gestalt therapy** is another kind of humanistic approach, even though its founder, **Fritz Perls**, was originally trained as a psychoanalyst. You may recognize the term 'gestalt' from our study of sensation and perception; there, it referred to the human tendency to organize perceptions of the world into meaningful wholes. The goal of gestalt therapy is to help the client become more "whole" by pulling together the separate parts of one's self. The gestalt therapist encourages the client to face the unresolved turmoil in his or her life in the present moment. Thus, Perls was breaking from the psychoanalytic focus on the past, while also emphasizing the humanistic view that the burden of recovery lies with the client.

When all the king's horses
and all the king's men failed,
they called in the gestalt therapists

### The Behavioral Model

The behavioral treatment model is built on the fundamental premises of classical and operant conditioning, along with social learning. Behavioral treatments per se are not *"talking cures"* like psychoanalysis or humanistic approaches. They do not seek underlying sources of psychological issues, but instead, directly address behaviors and the conditioning that supports them. You may wish to review the chapter on Learning Theory to refresh your memory on the work of important behaviorists like B. F. Skinner and John B. Watson. Look as well at Ivan Pavlov's work in the classical conditioning of dogs, and Albert Bandura's concept of observational learning.

**Mary Cover Jones** is often credited with being the first to propose behaviorist methods for reversing conditioned fears. One of those approaches is called **counterconditioning**, in which one pairs an object that a patient fears with a pleasant stimulus. For example, if you want to countercondition a child's fear of rabbits you might gradually bring a rabbit ever closer to the child while the child is eating their favorite snack. Theoretically, the positive feelings associated with the snack would replace the fear that the child had previously felt when exposed to rabbits. Many **exposure therapies** use the same technique of gradually exposing a patient to the object of their fear.

**Joseph Wolpe** used these basic principles to develop **systematic desensitization**. Statistically, this is the most successful of all treatment approaches for phobias. The basic behavioral argument is that phobias are conditioned fears, so it is not surprising that those theorists believe simply in de-conditioning those responses. In order to extinguish an intense fear of rodents, for example, a behaviorist would first teach the patient some basic breathing and relaxation techniques. He or she would then ask the patient to list events associated with rodents that cause the patient fear. Such a list is called an *anxiety hierarchy*, and might include seeing a photograph of a rat, knowing that rats may be nearby, being in the same room as a rat and so on. The events would then be placed in order of intensity by the patient, with the most intense trigger at the top of the list.

The next step in this behavioral process involves exposure to the least provocative event on the list. The patient utilizes relaxation techniques to modulate their level of fear. When the patient learns to substitute relaxation for fear at this level of exposure, therapist and patient move onto the next most stressful event on the anxiety hierarchy, and so on up the ladder of intensity.

In some rare cases, individuals have overcome phobias through full intensity exposure to the object of fear. It's possible, for example, that a person with a deep seated fear of leaving the home could be "cured" if forced out of the home by a fire or other emergency. If, after the expected period of extreme anxiety, the individual arrived at the realization that there was no danger in that environment, the phobic response might reach extinction. This kind of **flooding** is not a desirable therapeutic approach, for obvious ethical reasons. Instead, a therapist may instead use "mental flooding", in which the patient is guided to visualize a highly stressful exposure to the object of the phobia. In this way, the individual can learn to greet that image with relaxation rather than fear. Recently, behavioral therapists have begun to use **virtual reality exposure therapy** toward the same end.

One might also extinguish a phobia through the use of **modeling**. An individual suffering from a mouse phobia might watch the therapist or another "model" playing with or handling a mouse and learn to imitate that modeled behavior.

Some behavioral modification plans such as **token economies** are built upon the principles of operant conditioning. In some schools and institutions, individuals are given reinforcers (tokens) for desired behavior. These reinforcers may have no intrinsic value, but they can be traded in at some later point for something that truly is reinforcing for the individual, such as pizza, or free time, or vacation extensions. In one study, a token economy was set up in which chimps performed tasks in exchange for poker chips, which they could then use to "buy" bananas. The animals quickly learned to value the poker chips even though they have no inherent worth to a chimp. Token economies are often successfully used in "skills training" programs for people with schizophrenia, and they are sometimes used with children to foster the development of desirable social skills.

**Aversive therapy** incorporates fundamentals of conditioning in attempting to stop problematic behaviors by pairing a problem behavior with an *unpleasant* stimulus. A common example involves the use of a drug, *antabuse*, for those who wish to stop drinking alcohol. The volunteer regularly takes antabuse, which has no effect unless it combines with alcohol. Such a combination induces nausea and vomiting. The idea is to associate the previously desirable act of drinking with unpleasant illness, resulting in an aversion to drinking.

A long-standing criticism of behavioral techniques is that they fail to address the root causes of the condition in question. They deal with the symptoms, critics say, but don't really get at the true issue. Some also critique behavioral approaches on the grounds that patients are conditioned and de-conditioned in the same way one might deal with pigeons or mice. These opponents argue that human emotion and thought processes are given short shrift in the behaviorists' world.

### The Cognitive and Cognitive-Behavioral Models

Perhaps because of the final criticism of behaviorism noted above, behaviorism is often wedded to the cognitive approach in therapy. **The cognitive-behavioral approach** combines the emphasis on overt behaviors from the behaviorist's perspective with the cognitivist's focus on the hurtful, irrational thought processes of the patient. A cognitive-behaviorist would therefore work to change the undesired behaviors of a patient while also attacking self-defeating cognitions held by the individual.

You might remember from earlier units some references to the concept of **explanatory styles**, as formulated by **Martin Seligman**. He argued that some people have a pessimistic explanatory style. That is characterized by the tendency to blame bad events on themselves and to expect such events to be long lasting and to negatively impact one's entire life. This is but one example of a cognitive explanation for unhappiness. Two other cognitive views of therapy come from **Albert Ellis** and **Aaron Beck**. Ellis was the founder of **rational-emotive behavior therapy (REBT)**, in which the therapist boldly challenges the irrational or unjustifiable cognitions of the patient. The goal is to see the world and one's place in it more accurately, and to reduce self-blame and self-denigration. Beck proposed the concept of the **cognitive triad**, in which he theorized that many unhappy people have negative thoughts about themselves, events that occur around them and the future. Beck's cognitive therapy emphasized taking a realistic, objective look at these interpretations.

Most cognitive therapies focus on the patient's negative self-talk and work toward **cognitive restructuring**, where patients are challenged to reformulate the way they view and interpret life events. These therapies are *directive* in that the therapist actively guides the patient in confronting and modifying their dysfunctional ways of thinking.

One criticism of the cognitive perspective is that sometimes things really *are* bad, and the patient's unhappiness is a quite reasonable and predictable response to difficult times. Some also find particular trouble with Ellis's REBT, because he was known to be rather confrontational with his patients.

### Group, Family and Community Approaches

There are many advantages to **meeting in a group with others who share similar problems**. It can be very reassuring early on simply to recognize that there are others who share similar problems. Those individuals can also offer thoughts and advice, based on their experiences, which may help the other members of the group. The simple act of affiliating with a group can be very comforting, and can offer opportunities to refine one's social skills and deepen all relationships in each member's life. Group therapy is also less expensive than one-on-one treatment. **Self-help groups** such as Alcoholics Anonymous (AA) offer the same benefits as group therapy, but are more likely to be run by someone with less of a background in clinical therapy.

**Family therapy** (or **family systems therapy**) brings the members of a family together to explore the dynamics within that complex group. This approach is based on the idea that each member of the family is part of a web of interdependence. Thus, the emphasis is on each individual as a part of the unit, and how the interactions between each component part of the group impact each member. The therapy may focus on improving communication between family members, and analyzing the power structures within the family unit.

**Community psychology models** focus, at a grass roots level, on prevention and early intervention. The goal is to help those with psychological problems at the local level, partly because many people cannot afford or do not have access to larger institutions. In fact, the movement toward deinstitutionalization, mentioned earlier in this unit, is part of the community psychology model. Ideally, individuals who are at risk for developing disorders, or who have already begun to exhibit symptoms, are cared for more quickly, comfortably and conveniently at the local level.

## The Biomedical Model

The obvious emphasis of the biomedical model is on physical interventions, which directly address the symptoms of various disorders. The biomedical model focuses on genetic predispositions, brain abnormalities and neurotransmitter and hormonal imbalances. The majority of treatments addressed here involve the use of psychotropic drugs to help alleviate the symptoms of various disorders. While some are highly effective, it's important to note that all of the drugs we describe carry the possibility of side effects, ranging from dry mouth to irritability to drowsiness to sexual dysfunction.

This section is a good place to review some of what you learned in the chapter on Research Methodology. The drugs we describe have all been tested against the placebo effect to ensure that they are indeed more effective than the mere expectation that one will get better. These clinical trials involve the use of a *double blind procedure* in which the people administering the drug and the participants in the drug study do not know who is in the experimental group and who is in the placebo group. You may recall that this is one effective measure to help eliminate participant and experimenter bias.

The major categories of psychotropic drugs that you will need to know for the AP Exam include the following: mood stabilizers, **antidepressant**, **antianxiety** and **antipsychotic** medications.

**Lithium carbonate** is a *mood stabilizer* that is very effective in treating those with bipolar disorder. It is also the one that you are most likely to encounter on the Advanced Placement Exam. Although the exact mechanism of how this works is unclear, it likely influences the neurotransmitters norepinephrine and glutamate. Lithium is mildly effective in treating the depressive side of bipolar, but it is especially successful in treating the manic episodes associated with the disorder. Because lithium has significant side effects and can even be toxic, there has been substantial research into other drugs that moderate moods with fewer side effects. One outcome of such research is the discovery that an anti-seizure medication called *Depakote* is also often an effective treatment for bipolar disorder.

Early antidepressants, such as **the tricyclics** and **MAO inhibitors**, operated by increasing norepinephrine and serotonin activity in the brain. But many patients were reluctant to take these drugs because they often caused severe side effects. In the late 1980s, a new category of antidepressants with fewer side effects was introduced. These widely used drugs are known as **selective serotonin reuptake inhibitors (SSRI's)**. As their name suggests, these medications slow the reuptake of serotonin, leaving more of it in the synapse. The resulting increase of serotonin activity has the effect of elevating one's mood. **Prozac**, **Zoloft** and **Paxil** are among the most commonly prescribed SSRI's. In addition to treating depression, these drugs have been highly successful in treating anxiety disorders (including OCD), eating disorders, and more.

The **antianxiety medications** (or tranquilizers) most likely to appear on the AP Exam are the benzodiazepines. Two well-known examples from this group are **Valium** and **Xanax**. In essence, these drugs stimulate inhibition. They increase levels of GABA activity causing the central nervous system to slow down - you may recall that GABA is the most plentiful inhibitory neurotransmitter in the brain. In addition to the regular list of side effects, benzodiazepines are highly addictive. It is also relatively common for patients to build up a tolerance to these drugs, resulting in a cycle of dependence. Other drugs, such as *BuSpar*, are gaining favor in the treatment of anxiety because they cause fewer side effects and have a lower incidence of addiction.

**Antipsychotic drugs** (also called **neuroleptics**), operate on the neurotransmitter dopamine and are generally used to treat schizophrenia. Schizophrenia is marked by unusually high levels of dopamine, and medications for it block or inhibit dopamine activity. Early antipsychotics like *Thorazine* and *Haldol* were very successful in treating the positive symptoms of schizophrenia including hallucinations and delusions. These were great breakthroughs, but they also led to serious side effects including impaired motor coordination. With extended use, some patients developed **tardive dyskinesia**. This condition is marked by facial tics and contortions, lip smacking and other involuntary movements, and can be irreversible if not caught early. Concerns about such side effects have lead to the development of newer drugs. A group of drugs called *atypical antipsychotics* offer promise in that they have fewer (although still significant) side effects, and they have been shown to have some success in treating the negative symptoms of schizophrenia (i.e. apathy, social withdrawal, flat affect). One such drug is *Clozapine* (or *Clozaril*), which seems to effect both dopamine and serotonin receptor sites.

## Other Biomedical Treatments

A dramatically controversial and now largely outmoded technique is that of **psychosurgery**. In the middle of the 20th century especially, surgical procedures were sometimes done on violent patients. **The prefrontal lobotomy**, for example, involved the disconnection of the frontal lobes (the "executive" portion of the cortex) from the rest of the brain. This often succeeded in eliminating aggression in the patients, but also tended to leave them emotionally and cognitively impaired for the rest of their lives. More sophisticated forms of psychosurgery are only rarely conducted today.

**Electroconvulsive therapy (ECT)** is another controversial treatment, which is still sometimes utilized today, although in a more evolved form than earlier in the 20th century. It is sometimes used as a treatment for severe depression that has been resistant to other forms of therapy. The patient receives muscle relaxants and is briefly put to sleep. Next, an electric current is administered. The goal is to induce a seizure, and something about the seizure often alleviates, at least temporarily, the symptoms of the depression. Though we still do not know exactly how the process "works", it has great short-term success in bringing patients out of severe depression. Unfortunately, the rate of relapse over the long-term is quite high. It is a popular misconception that these "shock treatments" are used as punishment in institutions. While ECT remains controversial, it is not used to threaten or punish patients. It is, however, still commonly marked by side effects such as memory impairment.

A very new procedure called **repetitive transcranial magnetic stimulation (rTMS)** is being proposed as an alternative to ECT. In it, the prefrontal cortex is stimulated using electromagnets. Like ECT, there are questions about just what it does and how it works, but many individuals who have not benefited from other therapeutic approaches have found relief from their depression after rTMS treatments.

Another technique that addresses the biological roots of a disorder is the use of **light therapy** for sufferers of seasonal affective disorder. SAD is characterized by depression that comes with the change of seasons. The reduced levels of light during winter seem to be at the root of this mood disorder, so patients are often systematically exposed to light in order to alleviate symptoms. However, some psychologists contend that any help it provides is largely the result of a placebo effect.

## Assessing Various Treatments

It is impossible to say in a sentence or two which therapeutic approach is best. As mentioned earlier, the success of talking cures seems more related to the relationship between sufferer and therapist than to the academic orientation of the professional. This emotional bond between doctor and patient is often referred to as the **therapeutic alliance**. The most successful alliances form when the therapist makes the client feel respected, accepted and understood. It's also quite important to recognize that the success of any particular treatment depends on the disorder. Systematic desensitization is a very effective treatment for phobias, but how would one apply it to schizophrenia? Naturally, no one would prescribe an antipsychotic medication to an individual suffering from generalized anxiety disorder. A talking therapy that focuses on early childhood trauma might be very appropriate for an individual with dissociative identity disorder but not someone with seasonal affective disorder. It seems wise to tailor the therapy to the specific needs of the patient.

As mentioned earlier, many therapists use an eclectic approach, combining elements of various treatment perspectives. There is some evidence indicating that combination therapies may have longer lasting effects than the "single method" approach. For example, depressed patients treated with *both* Cognitive-Behavioral Therapy (CBT) and SSRI's, had fewer relapses than those only treated with one of those methods. It seems clear that there is no single "best" approach to treatment, but enough demonstrably valuable methods exist to provide most struggling patients with some hope.

### Name Hall of Fame

**Sigmund Freud** and **B.F. Skinner**.... sound familiar?

There are other people to know in this unit. On the AP Examination, the name **Albert Ellis** is usually mentioned in the same breath with his rational-emotive therapy, from the cognitive school of thought. **Aaron Beck** may deserve just as much recognition in that area, although in the past he has shown up less often on the exam. You met **David Rosenhan** in the last unit on Abnormal Psychology and his research on institutionalization and labeling fits in this chapter as well, and **Abraham Maslow's** name has figured prominently in units on Motivation and Personality Theory, along with this one.

**Carl Rogers** is so closely linked to his client or person-centered therapy that it is often referred to as a "Rogerian" approach, so know his name as well. In the history of treatment, **Mary Cover Jones** and **Joseph Wolpe** are important figures, but they are not likely to be the answer to a multiple-choice item on the AP Exam.

### Essay Themes

As we mentioned in the last unit, clinical psychology has been a common topic for free response items on past Advanced Placement Examinations. Fortunately, your grasp on the treatment unit should have been enhanced by your earlier study of Personality Theory. As you saw there, knowing about **the major schools of psychological thought** is of paramount importance for success on the big test.

# Treatment of Psychological Disorders

## Introduction to Treatment

- The history of 'treatment'
- Phillipe Pinel; Dorothea Dix
- psychiatrist vs. psychologist

- Commonalities in the talking cures
  - An eclectic approach

## The Psychoanalytic Approach

- The focus is on unresolved unconscious conflict; the goal is to break down defenses, achieving insight into that concealed conflict
- Resistance
- Transference
- Catharsis

- Freud, Jung
- Free association
- Dream interpretation
  - Criticisms?

## The Behavioral Approach

- The focus is on how maladaptive behaviors have been learned, and how they can be unlearned
- Behavior Modification programs
  - Token Economies
  - Aversive Therapy
  - Modeling
  - In combination with cognitive?

- Systematic Desensitization: a kind of counterconditioning
- Flooding
- Virtual Reality Therapy
  - Criticisms?

## The Cognitive Approach

- The focus is on modifying self defeating, maladaptive thoughts and interpretations of events
  - In combination with behavioral?

- Ellis and REBT
- Seligman's Explanatory Styles
- Beck's Cognitive Triad
  - Criticisms?

# Treatment of Psychological Disorders (Continued)

- Focus: problems are often rooted in a gap between one's "ideal self" and one's "real self"
  - The client is ultimately responsible for his/her own advancement

## The Humanistic Approach

- Maslow, and frustrated attempts at self-actualization
- Rogers and 'client centered' / 'person centered' therapy
- UPR vs. 'conditions of worth'
  - Criticisms?

- Review: how psychoactive medications operate
- Tolerance, Withdrawal, Side Effects (such as tardive dyskinesia)

- Antianxiety meds
- Antidepressant meds
- Antipsychotic meds

## The BioMedical Approach

- Lithium Carbonate
  - ECT
  - rTMS
  - History of psychosurgery
    - Criticisms?

- Pros and Cons of Group Therapy
- Self-Help Groups

## Group, Family and Community Therapies

- Family Therapy: the goal is to look at the family as a system, not at individual dispositions or attitudes
- Community Psychology: the goal is prevention or early intervention

- Review: Rosenhan's study on institutionalization
  - Deinstitutionalization: goals? impact?

## Institutions; Evaluating Treatments

- Which therapeutic approach is best?
  - The therapeutic alliance

263

### Practice Items

- **Time yourself** on this section, and record how long it takes you. It should take you between 10 and 11 minutes

- These section items are **not** in order of difficulty

1. A humanistic therapist would most likely criticize a behavioral therapist on the following grounds:

   (A) Behavioral approaches tend to get stuck in interpretations of the root causes of the patient's behaviors
   (B) Behavioral approaches ignore the importance of uncovering the powerful unconscious conflict rooted in early childhood
   (C) Behavioral approaches lack empirical support for their claims of success
   (D) Behavioral approaches are not empathetic and supportive enough of the whole person
   (E) Behavioral approaches put too much of the burden on the client for their own healing

2. In a therapy session, a patient says, "After this break-up, I know I'll never meet anyone who cares about me again." His therapist challenges the irrational, self-defeating nature of that statement. The therapist is practicing a technique most closely associated with

   (A) Freudian analysis
   (B) psychodynamic therapy
   (C) rational emotive behavior therapy
   (D) person-centered therapy
   (E) behavior modification programs

3. In one of Jorge's earliest treatment sessions, his therapist helped him create an anxiety hierarchy as a starting point to help Jorge overcome his fear of flying. His psychologist likely adheres to which of the following treatment perspectives?

   (A) The behaviorist model
   (B) The biomedical model
   (C) The existential model
   (D) The cognitive model
   (E) The psychodynamic model

4. A behaviorist would likely criticize the psychoanalytic or psychodynamic approach on the grounds that psychoanalysts

   (A) focus too much attention on the self-defeating thoughts of the patient
   (B) overemphasize the impact of current family dynamics on the individual's dysfunction
   (C) progress so quickly that the patient does not reap long-term benefits
   (D) expend too much effort on alleged, unobservable causes of problems that may have nothing to do with the patient's current behaviors
   (E) look to foster self-actualization at the expense of addressing the actual symptoms of disorders

5. Which of the following therapists would argue that the most important thing one can do to help a client is provide empathy and unconditional positive regard, as the client strives to close the gap between his real self and ideal self?

   (A) Carl Jung
   (B) Albert Ellis
   (C) Joseph Wolpe
   (D) Carl Rogers
   (E) B.F. Skinner

6. Today, electroconvulsive therapy is generally used only to treat

   (A) severe cases of depression
   (B) recurrent episodes of panic attacks
   (C) paranoid schizophrenia
   (D) dissociative identity disorder
   (E) extreme cases of mania

7. A family systems therapist would most likely

   (A) focus attention on the thoughts and actions of the most maladjusted family members
   (B) focus attention on the thoughts and actions of the most well adjusted family members
   (C) view each family member not in isolation but as a part of the whole family unit
   (D) explore the individual perspectives of each family member to encourage a sense of personal autonomy in relation to the family unit
   (E) encourage each individual member of the family to examine the contingencies of reinforcement which have governed their behaviors in the family unit

8. Tardive dyskinesia is

(A) a major potential side effect of some antipsychotic medications
(B) a recently developed antianxiety medication
(C) a recently developed anti-depressant medication
(D) likely to result from electroconvulsive therapy
(E) the most common form of psychodynamic therapy

9. Both Xanax and Valium

(A) increase the availability of GABA in the brain
(B) decrease the amount of serotonin in the synapse
(C) are effective in treating the positive symptoms of schizophrenia
(D) have been found to be the most effective drug treatments for bipolar disorder
(E) cause more dopamine to be released in areas of the brain near the prefrontal cortex

10. Which of the following techniques would likely be most effective in treating an intense fear of elevators?

(A) Aversive conditioning
(B) Dream analysis
(C) Systematic desensitization
(D) Beck's Cognitive Therapy
(E) rTMS

11. Jamal's therapist does not offer interpretations of his comments or give him specific directions as to how to improve his life. Instead, the therapist listens and encourages Jamal to pursue things that help him achieve a sense of personal satisfaction. Which type of therapy is likely being used?

(A) Free association
(B) Aversive therapy
(C) A token economy
(D) Cognitive restructuring
(E) Client-centered therapy

12. When paired with alcohol, the drug antabuse causes significant nausea and sickness. A therapist using antabuse to treat an alcohol addiction is using which of the following?

(A) Psychoanalytic therapy
(B) Aversive therapy
(C) Existential therapy
(D) Gestalt therapy
(E) Exposure therapy

13. Which of the following psychologists would most agree with the following statement? "There are three musts that hold us back - I must do well. You must treat me well. And the world must be easy."

    (A) Mary Cover Jones
    (B) John Watson
    (C) Albert Ellis
    (D) Sigmund Freud
    (E) Fritz Perls

14. Which of the following drugs works by blocking the reuptake of the neurotransmitter serotonin?

    (A) Lithium
    (B) BuSpar
    (C) Xanax
    (D) Thorazine
    (E) Prozac

15. Aaron Beck's cognitive triad refers to a patient's thoughts about

    (A) themselves, events in their life and the future
    (B) themselves, significant others and peripheral others
    (C) significant others, peripheral others and self image
    (D) the past, the present and the future
    (E) the world, the self and others

NO TESTING MATERIAL ON THIS PAGE

GO ON TO THE NEXT PAGE

# Chapter 14
## *Social Psychology*

(Sullivan, Blanchard)

## • "Too little, too late" •

### Introduction

Social psychology examines the impact of groups on individuals. It is essentially the study of the interconnectedness of humans. Perhaps it is an illusion to think of ourselves as "independent" beings at all - each of us is so interdependent with the environment and the people around us. Some Buddhist meditation masters call this "interbeing" and point out how difficult it is to separate "ourselves" from everything and everyone else. Social psychology specifically explores the human interplay between self and others.

You should expect 8 to 10 items on Social Psychology on the multiple-choice section of the AP Exam. The following are some of the intriguing questions that will emerge in this chapter:

- To what extent do our group affiliations influence our individual behavior? Has your sense of personal responsibility ever been affected by the fact that you were part of a group?

- How do groups make decisions?

- Despite our stated beliefs in our own independence, to what degree are humans vulnerable to obedience to authority figures? To conformity to group pressure?

- When do people help others, and under what conditions are people less likely to do so?

- Do humans have a natural tendency to compete with each other? Despite this, is it in our evolutionary best interests to cooperate?

- Is it natural for humans to discriminate between people who are "like me" and those that are "not like me?"

- How do we explain our own behaviors? Are those explanations different from our attempts to understand similar behavior in others?

- Why do we connect with certain people and not others? What explains friendly and romantic attraction?

You learned about Industrial and Organizational Psychology in an earlier unit on Motivation and Emotion. I-O Psychologists apply their understanding of psychology in various organizations and the workplace. There are clear linkages between it and this unit, because I-O Psychologists often study worker attitudes and functioning in such group settings. They also examine effective leadership styles, and may help to identify the strengths of the individual workers, in the hope of placing them appropriately within the whole system. At least part of that would also involve an understanding of how individuals in a company or other professional setting function within the group dynamic.

You might want to explore a subfield of I-O Psychology called **Human Factors**. Versions of this actually go by many names, including Human Factors Technologies, Human Factors Engineering, Human Factors Science and Ergonomics. Basically it involves applying one's understanding of psychology (especially in terms of perception and cognition) to designing optimal systems and work environments. They wrestle with the question, "How do I design this product or environment to make it safe and user-friendly, while maximizing productivity?"

## Group Interactions

If you have ever done something in a group that you would not have done when alone, then you already have some knowledge about social psychology. **Deindividuation** is a term coined to account for atypical individual behaviors that unfold in a group setting. It describes the sense of the loss of identity and personal responsibility in a crowd. Deindividuation helps to explain why an otherwise kind-hearted, law abiding person commits a theft during a riot. It accounts for why individuals do things at a huge concert or a packed sporting event that they would not imagine doing otherwise. It may be at the root of cyber-bullying - it is obviously easier to make fun of someone if you can then melt into the crowd of the Internet. In sum, certain group situations can apparently make us feel invisible, and thus less accountable for our actions.

Sometimes individuals behave in ways that are unproductive simply because they fear *others* might do so. This is a **social trap**. When trying to merge onto a road in a crowded city, it would probably be best for all if every individual driver were patient and cooperative. An ethic based on the idea, "First you go and then I'll go" might actually help everyone involved. However, each individual involved not only has to play along but has to believe that everyone else will play along too. Cooperation would serve the self-interest of all, but everyone must cooperate and trust that others will do the same. The so-called **tragedy of the commons** is a kind of social trap. Imagine a group of shepherds who share a common grazing area that is just the right size to accommodate their flocks. One shepherd, with a perfectly reasonable desire for self-improvement, decides that if he acquires one or two more animals, he can do his work better and turn a better profit besides. This self interested but understandable act will have a ripple effect on all the other shepherds, who now must share the common ground with too many sheep. If more than one shepherd has such an inclination, the problem is exacerbated. Eventually, even those who first moved to expand can also be hurt. Even when one's long term self-interest is best supported by cooperation, people often end up competing, to the detriment of all.

The **prisoners' dilemma** explores the same theme, within the context of game theory. Imagine that Lewis and Clark are arrested on suspicion of committing a felony. Unfortunately, the police have little evidence to support their suspicions, although they are confident they are correct. They separate the two, and offer each of them a deal – speak against your partner, and you can walk away with no jail time, while he will serve ten years in prison.

In one classic version of this scenario (there are several), Lewis and Clark would each get five years in prison if they both talk. If neither talks, they will serve only six months apiece. Of course, Lewis does not know what Clark is up to in his interrogation room, and vice versa.

From the perspective of Lewis and Clark, the best option seems to be to give up the other. But if they both do so, they will both be worse off than if they had remained silent. Thus, the members of a group who quite rationally look out for their own self-interest can end up hurting themselves, *and* everyone else. Even though cooperation is probably the best strategy, it is difficult to see how two people in such a scenario *would* cooperate.

It does seem possible to unite groups in a common cause through the introduction of **superordinate goals**. If a group, even a contentious one, is given a task that can be accomplished only with the cooperation of all members, that group tends to bond. Members rally around the cause to attack that overarching problem, and the effort ties them together as one.

It is not the case, however, that individuals always *want* to be "tied together as one". Research into personal space demonstrates that. While there is significant cultural and situational variation, as a general rule individuals tend to possess a sense of **personal space** that is not to be invaded without permission. In the 1960's researcher Edward Hall (who used the term **proxemics** to describe the dynamic between space relationships and personal comfort levels) postulated that Americans set the boundaries of their personal territory at two or three feet. In other cultures, the bubble is bigger or smaller, but there *is* a bubble nonetheless. When that bubble is broken, people may avoid eye contact, cross arms or legs, shift the body or actually move away to reestablish a comfortable relationship. There are numerous exceptions to this of course. Intimacy is often expressed through physical closeness, the rules may be different at a crowded party as compared to a library, and Hall also discussed issues of *public space* which may manifest at a quiet beach or on a relatively empty bus.

Two very important concepts related to more formal group activities are groupthink and group polarization. In **groupthink**, members of a group find themselves "going along" with the flow of the group or the apparent wishes of that group's leader. Criticisms are no longer raised, alternative solutions no longer offered. Sometimes this results from each individual member's desire for a harmonious group environment, sometimes because members are deferring to a strong, perhaps even feared, leader. Today, some wise group leaders actually designate specific members of the group to be naysayers. It is that person's primary job to pose questions, offer critiques, and generally insure that groupthink does not occur.

In **group polarization**, group decisions end up as extreme versions of the individual members' predispositions. Get a bunch of violent people together to discuss possible military strategies and it is likely that the final group proposal will be a more aggressive one than any of the individual participants would have offered. It was once thought that groups tended to make more dangerous decisions in general than the individual members would have (the so-called *risky shift*), but research suggests it is more accurate to say that the group simply exaggerates the predispositions of the individuals.

In **social loafing** individuals in a group exert less effort than they would if on their own. This can be conscious, but is more usually unconscious. In a tug of war game, teammates might each report they were pulling with all their might, and they might even believe that was so, but research suggests that the efforts of the entire group make it easier for each *individual* member to slack a bit.

Finally, we look at how a group of people observing an individual can influence that person's performance. If you are participating in a spelling bee competition or a math team event, does having an audience watching hurt you or help you? How about playing in a softball game or running in a track meet- does a big crowd help you to do better? Research in Social Psychology suggests that the audience influences you in ways that depend upon the task you are performing. If it is a task that you know well, and is one in which you have had success, the audience tends to aid your performance. This is known as **social facilitation**. If, on the other hand, an audience gathers round when you are trying to do something you've never done before, it's likely their presence will hinder your performance. This is called **social inhibition**. If you have won spelling competitions in each of the last five years, you'll get an additional boost from the presence of others this time around. If you sometimes misspell your own name, an audience will probably cause you to stumble even more in your spelling efforts.

## Prosocial Behavior – Helping Others

When do people help others, and what factors contribute to that sort of pro-social behavior? These are questions that have probably been asked for a very long time, and they were asked again in the 1960's when a woman named Kitty Genovese was stabbed to death in New York City. Over the course of approximately 30 minutes one evening, Genovese was stabbed repeatedly while being chased by a man in the immediate area of her own apartment building. She eventually died from her wounds. Social psychologists became very interested in this tragedy because it appeared no one helped Ms. Genovese, although police later discovered that over three dozen individuals heard at least part of the commotion. One neighbor did eventually call the assault into police, but only after Ms. Genovese was dead, and apparently only after first calling a friend to ask for advice.

The story is intensely dramatic, but it now appears that the details of the alleged apathy of the bystanders were exaggerated. Did any one person actually witness the assault in its entirety? Did some observers really turn up the volume of their television sets to mask the cries of Ms. Genovese? It now appears that both are unlikely, yet the incident endures in the minds of many as the definitive case study of bystander apathy.

Psychologists offer some explanations for when and why people help others in what is called **the bystander effect**. The more numerous the number of people witnessing an assault or other frightening event the less likely it is that any one person will do anything to help. This is known as **diffusion of responsibility**. In such a situation, bystanders seem to think, "Someone else will do it." Worse, the longer things go with nobody intervening the more likely it is that each individual will come to doubt whether anything actually needs to be done. This is called **pluralistic ignorance**. It means that while every individual may believe that help is required, each wrongly assumes that no one else feels that way – thus, no one does anything.

Of course, there is also an element of fear in such a scenario. Individuals may fear embarrassment if they intervene in a situation when help really wasn't needed (And, again, the longer no one helps, the more it can appear that help is *not* needed). Further, in the Genovese case, fear of physical harm might also have been a factor in the bystander's apparent inaction.

John Darley and Bibb Latane conducted research in response to the Genovese case that supported all of this. They found that individuals who were led to believe that a person nearby was having a seizure were more likely to help, more quickly, if they felt they were the only person aware of the situation.

Recent research has uncovered evidence of purposeful helping behavior in children as young as eighteen months old. Even those little ones spontaneously help others to retrieve objects and open doors. Does that suggest an inborn inclination toward altruism? The jury remains out on that question.

### Obedience to Authority

Some people use the terms 'obedience', 'compliance' and 'conformity' interchangeably, but there are definite distinctions between them. To *conform* is to adjust your thoughts or actions to agree with a reference group or a norm. **Obedience** refers to doing a thing because someone, often an authority figure, told you to do so, whether you like it or not. It's a bit harsher than compliance - there's an order and a person follows that order. If someone wins your *compliance*, they have essentially persuaded you to choose to do what they want you to do; to comply with a request implies some level of agreement on your part. We will say more on that in a moment. First, we turn to obedience.

Stanley Milgram's study in the early 1960's on obedience to authority remains one of the most famous and controversial studies in all of psychology. Milgram wrote an entire book on the subject, and it is difficult to do justice to his work and all of its implications in this space. Simply stated, Milgram created a situation in which an authority figure (in this case, a man in a lab coat, at Yale University) ordered a volunteer to "teach" another volunteer, and to punish that "learner" if and when he made a mistake (in Milgram's original work, the learners and teachers were all men). The volunteers were led to believe that they were participating in a study on the effects of punishment on learning and memory, but Milgram was actually interested in the behavior of the "teachers" - would they physically punish another volunteer if commanded to do so?

Electric shocks were used as the alleged punishment. The teacher believed he could administer over two-dozen levels of increasingly severe shock to the learner, up to a maximum of 450 volts. The teacher was given a low level "sample shock" before the session began, to give him a sense of what the shocks were like. The teacher was also personally introduced to the learner before things got underway. The teaching and learning was conducted via microphone - there was no visual contact after the teacher was allowed to see the learner hooked up to the shock apparatus. The teacher and learner could each hear the other quite easily; the verbal exchange alternated between questions, answers and grunts or cries of pain from the frequently incorrect learner.

Before running his study, Milgram asked many respected colleagues to forecast the outcome. They predicted that only one teacher in a thousand would administer the maximum amount of shocks, up to 450 volts, and that most would stop at around 120 volts. That would have required 3 or 4 wrong answers from the learner, and the subsequent punishments delivered by the teacher.

In Milgram's original study, with 40 male teachers ranging in age from 20 to 50, approximately 2/3 went "all the way", and *all* teachers administered at least some shocks. This despite the fact that the learner, who had openly complained of a past heart condition upon meeting the teacher, groaned, screamed, refused to answer, screamed some more, and then stopped responding altogether in the course of the session.

In fact, no shocks were really given. The "learner" was actually in on the whole operation with Milgram. His responses and cries of pain were scripted, such that each teacher heard the same reactions to the same questions at the same points in the process. Of course the volunteer teacher didn't know any of that.

The ethical guidelines for psychological research we discussed in the chapter on Research Methodology are in many ways derived from Milgram's research. If these volunteers had been told, for example, that "they had the right to discontinue participation at any time," as would be required today, Milgram would not have had much of a study.

There is much else to discuss in regard to this study, including the numerous variations later built into replications of it. For the purposes of your AP Exam preparation and laying a foundation for your future study of psychology, know that Milgram attributed the behavior of the teachers to the power of the situation. In watching film of Milgram's sessions, it is difficult not to be judgmental about the personalities of the people involved. How could they inflict this pain on a screaming man with a heart condition? Milgram would likely ask us how certain we are of what *we* would do in such a situation. In fact, when the situation was somewhat less overwhelming, results *were* a bit different. If, for example, a volunteer teacher was allowed to see another teacher refuse to continue, rates of obedience in the first teacher went way down. When the authority figure left the room or delivered instructions by phone, obedience levels were again reduced. In the original setup, the authority figure never threatened the teacher (although they did prompt teachers with phrases like, "You must continue" or, "The experiment requires that you continue"), but it appears the physical presence of that authority did make it harder to disobey.

## Compliance

Politicians, advertisers (and even teachers) use various methods to persuade you to do what they want you to do. **The central route to persuasion** (sometimes called *systematic persuasion*) is based upon presenting facts and evidence in a rational attempt to win you over to one argument or another. In this approach, a car sales executive might present you with a "fact sheet" emphasizing the various strengths of her car over others. **The peripheral route to persuasion** (which may also be referred to as *heuristic persuasion*) appeals to emotions, reflexive responses and conditioning. Most television commercials for automobiles operate on this level.

One way to get people to do something for you is simply to do something for them. This is based on **the norm of reciprocity**. Generally speaking, we tend to treat others as they have treated us. If a charity group includes a free set of mailing labels with their request for a donation, those receiving the labels feel an obligation to give something in return, making them more likely to contribute to the charity.

Because it may serve you well in the real world, we'll look at two more specific methods of persuasion used to win compliance. They go by interesting names: the foot-in-the-door technique and the door-in-the-face technique.

If you hope to make a big commission by selling the most expensive guitar possible to a prospective buyer, you might employ **the foot-in-the-door technique** by first showing guitars of lesser value, while encouraging the shopper to commit to the idea of buying from you. You might invite the shopper to test out one or more of your guitars, again in an attempt to win a small commitment from him or her. Only then would you move onto the more expensive models, now that the shopper has committed, even in small ways, to the idea of buying. The technique is based on methods sometimes employed in the past by door-to-door salespeople, who operated on the assumption that if they could just "get their foot in the door", their chance of sales success was high.

**The door-in-the-face technique** involves starting big and then "settling". To sell the most expensive guitar possible, you might begin by showing a custom made model with a price affordable only to the wealthiest of buyers. After rejecting that purchase, coming down to a lower price is much easier for the potential buyer. A $900 guitar looks quite inexpensive compared to a $10,000 instrument. The seller thus invites the buyer to slam the door in his face, at first, in order to win compliance on a less expensive but still profitable sale. When lawsuits are filed requesting exorbitant settlements, or when professional athletes publicly ask for astronomical salaries, the rationale behind the strategy might well be built on the door-in-the-face approach, which is also appropriately referred to as *rejection and retreat.*

## Conformity

As you saw in the last section, **conformity** refers to a kind of "going along" with others or with some societal expectation. **Solomon Asch** conducted studies in the 1950's on conformity to group pressure. He seated a number of individuals together and asked them to verbally respond to some questions. All but one of the participants were confederates of Asch's. On some of the questions, he had coached them to give obviously incorrect answers. The idea was to see if the target volunteer went along with those answers, even against his better judgment. Asch discovered that people were quite likely to conform to the group pressure, even on items that a control group (whose members had been asked the same questions without the public group pressure) almost never answered incorrectly. It was, therefore, not the case that those in his experimental setup didn't "know" the correct answers, but that having as few as three others give different responses made it very hard to resist the group consensus. Asch found that rates of conformity increased as the size of the group increased, up to a ceiling of six or seven members; after that point, adding more confederates did not impact the results. The factor that was even more important than the size of the group was *the unanimity of the group.* As you might imagine, if even one confederate did not go along with the group, that made it much easier for the target volunteer to avoid conforming as well.

Another study you must know about is **Philip Zimbardo's "mock prison"** of the early 1970's. Zimbardo asked for student volunteers to play roles in a "prison" established at Stanford University. He was interested in the dynamics of incarceration and prison psychology. Volunteers were randomly assigned as guards and prisoners in what was designed to be a two-week role-play of prison life. Zimbardo had to discontinue the study after less than one week, because the volunteers had gotten too immersed in their roles. Many of the guards conformed so much to what was "expected" of the role that they began to punish, humiliate and generally make life miserable for the prisoners, who largely tended to play the roles of powerless inmates. This study is another that contributed to today's ethical guidelines in psychological research, as many felt and still feel it was unnecessarily dangerous. You can probably think of one or two of your schoolmates that you would not want to have as a guard at *your* mock prison.

278 Chapter 14

Recent survey data gathered from The International Social Survey Programme and The World Values Survey challenge some long-held assumptions about American non-conformity and individualism. These data suggest that Americans are more inclined toward **collectivist** values (defining the self in relation to social roles and expectations) than is often thought. This despite the fact that people intuitively label Americans as being of an **individualistic** bent – that is, focused more on one's unique individuality than on the interests of the group at-large.

You might think of collectivist cultures in terms of **interdependent self-systems**, and individualistic cultures in terms of **independent self-systems**. Members of an interdependent self-system think of themselves in terms of group norms and the well being of the collective community. Those in independent self-systems focus more on establishing one's independence from others.

Of course, it seems problematic to label any one group of people as being strictly "collectivist" or "individualistic." Such general labels may at times help us as we talk about different cultures, but how often do they do us a disservice? And what sort of survey item can actually reveal such tendencies? Does a positive response to the statement, "People should support their country even if the country is in the wrong" suggest an affinity for collectivism, or is it more a statement of patriotic nationalism? Clearly, generalizations about groups of people have inherent pitfalls, especially when discussing characteristics that are difficult to quantify.

### Attribution Theory

In the 1950's, Fritz Heider proposed **attribution theory** to account for how each of us assigns responsibility for decisions and outcomes. He coined two terms for this: **dispositional (or personal) attributions** and **situational attributions**. If you win an important tennis match, you may be more likely to attribute your success to your hard work and exceptional ability (a dispositional attribution). If you lose a key match, you may be more likely to attribute the loss to external factors, such as bad weather or a poor umpire (a situational attribution). Heider argued that humans are often prone to the **fundamental attribution error** (or **FAE**), in which they tend to disproportionately make dispositional attributions over situational ones when accounting for the behaviors of others. This is especially likely if the behavior is distressing or ambiguous, and if it is *consistent* ("That's what he usually does in that situation"), *non-distinctive*, ("He's also like that in other situations") and low in *consensus* ("No one else does that sort of thing").

We often commit the FAE while driving in traffic - that person who is traveling so slowly in front of us must simply be an incompetent driver. There are many possible situational factors influencing that person's driving, but we typically give those less weight. However, we give such variables lots of weight when *we* are the ones driving slowly. In such a case, we tend toward **the self-serving bias**. We make situational attributions for our own unfortunate behaviors, even though we would have made a dispositional attribution to explain the same bad acts in others. If our behavior is irritating to others, it surely was a matter of an overwhelming or unavoidable circumstance, not a weakness of our own. Of course, we also lean toward dispositional attributions when we succeed – that success was surely due to my superior abilities! Collectively, the FAE and the self-serving bias are often referred to under the umbrella term, **the actor-observer bias**.

Many of us commit the fundamental attribution error when learning about Stanley Milgram's obedience study described earlier. We're inclined to think there's something wrong with the character of volunteers who obeyed the authority figure and we give less attention to the impact of situational forces on their decisions.

In **self-handicapping**, a person offers a kind of preliminary "excuse" which they can then fall back on if they indeed do poorly on a task. If a man fears that he will fail miserably in his concert tomorrow, he may stay up very, very late tonight, and make certain everyone *knows* that he did. This provides a ready-made excuse (or attribution) if his performance *is* disappointing.

**• Self-handicapping in the wild •**

There is subtle but strong psychological incentive to want to believe that the universe has an inherent balance, and that people largely get what they deserve. This is called **the just world phenomenon**. It allows us to explain the misfortunes others suffer as being the result of some behavior of theirs - and *we* will be careful not to behave that way ourselves. This creates a sense of control in one's life. Some people may even read the obituary of a peer and look for evidence in the story of behavior that may have led to the death (heavy cigarette smoking or drinking, for example). That may allow that person to conclude the passing was not random, that it had a "cause", and that *he* can avoid the dangerous behaviors that placed the deceased in jeopardy.

Some psychologists believe that many of our actions are driven by **the illusion of control** - why do people so commonly push a button calling for the elevator when that button is already pushed? Some argue that it gives one a sense that it is they who are calling for the elevator - no one else is in control of their destination or how they plan to get there!

## Attitudes

What comes first - attitudes or behaviors? Do we have views and judgments that in turn govern our behaviors, or do we first act and then *account for* those actions by constructing attitudes that are consistent with the behaviors?

In the unit on Motivation, we touched on **cognitive dissonance theory**. It addresses this interplay between behaviors and attitudes. Essentially, we seem to strive to keep our behaviors, cognitions and attitudes consistent with one another. When they are not in agreement, the result is cognitive dissonance, a term Leon Festinger coined to describe the internal tension we experience when what we think doesn't agree with what we do. If you claim to have a passionate interest in conservation, you will want to act in ways that are in line with that attitude. If one day you find yourself throwing plastic bags carelessly around a pristine campsite, you are likely to feel some anxiety. To relieve this dissonance, you must either change your behaviors or modify your stated attitude.

In the earlier unit on Thought and Language, we looked at **confirmation bias**, which is relevant to this section as well. Once we have an attitude or opinion, we tend to look to support it, while sometimes overlooking evidence that might refute it. Thus, long held beliefs and attitudes can be quite resistant to change.

Another concept that is relevant to many units in introductory psychology is the **self-fulfilling prophecy**. We mentioned it specifically in the earlier section on Testing and Individual Differences, and the chapter on Psychological Disorders. In it, our own expectations actually cause them to come true. At times our attitudes about someone or something can be transparent enough that they actually influence outcomes. In a study in the late 1960's, elementary school teachers were led to believe that their class of new students was especially ready to blossom academically. In fact, the students were chosen at random. But, by the end of the school year those students *had* significantly improved from the year before and in comparison to their classmates, who did not benefit from the apparently unconscious treatment the teachers' gave to the targeted kids. Those teachers *believed* that the students were going to do well, and thus they did.

**Bias/Prejudice/Stereotyping**

You may have been exposed in history classes to a study conducted by a third grade teacher in Iowa in the late 1960's which is sometimes called **the blue eyes/brown eyes study**. The teacher told her class that people with blue eyes were superior to those with brown eyes. Blue-eyed students in her class were allowed to place a stigmatizing collar on the brown-eyed kids, and in general the teacher began to treat the brown-eyed children as inferior. So too did the blue-eyed children, and very quickly at that. Many people still question the wisdom of this study, although the teacher has conducted follow-up sessions with the class that seem to indicate little long term negative fall out. The study certainly did seem to demonstrate how quickly and easily an authority figure can turn one group of people against another. History tells us it is all too easy to **scapegoat** those you deem inferior, blaming them for all wrongs.

This may be attributable to **in-group bias**. Humans seem to have a strong tendency to favor the groups to which they belong. "We" are the in-group, and "they" are the out-group.

"We" share common values and attitudes; "they" are different from us. **Ethnocentrism** is a related term referring to the tendency to think that your nation or culture is superior to others. This can also result in a tendency to see other cultures as simply versions of one's own; it's hard to appreciate another society or culture if you are trapped in an ethnocentric view of the world.

Interestingly however, while members of out-groups are seen to be different from those in the in-group (and, obviously, that relationship is all relative - you see the groups to which you belong as in-groups, while others may think of you as part of an out-group), often the members of that out-group are *not* seen as being particularly different from *each other*. This is called **out-group homogeneity bias**. Those who are in a group to which you do not belong and with which you are unfamiliar are judged to be more similar (or homogenous) than they really are. Thus, a Hispanic man who witnesses a crime perpetrated by an Asian man may genuinely have difficulty distinguishing between that man and other Asians, not because, "He's a racist" but because he has not had enough experience and interaction with Asian people.

**Stereotyping** is linked to out-group homogeneity bias. For example, a woman who is unfamiliar with the members of a group to which she does not belong may simply rely on generalizations about those members. You might remember from our study of Sensation and Perception that we often rely on such **schemas** in arriving at our perceptions of the world, and we seem to have cultural, racial and gender schemas as well. We see in people what we expect to see, and we're inclined toward *perceptual confirmation*, attending most to evidence that supports our predispositions.

Interestingly, humans also tend to attribute positive characteristics to physically attractive people. This **halo effect** results in us assuming that physically attractive people are smarter, nicer and more talented than those of us who are more aesthetically challenged. Perhaps this is related to the human tendency to stick with our first impressions of others. Rightly or wrongly, physical appearance *is* our first impression of most people. It is risky to assume that nice-looking people are always nice-acting people, but we are apparently prone to do so.

### Attraction and Relationships

Research in Social Psychology indicates that one of the most important factors in successful relationships is **similarity**. It may at times be true that "opposites attract," but that does not predict particularly well for longevity in a relationship. Also, initial attraction is often simply dependent on physical **proximity**. Even though many of us have romantic ideas about seemingly preordained meetings with those we are supposed to be with, it appears that we are simply more likely to link up with people who are nearby. We tend to like people and things that are familiar to us.

Gordon Allport once argued that we have "a fear of the strange." **The mere exposure effect** is based on the idea that we have more positive feelings about things (and people) to which we are frequently exposed. An outgrowth of this is **the contact hypothesis**. It suggests that bringing those in conflict together will in itself help to reduce the conflict. But it seems clear that this reduction of tension will not simply happen on its own. It requires a mutual sense of equality and interdependence in a positive environment. But, if you recall our earlier discussion of superordinate goals, you may see a value in bringing opponents together in the shared attempt to reach common goals.

We will end this chapter with a very brief look at an upbeat topic: love. Robert Sternberg (who also offers a well-respected Triarchic Theory of Intelligence, which we outlined in the unit on Testing and Individual Differences) has attempted to define certain types of love, a bold move in a world where so many people prefer to think of it as a mysterious, indefinable energy. In Sternberg's **triangular theory of love,** he argues that *consummate love* is made up of **passion** (the intense desire to be with the other person), **intimacy** (emotional closeness, openness and sharing) and **commitment** (the desire to maintain the relationship). Other forms of 'love' are made up of different combinations of these three elements. For example, *romantic love* has passion and intimacy but lacks commitment, *companionate love* is made up of intimacy and commitment but lacks passion, *empty love* has commitment but lacks intimacy and passion, and *infatuation* has passion but no commitment or intimacy. It's unlikely you will have to identify these types on the Advanced Placement Examination, but the theory certainly offers fodder for discussion.

## Name Hall of Fame

You first saw **Stanley Milgram's** name way back in the first unit on Research Methodology. His is a name you ought to know for the AP Exam. The same can be said of **Solomon Asch**, famous for his studies on conformity to group pressure, and **Philip Zimbardo**, who conducted the controversial "mock prison" study at Stanford University. You need to know attribution theory well, but probably not the name **Fritz Heider**, even though his is the name most associated with it. The name of **Kitty Genovese** should cue your recall of the basic elements of the bystander effect, and most anyone who claims to know about psychology recognizes her name.

## Essay Themes

It is not too hard to imagine an item that asks about obedience and conformity, perhaps with direct reference to the work of Milgram and Asch. Attribution theory, the study of attitudes and the concept of prejudice could all easily be tied into elements of other units, which makes them especially attractive to the authors of the test. One essay in the past assessed student grasp of experimental design using a study that was an almost exact replica of Darley and Latane's work on the bystander effect. So, you can see that this is a very important unit indeed.

# Social Psychology

- Cooperation and Competition
  - Social Traps
  - "The Prisoner's Dilemma"

- Deindividuation
- Social Loafing

- Social Facilitation
- Social Inhibition

- Personal space/proxemics

## Group Interactions

- Group Dynamics:
  - Groupthink
  - Group Polarization
  - Superordinate Goals

- Individualism and collectivism

- Milgram's Obedience study: details, variations

- Under what conditions are we least likely to obey?

## Obedience to Authority

- Winning compliance:
  - The foot-in-the-door
  - The door-in-the-face

- The central route to persuasion
- The peripheral route to persuasion

- Asch's "Line Comparison" study and conformity to a reference group

- Zimbardo's "Mock Prison" study and conformity to role expectations

## Conformity

- Under what conditions are we least likely to conform?

- The norm of reciprocity

- Darley and Latane's "seizure experiment"

## Altruism

- Case Study: The Genovese Stabbing

- The Bystander Effect:
  - Diffusion of responsibility
  - Pluralistic ignorance

# Social Psychology *(Continued)*

## Attribution Theory

- Dispositional vs. Situational attributions
- Actor-Observer Bias
  - The FAE
  - The self-serving bias
- The Just World Phenomenon
- The illusion of control
- Self-handicapping

## Attitudes

- Self-Fulfilling Prophecies
- Independent vs. interdependent self systems
- Links to other units:
  - Cognitive Dissonance
  - Confirmation Bias

## Bias/Prejudice

- In-Group Bias
- Out-Group Homogeneity Bias
- "Blue Eyes, Brown Eyes"
- Schemas
- Ethnocentrism
- Scapegoating

## Attraction and Relationships

- Sternberg's Triangular Theory of Love
- "Beautiful is good" - A Halo Effect
- Similarity
- Proximity
- Mere exposure; contact hypothesis

## Practice Items

- **Time yourself** on this section, and record how long it takes you. It should take you between 10 and 11 minutes

- These section items are **not** in order of difficulty

1. Research in social psychology indicates that inter-group conflict can best be resolved by

    (A) reciprocal determinism
    (B) the introduction of a common enemy
    (C) the introduction of a superordinate goal
    (D) extrinsic reinforcers
    (E) the threat of unpleasant outcomes if conflict continues

2. According to research in social psychology, which of the following is true of conformity?

    I.   Males conform more than females

    II.  Individuals are most likely to conform when the reference group is unanimous in its judgment or behavior

    III. The size of the reference group has little or no effect on rates of conformity

    (A) I only
    (B) II only
    (C) III only
    (D) I and II
    (E) II and III

3. In which of the following variations would you expect the lowest levels of obedience in Stanley Milgrams's "electric shock" study on obedience to authority?

    (A) When the "learner" is a male
    (B) When the "learner" is kept out of visual contact with the "teacher"
    (C) When the "teacher" can instruct another participant to administer the punishment
    (D) When the authority figure does not threaten but only verbally prompts the "teacher"
    (E) When the authority figure leaves the room after giving the instructions

4.  A classmate loudly announces that he is certain he will do poorly on that morning's national exam because he had to stay up the entire previous night with a distraught friend. This public pronouncement could be viewed by a psychologist as an example of

    (A) assimilation
    (B) self-efficacy
    (C) self-modulation
    (D) self-handicapping
    (E) cognitive dissonance

5.  A basketball coach is told that a new player on her team is not very intelligent. As a result, the coach asks very little of the player, assuming she can't understand everything about the team's offense. As a result, the player never fully learns the offense and is then thought to be "dumb" by her coach and her teammates. This situation illustrates the dangers of

    (A) an internal locus of control
    (B) an external locus of control
    (C) actor-observer bias
    (D) the self-fulfilling prophecy
    (E) a social trap

6.  The central conclusion from Philip Zimbardo's "mock prison" study at Stanford University was that

    (A) student volunteers will obey older authority figures
    (B) college students are prone to aggression
    (C) many individuals exhibit strong tendencies toward autocratic behavior and therefore should not be placed in positions of authority
    (D) highly suggestible volunteers should not be chosen as research participants
    (E) individuals tend to conform to role expectations

7.  According to the theory of diffusion of responsibility, the single biggest factor predicting whether a bystander will help someone in need is

    (A) the number of other bystanders
    (B) the duration of the incident
    (C) whether the person in need verbally requests assistance
    (D) the amount of potential threat involved
    (E) whether they themselves have been helped by others in the past

8. The head of a government agency proposes an idea to a group of advisors. The group quickly reaches consensus, as no contradictory or critical opinions are offered, despite the fact that there are substantial weaknesses in the boss's proposal. This is an example of

   (A) the risky shift
   (B) social loafing
   (C) social inhibition
   (D) group polarization
   (E) groupthink

9. In research conducted on social facilitation, it was discovered that skilled pool players who were watched by an audience

   (A) attempted fewer risky shots
   (B) attempted more risky shots
   (C) later reported being negatively affected by the spectators
   (D) performed better than their usual level of performance
   (E) made a substantially lower percentage of their shots than normal

10. An advertiser says to his boss, "I propose we flood the airwaves with commercials. After awhile, with that kind of repetition, consumers will come to like our product even if they don't even *know* they do!!" This is an application of

    (A) social desirability
    (B) the norm of reciprocity
    (C) the bandwagon effect
    (D) the mere exposure effect
    (E) hindsight bias

11. Students watch video of a study in conformity and laugh raucously at the conforming participants while calling them names and referring to them as 'weak' and 'stupid'. Their failure to consider the power of the situation in the study is an example of

    (A) collectivism
    (B) individualism
    (C) the fundamental attribution error
    (D) cognitive dissonance
    (E) pluralistic ignorance

12. Group polarization

    (A) describes the role a dominant leader can play in engineering a false consensus within a group
    (B) refers to the tendency of group interaction to strengthen the predisposed positions of the individuals in the group, resulting in a more extreme group decision
    (C) highlights the differences between dominant and submissive members in a group dynamic
    (D) predicts that males are more likely to make "risky" decisions when in a group than females, especially when that group is led by a male
    (E) explains why individual allegiance to a group tends to dissolve over time

13. Of the following, which is the best predictor of attraction between two people?

    (A) Similarity of attitude and values
    (B) Divergent attitudes and values that somehow "work" together
    (C) Working in the same profession
    (D) Approximate equality of levels of self-esteem
    (E) Approximate socioeconomic equality

14. Which of the following is the clearest example of deindividuation?

    (A) A student signs a petition because many of his peers have done so
    (B) An individual moves from a highly individualistic culture to a collectivist culture
    (C) A teacher publicly humiliates a student
    (D) An incoming college freshman attempts to blend into the background during the first day of freshman orientation
    (E) A normally calm, well-mannered 55-year-old woman joins the crowd in shouting obscenities at the referee of an emotional football game

15. A researcher wants to see if she can entice people to volunteer two hours a week working with recently released felons. She first asks potential volunteers if they believe in giving a helping hand to former prisoners who've served their time. Most say 'yes.' Several weeks later, she returns to those who answered 'yes' to that survey question and asks if they are willing to work with a group of ex-convicts. A large percentage of them agree to do so. The researcher has utilized

    (A) the foot-in-the-door approach
    (B) the door-in-the-face approach
    (C) the scarcity technique
    (D) the norm of social responsibility
    (E) the norm of reciprocity

# Chapter 15
# *Preparation to Take the Examination*

On the Advanced Placement Psychology exam you will have **70 minutes** to answer **100 multiple-choice questions**. After a break, you will then have **50 minutes** to respond to **two free response questions**. The free response section of the exam is administered only after the multiple-choice portion is completed - you can't go ahead to it if you finish the multiple-choice early.

The directions provided for you before the multiple-choice section don't tell you much of anything - besides, you probably have more than your share of experience with such tests. However, the directions for the free response section are worth looking at beforehand:

*__Directions__: You have 50 minutes to answer BOTH of the following questions. It is not enough to answer a question by merely listing facts. You should present a cogent argument based on your critical analysis of the question posed, using appropriate psychological terminology.*

Pay special attention to the words **cogent argument** and **appropriate psychological terminology**. The exam readers, who are highly qualified high school advanced placement psychology teachers and college psychology professors, find it difficult to score responses that circle around the question with a collection of facts but never really offer an argument supported by evidence. A list of definitions will simply not do. Readers can also be annoyed by responses that rely mostly on "pop psychology" or man-in-the-street knowledge and intuition. You want to show them you took a rigorous, college-level psychology course, and that you have a firm grasp of actual psychology terminology and concepts.

As you develop your answers you also ought to think about making the reader's job as easy as possible. You might even consider highlighting key terms as you go. In the end, focused and clear writing will please them and thus benefit you.

At this point you may want to look back at the first chapter in this book to review the "Top Ten Tips" for success on each section of the examination. On the next two pages, we provide an abbreviated version of those suggestions.

## Tips for the Multiple-Choice Section

- **Slow down**. Be aware of the clock, yes, but remember that 70 minutes is a pretty reasonable amount of time for 100 items, if you're well prepared.

- Remember that **the multiple-choice items are arranged in order of difficulty**. It's a decent general rule not to talk yourself out of answers that come easily to you. And, if you're well prepared, the first 20 or so items will likely *be* fairly easy for you.

- If you have time to review a bit at the end of the 70-minute session, try to discipline yourself to **revisit only those items you'd marked** as being potentially problematic. Re-evaluating and changing answers isn't a bad thing per se, but you obviously want to avoid talking yourself out of responses that don't need changing.

- Remember that this section is **worth 66% of your total exam score**. Even though you may get tired as the section progresses, hang in there, because these items carry a lot of weight.

- If you've worked conscientiously through this book you should be able to use **process of elimination** and thus arrive at a reasonable answer choice even on the most difficult items on the exam. Since the so-called "guessing penalty" (in which ¼ point was deducted for each wrong answer) is no longer in force, it's best to answer all questions.

- Don't look for patterns in your responses. In the end, the exam will likely have a pretty balanced distribution of A's, B's, C's, D's and E's, but you should never answer a question based on reasoning like, "That's too many 'B's in a row." You could conceivably have four B's' in a row - don't worry about it.

- One effective strategy is to cover the answer choices and answer the question to yourself before even looking at the options. This makes it less likely that you will be lured off-track by appealing distractors, which can spare you valuable time that might otherwise be lost debating with yourself about an item you really do know.

### Tips for the Free Response Section

- The sample exams that follow will give you a chance to **practice pacing**, which is very important on the essays.

- **Budget your time and stick to that plan** - 50 minutes will pass quickly!

- Your exam proctor should give you a warning at the 25-minute mark that you're halfway home - you may want to specifically ask for that. If you haven't begun your second essay by then, go to it.

- **Do the question you know best first**. It'll be very frustrating if you take an inordinate amount of time struggling with essay #1 only to find you have limited time to answer the second question that you know very well. Take the same approach *within* each question - answer the parts you know well first, then give your best attempt at whatever remains.

- Remember that **the two essays each carry the same scoring weight**. Even if one looks bigger or appears to have more points to earn in it, don't be deceived.

- **Know what the question is specifically asking** and systematically address all of it. That seems obvious, but a large percentage of test takers simply don't do it.

- Your job is to tell the readers what you know. It can be helpful to pretend that they don't know anything - **they're smart but don't know psychology, and you're explaining it to them**, using appropriate psychological terminology.

- For those of you who are handwriting-impaired, have mercy on your readers. They sit for several hours a day for over a week reading responses to the same free response item, which is challenging under any circumstances. But completely illegible penmanship can be exasperating for a reader, because he or she can't really decipher what you know. The readers want to give you the credit you deserve- they really do. Make it easy for them.

On the next three pages, we provide you with a timeline of the history of psychology, which might be of use as you get ready for the exam. It is not exhaustive, but it could serve as a helpful overview of the entire course.

Good luck!

**Timeline: The History of Psychology**

1793    Philippe Pinel works to reform treatment of mental patients, arguing that they should be treated more humanely

1848    Phineas Gage is seriously injured in an accidental explosion, and becomes an enduring psychological case study

1860    Gustav Fechner publishes *Elements of Psychophysics*, outlining the experimental study of what would now fall under the heading of "Sensation and Perception"

1861    Paul Broca discovers that damage to a particular region in the left hemisphere of the brain impairs language

1869    Francis Galton publishes *Hereditary Genius* in which he argues that intelligence is inherited; he later coined the term 'nature vs. nurture'

1879    Wilhelm Wundt establishes the first experimental psychology laboratory at the University of Leipzig

1883    G. Stanley Hall establishes the first American psychology laboratory at Johns Hopkins University

1885    Hermann Ebbinghaus publishes his research on memory and forgetting, coining the term "the forgetting curve"

1890    William James publishes *Principles of Psychology*, soon to become a standard text for American students of psychology

1891    Mary Whiton Calkins, with help from William James, establishes a psychology laboratory at Wellesley College, the first at a women's college; she is later the first female president of The APA

1892    The American Psychological Association (The APA) is founded by G. Stanley Hall (First budget = $63, original membership = 42)

1894    Margaret Floy Washburn is the first woman to receive a PhD in psychology, from Cornell University

1898    Edward Thorndike publishes research on animal learning; his "law of effect", formulated later, would become the foundation of operant conditioning

1900    Sigmund Freud publishes *The Interpretation of Dreams*

1903    Ivan Pavlov begins laying the foundation for his groundbreaking work in classical conditioning

1904    Charles Spearman first publishes work on his theory of "G", or general intelligence

1905    Alfred Binet and Theodore Simon develop the first widely used intelligence test

1913   John B. Watson publishes *Psychology as the Behaviorist Views It*, arguing that psychology should place its focus on the study of observable behaviors, rather than untestable, unseen mental processes

1920   John B. Watson conducts his classical conditioning study with "Little Albert"

1920   Jean Piaget publishes *A Child's Conception of the World*, an important look at the cognitive development of children

1921   Swiss psychiatrist Hermann Rorschach introduces his 'inkblot' projective test

1925   Wolfgang Kohler publishes *The Mentality of Apes*, focusing on the problem-solving abilities of certain primates

1936   Egas Moniz publishes work on the first frontal lobotomies in humans

1938   B.F. Skinner publishes *Behavior of Organisms: An Experimental Analysis*, outlining the basic principles of operant conditioning

1939   David Wechsler develops his earliest intelligence tests, foreshadowing the WISC and the WAIS

1941   A 'clinical psychology' boom begins in the United States in response to the greater need for such services stemming from World War II and its aftermath

1943   The MMPI is first published

1946   The American Psychological Association broadens its membership to include clinical psychologists as well as research psychologists

1951   Carl Rogers begins the humanistic movement with his book *Client Centered Therapy*

1953   Eugene Aserinsky and Nathaniel Kleitman first coin the term REM

1954   Abraham Maslow boosts the humanistic movement with his book *Motivation and Personality*

1955   Solomon Asch conducts his classic research on conformity to a peer or reference group

1959   Harry Harlow publishes work indicating that monkeys require social affiliation and "contact comfort" for healthy development

1962   David Hubel and Torsten Wiesel publish Nobel Prize-winning research reporting the discovery of feature detector cells in the brain

1963   Stanley Milgram conducts his controversial research on obedience to authority

1967   Martin Seligman publishes research on learned helplessness in dogs

1968   John Darley and Bibb Latane publish research on the bystander effect

1969    Candace Pert and Solomon Snyder discover that there are receptor sites in the brain for opiates, laying the groundwork for the discovery of naturally produced pain blockers which came to be called endorphins

1971    Albert Bandura publishes *Social Learning Theory*

1973    Ethologists Konrad Lorenz, Karl von Frisch and Niko Tinbergen win a Nobel Prize for their work on the instinctive behavior of animals

1976    Richard Dawkins publishes *The Selfish Gene*, popularizing evolutionary theory

1978    Herbert Simon wins a Nobel Prize for work on computer simulations of human problem solving processes

1981    Roger Sperry wins a Nobel Prize for his research on split brain patients

1982    Daniel Kahneman and Amos Tversky publish *Judgment Under Uncertainty – Heuristics and Biases*; Kahneman later wins a Nobel Prize for his work on human judgment and decision-making

1983    Howard Gardner first publishes work on his theory of multiple intelligences

1987    The Food and Drug Administration approves SSRIs like Prozac and Paxil

1991    Martin Seligman publishes *Learned Optimism*, a starting point for the Positive Psychology movement

# Sample Examination I

## Section 1

1. If a personality test lacks validity,

   (A) it cannot be consistently scored
   (B) it does not measure the elements of personality that it claims to measure
   (C) it has not been normed with a group that is representative of the population
   (D) it will not have good test-retest reliability
   (E) it is too subjective to be scored accurately

2. Which brain structure seems most responsible for the formation of new memories?

   (A) The hippocampus
   (B) Broca's Area
   (C) Wernicke's Area
   (D) The amygdala
   (E) The caudate nucleus

3. In the following group of values, what is the mode?: 8, 9, 10, 10, 12, 15, 15, 15

   (A) 10.50
   (B) 11.00
   (C) 11.75
   (D) 12.00
   (E) 15.00

4. A six-year-old child reports that the two sets of coins in the following arrays have the same amount:

O O O O O O O
O O O O O O O

The same child is then shown this array and reports that the bottom row "has more":

O O O O O O O
O O O O O O O

The child's responses indicate she has not yet mastered

(A) object permanence
(B) transitional objects
(C) conservation
(D) assimilation
(E) accommodation

5. In the first part of the 20th century, several German psychologists argued that humans consistently attempt to organize sensory stimuli into coherent wholes. This contention became the theme of

(A) the cognitive perspective
(B) gestalt psychology
(C) the community mental health movement
(D) the behavioral perspective
(E) spatial tests of intelligence

6. Which of the following sleep disorders is marked by sudden lapses into REM sleep, often during times of excitement or high emotion?

(A) Hypersomnia
(B) Enuresis
(C) Narcolepsy
(D) Apnea
(E) Somnambulism

7. Carl Jung's personality theory differs from traditional Freudian psychoanalytic theory in that

   (A) Jung believed reinforcements played a primary role in personality development
   (B) Jung believed birth order was the key to personality
   (C) Jung did not accept that the unconscious played a role in personality development
   (D) Jung believed humans had inherited a collective unconscious with memory traces of the history of our species
   (E) Jung believed personality develops out of the unconditional love we receive from our parents and friends

8. According to Erik Erikson, the psychosocial task of adolescence is to resolve the conflict between

   (A) initiative vs. guilt
   (B) identity vs. role confusion
   (C) intimacy vs. isolation
   (D) industry vs. inferiority
   (E) generativity vs. stagnation

9. If a researcher was looking to demonstrate that aggression is caused directly by frustration, they would need to use which type of methodology?

   (A) A correlational study
   (B) A cross-sectional study
   (C) Survey methodology
   (D) A controlled experiment
   (E) Naturalistic observation

10. The false belief that one is constantly under surveillance by the FBI and CIA is an example of

   (A) dissociative identity disorder
   (B) a delusion
   (C) overgeneralization
   (D) a hallucination
   (E) egocentrism

11. Daniel suffers from sleep disturbance, irritability, difficulty concentrating, and recurrent, intrusive recollections and dreams about a previously threatening event. Experts would likely diagnose this as

    (A) major depressive disorder, recurrent
    (B) major depressive disorder, single episode
    (C) Tourette's disorder
    (D) generalized anxiety disorder (GAD)
    (E) posttraumatic stress disorder (PTSD)

12. The mood disorder marked by shifts between deep depression and euphoric, wildly optimistic mania is called

    (A) bipolar disorder
    (B) dysthymia
    (C) seasonal affective disorder
    (D) unipolar depression
    (E) conversion disorder

13. Surveys demonstrate that people tend to view themselves as above average in most categories including intelligence, competence and physical attractiveness. These findings are consistent with

    (A) the self-serving bias
    (B) interdependent self-systems
    (C) self-perception theory
    (D) Roger's person centered approach
    (E) convergent thinking

14. Diffusion of responsibility is a central characteristic of

    (A) prototype matching theory
    (B) the bystander effect
    (C) the law of effect
    (D) sociobiology
    (E) attribution theory

15. Autism is characterized by

   (A) hyperactivity
   (B) rapidly cycling mood swings
   (C) impaired social interaction and communication
   (D) deceitfulness and an apparent lack of remorse or empathy
   (E) visual and auditory hallucinations

16. What psychological perspective is the concept of unconditional positive regard most associated with?

   (A) Trait Theory
   (B) Psychoanalytic Theory
   (C) Cognitive Theory
   (D) Behavioral Theory
   (E) Humanistic Theory

17. Which structure within the limbic system seems most responsible for regulating appetite, thirst and core body temperature?

   (A) The basal ganglia
   (B) The pons
   (C) The hypothalamus
   (D) The medulla
   (E) The cerebellum

18. According to Sigmund Freud, dreams can be interpreted for their underlying symbolism, which he referred to as

   (A) latent content
   (B) manifest content
   (C) catharsis
   (D) transference
   (E) discrimination

19. Deep sleep is characterized by

    (A) the loss of control of the major muscle groups
    (B) the presence of delta wave activity on an EEG
    (C) the presence of alpha wave activity on an EEG
    (D) the presence of sleep spindles on an EEG
    (E) the presence of low amplitude, very rapid electrical brain wave activity

20. Which of the following sets of techniques is most closely associated with behavioral treatment?

    (A) Aversive therapy, virtual reality therapy, token economies
    (B) The empty chair, reflective listening, cognitive restructuring
    (C) Rational emotive behavior therapy, flooding, transference
    (D) Transference, countertransference, dream analysis
    (E) Free association, word association, flooding

21. Harry Harlow discovered that infant monkeys would seek safety from a soft, cloth surrogate mother rather than a hard, wire surrogate mother, even when the wire mother was the only one to provide food to the infant. Harlow's finding supports the notion that infants require

    (A) socialization
    (B) contact comfort
    (C) psychosocial development
    (D) constancy
    (E) continuity

22. One major problem threatening the validity of a "naturalistic observation" is that

    (A) the subjects may react to or be influenced by the observation if they realize they are being observed
    (B) the subjects' behavior cannot be controlled at any period during or after the naturalistic observation has taken place
    (C) the observer is unable to predict the behaviors of the subjects
    (D) the observer cannot statistically analyze the findings in a meaningful way
    (E) the observer will have difficulty establishing the necessary control group

23. Which of the following behaviorists famously conducted a study to condition a baby, called Little Albert, to fear a rat that the baby previously did not fear?

    (A) B.F. Skinner
    (B) John Garcia
    (C) Albert Ellis
    (D) John Watson
    (E) Joseph Wolpe

24. The contention that basic human emotions are universally expressed and understood is supported by Paul Ekman's research into

    (A) body language
    (B) linguistic relativity
    (C) chimpanzees and their emotional responses
    (D) facial expressions
    (E) the limbic system

25. Which of the following best describes the capacity of short-term memory in humans?

    (A) It seems to have unlimited capacity
    (B) It can hold 7 + or - 2 unrelated pieces of information
    (C) It can hold material for several minutes even with no specific rehearsal
    (D) It can hold material for a maximum of a second or two if no other cognitive processing takes place
    (E) No valid studies of short-term memory have been conducted to accurately ascertain its capacity

26. Electroconvulsive therapy (ECT) is sometimes used as a treatment in cases of severe

    (A) bipolar disorder
    (B) anti-social behavior
    (C) schizophrenia
    (D) depression
    (E) dysthymia

27. According to research conducted by Solomon Asch, individuals are least likely to conform to group pressure when

    (A) the group size reaches as high as six or seven individuals
    (B) the behavior by the group is clearly inappropriate or incorrect
    (C) there is no unanimity within the group
    (D) the conformity experiment is conducted by a female instructor
    (E) the individual did not previously know any of the members of the group

28. Which of the following is the order in Abraham Maslow's "hierarchy of needs", ranging from the bottom of the hierarchy to the top?

    (A) Psychological needs, safety needs, need to belong, need for self-efficacy, need to survive
    (B) Physiological needs, safety needs, need to belong, esteem needs, self-actualization
    (C) Physiological needs, esteem needs, need to belong, need for self efficacy, self actualization
    (D) Physiological needs, need to belong, esteem needs, need to pursue happiness, self actualization
    (E) Need for survival, esteem, need for control, need to pursue happiness, need for safety

29. A statistician looks at the amount of agreement between three different judges who score the performances of Olympic ice skaters. The statistician is most probably investigating

    (A) test bias
    (B) ethnocentrism
    (C) inter-rater reliability
    (D) intra-rater reliability
    (E) the normal curve

30. Which of the following would most heavily involve episodic memory?

    (A) A student gives an in-class report entitled "How I Spent My Summer Vacation"
    (B) A child can immediately repeat five digits that they have just heard
    (C) A woman retains the ability to ski after years of not doing it
    (D) A student remembers his old locker combination but forgets his current combination
    (E) A student recalls the first 15 US presidents

31. Gloria has been experiencing depressed moods, and her appetite and sleep patterns have been unpredictable. Which of the following chemicals would her doctor most likely investigate to see if it was influencing the symptoms she has been experiencing?

    (A) Glutamate
    (B) Serotonin
    (C) Oxytocin
    (D) Thyroxine
    (E) Dopamine

32. An aptitude test would be used to

    (A) assess the extent to which an individual has mastered a body of information
    (B) assess how well an instructor taught a body of information
    (C) establish a baseline for comparison to other assessments
    (D) predict the correlation between two variables
    (E) determine how well suited the test taker is for a particular job or role

33. Which of the following is an advantage of longitudinal studies over cross-sectional studies?

    (A) Subject mortality is more likely in longitudinal studies
    (B) The independent variable is more easily manipulated in longitudinal studies
    (C) The dependent variable is more easily measured in longitudinal studies
    (D) It is easier to control sample size in longitudinal studies
    (E) The sample is consistent in longitudinal studies

34. In human language acquisition, babbling is typically followed by

    (A) cooing and telegraphic speech respectively
    (B) cooing and holophrastic speech respectively
    (C) semantics and meta-linguistics respectively
    (D) telegraphic speech and holophrastic speech respectively
    (E) holophrastic speech and telegraphic speech respectively

35. The central emphasis in family therapy is to

    (A) modify the contingencies of reinforcement inherent in the family dynamic
    (B) look at the family as a collection of very distinct and independent individuals
    (C) place the burden for healing on each of the family members themselves
    (D) view the family as a web of interdependent relationships
    (E) explore the unconscious sources of conflict within the family unit

36. People tend to believe that good things happen to good people and bad things happen to bad people. This tendency in thinking represents

    (A) the actor-observer bias
    (B) Maslow's hierarchy of needs
    (C) pluralistic ignorance
    (D) the just world hypothesis
    (E) the theory of objective self-awareness

37. In classical conditioning, extinction is produced

    (A) only when punishments are consistently used
    (B) only when reinforcements are consistently used
    (C) by repeatedly presenting the conditioned stimulus without the unconditioned stimulus
    (D) by utilizing a continuous schedule of reinforcement
    (E) by allowing a substantial amount of time to pass between conditioning trials

38. The section of the human brain that is most responsible for higher-level reasoning, social judgment and planning is

    (A) the frontal lobe
    (B) the parietal lobe
    (C) the occipital lobe
    (D) the somatic nervous system
    (E) the autonomic nervous system

39. A pigeon is reinforced with food for pecking at a red disk. However, the pigeon does not peck at other red objects. This is called

    (A) second order conditioning
    (B) higher order conditioning
    (C) discrimination
    (D) stimulus generalization
    (E) latent learning

40. Activation of the parasympathetic branch of the autonomic nervous system would result in

    (A) dilation of the pupils
    (B) an increase in heart and respiration rates
    (C) a decrease in salivation and digestive activity
    (D) inhibition of bladder constriction
    (E) a decrease in heart rate

41. Julia buys herself a new car, and now notices far more of the same model and color of car than she ever did before her purchase. This is an illustration of

    (A) top-down processing
    (B) bottom-up processing
    (C) a stimulus variable
    (D) the phi phenomenon
    (E) context dependence

42. Glial cells

    (A) nourish, support and protect neurons throughout the brain
    (B) are found only in the parietal lobes of the brain
    (C) carry messages from the skin receptors to the central nervous system
    (D) carry messages from the central nervous system to the muscles and glands
    (E) lack a nucleus

43. As objects move closer or further away from you, your lens changes shape to help bring that object into focus. This monocular depth cue is called

    (A) convergence
    (B) accommodation
    (C) retinal disparity
    (D) overlap
    (E) linear perspective

44. In an experiment examining the impact of uniform color on referee's perceptions of aggression in football games, the referee's perception of aggression is

    (A) an extraneous variable
    (B) a confounding variable
    (C) the independent variable
    (D) the dependent variable
    (E) the intervening variable

45. Which of the following is an example of a negative correlation?

    (A) A statistical analysis indicates there is no clear relationship between IQ and levels of prejudice
    (B) A dog learns that chewing on the furniture consistently leads to an unpleasant consequence, so it stops chewing the furniture
    (C) A study suggests a strong upward connection between hours spent watching television and weight in pounds of American adolescents
    (D) A school district reports that their low scores on a national achievement test are directly related to low salaries for teachers in the district
    (E) A researcher discovers that as education levels increase, levels of obedience to authority decrease

46. Two mountaineers are carrying packs of identical weight. Each time they stop to rest, one secretly puts a light object from his pack into his companion's pack. He hopes to lighten his own load, and reasons that his companion will not notice such small changes in a pack that is already heavy. Such reasoning is an application of

    (A) Weber's Law
    (B) Yerkes-Dodson Law
    (C) the Law of Pragnanz
    (D) the Whorfian Hypothesis
    (E) the gestalt principle of good continuation

47. After living in a new apartment for over a year, you have become so accustomed to the nightly passing of a train near your window that you no longer notice it until one night it does *not* pass by. This is an illustration of

    (A) dichotic listening
    (B) opponent process theory
    (C) sublimation
    (D) habituation
    (E) sensory adaptation

48. According to Albert Bandura, under which of the following conditions would a child be most likely to imitate a modeled behavior?

    (A) When the model is unknown to the child
    (B) When the model is the same age as the child
    (C) When the modeled behavior is reinforced and the child has a sense of self-efficacy
    (D) When the model is the same sex and approximate size of the child
    (E) When the modeled behavior is not harmful to self or others

49. In the study of language, morphemes refer to

    (A) the rules that govern the order of words or phrases
    (B) the basic sounds of a language
    (C) the smallest units of meaning
    (D) two word phrases used by children to get their message across
    (E) groups of words that convey a thought

50. A child who solves an unfamiliar arithmetic problem explains how he arrived at his solution. This is an example of

    (A) metacognition
    (B) an internal locus of control
    (C) an external locus of control
    (D) self handicapping
    (E) self-actualization

51. A preoperational child nods her head repeatedly while speaking on the phone, seemingly unaware that the listener cannot see what she is doing. Jean Piaget would likely view this as evidence of

    (A) egocentrism
    (B) reversibility
    (C) artificialism
    (D) animism
    (E) habituation

52. According to George Kelly, individuals build and revise their own personal constructs that help them to understand and explain the world to themselves. Such a conception fits best under

    (A) cognitive theory
    (B) gestalt theory
    (C) behavioral theory
    (D) introspection
    (E) functionalism

• **Items 53 and 54 each refer to the following scenario:**

Researchers design an experiment to test the effect of reading aloud on retention of the material read. One group of randomly assigned volunteers will read a story quietly to themselves, and a second group of randomly assigned volunteers will read the same story aloud. Both groups will later be assessed for retention of what they've read using a multiple-choice test.

53. What is the independent variable (IV) in this experiment?

    (A) Retention of facts in the story
    (B) The story itself
    (C) The reading of the story aloud
    (D) The items on the multiple-choice test
    (E) Reading

54. Which of the following would be a confounding variable in this experiment as it is presently set up?

    (A) One group reads the story aloud but the other reads it quietly
    (B) The "reading aloud" group reads the story in the classroom, and the "reading silently" group reads the story at home for homework
    (C) The brightest students are randomly distributed between the "reading aloud" group and the "reading silently" group
    (D) The story is familiar to all the students
    (E) The story is unfamiliar to all the students

55. Under which of the following conditions were volunteers in Stanley Milgram's "electric shock" obedience study most likely to obey an authority figure?

    (A) When the volunteers were female
    (B) When the volunteers were paid
    (C) When the authority figure threatened the volunteers with physical harm if they did not obey
    (D) When the volunteers were allowed to instruct a second party to actually execute the orders of the authority figure
    (E) When the orders given by the authority figure were deemed to be dangerous by the volunteers

56. According to arousal theory,

    (A) females score consistently higher on measures of baseline physiological arousal than males
    (B) males score consistently higher on measures of baseline physiological arousal than females
    (C) there is little statistical correlation between levels of physiological activation and task performance
    (D) organisms will perform challenging tasks best if they have a moderate level of activation
    (E) the great majority of humans tend to seek high levels of sensation and arousal

57. Broca's Area and Wernicke's Area play a very important role in

    (A) language expression and understanding
    (B) logical reasoning
    (C) our ability to make sounds and our ability to hear
    (D) determining the emotional relevance of incoming messages
    (E) motor movement throughout the somatic system

58. In statistics, the standard deviation is a measurement of

    (A) the spread of scores in relation to the mean
    (B) the difference between the lowest and highest scores in a distribution
    (C) the typical difference between the independent variable and the dependent variable
    (D) the typical difference between any experimental group and the control group
    (E) central tendency

59. Which of the following is NOT a defensible conclusion based on current research into the biological basis of schizophrenia?

    (A) The presence of the disease is correlated with frontal lobe dysfunction
    (B) The ventricles in the brain of sufferers tend to be enlarged
    (C) An excess of dopamine activity is correlated with the disorder
    (D) A child is at a significantly higher risk if their mother had a viral disease during pregnancy
    (E) A child's risk of developing the disorder does not change when both his biological parents have the disease

60. If someone has an internal locus of control,

    (A) they tend to believe that they do not have much control over what happens to them
    (B) they often believe that negative events won't happen to them
    (C) they believe that they are in control of their own destiny
    (D) they are motivated primarily by extrinsic incentives
    (E) they tend to be pessimistic and blame themselves for things that go wrong

61. Gordon Allport used the term *cardinal trait* to refer to

    (A) one of the five or so most important personality characteristics in an individual
    (B) personality traits that are consistently found in most individuals across cultures and over time
    (C) a single characteristic in an individual that is dominant in every situation and stable over time
    (D) the most primitive, survival-based human characteristics
    (E) the characteristics in humans that arise only when under severe and enduring stress

62. Humanistic personality theory is most frequently criticized on the grounds that it is

    (A) too restrictive of human freedom
    (B) unrealistically optimistic about human nature and motives
    (C) too pessimistic about the individual's willingness to control his or her own destiny
    (D) heavily biased in favor of the influence of early childhood experiences
    (E) heavily biased in favor of the male perspective at the expense of female experience

63. Which of the following does a healthy newborn human possess from birth?

   (A) The moro reflex
   (B) Stranger anxiety
   (C) Separation anxiety
   (D) Attachment to the primary human food source
   (E) A sense of object permanence

64. Which of the following is the most likely criticism a psychoanalyst would make of behavioral therapeutic approaches?

   (A) The behaviorist pays too much attention to the emotional needs of the patient
   (B) The behaviorist focuses too heavily on the unhealthy relationships in a patient's life
   (C) The behaviorist gives too little attention to the underlying, unconscious causes of disorders
   (D) There is no measurable evidence to assess the success or failure of behavioral techniques
   (E) There is no theoretical framework upon which behavioral techniques are built making them far too subjective for science

65. A history examination purportedly assessing knowledge of the pre-Civil War American South has several items on it about post-war Reconstruction. The exam lacks

   (A) appropriate standardization
   (B) reliability
   (C) content validity
   (D) criterion validity
   (E) test-retest reliability

66. Psychologists who adhere to the evolutionary view of motivation would argue that natural selection favors behaviors that

   (A) allow people to self-actualize
   (B) satisfy psychological needs over physiological needs
   (C) allow one to accumulate as much wealth as possible
   (D) meet one's interpersonal needs
   (E) encourage reproductive success

67. In order to "standardize" an assessment, a group is administered the test

    (A) to determine if it is reliable
    (B) to determine if it is valid
    (C) to establish the extent to which the sample is representative
    (D) and those results are used as the norm against which future test takers are compared
    (E) and it is evaluated for its accuracy in testing what it claims to be testing

68. Raymond Cattell argued that there are two basic kinds of intelligence; of those, which is most closely associated with reasoning, novel problem solving and understanding of the relationship between ideas?

    (A) Fluid intelligence
    (B) Practical intelligence
    (C) Crystallized intelligence
    (D) Analytical intelligence
    (E) Primary intelligence

69. Psychologist David Rosenhan and seven others had themselves admitted to mental institutions by falsely claiming to hear voices. Once admitted, each pseudopatient acted perfectly normally and never again reported hearing voices. Which of the following best summarizes the results of this study?

    (A) Both the staff and the patients already residing in the institutions discovered the pseudopatients were misrepresenting their symptoms within one week
    (B) The study had to be discontinued after one week because each of those taking part had become dangerously overmedicated
    (C) No members of the staff caught onto the charade, interpreting the day-to-day behaviors of the pseudopatients only in the context of the diagnosis each had been given
    (D) The pseudopatients were kept against their will in the institutions for periods ranging from twelve to fifteen months and were only released after an intensive investigation
    (E) The original diagnoses of each of the pseudopatients were changed at least three times within an average of two months

70. Amos Tversky and Daniel Kahneman demonstrated that people often judge the likelihood of an event based on how easily other examples of that event come to mind. What term did they use to describe this tendency?

    (A) Prototype theory
    (B) Implicit cognition
    (C) Confirmation bias
    (D) The representativeness heuristic
    (E) The availability heuristic

71. Which of the following psychologists proposed theories that support the idea of multiple intelligences?

    (A) Robert Sternberg and Charles Spearman
    (B) Martin Seligman and Roger Sperry
    (C) Howard Gardner and Charles Spearman
    (D) Walter Mischel and George Kelly
    (E) Howard Gardner and Robert Sternberg

72. After witnessing a near fatal accident involving his sister, a young boy is suddenly stricken with blindness for which there seems to be no physiological cause. Which of the following psychological disorders bests fits the above symptoms?

    (A) Panic disorder
    (B) Generalized anxiety disorder
    (C) A fugue episode
    (D) Hypochondriasis
    (E) Conversion disorder

73. The debate over whether development occurs gradually and almost imperceptibly, or in a stage-like way marked by clearly observed divisions is an argument over

    (A) cognitive vs. social forces
    (B) continuity vs. discontinuity
    (C) nature vs. nurture
    (D) adaptation and habituation
    (E) situational or dispositional attributions

74. All auditory, visual, touch and gustatory signals are routed through this large structure in the center of the brain:

   (A) the thalamus
   (B) the hypothalamus
   (C) the cerebellum
   (D) the association cortex
   (E) the pons

75. The fact that weak incoming stimuli do not result in the transmission of weak neural messages is evidence for

   (A) the existence of a relative refractory period
   (B) the existence of an absolute refractory period
   (C) the all-or-none law
   (D) reuptake
   (E) the process of neural networking

76. Edward Tolman discovered that rats that had been exposed to a maze would not actually demonstrate their learning unless reinforced for doing so. He called this

   (A) trial and error learning
   (B) latent learning
   (C) insight learning
   (D) temporal conditioning
   (E) positive transfer

77. Alyson, who feels deep seated discomfort about her physical appearance, tells her partner "I know you think I'm fat," and the partner vigorously disputes her claim. A psychoanalyst might interpret Alyson's statement as being an example of

   (A) projection
   (B) identification
   (C) rationalization
   (D) reaction formation
   (E) displacement

78. As students return from college to visit a high school teacher, the teacher finds she has difficulty remembering some of their names. She explains this by saying that she's learned so many new names during the current school year that she now has trouble recalling all of her former students. This is an example of

    (A) constructive memory
    (B) reconstructive memory
    (C) situational schemas
    (D) proactive interference
    (E) retroactive interference

79. Research demonstrates that if a person is skilled at the game of billiards, they tend to play better when in front of an audience. What term is used to describe this finding?

    (A) Social ingratiation
    (B) Social loafing
    (C) Social acceleration
    (D) Social facilitation
    (E) Social inhibition

80. Negative reinforcement

    (A) decreases the probability of a behavior
    (B) occurs when a learner is given something they want after performing a behavior
    (C) requires the regular delivery of an aversive consequence immediately following an undesired behavior
    (D) is the schedule of reinforcement that leads to the highest rate of responding by an organism
    (E) increases the probability of a behavior because it results in the removal of an unpleasant stimulus

81. Recalling and naming the glands of the endocrine system is an example of

    (A) semantic memory
    (B) procedural memory
    (C) working memory
    (D) maintenance memory
    (E) constructive memory

82. According to this theory, the auditory cortex identifies the pitch of 40 Hz sounds because neurons along the basilar membrane processing that auditory input fire 40 times per second:

    (A) place theory
    (B) prototype theory
    (C) feature analysis theory
    (D) frequency theory
    (E) volley theory

83. The kinesthetic system

    (A) is housed in the parietal lobe
    (B) is housed in the inner ear
    (C) tells you where your body parts are in relation to space and to each other
    (D) provides information on whole body balance and head position
    (E) provides information about sensations of temperature and pressure

84. Which of the following is the best example of state-dependent memory?

    (A) An eyewitness supplies two different versions of events to two different questioners
    (B) An eyewitness supplies two different versions of events because of the different ways questions are put to him
    (C) A girl who learned a vocabulary list in room 207 feels she will do better on a test of those words if she can take the test in room 207
    (D) A man who learned new material after an epinephrine injection does better in recalling that material when in a similarly aroused condition
    (E) The victim of a crime does not recall details of the crime well because of the highly emotional nature of the events

85. If a therapist asks a client to design an anxiety hierarchy as an early step in helping the client to overcome his fear of heights, the therapist is likely using which technique?

    (A) Rational emotive behavior therapy
    (B) Flooding
    (C) Aversive conditioning
    (D) Systematic desensitization
    (E) Implosive exposure therapy

86. The original Wechsler Intelligence tests

    (A) were designed only for children
    (B) were designed only for adults
    (C) required greater language skills than previous intelligence assessments
    (D) were more performance-based than the previous language-based assessments
    (E) were the first to sample a wide range of individuals

87. Which of the following behaviors are being reinforced on a variable interval schedule of reinforcement?

    (A) A child is rewarded for every five toys he picks up
    (B) After many attempts a child gets a hit in baseball
    (C) A worker receives a paycheck after seven full days of work
    (D) A man wins the state lottery after buying hundreds of tickets
    (E) A student studies regularly, in case of an unannounced pop quiz in chemistry class

88. Robert Rescorla argued that classical conditioning would only occur if there was contingency, which means

    (A) the UCS reliably predicts the presentation of the CS
    (B) the CS reliably predicts the presentation of the UCS
    (C) the CS is previously unknown to the learner
    (D) the learner has had previous exposure to the CS and the UCS
    (E) the CS and the UCS are also presented in reverse order

89. Which of the following play a key role in stimulating our biological motivation to eat?

    (A) The ventromedial hypothalamus and leptin
    (B) The lateral hypothalamus and insulin
    (C) The medulla and epinephrine
    (D) The caudate nucleus and dopamine
    (E) The somatosensory cortex and GABA

90. Positron Emission Tomography (PET)

    (A) mimics the activation of the sympathetic nervous system to allow for study of human emotional response
    (B) tracks and measures the flow of slightly radioactive glucose to determine the location and level of neural activity
    (C) records brain wave activity
    (D) is used in conjunction with polygraphs in work with lie detection
    (E) is used to treat major depression when the patient has not responded to drugs

91. Blocking neural receptor sites for acetylcholine would most likely result in

    (A) hypersomnia
    (B) a disturbance in memory formation
    (C) insomnia
    (D) erratic emotional behavior
    (E) delusional thinking marked by paranoia

92. A child waits all afternoon for his father to arrive home to punish the boy for his misbehavior earlier in the day. The sound of his father's car on the gravel in the driveway signals his arrival, and the boy is then spanked for his earlier transgression. For some time afterward, the boy feels a sense of anxiety whenever he hears the sound of a car on gravel. In this scenario, what are the conditioned stimulus, unconditioned stimulus, unconditioned response and conditioned response respectively?

    (A) Anxiety, pain from the spanking, the sound of the gravel, fear of his father
    (B) The spanking, his father, pain from the spanking, anxiety
    (C) The spanking, his father, anxiety, pain from the spanking
    (D) The sound of the gravel, anxiety, the spanking, pain from the spanking
    (E) The sound of the gravel, the spanking, pain from the spanking, anxiety

93. Which of the following theories of emotional response proposes that the thalamus processes awareness of physiological changes and the psychological experience of an emotion simultaneously?

    (A) Opponent process theory
    (B) James-Lange Theory
    (C) Cannon-Bard Theory
    (D) Selye's General Adaptation Syndrome
    (E) Schachter-Singer Theory

94. Cross-cultural research between collectivist and individualistic cultures demonstrates that people in collectivist cultures

    (A) show higher levels of the self-serving bias
    (B) tend to use stereotypes more frequently
    (C) often experience lower levels of cognitive dissonance
    (D) are less prone to making the fundamental attribution error
    (E) typically make dispositional attributions when accounting for the behavior of others

95. While Jean Piaget argued that children largely develop through biological maturation, Lev Vygotsky argued for internalization, which is

    (A) a process by which children develop by absorbing information from the social context they inhabit
    (B) largely dependent on the physical health and cognitive processes of the child in the first year of life
    (C) driven by instinctive, reflexive responses
    (D) strictly based upon biological imperatives
    (E) most influenced by birth order variables

96. Which of the following best illustrates the fundamental attribution error in your attempt to account for why a lone driver would not stop to help you while your car was broken down by the side of the road?

    (A) "He must have believed it was too dangerous to stop."
    (B) "He's obviously not a considerate person."
    (C) "You just can't figure out why people do what they do."
    (D) "No one else would've stopped either."
    (E) "I must have been too sloppily dressed."

97. A study reveals that Asian volunteers have difficulty identifying different Hispanic individuals if the volunteers have had little or no previous exposure to Hispanic people. This is supported by the concept of

    (A) pluralistic ignorance
    (B) scapegoating
    (C) bottom up processing
    (D) in-group bias
    (E) out-group homogeneity bias

98. Damage to the suprachiasmatic nucleus in the hypothalamus would likely

    (A) cause a disruption in the auditory and vestibular systems
    (B) lead to serious impairment in semantic and episodic memory
    (C) create significant disruptions in the somatic nervous system
    (D) disrupt circadian rhythms and melatonin production
    (E) inhibit communication between the left and right hemispheres

99. Chris has a period of relative calm shattered by a rush of intense anxiety and worry and physiological arousal which seem to have no apparent cause. These symptoms are most consistent with a diagnosis of

    (A) posttraumatic stress disorder
    (B) agoraphobia
    (C) generalized anxiety disorder
    (D) panic disorder
    (E) somatization disorder

100. When sodium channels on a cell membrane open, the electrical charge within the cell briefly becomes more positive than the charge outside of the cell. This is called

    (A) self-propagation
    (B) the absolute refractory period
    (C) the relative refractory period
    (D) polarization
    (E) depolarization

# Section II

Directions: You have 50 minutes to answer BOTH of the following questions. It is not enough to answer a question by merely listing facts. You should present a cogent argument based on your critical analysis of the questions posed, using appropriate psychological terminology.

1. Imagine that you are an eyewitness to a crime. How would each of the following be involved in your experience and recollection of that event?

   - The amygdala
   - Epinephrine
   - Flashbulb memory
   - Schema
   - The misinformation effect
   - Context-dependent memory
   - The bystander effect

2. Toni is running a political advertising campaign for a candidate who has many controversial beliefs.

   Explain how Toni might use each of the following in her advertising campaign:

   - The central route to persuasion
   - The mere exposure effect
   - Classical conditioning
   - Scapegoating

   Explain how Toni might be affected by each of the following while she is working on the campaign:

   - Belief perseverance
   - Cognitive dissonance
   - An approach-avoidance conflict

GO ON TO THE NEXT PAGE

# Sample Examination II

## Section 1

1.  The purpose of a placebo is to

    (A) determine if the expectation of receiving a treatment has an effect apart from the treatment itself
    (B) measure the effect of various confounding variables on the independent and dependent variables
    (C) control possible experimenter bias
    (D) prevent social desirability bias
    (E) prevent demand characteristics

2.  A man who is a heavy smoker self-administers an electric shock every time he desires a puff of a cigarette. This is an example of which behavior modification strategy?

    (A) Systematic desensitization
    (B) Modeling
    (C) Aversive conditioning
    (D) VRT
    (E) Shaping

3.  A teenage girl vividly recalls her first day of preschool – what she was wearing, the food she ate for breakfast and her activities throughout the day. This is an example of

    (A) iconic memory
    (B) procedural memory
    (C) state-dependent memory
    (D) episodic memory
    (E) eidetic imagery

4.  Which of the following is the most accurate statement about the capacity and duration of short-term memory?

    (A) It theoretically has an unlimited capacity over an unlimited period of time
    (B) Its capacity and duration invariably increase after adolescence
    (C) Typically, an individual can hold 7 + / - 2 items in it, for 20 to 30 seconds
    (D) Its capacity and duration invariably decrease after adolescence
    (E) It is so variable from one individual to another that it is meaningless to generalize about its capacity or duration

5.  While playing with your eight-month-old cousin, you hide behind the couch out of her sight. A moment later, she crawls around the couch and "finds" you. She has demonstrated a grasp of

    (A) object permanence
    (B) conservation
    (C) animism
    (D) artificialism
    (E) reciprocity

6.  If an individual were to reach his or her fullest potential, becoming a fully creative, productive, spontaneous and empathetic person, Abraham Maslow would say they were

    (A) high functioning
    (B) homeostatic
    (C) self-actualized
    (D) in an approach-approach mode
    (E) acculturated

7.  Increased recall for items placed early in a list one is trying to remember is called

    (A) the primacy effect
    (B) the recency effect
    (C) the distinctiveness effect
    (D) semantic memory
    (E) crystallized memory

8- A child's story is given the following scores by seven different raters using a ten point scale to evaluate the creativity of the child's work: 4, 3, 4, 5, 7, 4, 5. What is the median score?

(A) 3.0
(B) 4.0
(C) 4.6
(D) 5.0
(E) 7.0

9. The earliest forms of intelligence tests compared the chronological age of each of the test takers to his

(A) physical appearance or phenotype
(B) performance on non-linguistic tasks
(C) mental age
(D) level of emotional development
(E) siblings

10. Those who suffer from this rare disorder have two or more distinct personalities housed in their one body:

(A) Schizophrenia
(B) Bipolar disorder
(C) Somatization
(D) Dissociative fugue
(E) Dissociative identity disorder

11. Which of the following is the most defensible conclusion one can reach from Stanley Milgram's "electric shock" obedience study?

(A) Obedience was usually a function of the particular personality types of those administering the shocks
(B) Volunteers with a history of rebelliousness and resistance to authority were much less likely to obey than others
(C) Obedience seems to be linked most to the nature of the orders given; people are highly unlikely to follow orders which inflict harm on others
(D) Obedience appears to be a function of the power of the situation and is less attributable to the personalities of those who receive the orders
(E) Individuals are much more likely to obey male authority figures than female authority figures

12. A young child learns to become conscious of being in the dream state and can control to some extent the progression of dream events. This is an example of

    (A) REM rebound
    (B) hypersomnia
    (C) lucid dreaming
    (D) latent content
    (E) manifest content

13. According to Jean Piaget, a child in the concrete operational stage of cognitive development learns that the amount of matter does not increase or decrease merely because of a change in its form or appearance. At this point, the child has mastered

    (A) conservation
    (B) functional fixedness
    (C) abstract thought
    (D) externalization
    (E) proximal development

14. To an ethologist, a complex pattern of organized, unlearned behavior that is species-specific is called

    (A) a drive
    (B) a need
    (C) an affective response
    (D) an instinct
    (E) a motive

15. A doctor gently strokes the cheek of a healthy newborn child. What will the neonate reflexively do in response?

    (A) A neonate would be unresponsive to such stimulation in the first hours of life
    (B) Pull her arms and legs into the midline of her body
    (C) Turn her head in the direction of the touch, rooting for a food source
    (D) Imitate the modeled behavior
    (E) Demonstrate visually directed reaching

16. Paul Ekman and his colleagues concluded from studies on facial expressions of emotions that

    (A) individuals vary widely in their ability to recognize genuine emotions via facial expression alone
    (B) there were specific and significant differences between residents of Brazil and Chile in recognition of facial expressions
    (C) trained professionals tend to outperform amateurs in lie detection through facial expression
    (D) facial expressions often contradict messages transmitted through body language
    (E) the meaning and understanding of basic facial expressions is universal across cultures

17. Lawrence Kohlberg's theory of the development of moral reasoning is characterized by

    (A) a progression from judgment based on reward and punishment, to reasoning rooted in social expectations and finally to a reliance on abstract moral principles
    (B) a consistent focus on age variations in moral reasoning, especially in adolescence and adulthood
    (C) the belief that humans are born with a sense of morality housed in the collective unconscious
    (D) an emphasis on just vs. unjust consequences for immoral or amoral behavior
    (E) the recognition of significant cultural differences in moral judgment and behavior

18. Which of the following interacts to help in regulating appetite and thirst?

    (A) The hippocampus and the cerebellum
    (B) The thalamus and the prefrontal cortex
    (C) The hypothalamus and the hippocampus
    (D) The hypothalamus and the pituitary gland
    (E) The pons and the prefrontal cortex

19. Daniel is investigating why his car won't start. He systematically looks at every part of the engine, one after another, believing that while it may take him a long time to find the problem, he is guaranteed to eventually find a solution. Daniel has used

    (A) a decision matrix
    (B) the representativeness heuristic
    (C) an algorithmic approach
    (D) brainstorming
    (E) concept perseverance

20. With which of the following theorists would you associate the following quote? "The ego's relation to the id might be compared with that of a rider to his horse."

    (A) Edward Thorndike
    (B) Sigmund Freud
    (C) B.F. Skinner
    (D) Albert Bandura
    (E) Carl Rogers

21. If the consequence of a behavior brings pleasure or satisfaction, it is likely the behavior will be repeated under similar circumstances. This is a description of

    (A) classical conditioning
    (B) the law of effect
    (C) omission training
    (D) aversive training
    (E) the law of pragnanz

22. _____, located on the back border of the frontal lobe, regulates voluntary movement in the various parts of the body.

    (A) Wernicke's Area
    (B) The central sulcus
    (C) The motor cortex
    (D) The Sylvian fissure
    (E) The caudate nucleus

23. Down Syndrome and Phenylketonuria (PKU)

    (A) both result from extreme early childhood abuse
    (B) are genetically determined
    (C) are both much more common among females
    (D) inevitably result in severe mental disturbance
    (E) are both related to heightened levels of serotonin activity

24. Systematic desensitization is a form of

    (A) implosive therapy
    (B) rational emotive behavior therapy
    (C) counterconditioning
    (D) countertransference
    (E) Freudian defense mechanism

25. The Diagnostic and Statistical Manual (DSM)

(A) offers guidelines on basic treatment of mental disorders
(B) provides statistical support for the use of certain treatment approaches over others
(C) provides a classification system for mental disorders
(D) is the most statistically reliable self-report assessment of personality
(E) explains the scoring system used in evaluating responses to Rorschach ink blots

26. Benzodiazepines like Valium are considered to be

(A) anti-depressant medications
(B) anti-psychotic medications
(C) anti-anxiety medications
(D) hallucinogens
(E) narcotics

27. Which of the following quotes most illustrates the possible effects of a self-fulfilling prophecy?

(A) "It is the weak who are cruel. Gentleness can only be expected from the strong."
(B) "If you are going through hell, keep going."
(C) "Doubt is not a pleasant condition, but certainty is absurd."
(D) "Believe those who are seeking the truth. Doubt those who find it."
(E) "Think you can or think you can't - either way, you're probably right."

28. Which of the following is likely damaged if an individual is showing difficulty in smooth, coordinated movement?

(A) The thalamus
(B) The hypothalamus
(C) The cerebellum
(D) The medulla
(E) The reticular activating system

29. Brianna has a persistent, longstanding and intensely exaggerated sense of her self-importance and uniqueness. This is most consistent with a diagnosis of

(A) dysthymia
(B) cyclothymia
(C) conduct disorder
(D) histrionic personality disorder
(E) narcissistic personality disorder

30. "Anything seems commonplace, once explained." This comment, made by Dr. Watson in a Sherlock Holmes mystery, illustrates

(A) special pleading
(B) hindsight bias
(C) the post hoc ergo propter hoc fallacy
(D) belief perseverance
(E) self-handicapping

31. Two major functions governed largely by the right hemisphere of the brain are

(A) intuition and perception of spatial relationships
(B) reading and speaking
(C) speaking and understanding speech
(D) athletic muscle movement and vision
(E) logical and linguistic skills

32. Which of the following is a negative symptom of schizophrenia?

(A) Hallucinations
(B) Delusions
(C) Disorganized thinking
(D) Disorganized speech
(E) Flattened affect

33. The sense of head position and whole body balance is called

(A) the kinesthetic sense
(B) the somasthetic sense
(C) synesthesis
(D) the vestibular sense
(E) redintegration

34. Two young soldiers are training to become radar operators, learning to detect the presence of aircraft in computer simulations. Their teacher positions a simulated aircraft on the respective screens of the trainees, but both fail to detect its presence. In signal detection theory, this is called

    (A) a hit
    (B) a miss
    (C) a false alarm
    (D) a false positive
    (E) an attribution error

35. Dichotic viewing and listening tasks have typically been used to study

    (A) selective attention
    (B) habituation
    (C) linear perspective
    (D) motion parallax
    (E) perception of distal and proximal stimuli

36. The fovea

    (A) houses all the receptors for vision
    (B) is located in the center of the retina and is responsible for visual acuity
    (C) falls in the center of the human "blind spot"
    (D) allows light to enter the eye
    (E) is the colored membrane in front of the eye

37. The inability to detect smells is known as

    (A) enuresis
    (B) anosmia
    (C) prospagnosia
    (D) aphasia
    (E) apraxia

38. According to opponent process theory, a boy who stares for a full minute at a red valentine sent to him by a classmate who then looks at a neutral background will experience

    (A) a green afterimage
    (B) a red afterimage
    (C) a blue afterimage
    (D) an upside-down afterimage
    (E) a black and white afterimage

39. Which of the following characterizes the statistical relationship between age and average amount of nightly sleep?

    (A) There is no consistent pattern in this relationship
    (B) The younger the child the less they sleep
    (C) The average amount of sleep any individual gets fluctuates regularly as we age
    (D) The two tend to be negatively correlated
    (E) The two tend to be positively correlated

40. Volunteers who are systematically deprived of REM during a controlled sleep study

    (A) are prone to hallucinations
    (B) are prone to paranoid delusions
    (C) show a marked drop in glutamate levels
    (D) spend a much larger percentage of sleep in REM when allowed to sleep normally
    (E) learn to sleep for extended periods while experiencing no REM sleep at all

41. The temporary reappearance, after extinction, of a previously conditioned response is called

    (A) acquisition
    (B) spontaneous recovery
    (C) retrieval
    (D) retroactive interference
    (E) remission

42. Which of the following is the best example of negative reinforcement?

    (A) Being spanked for failing to clean your room
    (B) Eating a handful of candy which reduces your sadness and boredom
    (C) Being threatened with physical punishment without its being carried out
    (D) Being made to sit quietly on a chair for exactly two minutes
    (E) Drinking a huge amount of water before competing in a long road race

43. For a mere five seconds, a woman is shown a drawing which contains pictures of thirty unrelated items. She is then able to recall each of the items and place them in their exact location in the original drawing. It is reasonable to assume this woman possesses

   (A) eidetic memory
   (B) flashbulb memory
   (C) associative memory
   (D) frontal lobe hypertrophy
   (E) an enlarged amygdala

44. Which of the following quotes best summarizes the concept of perceptual set?

   (A) "We forfeit ¾ of ourselves to be like other people" (Arthur Schopenhauer)
   (B) "People only see what they are prepared to see" (Ralph Waldo Emerson)
   (C) "How bold one gets when one is sure of being loved" (Sigmund Freud)
   (D) "A great many people think they are thinking when they are merely rearranging their prejudices" (William James)
   (E) "Everything that irritates us about others can lead us to an understanding of ourselves" (Carl Jung)

45. The brief period after the "firing" of a neuron during which the neuron cannot be reactivated is called

   (A) sublimation
   (B) kinesis
   (C) depolarization
   (D) the refractory period
   (E) the resting state

46. The large band of fibers connecting the left and right hemispheres of the cortex, allowing those two sides of the brain to communicate with each other, is called the

   (A) cerebellum
   (B) cerebrum
   (C) corpus callosum
   (D) septum
   (E) reticular formation

47. Which of the following is a transitional object?

    (A) A wedding ring
    (B) A birth certificate
    (C) A child's first reading book
    (D) A cup of juice
    (E) A stuffed animal

48. Tommy and Jessica's parents have many rules in place at home but are quick to explain the reasons for them and remain open to modifying those rules as Tommy and Jessica develop. This is an example of which of the following parenting styles?

    (A) Permissive
    (B) Laissez-faire
    (C) Democratic
    (D) Authoritative
    (E) Authoritarian

49. A researcher calculates the standard deviation of a data set and determines that SD = 9. In this set of data what is the variance?

    (A) 3
    (B) 18
    (C) 45
    (D) 63
    (E) 81

50. Set point theory suggests that humans possess

    (A) an internal mechanism that regulates how much fat the body will carry
    (B) a culturally established range of expectations for male and female role behaviors
    (C) an individually established range of expectations for male and female role behaviors
    (D) a biological tendency to seek safety and control
    (E) an innate drive toward affiliation

51. Which of the following is an example of overregularization in a child's language development?

   (A) "All dogs are mean."
   (B) "Me cup."
   (C) "I runned to mommy."
   (D) "Pardon me."
   (E) "Up!"

52. A police officer ignores evidence that might exonerate a suspect because the officer is already convinced of the suspect's guilt. This is an example of

   (A) factor analysis
   (B) confirmation bias
   (C) hindsight bias
   (D) cognitive consistency
   (E) prototype matching

53. According to Yerkes-Dodson Law, for optimum performance on a difficult task

   (A) the performer must have prior experience with the task
   (B) a high level of arousal is required
   (C) a moderate level of arousal is desirable
   (D) distractions must be eliminated
   (E) emotionality must be essentially absent

54. A mother publicly demonstrates exaggerated concern and love for her children, although she unconsciously feels trapped and frustrated by motherhood. To a Freudian psychoanalyst this is an example of

   (A) suppression
   (B) repression
   (C) regression
   (D) reaction formation
   (E) projection

55. At the start of her course, a chemistry professor administers an assessment designed to measure aptitude in the study of chemistry. At the end of the course she finds a strongly negative correlation between scores on the aptitude test and final grades for the chemistry course. This result suggests the aptitude test lacks

    (A) split-half reliability
    (B) intra-rater reliability
    (C) test-retest reliability
    (D) test-retest validity
    (E) predictive validity

56. Volunteers are shown a photograph and asked to write a story about it. The stories are then scored and analyzed. This is most likely a

    (A) Q-Sort
    (B) Strong Preference Test
    (C) Thematic Apperception Test (TAT)
    (D) Rorschach Test
    (E) Myers-Briggs Inventory

57. Conversion disorder is characterized by

    (A) physical symptoms which have no apparent physiological basis
    (B) heightened levels of arousal in the central nervous system
    (C) reduced levels of arousal in the central nervous system
    (D) persistent fear of becoming mentally ill
    (E) persistent changes in gross motor function

58. Research into fluid intelligence suggests

    (A) a 20-year-old man will generally outperform a 70-year-old man in measures of it
    (B) a 70-year-old man will generally outperform a 20-year-old man in measures of it
    (C) that females generally outperform males in measures of it
    (D) that it is culture-specific
    (E) that it develops after adolescence

59. In one statistical study, the correlation coefficient for the IQ scores of identical twins raised separately is found to be +.80. This

(A) suggests that there is no basis for hypothesizing a genetic predisposition for intelligence
(B) serves as fairly strong evidence for the argument that there is a genetic component to intelligence
(C) means there is no clear connection between upbringing and performance on assessments of intelligence
(D) demonstrates that correlational research is not useful in looking at a variable such as IQ
(E) highlights flaws in the operational definitions of intelligence

60. Which of the following is the best example of a problem with inter-rater reliability?

(A) Two different inventories are found not to measure what they claim to measure
(B) A musician performs badly in rehearsals but excels during actual performance
(C) A college professor has one of her teaching assistants grade all her students' exams
(D) Two driving schools use very different approaches in teaching their driving students
(E) Three talent show judges have widely divergent views of who the best contestant is

61. David Rosenhan's research in which healthy people were admitted for varying amounts of time to mental hospitals, unbeknownst to the hospital staff, showed that

(A) such pseudo-patients are quickly detected by the trained staff at such institutions
(B) clinical labels often endure, even in the face of behavioral evidence to the contrary
(C) deception is unacceptable in research
(D) treatment in mental hospitals is not effective
(E) the deinstitutionalization movement has been highly successful

62. Historically, one especially serious side effect to heavy dosages of anti-psychotic medications has been

(A) maintenance insomnia
(B) excessive weight loss
(C) mania
(D) tardive dyskinesia
(E) significant loss of short-term memory capacity

63. A hospital housing the mentally ill wishes to confirm the preliminary diagnosis on a patient. Of the following assessments, which would staff members most likely use?

    (A) The WISC
    (B) The WAIS
    (C) The California Psychological Inventory
    (D) The Bulit-R
    (E) The Minnesota Multiphasic Personality Inventory (MMPI)

64. Nobel Prize winner Roger Sperry found that when he instantaneously displayed images to patients who had recently undergone split brain surgery that

    (A) they were able to verbally report what had been shown to their right visual field but not what had been shown to their left visual field
    (B) they were able to verbally report what had been shown to the left visual field but not what had been shown to their right eye
    (C) they were unable to verbally report having seen anything at all displayed to either portion of the visual field, but could draw what they had seen
    (D) they were unable to report, verbally or in writing, anything they had seen in any portion of their visual field
    (E) even though they had just had the surgery they learned to adapt immediately and could thus verbally report anything that had been displayed in their visual field

65. Renee is a Human Factors Psychologist. She is most likely to be

    (A) helping children move closer to self-actualization
    (B) studying the universality of facial expressions of emotions
    (C) tutoring therapists in ways to interact with their patients in a more positive manner
    (D) examining the design of machines in a workplace to determine if they are set-up for optimum human performance
    (E) observing and then attempting to define "peak experiences" or "flow" in various interpersonal relationships

66. The developmental process in which an individual modifies preexisting schemas to account for new information or learning is called

    (A) synthesis
    (B) accommodation
    (C) assimilation
    (D) summation
    (E) elaboration

67. A fund-raiser hopes to get nearby residents to contribute money to a charitable endeavor. First, she has volunteers visit those residents, asking them to display a small sticker in their windows that states support for that cause. One month later, the volunteers return to ask for a contribution to the cause, and they easily reach their goal. The fund-raiser relied on which of the following persuasion techniques?

    (A) Reciprocity
    (B) Mutuality
    (C) The self-enhancement technique
    (D) The door-in-the-face technique
    (E) The foot-in-the-door technique

68. Which of the following is the best example of the defense mechanism known as sublimation?

    (A) Michael is concerned about the size of his ears and feels certain that everyone is constantly looking at them
    (B) Karen does poorly on a biology exam and says, "I don't want to be a biologist anyway"
    (C) Anne has powerful, unconscious aggressive urges and decides to become a surgeon
    (D) Dustin is attracted to pornographic material but he also leads a community censorship program against pornography
    (E) Shaunna and Ed are told that their child has a terminal illness but remain convinced the child will recover

69. An early perspective in the field of psychology focused on identifying the fundamental elements of conscious experience. This was called

    (A) gestalt
    (B) structuralism
    (C) functionalism
    (D) introspection
    (E) naturalism

70. The introduction of a superordinate goal would likely

    (A) contribute to increased cooperation and liking between two groups
    (B) reduce levels of intrinsic motivation
    (C) serve as a secondary reinforcer
    (D) cause friction in a group of more than three members
    (E) extinguish a conditioned response

71. Which of the following best summarizes Albert Bandura's Social Learning Theory?

    (A) "You can't fool all of the people all of the time"
    (B) "Better safe than sorry"
    (C) "Monkey see, monkey do"
    (D) "The eyes don't lie"
    (E) "Speak softly and carry a big stick"

72. _____ seems involved in transmission of messages regarding muscular control and of pleasure.

    (A) Substance p
    (B) Dopamine
    (C) Acetylcholine
    (D) Beta-endorphin
    (E) Noradrenaline

73. A hypnotist claims that he can end smoking addictions in three hypnosis sessions, and a researcher wants to test this assertion. The null hypothesis states that

    (A) levels of addiction will actually increase as a result of the hypnosis sessions
    (B) the experimental results are not falsifiable
    (C) the dependent variable does not cause the independent variable
    (D) the hypnosis sessions will have no effect on the level of addiction
    (E) the hypnosis sessions will reduce addiction

74. REM sleep is often referred to as "paradoxical sleep" because in it brain activity is quite high while there is

    (A) a reduction in blood pressure
    (B) a slowed heart rate
    (C) a slowed rate of breathing
    (D) a sharp decrease in voluntary muscular control
    (E) an increase in delta wave activity

75. Humanistic personality theorists would likely object to psychoanalytic and behavioral approaches on the grounds that

    (A) neither is applicable to mentally healthy individuals
    (B) the claims of both are not empirically measurable
    (C) each is too idealistic about human nature
    (D) each is too pessimistic and deterministic
    (E) they are needlessly complex

76. According to Erik Erikson, in the second stage of psychosocial development a child focuses attention on toilet training and other issues of control over his or her environment, thus wrestling with the conflict between

    (A) trust and mistrust
    (B) integrity and despair
    (C) assimilation and accommodation
    (D) generativity and stagnation
    (E) autonomy and doubt

77. If the human brain were an orchestra, which of the following regions would be most analagous to the conductor of that orchestra?

    (A) The left hemisphere
    (B) The right hemisphere
    (C) The somatic system
    (D) The prefrontal cortex
    (E) The hindbrain

78. Blocking the reuptake of a neurotransmitter would result in

    (A) increased transmission of that neurotransmitter's signals
    (B) the cessation of activity in the central nervous system
    (C) the cessation of activity in the peripheral nervous system
    (D) seizures
    (E) coma

79. The chemicals leptin and ghrelin are most involved in

    (A) depression
    (B) hunger
    (C) sexual motivation
    (D) aggression
    (E) anxiety

80. Which of the following best summarizes the essence of cognitive theory?

    (A) "Men are disturbed not by things but by the views they take of them" (Epictetus)
    (B) "Nothing is so carefully secured as this, that whilst we live we shall learn" (Ralph Waldo Emerson)
    (C) "You can discover what your enemy fears most by observing the means he uses to frighten you" (Eric Hoffer)
    (D) "Be not afraid of life" (William James)
    (E) "Human temperaments are combinations of psychological profiles, behaviors, thoughts and emotions along with their presumed biological foundation" (Jerome Kagan)

81. With slight changes in word emphasis, the three-word sentence, "Eat your food" can have at least three different underlying meanings. Those meanings are examples of

    (A) linguistic relativity
    (B) linguistic ambiguity
    (C) lateral inhibition
    (D) the surface structure of language
    (E) the deep structure of language

82. The tendency for decisions made by a group to be more extreme than those that would've been made by any single member of the group is called

    (A) group polarization
    (B) group compliance
    (C) groupthink
    (D) pluralistic ignorance
    (E) the autokinetic effect

83. A teenager who is normally shy and reserved and has not been drinking dances wildly while shirtless in the midst of a large crowd at a concert. His atypical behavior is best explained by

(A) social inhibition
(B) attribution theory
(C) pluralistic ignorance
(D) false consensus
(E) deindividuation

84. Telegraphic speech

(A) is semantically correct and thus qualifies as prescriptive grammar
(B) qualifies as neither prescriptive nor descriptive grammar
(C) occurs developmentally during adolescence
(D) involves expressions of single words which still convey meaning
(E) meets the criteria to characterize it as descriptive grammar

85. A woman who is furious about issues at her workplace returns home and spanks her child for no apparent reason, then explains the behavior by saying, "Discipline is good for a child." What two defense mechanisms are at work here?

(A) Identification and suppression
(B) Suppression and identification
(C) Displacement and rationalization
(D) Displacement and projection
(E) Internalization and identification

86. According to developmental psychologists, adolescence is marked by

(A) abstract thinking and acquisition of conservation
(B) acquisition of gender constancy and gender role
(C) identity issues and the personal fable
(D) identity issues and loss of primary sex characteristics
(E) acquisition of object permanence and development of secondary sex characteristics

87. The use of Virtual Reality Therapy has proven to be effective in

    (A) reducing catatonia in some schizophrenia patients
    (B) uncovering the root causes of dissociative identity disorder
    (C) recovering the memories of those with dissociative fugue
    (D) treating conversion disorder
    (E) extinguishing phobias

88. Damage to Broca's Area would most likely result in

    (A) Parkinson's Disease
    (B) obsessive compulsive disorder
    (C) PTSD
    (D) expressive aphasia
    (E) asynchronous physical development

89. A criticism of trait theory is that

    (A) there is no reasonable way to measure the presence of personality traits
    (B) there may be relatively little consistency in personality traits across situations
    (C) it is too optimistic about essential human nature
    (D) it is too pessimistic about essential human nature
    (E) it overemphasizes the role of human decision making in the growth of personality

90. A woman is saddened by a romantic breakup. She decides to date several different men in an attempt to forget her old partner, but she sometimes finds herself accidentally calling her new dates by her old boyfriend's name. This is an example of

    (A) inhibition theory
    (B) encoding specificity
    (C) structural encoding
    (D) proactive interference
    (E) retroactive interference

91. A cat has become classically conditioned to run into a room in response to the sound of a can opener, after that sound has been repeatedly paired with the presentation of food. Next, the researcher conducts several trials in which she presents a red light, followed by the presentation of the sound of the can opener, and the cat soon learns to run into the room at the sight of the red light. This is called

    (A) higher order conditioning
    (B) temporal conditioning
    (C) trace conditioning
    (D) vicarious conditioning
    (E) successive conditioning

92. Psychologist Robert Sternberg points out that it is a "fatal scientific error ... to assume that genetic variation, which can account for differences among individuals within a group, is also the reason for differences between groups". This quote illustrates the complexity of

    (A) heritability
    (B) Turner's Syndrome
    (C) Williams Syndrome
    (D) expressive aphasia
    (E) biological preparedness

93. Activation-synthesis theory proposes that

    (A) humans seek physical activity and arousal in an attempt to make sense of their internal disequilibrium
    (B) dreams are the product of the individual's cognitive attempts to make sense out of essentially random neural activity
    (C) physical activity during sleep is frequent and often uncontrolled
    (D) people tend to try to organize their perceptions into meaningful units
    (E) group members with similar interests tend to engage more actively in the group

94. According to the learning principle of overjustification

    (A) subjects learn best through extrinsic motivation
    (B) motor skills are easily overlearned
    (C) cognitive skills are easily overlearned
    (D) intrinsic motivation may be reduced by the offer of extrinsic reinforcers
    (E) punishment and reinforcement are equally successful tools in operant conditioning

95. Which of the following quotes would most likely be associated with Gustav Fechner, a 19th century researcher into "psychophysics"?

    (A) "Each cell in the visual cortex seems to have its own specific duties."
    (B) "There are wholes, the behavior of which is not determined by that of their individual elements."
    (C) "The method of just noticeable differences consists in determining how much two weights have to differ so that they can be discriminated."
    (D) "What a man can be, he must be."
    (E) "The subtests of the WAIS are different measures of intelligence, not measures of different kinds of intelligence."

96. Volunteers in an experiment are given an injection of epinephrine, although they are not told this. The injection results in an increase in heart, pulse and respiration rates. One half of the volunteers, when placed in a room with a confederate of the researchers who pretends to be angry and agitated, interpret the physiological changes caused by the injection to be representative of anger. The other volunteers, given the same injection, are placed in a room with a confederate who pretends to be happy and excited; these volunteers report their physiological changes as being representative of excitement. These results most support which of the following theories of human emotional response?

    (A) Universality theory
    (B) Opponent process theory
    (C) Cannon-Bard Thalamic Theory
    (D) James-Lange Theory
    (E) Schachter-Singer Two Factor Theory

97. In discussing a kitten's attempt to escape a box in order to reach some nearby food, Edward Thorndike said, "... there is no thinking about things, no putting two and two together; there are no ideas - the animal does not think of the box or of the food or of the act he is to perform." This quote would best be used as

    (A) a summary of social learning
    (B) a summary of classical conditioning
    (C) a behaviorist's criticism of cognitive theory
    (D) a cognitive theorist's explanation for a pessimistic explanatory style
    (E) an example of The Premack Principle

98. The most plentiful excitatory neurotransmitter in the human brain is

    (A) glutamate
    (B) GABA
    (C) serotonin
    (D) enkephalin
    (E) epinephrine

99. "In my early professionals years I was asking the question - How can I treat, or cure, or change this person? Now I would phrase the question in this way: How can I provide a relationship which this person may use for his own personal growth?" Which of the following people is most likely to have said this?

    (A) Karen Horney
    (B) Aaron Beck
    (C) William James
    (D) Alfred Adler
    (E) Carl Rogers

100. A high school administrative committee evaluating the effectiveness of the school's discipline procedures concludes that three-hour "Saturday School" punishments have not deterred bad behavior among the most frequent student rule-breakers. A learning theorist might argue that the failure of this approach is due to the lack of contingency in how it is applied, which would mean

    (A) that students believe "Saturday School" is a good thing
    (B) the threat of punishment never actually deters undesired behavior
    (C) punishments tend to be ineffective if they are not designed and implemented by those who are most likely to experience them
    (D) the punishment is ineffective because it's name suggests it is something that it  is not, and thus frequent offenders do not take it seriously
    (E) the punishment is ineffective because it is not certain and immediate enough for students to associate their unacceptable behavior with the consequence

# Section II

Directions: You have 50 minutes to answer BOTH of the following questions. It is not enough to answer a question by merely listing facts. You should present a cogent argument based on your critical analysis of the questions posed, using appropriate psychological terminology.

1.  An executive at a processed foods company is presented with some evidence that the company's leading product may contribute to long-term health problems for its consumers.

    Discuss how she may react to this information. Include specific reference to each of the following in your analysis:

    *   Cognitive dissonance
    *   Belief perseverance
    *   Incentive theory
    *   Diffusion of responsibility
    *   Learned helplessness
    *   The self-serving bias
    *   An avoidance-avoidance conflict

2.  A researcher wants to study the effect of homework load on learning in public schools. Describe one advantage and one disadvantage in using each of the following approaches in conducting this research:

    *   Experimental methodology
    *   Survey methodology
    *   Case study approach
    *   Longitudinal research
    *   Correlational research

# Sample Examination III

## Section 1

1. A baby looks behind a door for a ball that has just rolled there. In developmental terms, this would serve as evidence that the child had mastered

   (A) reversibility
   (B) object permanence
   (C) circular movement
   (D) conservation
   (E) attachment

2. B.F. Skinner's name is most associated with which of the following?

   (A) Studies of latent learning in rats
   (B) Operantly conditioning animals
   (C) Classically conditioned taste aversions
   (D) The cognitive triad of therapy
   (E) Conducting split-brain research

3. A researcher is conducting an experiment on the effects of subliminal perception. At random, she assigns 50 volunteers to group #1 who will knowingly listen to a tape with an "appetite suppressant" subliminal message (masked by pleasant ocean wave sounds) and 50 volunteers to group #2 who are told nothing and who listen to an "ocean sounds" tape that has no subliminal message on it. She further assigns 50 volunteers to group #3 who are told that they are hearing a subliminal "appetite suppressant" tape even though they hear a tape with no message at all, and 50 more volunteers to group #4 which receives an oral lecture on appetite control. Which of the following is the "placebo" group in this study?

   (A) Group # 1
   (B) Group # 2
   (C) Group # 3
   (D) Group # 4
   (E) There is no placebo group in this study

4. Which of the following is most predictive of attraction between two humans?

   (A) Similarity of attitudes and physical proximity
   (B) Complementarity and shared cultural experience
   (C) Age similarity and IQ similarity
   (D) Socioeconomic background
   (E) Education level

5. Free association and dream analysis are therapeutic techniques most associated with

   (A) gestalt therapy
   (B) psychoanalysis
   (C) rational-emotive behavior therapy
   (D) client-centered therapy
   (E) counterconditioning

6. Telephone and social security numbers both illustrate which concept in memory:

   (A) rehearsal
   (B) the link method
   (C) the method of loci
   (D) confabulation
   (E) chunking

7. The inability to solve a problem because some element of it is viewed only in terms of its most typical uses is called

   (A) functional fixedness
   (B) meta-analysis
   (C) metacognitive analysis
   (D) regularization
   (E) polarization

8. In Albert Bandura's "Bobo Doll" experiment on social learning, the control group

   (A) immediately beat Bobo upon being placed in a room with the doll
   (B) were shown a video in which Bobo was attacked by adult models
   (C) did not view the video showing adults beating up Bobo
   (D) hesitated at first but eventually beat Bobo when placed in a room with the doll
   (E) behaved identically to the experimental groups in the experiment

9. According to Martin Seligman, the belief that one cannot control unpleasant outcomes is called

   (A) learned helplessness
   (B) social inhibition
   (C) self-handicapping
   (D) latent learning
   (E) transference

10. A student is informed that she has finished in the 49th percentile on a national achievement test. What does this indicate?

   (A) She got 49% of the items on the test correct
   (B) She got 51% of the items on the test correct
   (C) There is a 49% likelihood that the test actually measures what it purports to measure
   (D) She performed as well as or better than 49% of those who took the same test
   (E) She performed as well as or better than 51% of those who took the same test

11. Which of the following has proven to be the most effective treatment for phobias?

   (A) Person-centered therapy
   (B) Psychotropic medications
   (C) Systematic desensitization
   (D) The cognitive triad
   (E) Repetitive transcranial magnetic stimulation

12. The type of schizophrenia marked most by physical immobility or repetitive, purposeless mannerisms is called

   (A) undifferentiated schizophrenia
   (B) paranoid schizophrenia
   (C) catatonic schizophrenia
   (D) hebephrenic schizophrenia
   (E) disorganized schizophrenia

13. Charles Spearman's concept of "g" refers to

   (A) the first stage in the grieving process
   (B) general intelligence
   (C) gender
   (D) groupthink
   (E) generativity in late adulthood

14. A 34 year-old man demonstrates poor self-control, impulsiveness, chronic deceitfulness and a seeming lack of empathy. These characteristics are most consistent with a diagnosis of

    (A) conversion disorder
    (B) post traumatic stress disorder (PTSD)
    (C) seasonal affective disorder (SAD)
    (D) anti-social personality disorder
    (E) schizoaffective disorder

15. A teacher reads an essay and gives it a grade of "B-". Three days later, the author of the essay submits the same paper again, amongst a pile of essays from another section of the course. This time, the teacher gives the essay a grade of "D". This result is an illustration of weak

    (A) criterion validity
    (B) face validity
    (C) norming
    (D) inter-rater reliability
    (E) intra-rater reliability

16. In order to study whether boys in elementary school are more aggressive in their interactions than girls, you decide to watch them at play during recess without their knowledge. You are conducting

    (A) an unethical study
    (B) correlational research
    (C) a longitudinal study
    (D) a cross-sectional study
    (E) a naturalistic observation

17. Janet receives the following quiz scores, calculated on a ten-point scale: 7, 9, 7, 7, 10, 7, 9. Which of the following is the most accurate representation of the central tendency of this distribution?

    (A) The standard deviation is >1, the mean is 8 and the mode is 7
    (B) The standard deviation is <1, the mean is 8 and the mode is 7
    (C) The mean is 8, the median is 7 and the mode is 7
    (D) The mean is 8, the median is 7 and the mode is 10
    (E) The mean is 8, the median is 10 and the mode is 7

18. In an experiment designed to examine whether crowding influences an individual's level of hostility, crowding is

    (A) an extraneous variable
    (B) a confounding variable
    (C) the result of the null hypothesis
    (D) the dependent variable
    (E) the independent variable

19. According to Jean Piaget, formal operational thinking is characterized by

    (A) language acquisition
    (B) the earliest forms of logical reasoning
    (C) the ability to reason abstractly and hypothetically
    (D) the inability to cognitively take the perspective of another
    (E) mastery of conservation of mass and liquid

20. Which of the following best describes the capacity of long-term memory (LTM)?

    (A) It can generally hold 5 to 9 unrelated pieces of information
    (B) It can generally hold only what the sensory memory can hold
    (C) There appear to be no limits to its capacity
    (D) It can hold about the same amount of information as short-term memory (STM)
    (E) There appear to be limits, but only in terms of retaining procedural memories

21. Symptoms of schizophrenia

    (A) usually manifest themselves during late adolescence or early adulthood
    (B) usually manifest themselves as a response to a clear environmental trigger
    (C) include the presence of two or more distinct personalities in one individual
    (D) always include either visual or auditory hallucinations
    (E) are often misinterpreted as characteristic of somatoform disorder

22. Theories of motivation that assume the presence of a biological need to maintain an ideally balanced internal state are considered

    (A) Darwinist
    (B) reductionist
    (C) hierarchical
    (D) sociobiological
    (E) homeostatic

23. According to Sigmund Freud, it is during this stage of psychosexual development, roughly between the ages of 3 to 6 years old, that a male child unconsciously experiences the Oedipal Conflict:

    (A) the genital stage
    (B) the latency stage
    (C) the phallic stage
    (D) the anal stage
    (E) the oral stage

24. Cells in the visual cortex that respond to specific lines and angles in the visual field are called

    (A) glucocorticoids
    (B) complex motion cells
    (C) simple cells
    (D) feature detector cells
    (E) bipolar cells

25. Hearing impairment caused by damage to hair cells or the auditory nerve is called

    (A) agnosia
    (B) Wernicke's aphasia
    (C) anosmia
    (D) sensorineural deafness
    (E) conductive deafness

26. The closer an object is to the viewer, the faster it appears to move. This depth cue is called

    (A) texture gradient
    (B) the phi phenomenon
    (C) interposition
    (D) the autokinetic effect
    (E) motion parallax

27. Daniel jumps out of the shower twice, wrongly believing he has heard the telephone ring. In signal detection theory, each would be termed

    (A) a correct rejection
    (B) a heuristic error
    (C) a false alarm
    (D) a false negative
    (E) a miss

28. In the last quarter of the 19th century, the study of the relationship between the physical stimuli in the world and the psychological interpretations of those stimuli was called

    (A) gestalt psychology
    (B) introspection
    (C) structuralism
    (D) psychophysics
    (E) cognitivism

29. Operant responses are easiest to extinguish when they are originally learned through which of the following reinforcement schedules?

    (A) Continuous
    (B) Negative
    (C) Intermittent
    (D) Variable ratio
    (E) Variable interval

30. Psychoactive drugs operate by

    (A) increasing myelinization at the neuronal level
    (B) increasing the rate of neurogenesis
    (C) increasing the firing threshold of neurons
    (D) stimulating or blocking the action of neurotransmitters at the synapse
    (E) stimulating the creation of hormones in the endocrine system

31. Research on the phenomenon of REM Rebound indicates that

    (A) babies tend to spend more time sleeping in the REM stage
    (B) after people turn 50, there is an increase in the amount of REM that people experience during a night's sleep
    (C) if a person is consistently deprived of REM sleep, they will spend more time in that stage when they are allowed to sleep normally
    (D) if a person is deprived of REM, they will dream much more frequently in the other stages of sleep
    (E) as the brain enters the REM state, brain wave activity fluctuates between wakefulness and deep sleep

32. In girls, breast development at puberty is an example of

    (A) accommodation
    (B) assimilation
    (C) a primary sex characteristic
    (D) a secondary sex characteristic
    (E) androgyny

33. Evidence indicates that, through interaction with the world, the human brain wires and rewires its synaptic connections throughout life. This is called

    (A) brain salience
    (B) biological preparedness
    (C) brain plasticity
    (D) depolarization
    (E) polarization

34. We might say that a man is rewarded for opening an umbrella in that it ends the unpleasantness of rain falling on him. This is an example of

    (A) simultaneous conditioning
    (B) negative reinforcement
    (C) positive reinforcement
    (D) primary reinforcement
    (E) omission training

35. During Erik Erikson's fourth stage of psychosocial development, a seven-year-old girl is repeatedly frustrated by her attempts to learn in math class. For the child this might result in a lifelong sense of

    (A) trust issues
    (B) stagnation
    (C) isolation from peers
    (D) inferiority
    (E) role confusion

36. According to incentive theorists, the thrust of human motivation is based on

    (A) survival of ones' genes
    (B) external goal attainment
    (C) inborn biological imperatives
    (D) pre-wired instincts that drive us to seek pleasure
    (E) the desire to reach self-actualization

37. Disturbances in mood, sleep and appetite are most likely correlated with reduced levels of

    (A) serotonin activity
    (B) GABA activity
    (C) activity in the medulla
    (D) function in the corpus callosum
    (E) insulin activity

38. The visual cliff is

    (A) both a monocular and a binocular depth cue
    (B) misperceived because of contrast effects
    (C) an example of a reversible figure
    (D) used by developmental psychologists to explore preference for familiar images
    (E) an apparatus used to examine depth perception in infants

39. A politician who has firmly held convictions about a particular economic policy no longer welcomes information or evidence that might contradict her beliefs. This is best explained by

    (A) the illusion of control
    (B) the availability heuristic
    (C) confirmation bias
    (D) hindsight bias
    (E) prototype matching theory

40. Which of the following is the best example of divergent thinking?

    (A) An author decides to stop writing altogether after she fails to sell any of her work

    (B) A group leader asks for input from one other person before making a decision

    (C) A fifth grader generates ten different possible answers to the question "what is half of thirteen?"

    (D) A high school math teacher subtracts ten points from the grade of any students who does not show their work on an assignment

    (E) A teacher insists that all students arrive at a solution in the same way

41. Wolfgang Kohler's research on insight learning in chimpanzees suggested that the chimps

    (A) had unusual difficulty understanding the problems given to them

    (B) could at best only mimic what Kohler himself first demonstrated to them

    (C) seemed unable to generalize their solutions to other similar problems

    (D) could not solve problems which required more than two or three steps in the solution

    (E) first reflected and then reached sudden solutions to the problems presented to them

42. Kristen is in love with the idea of becoming a social worker, but also has a deep desire to attend the local university to study law. This is an example of

    (A) an approach-approach conflict

    (B) an approach-avoidance conflict

    (C) an avoidance-avoidance conflict

    (D) a multiple approach-avoidance conflict

    (E) a multiple approach-approach conflict

43. Telegraphic speech

    (A) begins in the first six months of childhood

    (B) usually develops as children reach the fourth year of life

    (C) serves as evidence for Behaviorists that children learn to speak through imitation of others

    (D) refers to the stage in language acquisition in which children express themselves in two word sentences, such as "Mommy juice"

    (E) is rarely seen in children who have been consistently exposed to more than one language from birth

44. "The feathers will get wet. There's no telling how fast the legs are moving. It would be nice to know where they plan to go". These sentences would be significantly easier to recall if you knew they were part of a story about ducks swimming in a pond. This is an illustration of

    (A) the primacy effect
    (B) the recency effect
    (C) semantic distinctiveness
    (D) the effect of context on memory
    (E) proactive interference

45. A high school student expects to receive a college acceptance letter on Saturday. The mail carrier always delivers the mail at precisely 10 AM on Saturdays; the student does not check for her letter before 10 AM, but does check immediately at that time. Essentially, the student is

    (A) undergoing extinction trials
    (B) experiencing classical conditioning
    (C) on a fixed ratio schedule of reinforcement
    (D) on a fixed interval schedule of reinforcement
    (E) on a variable interval schedule of reinforcement

46. A man is warned to expect poor behavior from his nephew during a weekend camping trip. As soon as the youngster arrives, the man behaves as if he expects trouble from the boy, and the boy does indeed behave rudely and irresponsibly for the entire trip. A social psychologist might account for this by citing the concept of

    (A) the self fulfilling prophecy
    (B) conformity
    (C) dispositional attribution
    (D) situational attribution
    (E) discrepancy theory

47. The motor cortex of the brain is located

    (A) right next to the visual cortex
    (B) in the frontal lobes of the brain
    (C) near the auditory cortex of the temporal lobe
    (D) adjacent to the reticular formation
    (E) in close proximity to the medulla and other brain stem parts vital to life function

48. In John B. Watson's classical conditioning of a fear response in a small boy called "Little Albert", the unconditioned stimulus was

    (A) fear of the white rat
    (B) fear of all white, furry things
    (C) Albert's attempt to escape
    (D) the white rat
    (E) the loud noise

49. The idea of catharsis as a kind of safety valve that releases unconscious aggression is most clearly associated with

    (A) arousal theory
    (B) drive reduction theory
    (C) sociobiology
    (D) psychoanalysis
    (E) the theory of natural selection

50. Carol Gilligan's criticism of Lawrence Kohlberg's theory of moral development is based on the argument that

    (A) Kohlberg misinterpreted cultural differences in responses
    (B) Kohlberg's stages are too narrowly defined
    (C) Kohlberg's theory underestimates the cognitive ability of younger children
    (D) Kohlberg's theory does not account well for differences between male and female responses
    (E) Kohlberg's "Heinz Dilemma" was poorly understood by most participants in the study

51. Which of the following is the best example of semantic memory?

    (A) Remembering exactly what you were doing on September 11, 2001
    (B) Knowing what acetylcholine is
    (C) Typing well even into old age
    (D) Remembering your seventh birthday party
    (E) Retaining the basic elements of your golf swing after years of not playing

52. The just noticeable difference (JND) is a

    (A) measure of the minimum amount of a stimulus that one can detect 50% of the time
    (B) measure of the minimum amount of detectable change between two stimuli
    (C) method of measuring levels of neural activity
    (D) method of viewing brain structure
    (E) manual used by therapists to help diagnose mental disorders

53. The cognitive developmental process of dealing with new information by attempting to fit it into previously held schemas is called

    (A) modeling
    (B) discrimination
    (C) synthesis
    (D) accommodation
    (E) assimilation

54. According to David Elkind, the phenomena of the personal fable and the imaginary audience are associated with

    (A) old age
    (B) middle age
    (C) young adulthood
    (D) adolescence
    (E) emerging adulthood

55. A researcher classically conditions a dog to salivate at the sound of a buzzer by repeatedly pairing that sound with the arrival of food. Next, the researcher repeatedly pairs an image of a black square with the sound of the buzzer; soon, the presence of the black square elicits a salivary response in the dog. This is an example of

    (A) extinction
    (B) higher order conditioning
    (C) discrimination conditioning
    (D) spontaneous recovery
    (E) generalization

56. Which of the following would serve as the best evidence in support of critical period theory?

   (A) A student runs out of time on a standardized test even though he knew the material very well
   (B) A three year-old child is not corrected when he repeatedly says "I eated candy this morning"
   (C) A child understands the meaning of certain sentences even though she cannot yet speak herself
   (D) A seven year-old child is penalized for frequently thinking divergently during whole- class discussions
   (E) A 12 year-old child with no previous exposure to spoken language now has great difficulty learning any language even with professional training

57. The gland of the endocrine system most responsible for the metabolization of glucose is

   (A) the adrenal medulla
   (B) the adrenal cortex
   (C) the pituitary
   (D) the thyroid
   (E) the pancreas

58. Which of the following is characteristic of the human "fight or flight" response?

   (A) Increased respiration, increased blood pressure, decreased blood flow to the digestive system
   (B) Constriction of pupils, increased heart rate, increased salivation
   (C) Decreased salivation, decreased respiration, dilation of pupils
   (D) Increased heart rate, decreased epinephrine activity, decreased salivation
   (E) Decreased heart rate, increased respiration, decreased blood flow to the digestive system

59. Which of the following would serve as the best argument against Abraham Maslow's hierarchy of needs?

   (A) Most humans aspire to reach their fullest potential
   (B) Animals and humans have different motivations
   (C) Motivation is a multi-layered, interactive phenomenon
   (D) Some individuals seek companionship even in the absence of satisfactory amounts of food and water
   (E) Human emotional response is too variable individual-to-individual to offer meaningful generalizations about it

60. Some theorists believe that dreaming is produced as the brain combines, interprets and adds meaning to the electrical input emanating from cells firing in the brainstem. This is a summary of which theory of dreaming?

    (A) Activation-synthesis theory
    (B) Psychoanalytic theory
    (C) Opponent-process theory
    (D) Adaptive non-responding theory
    (E) Information-processing theory

61. According to neo-Freudian Carl Jung, the fact that similar themes appear in folk and fairy tales of many different cultures over centuries is evidence for the existence of

    (A) anima and animus
    (B) archetypes in the collective unconscious
    (C) an inborn basic anxiety
    (D) the typical human progression through psychosexual stages of development
    (E) cultural transmission of central human problems and methods for addressing them

62. In Philip Zimbardo's "mock prison" study

    (A) student volunteers conformed, sometimes to dangerous extremes, to the role expectations associated with 'guards' and 'prisoners'
    (B) riots broke out among all those acting as inmates, in protest against their treatment by those playing the roles of guards
    (C) the social hierarchy of the prison population was substantially different from the social hierarchies which tend to develop in actual prisons
    (D) the 'guards' in the prison affiliated with the 'prisoners', in joint opposition against the warden
    (E) it was difficult to obtain a representative sample of volunteers because so few individuals were willing to play the role of 'prisoner'

63. An ethologist would be most concerned with examining

    (A) sign stimuli and instinctive fixed action patterns
    (B) cultural influences on individual behavior
    (C) human emotional potential
    (D) human intellectual potential
    (E) human neural circuitry

64. John Milton's quote, "The mind is it's own place and in itself can make a heaven of hell, a hell of heaven" best summarizes

    (A) the cognitive perspective in psychology
    (B) the behavioral perspective in psychology
    (C) the humanistic perspective in psychology
    (D) the eclectic perspective in psychology
    (E) the biopsychosocial perspective in psychology

65. Which of the following is the best example of the defense mechanism known as displacement?

    (A) David claims his co-workers don't work hard enough, although they all see him as the laziest person in their workplace
    (B) Ty throws himself into volunteer work after being laid off from his job
    (C) Craig misses work for several days but does not take responsibility by calling his superiors
    (D) Tom tells his friends that the teacher of his art history class hates him, but those who know him believe that it is actually Tom who hates the teacher
    (E) Anna's former boyfriend calls her to report he is engaged to another woman; Anna congratulates him, but after hanging up the phone throws a plant against the wall

66. According to Carl Rogers, what is the result for individuals who are in relationships characterized by unconditional positive regard?

    (A) They become spoiled and narcissistic
    (B) They reject genuine affection when it is offered later in life
    (C) They are more open to love but simultaneously more distrustful of it
    (D) They become more defensive, withdrawn and cynical about the real motives of others
    (E) They are happier, better adjusted and closer to their ideal sense of self

67. Which of the following is NOT characteristic of a manic episode?

    (A) Inflated self esteem or grandiosity
    (B) Persistently elevated mood
    (C) Heightened attention
    (D) Talks more frequently and feels the need to talk for longer durations
    (E) Engagement in activities that have a potential for painful consequences

68. These provide neurons with nutrients while also insulating them and essentially holding them in place:

    (A) glial cells
    (B) afferent neurons
    (C) efferent neurons
    (D) neurotransmitters
    (E) neuromodulators

69. A developmental psychologist would be most likely to utilize which of the following to examine an infant's preferences?

    (A) Habituation techniques
    (B) Feature detection
    (C) Feature analysis
    (D) Longitudinal methodology
    (E) Stimulus generalization

70. For nearly two years you have been working at a job that makes you very tense and unhappy, but find yourself telling your friends that it's really a very nice work environment that you enjoy. Researchers like Leon Festinger would argue that your words are an attempt to relieve a state of

    (A) homeostasis
    (B) belief perseverance
    (C) overjustification
    (D) self-actualization
    (E) cognitive dissonance

71. Sam is highly emotional and dramatic, and has a seemingly insatiable desire to be the center of attention. This is most consistent with a diagnosis of

    (A) narcissistic personality disorder
    (B) borderline personality disorder
    (C) histrionic personality disorder
    (D) anti-social personality disorder
    (E) dependent personality disorder

72. Jamal's psychiatrist prescribed him a psychotropic drug that will limit the amount of dopamine available in certain parts of his brain. Its likely that Jamal is suffering from

    (A) major depressive disorder
    (B) hypochondriasis
    (C) dissociative identity disorder
    (D) conduct disorder
    (E) schizophrenia

73. Which of the following describes the autokinetic effect?

    (A) A child imitates the physical movements of an admired adult
    (B) A weightlifter reaches her performance ceiling and is unable to lift more weight
    (C) A point of light when viewed in a totally darkened room appears to move
    (D) A series of lights turned on one after another appears to be moving in a steady stream
    (E) A distant vehicle appears to move more slowly than a similar vehicle that is close by

74. Which of the following is NOT a component of Howard Gardner's theory of multiple intelligences?

    (A) Naturalistic intelligence
    (B) Fluid intelligence
    (C) Interpersonal intelligence
    (D) Logical-mathematical intelligence
    (E) Bodily-kinesthetic intelligence

75. Token economies are based on the principles of

    (A) operant conditioning
    (B) classical conditioning
    (C) modeling
    (D) social learning
    (E) humanism

76. Which of the following is NOT generally seen as an advantage of group therapy approaches?

    (A) Group therapy minimizes the sense that one authority figure must "cure" the patient
    (B) Group therapy helps individuals to see that others do indeed share their problems
    (C) Group therapy discussions can focus entirely on each member's personal stories
    (D) Group therapy allows patients to hear how others cope with similar problems
    (E) Group therapy is less expensive than one on one therapy

77. Two individuals decline to cooperate with each other even when cooperation would actually have served the self-interests of both. This describes

    (A) the concept of self-monitoring
    (B) the predominance of superordinate goals
    (C) social polarization
    (D) confirmation bias
    (E) a social trap

78. Jessie and Jon are driving on the highway at rush hour when a car suddenly cuts in front of them in order to reach a poorly marked exit. Jon loudly criticizes the driver of the other vehicle for his poor judgment and driving skills, while Jessie points out that the circumstances may have required the other driver to do what he did. Jon's response is best explained by

    (A) the availability heuristic
    (B) the fundamental attribution error
    (C) social diffusion
    (D) the norm of social responsibility
    (E) impression formation theory

79. In a study on group problem-solving it is discovered that individual members of groups tend to exert less effort than they would have if working alone. This is called

    (A) the tragedy of the commons
    (B) groupthink
    (C) contingency
    (D) social loafing
    (E) social inhibition

80. Paul is a 44 year-old male who is found living in a large city almost 900 miles from his home, where he has assumed a new identity. His wife identifies him based on his appearance, but he has no recollection of his life with her. This is most consistent with a diagnosis of

   (A) dissociative fugue
   (B) dissociative identity disorder
   (C) Turner's Syndrome
   (D) post traumatic stress disorder
   (E) borderline personality disorder

81. The "flow" of a neural message is

   (A) cell body to axon to terminal buttons to axon hillock
   (B) cell body to axon hillock to dendrites to terminal buttons
   (C) axon hillock to cell body to terminal buttons to axon
   (D) dendrites to cell body to terminal buttons to axon
   (E) dendrites to cell body to axon to terminal buttons

82. Which of the following psychotropic drugs operates by blocking the reuptake of serotonin?

   (A) Clozapine
   (B) Prozac
   (C) Valium
   (D) Librium
   (E) Xanax

83. Which of the following clusters of disorders is not categorized by the DSM-IV-TR as an Axis I disorder?

   (A) Anxiety disorders
   (B) Mood disorders
   (C) Personality disorders
   (D) Somatoform disorders
   (E) Dissociative disorders

84. Which of the following is the most likely value for "r" resulting from a study of the correlation between air temperature and the incidence of urban violence?

    (A) -1.0
    (B) +1.0
    (C) -.74
    (D) +.53
    (E) +.14

85. A man who unconsciously resents a rival in the workplace frequently showers that rival with praise. According to a proponent of Freudian psychoanalytic theory, this is an example of

    (A) sublimation
    (B) reaction formation
    (C) identification
    (D) regression
    (E) suppression

86. A researcher administers a battery of ten personality tests to a client. When she statistically analyzes the results, she discovers that the results from tests 3, 5 and 7 are highly correlated with each other, and concludes that those three assessments all measure the same key component of personality. The researcher has utilized

    (A) factor analysis
    (B) criterion validity
    (C) concurrent validity
    (D) test/retest reliability
    (E) standardization

87. Which of the following quotes is most closely associated with humanistic personality theory?

    (A) "People largely disturb themselves by thinking in a self defeating, illogical, and unrealistic manner"
    (B) "The goal of the human soul is conquest, perfection, security, superiority"
    (C) "It's as if Freud supplied to us the sick half of psychology and we must now fill it out with the healthy half"
    (D) "That we have found the tendency to conform in our society so strong ... is a matter of concern"
    (E) "The essence of obedience is that a person comes to view himself as the instrument for carrying out another person's wishes, and he therefore no longer regards himself as responsible for his actions"

88. If the variance for a set of data is 100, what is the standard deviation for this set of data?

   (A) 5
   (B) 10
   (C) 20
   (D) 25
   (E) 50

89. A 55-year-old man suffers a stroke that leaves him with anterograde amnesia. This means he is

   (A) able to recall what he experiences but only with the use of mnemonics
   (B) able to recall semantic memories only
   (C) unable to recall his own identity, old friends and family members
   (D) unable to retain memory of events which have occurred after the stroke
   (E) unable to recall details of the stroke itself, but the rest of his memory remains intact

90. A Human Factors psychologist would likely be involved in studying which of the following?

   (A) The interpersonal dynamics in the relationships of family members
   (B) The assessment of and treatment for those with psychological disorders
   (C) Designing safe and user-friendly machines
   (D) The application of psychological principles in the legal profession
   (E) Ways to promote wellness and prevent disease at the community level

91. The change in the electrical charge of a neuron when it "fires" its neural message is called

   (A) reuptake
   (B) the action potential
   (C) refraction
   (D) relative refraction
   (E) potentiation

92. Afferent neurons

   (A) carry neural messages into the central nervous system
   (B) are also known as motor neurons
   (C) are also known as interneurons
   (D) support the function of glial cells
   (E) carry neural messages away from the central nervous system

93. In group polarization

   (A) the individual members of a group leave the group setting with an inflated sense of their own importance to the group
   (B) the individual members of a group leave the group setting with an unrealistically negative view of their contributions to the group
   (C) members of a group tend to divide themselves into opposing "sides" even when such a division did not exist before the group came together
   (D) group size becomes the major determinant as to whether the group effectively completes its assigned tasks
   (E) a group's judgments and decisions tend to be more extreme than those of any individual member of the group

94. Which of the following statements most accurately describes the Schachter-Singer (Two Factor) Theory of emotional response?

   (A) There are universal emotions that are expressed similarly in all cultures
   (B) We experience a physiological response and an emotion at exactly the same time
   (C) We feel a physiological response first and we later experience emotion as we interpret that response in the context of the circumstances we are in
   (D) There are substantial cross-cultural differences in "display rules", affecting when and how dramatically an individual shows his or her emotions to others
   (E) Human emotional response is largely learned, through observation, imitation and reinforcement

95. If a set of AP exam scores is positively skewed,

   (A) the majority of the scores are higher than the mean
   (B) the mean, median and mode would be exactly the same
   (C) the standard deviation would be greater than the mean
   (D) the distribution of scores would form a normal curve
   (E) low scores will outnumber high scores on the exam

96. A drug that is an antagonist for the neurotransmitter acetylcholine (ACh), would most likely

    (A) lead to significant changes in appetite
    (B) induce a manic state of euphoria
    (C) cause intense feelings of pleasure
    (D) cause an inability to move voluntary muscles
    (E) speed up most functions of the central nervous system

97. Which of the following therapists was known for challenging a patient's irrational thought patterns, often in a confrontational manner?

    (A) Albert Ellis
    (B) Aaron Beck
    (C) Joseph Wolpe
    (D) Carl Rogers
    (E) Carl Jung

98. An assessment of 'intelligence' that has an insufficient operational definition of the concept would most likely lack

    (A) norms
    (B) a representative sample
    (C) confounds
    (D) intra-rater reliability
    (E) construct validity

99. Ms. Williams teaches at a high school where students are randomly assigned to classes without reference to past performance or supposed ability level. After her first unit of the course, she gives a history exam to one class of 25 seniors during first period in room 204. She administers the same test to a second class of 25 seniors during the last period of the day in room 105. The mean performance of the first class is nine points higher than that of the second class, and Ms. Williams concludes that it is her "smart class". Which of the following are confounding variables in this scenario?

    (A) The exam itself and Ms. Williams
    (B) The time of administration of the tests and the two rooms
    (C) Ms. Williams and the two classes
    (D) The two classes and the two rooms
    (E) The high school and the two classes

100. A man who runs a horse stable gives a tour to a friend, introducing each individual horse by name, although the friend cannot discriminate one animal from another. This is best accounted for by

(A) scapegoating
(B) the self-serving bias
(C) social inhibition
(D) pluralistic ignorance
(E) outgroup homogeneity bias

# Section II

Directions: You have 50 minutes to answer BOTH of the following questions. It is not enough to answer a question by merely listing facts. You should present a cogent argument based on your critical analysis of the questions posed, using appropriate psychological terminology.

1. Describe each of the following concepts and explain how each might play a role in applying to college and making your final decision about which school to attend.

   - The prefrontal cortex
   - A heuristic approach to problem solving
   - Mental set
   - Incentive theory
   - An approach-approach conflict
   - The mere exposure effect
   - Erikson's psychosocial stage of identity vs. role confusion

2. Expectations can have a major impact on human behavior and mental processes. Describe the following concepts and tell how expectations play a role in each.

   - Self-fulfilling prophecy
   - Stereotype threat
   - A placebo in an experiment on pain medication
   - Rosenhan's study on institutionalization
   - The social clock
   - Contingency in operant conditioning
   - A demand characteristic in taking a survey
   - A double-blind condition

biopsychosocial perspective 224
bipolar cells 54
bipolar disorder 32, 225, 227-228, 258
birth order theory 148, 191
blind spot 54
blocking in classical conditioning 93, 99
blood-brain barrier 81
blue eyes/brown eyes study 281
body dysmorphic disorder 233
borderline personality disorder 239-240
bottom-up processing 49, 56, 60
Bowlby, John 149, 156
brain plasticity 39, 43
brainstem 34, 74, 79
brightness as a depth/distance cue 63
Broca's Area 37, 133
bulimia nervosa 169, 238
bystander effect 11, 274, 284, 295

# C

caffeine 29, 82
Cannon-Bard/Thalamic Theory 171
cardinal traits 185
case studies 11-12, 38, 131, 142, 185, 190
   weaknesses of 12
catatonic schizophrenia 234-235
categories (basic, subordinate, superordinate) 126
catharsis 170
Cattell, Raymond 185, 196, 204
caudate nucleus 116, 231
central nervous system 29, 31-33, 259
central route of persuasion (systematic persuasion) 276
central tendency 13-15
central traits 185
cerebellum 34, 60, 116, 238
chaining 95
change blindness 52
Chomsky, Noam 131-133, 136
chunking 109, 111
circadian rhythms 75

classical conditioning 6, 18, 89-93, 99-100, 254, 294-295
Clever Hans 18
client centered/person centered therapy 194, 231, 253, 295
clinical psychologists 250, 295
clinical psychology 226, 241, 249-250, 261, 295
closure 62
Clozapine 259
cocaine 30, 82
cochlea 56
cognitive- behavioral approach 192, 256, 260
cognitive consistency 166
cognitive development 146-148, 155-156, 295
cognitive dissonance 130, 166, 175, 280
cognitive learning 89, 98
cognitive maps 98
cognitive perspective 192, 238
cognitive restructuring 257
cognitive therapy 257
cognitive triad 228, 257
cohort effect 141
collectivist cultures 195, 278
collective unconscious 191
color afterimages 56, 172
color blindness 55
community psychology 257
compliance 274, 276-277
compulsions 230
computerized axial tomography (CAT) 38
concepts 125-126
concrete operational stage of cognitive development 148
conditioned reinforcers 96
conditioned response (CR) 91-93
conditioned stimulus (CS) 89-91, 93
conditions of worth 194, 253
conduct disorder 237-238
conduction deafness 56
cones 54-56
confabulation 109
confidentiality 6
confirmation bias 4, 130, 280
conformity 12, 270, 274, 277-278, 284, 295

confounding variables 2, 214
conscious mind 187
conservation 148
constancy 63, 66
constructive memory 109, 119
contact comfort 143, 295
contact hypothesis 283
context and memory 108-109
context and perception 62
context dependent memory 112
contiguity 90
contingency 89-90, 97, 100
continuity theories 141, 156
continuous schedules of reinforcement 96
contrast effects 62
control group 3-5, 99, 277
conventional level of moral reasoning 155
convergence 64
convergent thinking 126
conversion disorder 233
cooing 133-134
cooperation vs. competition 271-272
correlation coefficients 8
correlational research 1, 8-9
cortex 33, 35-36, 43, 50, 54, 56-59, 63-64, 74, 78, 116, 117, 228, 259-260
cortisol 40, 228
counselors 250
counterconditioning 255
criteria for psychological abnormality 225
critical period theory 132, 136, 142-143
cross-sectional studies 2, 13, 141
crystallized intelligence 204, 217
cyclothymia 227

# D

dark adaptation 55
Darley, John 274, 284, 295
Darwin, Charles 165
Debriefing 6-7
decay in memory 117
declarative/explicit memory 113, 116

hypnosis 73, 80-81, 118, 232
hypochondriasis 233-234
hypocretins 77
hypothalamus 34-35, 39, 76, 168
hypothesis 2, 5

# I

IACUC 8
id 188
ideal self 194, 231, 253
identification 190
identity vs. role confusion 152
illusion of control 280
illusory superiority 131
imaginary audience 153
implicit assumptions 127-128
implicit memory 113
imprinting 143
inappropriate affect as a
    symptom of schizophrenia 234
inattentional blindness 52
incentive theory 166
incubation 127
independent self-systems 278
independent variable 2, 5
individualistic cultures 195, 278
individual tests 213
industry vs. inferiority 152
industrial/organizational
    psychology (I-O Psych) 164,
    270
inferential statistics 13
inferiority complex 191
information processing model of
    memory 108, 111
information processing theory of
    sleep 76
informed consent 6
in-group bias 281-282
inhibitory neurotransmitters and
    receptor sites 29, 31, 238
inner speech 148
initiative vs. guilt 152
insanity defense 226
insight 127
insight learning 98, 100
insight therapies 251-252
insomnia 77
instinct 164

instinct theories 164-165
instinctual drift 97
institutional review board (IRB)
    6, 8
instrumental aggression 170
instrumental conditioning 94
insulin 40, 168
integrity vs. despair 152
intellectual disability 208
intelligence quotient (IQ) 207
intelligence testing 206-208
interactionist model of language
    133
interdependent self-systems 278
intermittent schedules of
    reinforcement 96
interneurons 33
intern's syndrome 226, 229
interposition/overlap 63
inter-rater reliability 11, 215, 225
intimacy vs. isolation 152
intrinsic motivation 164, 167
introspection 50, 83

# J

James-Lange Theory 171, 173
James, William 18-19, 83, 117,
    203, 294
Jones, Mary Cover 255, 261
Jonestown Case Study 12
Jung, Carl 191, 196, 250
just noticeable difference (JND)
    50-51
just world phenomenon 279

# K

Kagan, Jerome 184
Kahneman, Richard 129-130,
    136, 296
Kelly, George 193, 196
kinesthetic sense 49, 60
Kohlberg, Lawrence 155-156
Kohler, Wolfgang 98, 100, 295
Kubler-Ross, Elisabeth 154, 156

# L

language acquisition device
    (LAD) 132
Latane, Bibb 274, 284, 295
latency stage of psychosexual
    development 189-190
latent content of dreams 79, 251
latent learning 98, 100
lateral hypothalamus 168
lateralization of the brain 37
law of effect 94, 100, 294
Lazarus, Richard 173, 175
learned helplessness 98, 100,
    193, 228, 295
leptin 168
leveling 114
lifespan development 151, 153-
    154
light therapy 260
limbic system 34, 43, 58, 60, 78,
    116, 168-169, 228, 231
linear perspective 63
linguistic relativity theory/
    Whorfian hypothesis 135
lithium carbonate 228, 258
Little Albert 6, 18, 92, 100, 230,
    295
locus of control 193, 196
Loftus, Elizabeth 114-115, 119
longitudinal studies 2, 12-13,
    141, 149-150, 184, 209-210
long term memory (LTM) 111,
    113, 119
Lorenz, Konrad 143, 175, 296
LSD 82
lucid dreaming 80

# M

magic number of short term
    memory capacity 111
magnetic resonance imaging
    (MRI) 38, 238
maintenance rehearsal 108
maladaptive behavior 188, 225,
    227, 230, 231, 239
manic-depression/bipolar
    disorder 225, 227
manifest content of dreams 79

penis envy 190, 191
percentiles 15-16, 209
perceptual confirmation 282
perceptual set/expectancy 61, 66, 81
performance based assessments 212
peripheral nervous system 33
peripheral route of persuasion (heuristic persuasion) 276
Perls, Fritz 253
permissive parenting 150
person centered/client centered therapy 194, 253, 261
personal attributions 278-279
personal constructs 193, 196
personal fable 153
personal space/territoriality 272
personality disorders 224, 226, 239-240
pessimistic explanatory styles 193, 228, 256
peyote 82
phallic stage of psychosexual development 189-190
phenotype 41
phenylketonuria (PKU) 42
pheromones 58
phi phenomenon 65
phobias 92-93, 229-231, 255, 260
phonemes 133-134
physical dependence 81
physiological needs 167
Piaget, Jean 146-148, 156, 203, 295
pineal gland 40, 76
Pinel, Philipe 249, 294
pituitary gland 35, 39
place theory 57
placebo 3-5, 20, 73, 258, 260
plasticity of the brain 39, 43
pleasure principle 188
pluralistic ignorance 12, 274
polygons 17
pons 34
positive correlation 8
positive psychology 154, 167, 194, 296
positive punishment 95
positive reinforcement 95
positive symptoms of

schizophrenia 235, 236, 259
positive transfer of learning 99
positron emission tomography (PET) 38, 80
postconventional level of moral development 155
postsynaptic neuron 28-30
posttraumatic stress disorder (PTSD) 230, 231
power tests 213
preconscious mind 187
preconventional level of moral development 155
prefrontal cortex 35-36, 43, 78, 116, 153, 228, 260
prefrontal lobotomy 259
prejudice 281, 284
Premack, David 97, 100
Premack Principle 97, 100
preoperational stage of cognitive development 147-148
prescriptive grammar 134
presynaptic neuron 28-29
primacy effect 114
primary appraisal 173
primary mental abilities 204
primary reinforcers 95-96
primary sex characteristics 40, 153
prisoners' dilemma 271
proactive interference 117
procedural memory 112, 113, 116
projection 188
projective tests 170-171, 213, 295
prosocial behavior 273
Prosser, Inez 19
prototype matching theory 63
prototypes 63, 125-126
proxemics 272
proximal stimulus 63
proximity and attraction 282
proximity as a gestalt principle 62
Prozac 228, 258, 296
psychiatrist 250
psychoactive/psychotropic drugs 81, 258
psychoanalytic perspective 79-80, 170, 187, 191, 228, 232

psychoanalytic theory and dreaming 79-80
psychoanalytic/psychodynamic therapy 170, 228, 232, 250, 252
psycholinguistics 131, 133, 135
psychometrics 206
psychophysics 50, 66, 294
psychosexual stages of development 189, 251
psychosocial development 151, 156
psychosurgery 259
puberty 40, 153
punishment 94, 95, 97

# R

random selection and assignment 3, 5
range 14
rapid cycling in bipolar disorder 227
rational emotive behavior therapy (REBT) 256-257
rationalization 188
reaction formation 188
reaction range 211
real self 194, 231, 253
reality principle 188
recall (vs. recognition) 113
recency effect 114
receptors 29
reciprocal determinism 192, 196
recognition (vs. recall) 113
redintegration 58
reflex arc 33
refractory period 29
regression 189
rehearsal 108, 110
relative height/elevation as a depth/distance cue 63
relative size as a depth/distance cue 64
reliability of assessments (equivalent form reliability, inter-rater reliability, intra-rater reliability, split half reliability, test/retest reliability) 215-216
REM sleep behavior disorder 78

vestibular sense 49, 60-61
Victor - The Wild Child of
    Aveyron 132, 136
virtual reality therapy (VRT) 255
visual cliff 145
visual cortex 35, 50, 54, 56, 63,
    64, 78
volley principle 57
Vygotsky, Lev 148, 156

## W

Wagner, Allan 89, 90
Watson, John B. 6, 18, 91-92,
    100, 192, 254, 295
Weber, Ernst 50, 66
Weber's Law 50-51
Wechsler, David 208, 217, 295
Wechsler intelligence tests 208,
    213, 216
    Wechsler Intelligence Scale for
    Children (WISC) 208, 295
    Wechsler Adult Intelligence
    Scale (WAIS) 208, 216, 295
    Wechsler preschool and
    primary scale of intelligence
    (WPPSI) 208
Weisel, Thorsten 66, 295
Wernicke's Area 37, 133
Whiton-Calkins, Mary 19, 294
Whorfian/Whorf-Sapir/
    linguistic relativity hypothesis
    135
Williams Syndrome 41
withdrawal (in reference to drug
    use) 81-82
Wolpe, Joseph 255, 261
womb envy 191
word salad 234
working memory 111
Wundt, Wilhelm 18-19, 50, 66,
    83, 294

## X

Xanax 231, 259

## Y

Yerkes-Dodson Law 166
Young-Helmholtz/trichromatic
    color vision theory 55-56

## Z

Zimbardo, Philip 277, 284
Zimbardo's "mock prison" study
    277
zones of proximal development
    (ZPD) 148
Zoloft 228, 258
z-scores 16
zygotic stage 143

# · N · O · T · E · S ·

# · N · O · T · E · S ·

# • N • O • T • E • S •

# • N • O • T • E • S •